SPORT AND LEISURE IN THE IRISH AND BRITISH COUNTRY HOUSE

# Sport and Leisure in the Irish and British Country House

Terence Dooley & Christopher Ridgway

EDITORS

FOUR COURTS PRESS

Set in EhrhardtMTPro 10.5pt on 12.5pt by
Carrigboy Typesetting Services, www.carrigboy.com, for
FOUR COURTS PRESS LTD
7 Malpas Street, Dublin 8, Ireland
www.fourcourtspress.ie
*and in North America for*
FOUR COURTS PRESS
c/o IPG, 814 N Franklin St, Chicago, IL 60610.



A catalogue record for this title is available
from the British Library.

ISBN 978-1-84682-806-5



Printed in England,
by CPI Antony Rowe, Chippenham, Wilts.

# Contents

# Illustrations

*Oliver Cox*

Images from the Portland Collection, Harley Gallery, Welbeck Estates, Nottinghamshire/Bridgeman Images.



*Ian d'Alton*



*Terence Dooley*



*Eugene Dunne*



*Brian Griffin*



*Tom Hunt*



*Antonia Laurence-Allen*

All images copyright National Trust for Scotland, Hill of Tarvit Mansion House and Gardens.

# Acknowledgments

The editors are grateful to the authors for their contributions to this volume, which began life as a series of presentations at the Sixteenth Annual Historic Houses Conference, held under the auspices of the Centre for the Study of Historic Irish Houses and Estates at Maynooth University in 2018, entitled 'Sport and leisure and the country house'.

The editors would also like to record their deep gratitude to Fred and Kay Krehbiel for their generous sponsorship, which made this conference possible, and also for their wider support of the work of the CSHIHE. The sponsorship of the Ireland Funds is also greatly appreciated. As ever, without the support of the Office of Public Works, and Mary Heffernan especially, research, annual conferences and publications such as this would not be possible. Our thanks also go to Cathal McCauley and his staff in the university library, and to Jacqueline Crowley for her administration of the conference and for helping to bring this publication to fruition by way of numerous tasks, and to Mattie Shinnors for all his continued advice and guidance. A special word of thanks to Prof. Marian Lyons, who had to step into the breach on day one of the conference when both conference convenors – the editors of this work – unexpectedly became indisposed. Thanks also to Dr Jacinta Prunty, head of the Department of History at Maynooth University (2015–18). We are grateful too to Den Stubbs for his design work, and, as always, to the staff of Four Courts Press for their support and professionalism.

In keeping with the tradition of similar published proceedings, the essays in this volume are aimed at the general reader, but will also interest specialists. They marry fresh research and archival investigation while also building upon the growing historiography in these subjects. These narratives affirm yet again the wealth of material that lies in archival collections belonging to country houses, in local and national repositories, but also sporting organizations, dedicated associations and charities, and digital newspaper archives. Without the assistance and support of those who look after these archival collections, publications such as this would not be possible.

# Introduction

In 1868 the journalist Francis Lawley confidently proclaimed that Britain and Ireland had created 'the largest and wealthiest leisure class that any country, ancient or modern, ever boasted'. He was also in no doubt that in future centuries this reputation would also be defined by achievements such as trial by jury, freedom of the press, social peculiarities such as the stove-pipe hat, the late dining hour and the laws of etiquette, but most of all this class would be celebrated for its contagious passion for the national pastimes of fox hunting and horse racing. He was not alone in recognizing that for the landed classes leisure was a serious subject requiring time, effort and money in its pursuit.[1]

Elite society has always been perceived as a leisured one – with ways and means for its members to spend time as they pleased; how such individuals occupied that time was rarely, if ever, linked to acquiring a means of living; and the divide between striving for pecuniary gain and not having to do so underpinned Thorstein Veblen's famous treatise *The theory of the leisure class*, published in 1899. With affluence came choice, and elite classes were able to jettison quotidian tasks in order to devote their time and wealth to more comfortable pursuits, which were not necessarily productive in any material sense.[2] The value or quality of this free time was perhaps harder to assess, and could encompass anything from the highbrow to the lowbrow, the worthwhile to the meaningless. This metric is subjective, gauged by feelings of pleasure, satisfaction and some kind of gain. It might result in one being a better shot or rider to hounds; a more proficient painter; a superior conversationalist; or developing a keener intellect. Of a different calibre is the hobby of the heir to the earl of Marchmain in Evelyn Waugh's *Brideshead revisited* (1945), whose spare time is devoted to collecting matchboxes. But pursuing a life of leisure does not automatically equate to indolence and frivolity. Leisure itself, as Veblen recognized, can be a productive pastime and involve satisfying pursuits – study, ceremony, etiquette, sporting prowess.

The range of activities and accomplishments chronicled in this volume demonstrate how varied and productive the world of leisure and sport could

1 'Horse racing' in Anthony Trollope (ed.), *British sports and pastimes* (London, 1868), pp 10, 18. Although Lawley repeatedly uses the terms British and English there seems little doubt this sweeping pronouncement encompassed Ireland. The essay on hunting in the volume was written by Trollope himself, who went so far as to consider hunting 'more Irish than English, so thoroughly has life in that country, both rural life and town life, become imbued with a love of the sport', p. 71. For a summary of Trollope's experiences hunting in Ireland see the entry in R.C. Terry (ed.), *Oxford reader's companion to Trollope* (Oxford, 1999), pp 264–6.
2 Thorstein Veblen, *The theory of the leisure class*, ed. Martha Banta (Oxford, 2007), especially chs 2 and 3.

prove to be. The individuals and families featured question the stereotypical view of the landed classes indulging in merely frivolous or meaningless pastimes. Granted, their privileged status gave them the affluence and free time to engage in these pursuits, but they applied themselves to them with a perseverance and industry that was variously muscular, competitive, intellectual and often driven by a desire for improvement. However, these activities cannot be viewed in isolation, since one person's leisure might rely upon another person's labour, and one pastime determine factors elsewhere. For better or worse there are political, economic or social consequences to these activities, which extend beyond the confines of the leisure class.

Einion Wyn Thomas, for example, describes the detrimental consequences, in the eyes of many locals, of Richard Lloyd Price's decision to turn his Rhiwlas estate in Wales into a sporting one, and in doing so he reveals how estates often engaged in contradictory uses of land. Amid widespread resentment over game laws, the employment of non-Welsh gamekeepers, and the prevalence of poaching, he presents a bottom-up view of estate management that appeared to assign more value to game than the agricultural welfare of tenants – a tension, it has to be said, that has been commonplace for centuries and endures even to this day.

Fergal Browne examines how hunting in County Cork could cross class boundaries and even cement local populations around a shared interest, an argument, he notes, that was invoked by many in 2004 when legislation was introduced that banned hunting in England and Wales. But the interdependence of various constituencies was also undercut by wider forces such as the Irish National League and the 1903 Land Act, which fuelled tensions between the hunt and local populations; this is another reminder of how use of land could prove incompatible with the interests of those outside the privileged few.

Political, economic, and class frictions were apparently of no concern for Harry Worcester Smith when he transported his pack of hounds from Massachusetts to Westmeath in 1912. This was, as Eugene Dunne remarks, a 'curious experiment'. For Smith hunting was more than just a pleasurable sport; it affirmed status. He was quick to interact with the aristocratic and gentry families of the county, and became master of the hunt. However the experiment was not a success, not least of all because of a committee decree forbidding American and Westmeath hounds from hunting together, a decision that marred his otherwise successful assimilation into hunting society. Laura Servilan Brown explores a less well-known side of the life of renowned author and seasoned rider Edith Somerville who, with her brothers away on military service, acted as head of the family at Drishane House, and in 1903 assumed the role of 'lady master' of the West Carbery Hunt. While she discharged these duties capably, Brown suggests that Somerville was not comfortable in these traditional male roles; and she was unable to halt the demise of the hunt in the years following the First World War.

What many of these examples show is how pursuing sporting enthusiasms often involved considerable outlays of money. For Oliver Cox the eighteenth-century world of horseflesh did not just mean gambling but also investment in horse breeding, building stables and commissioning paintings, forms of conspicuous consumption that were directed towards affirming pedigree and status – human and equine. Such was the importance of the calendar of race meetings in this factional world that horse racing might be described as the pursuit of politics by other means, beyond the debating chamber in Westminster. For Ian d'Alton yachting and sailing created a marine Freemasonry bound by strict protocols regarding form, dress, communication and reward, which also demanded levels of nautical skill in order to compete successfully and enhance the reputation of sailor and club alike. For Tony McCarthy, the example of George Wyndham confirms the sporting and intellectual prowess of an elite group who were equally at home composing poetry, debating philosophical questions, playing tennis and riding to hounds. For this caste of high-minded Tories, the recreative world flowed seamlessly into the world of politics, and vice versa; they worked hard and they played hard, even if they were at pains to disguise the effort involved.

Terence Dooley describes how golf and Edwardian politics were closely intertwined, especially in Ulster, with the formation of exclusive clubs whose memberships were defined by class and sectarian identities. Moreover, he demonstrates how some landowners were quick to exploit the real estate potential of their land in the face of growing middle-class participation in recreational sports. In certain cases land and property could yield a better return in the service of golf courses, especially when linked to growth in tourism, a phenomenon that would become widespread in the late twentieth century. For Antonia Laurence-Allen, Frederick Sharp's golf course at Hill of Tarvit in Fife characterized a new class of leisured elite: the successful businessman or entrepreneur directing his wealth towards the traditional trappings of elite status. He bought a country mansion, in this case designed to the most up-to-date specification by the architect Robert Lorimer, and with sufficient land for a nine-hole golf course; and this Scottish arriviste's outdoor pursuits were matched by a desire to build up a fine art collection.

Annie Tindley discusses collecting of an altogether different kind – the taxidermy displays of wildlife and game that adorned many houses as hunting trophies. This was an affirmation of the conquest of nature as much as it was a status symbol for those who had the social and economic means to shoot and fish, especially if it involved travel to exotic parts of the globe. Like hunting or horse racing, taxidermy spawned a whole infrastructure of related trades and professions that could supply this particular demand. By contrast, Kerry Bristol discusses the passion of the Winn family of Nostell Priory in Yorkshire for collecting living creatures, whether dogs, birds, goldfish or marmosets. Their expanding menagerie was not just an instance of conspicuous consumption, or simply a case of Sir Rowland Winn catering to the whims of his wife in the country. These creatures were acquired in the spirit of scientific enquiry and reveal, so Bristol argues, the contradictions inherent in Enlightenment attitudes towards hierarchies of sentient life.

Lesley Whiteside writes about Adela Richards of Monksgrange, County Wexford, who shared with her father a fascination with astronomy. Together, Adela and Edward Richards read widely on the subject, met with astronomers, patronized instrument-makers, and even built an observatory at Monksgrange in the 1870s. Within a few years this privileged bubble of leisure came to an end, with the observatory dismantled and the telescope sold as money became tight with falling rents and fears over agrarian agitation. Monksgrange is also the subject of Philip Bull's essay, which focuses on the social and sporting pursuits of the Orpen and Richards families, who he describes as 'achievers'. Thus Goddard Orpen, husband to Adela Richards, was able to abandon his legal career thanks to his wife's inheritance, and devote himself to scholarly pursuits, which resulted in his four-volume *Ireland under the Normans*, published between 1911 and 1920; but he was able to balance the scholar's life with an enthusiasm for tennis and cycling, as well as photography.

Ciarán Reilly demonstrates how politics and sport mingled at the end of the nineteenth century, revealing surprising connections between two sports that could be said to be ideologically opposed to one another: cricket and hurling.[3] As Reilly remarks, the GAA and the world of the Big House made for unlikely bedfellows but in certain localities a *modus vivendi*, or *modus ludendi*, was possible. In a similar vein Tom Hunt describes Charles Stewart Parnell's passion for cricket and the matches played at his Avondale home in County Wicklow; but in his role as patron of the GAA Parnell also made his home ground available for hurling and football matches. Both essays reveal how the boundaries between English and Irish sports were more porous than has been supposed; furthermore, echoing points made by Thomas and Dooley, they also demonstrate how land had competing sporting, agricultural, amenity and investment values, and that it could in fact accommodate more than one sport for the benefit of different people, sometimes harmoniously, at other times less so.

Maeve O'Riordan discusses the enclosed world of Lady Castletown, whose scrapbook compiled during the later decades of the nineteenth century sits in a long tradition of assembling words, images and private tokens into keepsakes. An example of a deeply reflective pastime, the album is more than just a random bricolage, and O'Riordan argues that it can be read as both a record of an era as well as an exercise in autobiography, every bit as eloquent as a penned memoir.

3 On Irish sport, politics and society, see R.V. Comerford, 'Sport' in *idem, Ireland* (London, 2003), pp 212–35.

Brian Griffin offers an intriguing perspective on the Great Famine of the 1840s, citing regular instances of celebration and plenty in rural districts, more often than not centred upon the Big House and its family. Prosperity and even a measure of social harmony existed at a time of deep immiseration elsewhere. These local instances of sporting events accompanied by drinking, feasting, fireworks and dancing disprove the received view that the whole of Ireland was overwhelmed with grief.

Finally, Allen Warren revisits the decline of the landed classes in the twentieth century and investigates the purpose of the aristocracy. Building on the idea of an ornamental elite, increasingly removed from the principal arena of political power, he shows how many families redefined their purpose at a county level, especially through support for the Boy Scout movement, the St John's Ambulance, the Anglican church, the justice system, and the conservation movement. This recalibration of civic duty away from a traditional engagement in national politics in the capital was fundamental in shaping many of the institutions and movements of the twentieth century, and Warren's examples drawn from families in Somerset include members of the aristocracy and the gentry, as well as successful business families such as the Wills, tobacco barons of Bristol. These case studies gainsay the remark made by one of the characters in Edith Wharton's novel of 1920, *The age of innocence*, that in the face of displacement 'decent people had to fall back on sport or culture'.[4]

While essays on sport and leisure have been combined here in a single volume a caveat should be sounded that the two topics are not synonymous; they are closely related insofar as their serious pursuit is possible on account of surplus time and wealth that enables people to devote themselves to a variety of recreational choices. These might be gregarious or more solitary and private; they might involve outdoors activity or spending time indoors; they might be cerebral or muscular. At the same time it would be misleading to view these individuals as entirely inactive in the world of work. Many of them were engaged in politics, philanthropy, raising families, managing estates or pursuing a profession. They were far from being the idle rich; life was calibrated between work and leisure in some measure or other, and many would have concurred with Samuel Smiles, that apostle of self-help, that there is a need to balance the 'gospel of labour' with the 'gospel of leisure and recreation', both of which were essential to well-being and happiness.[5]

Both sport and leisure as topics have attracted the attention of writers for at least a century. Veblen's *Theory of the leisure class* was written at a moment when many of these individuals and families were occupied by how to spend their time and money in ways that were productive and meaningful to them, whether in terms of personal self-development, wider social engagement, or simple

4 Edith Wharton, *The age of innocence* (London, 1974), ch. 14, p. 106. 5 Samuel Smiles, *Life and labour; or characteristics of men of industry, culture and genius* (London, 1912), p. 310.

pleasure. Since then the concept of leisure has received extensive treatment in the hands of historians, sociologists and literary historians.[6]

In the nineteenth and twentieth centuries, aristocrats and sporting enthusiasts drawn from the landed classes wrote enthusiastically about sport and their sporting pursuits, sometimes in monographs on their favourite sports, such as hunting or shooting, or as an obligatory part of their published memoirs.[7] In the last twenty years or so historians have begun to write on the history of Irish sport; today, it forms an important component in wider Irish historiography.[8] The growth in interest has much to do with the interest of professional historians in Britain in the emergence of organized and regularized sport in Victorian and Edwardian Britain.[9] In the Irish case, R.V. Comerford has pointed out that the years between 1850 and the First World War were the most critical period in the general history of sport in Ireland, when 'various games and pastimes were changed to become codified, centrally administered and organised on a national basis'.[10] In turn, he argues, 'sport played a significant part in the invention of nationality, in Ireland and elsewhere', concluding:

> A familiar paradigm can be observed: sport has an existence ontologically prior to nationality; as it is put on a modern basis, its organisational structures become coterminous with the state and it becomes in that sense national; once visibly national it is available to be invested with meaning and significance by nation inventors.[11]

6 See, variously: Stanley Parker, *The sociology of leisure* (London, 1976); Peter Bailey, *Leisure and class in Victorian England* (London, 1978); David Cannadine, 'The theory and practice of the English leisure classes', *The Historical Journal*, 21:2 (June 1978), pp 445–67; Neil McKendrick, 'The commercialization of leisure' in Neil McKendrick, John Brewer and J.H. Plumb (eds), *The birth of a consumer society: the commercialization of eighteenth-century England* (Bloomington, 1982), pp 337–78; Andrew Adonis, *Making aristocracy work* (Oxford, 1993); Peter Burke, 'The invention of leisure in early modern Europe', *Past & Present*, 146 (Feb. 1995), pp 135–50; Patricia Meyer Spacks, *Boredom: the literary history of a state of mind* (Chicago, 1995); Rudy Koshar (ed.), *Histories of leisure* (Oxford, 2002); Hugh Cunningham, *Time, work and leisure: life changes in England since 1700* (Manchester, 2012); Jeffrey A. Auerbach, *Imperial boredom, monotony and the British empire* (Oxford, 2018). 7 See for example, 'Desdichado', *Fox hunting in Meath: an imperfect record of a hunting season in Meath, 1883–84* (Dublin, 1884); J.B. Drought, *A sportsman looks at Ireland* (London, n.d.); Earl of Mayo and W.B. Boulton, *A history of the Kildare Hunt* (London, 2013); Earl of Dunraven, *Past times and pastimes* (London, 1922); Lord Castletown, *Ego: random records of sport, service, and travel in many lands* (London, 1923). 8 Comerford, 'Sport'. 9 See for example, Joe Maguire, 'Images of manliness and competing ways of living in late Victorian and Edwardian Britain', *International Journal of the History of Sport*, 3:3 (1986), pp 265–87; Richard Holt, *Sport and the British: a modern history* (Oxford, 1989); David Neave, '"Violent idleness": the 18th-century east riding gentleman at leisure', *Journal of Regional and Local Studies*, 11 (1991), pp 3–15; Derek Birley, *Land of sport and glory, sport and British society, 1887–1910* (Manchester, 1995); Neil Tranter, *Sport, economy and society in Britain, 1750–1914* (Cambridge, 1998). 10 Comerford, 'Sport', p. 212. 11 Ibid., p. 213.

Thus, the major emphasis that has very often been placed on the role of the Gaelic Athletic Association, founded in 1884, to revitalize native Irish sports.[12]

In recent years a number of major monographs on the history of sport in Ireland have appeared which, while broad in their scope, have developed various aspects of the history of country-house sport, including Tom Hunt, *Sport and society in Victorian Ireland: the case of Westmeath* (2017); James Kelly, *Sport in Ireland, 1600–1840* (2014); and Paul Rouse, *Sport and Ireland: a history* (2015).[13] Sporting and leisure pursuits of the aristocracy and gentry class have also been touched upon in general histories of these classes and their houses and estates.[14]

In 2005, Sport History Ireland was founded to 'provide an ongoing forum for the discussion, encouragement and promotion of sports history in Ireland'. The body has held an annual conference since 2005 where a variety of papers on country-house-related sports activities have addressed topics including cricket, the sporting activity of women in the country house, polo in Westmeath and Sinn Féin's attempts to prevent hunting in 1919. In recent decades a number of scholarly journals on the subject of sport and leisure have appeared.[15] The essays in this volume therefore contribute to this growing understanding of the role of sport and leisure in landed society.

12 See, for example, Gearóid Ó Tuathaigh, 'Introduction' in Gearóid Ó Tuathaigh (ed.), *The GAA and the Irish revolution, 1913–1923* (Cork, 2015), p. 11. 13 See also Brian Griffin, *Cycling in Victorian Ireland* (Dublin, 2006); *idem*, 'The Big House at play: archery as an elite pursuit from the 1830s to the 1870s' in Ciaran O'Neill (ed.), *Irish elites in the nineteenth century* (Dublin, 2013), pp 153–71; Jennifer Kelly and R.V. Comerford, *Associational culture in Ireland and abroad* (Dublin, 2010); Patricia McCarthy, 'Master of the hounds and "father of the turf": Tom Conolly and his equine exploits', *Irish Architectural and Decorative Arts*, 20 (2017), pp 70–83. 14 See, for example, Fergus D'Arcy, *Horses, lords and racing men* (Kildare, 1991); Terence Dooley, *The decline of the Big House in Ireland* (Dublin, 2001), pp 51–64, 258–70; Toby Barnard, *Making the grand figure: lives and possessions in Ireland, 1641–1770* (London, 2004); M.J. Powell, 'Hunting clubs and societies' in James Kelly and M.J. Powell (eds), *Clubs and societies in eighteenth-century Ireland* (Dublin, 2010), pp 392–408; Adrian Tinniswood, *The long weekend: life in the English country house between the wars* (London, 2016); John Stobart and Andrew Hann (eds), *The country house, material culture and consumption* (Swindon, 2016); Patricia McCarthy, *Life in the country house in Georgian Ireland* (London, 2016); Maeve O'Riordan, *Women of the country house in Ireland, 1860–1914* (Liverpool, 2018). 15 For example, the *Journal of Sport History* was founded in 1974; the *International Journal of the History of Sport* was launched in 1984; the *Sports Historian* founded in 1983 was re-launched as *Sport in History* in 2003. More generally, see Richard Cox, *British sport: a bibliography to 2000*, 3 vols (London, 2003), and Paul Rouse, *Sport and Ireland: a history* (Oxford, 2015). The *Journal of Leisure Research* was founded in 1969, followed by *Leisure Studies* in 1982 and, in 2009, the *Journal of Tourism History* was launched.

# Marmosets and mynah birds: exotica and other pets at Nostell, *c.*1759–1806

KERRY BRISTOL

Tucked away in a once-secluded spot on the West Yorkshire estate of Nostell sits a small Gothick building known as the Menagerie House, its doors and windows fastened shut and its once-elegant interior now in a ruinous condition (fig. 1.1).

This is all that remains of the Menagerie Garden created in the 1750s for Sir Rowland Winn, 4th baronet; augmented in the 1760s and 1770s by his son Rowland, the 5th baronet; and maintained into the nineteenth century by his grandson, yet another Rowland, the 6th and last baronet of Nostell. Today the birds and animals are long gone and with them went any sense that collecting exotica had been a fashionable pastime for the Georgian elite. Yet, as Caroline Grigson observed in her recent survey, 'no park was complete without an aviary of exotic and native birds, or a menagerie containing birds or a few exotic mammals'.[1] Far from being an esoteric interest of the few, middle-class and aristocratic ownership of foreign species was widespread in the eighteenth century. It demonstrated access to a global trade made possible by the rapid expansion of the British empire, the leisure time to appreciate a bird or animal's presence and the financial resources needed to devote to its specialized care. For many, amassing a collection of exotica was an end in itself and did not require much interest in natural history or the new modes of scientific investigation fostered by the Enlightenment, although there were some who used their collections as the basis for experiments in a 'search to find something of use to the general improvement of mankind and the nation'.[2] As will be argued, the Winns fall into the former category, but this highlights rather than negates their importance. As the exceptional 'few', rather than the ordinary 'many', have been the focus of much recent scholarship, this investigation into the Winns' menagerie not only sheds new light on daily life at Nostell but raises important questions about the gentry at leisure in the Georgian country house.

It is, of course, one thing to know that a menagerie existed and another to discover of what it actually consisted. This quest has not been straightforward. The absence of any lists of what the Winns owned leaves one reliant on

1 Caroline Grigson, *Menagerie: the history of exotic animals in England, 1100–1837* (Oxford, 2016), p. 150. Forty-three menageries are listed in Sally Festing, 'Menageries and the landscape garden', *Journal of Garden History*, 8:4 (Oct.–Dec. 1988), pp 104–17 at pp 111–15.
2 Robert Huxley, 'Natural history collectors and their collections: "simpering macaronis" and instruments of empire' in Kim Sloan with Andrew Burnett (eds), *Enlightenment: discovering*

1.1 Menagerie House, Nostell, West Yorkshire, May 2018. Photo: author.

memoranda in English and French (the 5th baronet's wife was a native French speaker born in Switzerland); passing comments in longer letters; and accounts from tradesmen, craftsmen and a painter that include charges for menagerie-related objects and supplies, all of which are scattered among the thousands of documents in the Winn papers held at West Yorkshire Archive Service at Wakefield. The results have been surprising, even though it has not always been clear whether a bird or animal was intended for the menagerie, for a scientific experiment or for the cooking pot: witness the case of William Leeke, who supplied the 6th baronet with '3 Song Birds and 9 hens' at the same time as he billed the young man's mother for turbot, lobsters, stockings and raisins.[3] Were the songbirds eaten, were they sacrificed in the name of science or did they live out their lives in the menagerie? The archive is silent on this matter.

## FROM FOREBEARS TO CONTEMPORARIES: ROYAL MENAGERIES AND OTHER EXEMPLARS

Menageries in Britain originated with the royal family. The first recorded was created for Henry I in Woodstock Park, Oxfordshire, followed by that at the

*the world in the eighteenth century* (London, 2003), p. 87. 3 Two bills from William Leeke, 1797 (West Yorkshire Archive Service (Wakefield) WYW 1352/3/4/3/1). Hereafter the Winn

Tower of London founded after Louis IX of France sent a gift of three leopards to Henry III in 1235.[4] What remained of the royal menagerie at Woodstock was moved to the Tower in 1252,[5] where at various times lions, bears, marmosets, an elephant and numerous birds were displayed. Because the Tower was notionally tied up with significant events in English history, its menagerie was one of the sights of the capital until the transfer of its inhabitants to what became London Zoo in the nineteenth century.

Under the Hanoverians, there were several burgeoning menageries, mostly masterminded by the royal consorts and open to the visiting public. Queen Caroline was instrumental in developing what had been a hunting ground at Kensington Palace into a menagerie. By 1726, tigers and civets were living in 'iron "dens" … and there were plans to introduce "East Indian" and "outlandish" birds', although the big cats were soon moved to the Tower.[6] At Richmond, Caroline amassed both plant and animal collections and is known to have had botanical and zoological books in her library.[7]

Princess Augusta is remembered for her transformation of the gardens at Kew – a project undertaken with advice from John Stuart, 3rd earl of Bute, and continued by George III and Queen Charlotte – but from the outset of her marriage to Prince Frederick in 1736 she collected canaries, parakeets, magpies and Virginia nightingales (North American cardinals), and in 1753 was given an American goldfinch, painted finch and blue linnet by the South Carolina plantation owner Eliza Lucas Pinckney.[8] By the 1760s, there were native songbirds such as bullfinches, larks, yellowhammers and chaffinches in a pseudo-Chinese aviary adjacent to a scented flower garden, and a chinoiserie menagerie ringed with cages for pheasants and larger birds, as well as a pond with goldfish.[9] The interest in oriental pheasants was closely allied with other imported goods from the Far East,[10] and naturally invited attendant architecture in a similar style.

Queen Charlotte's well-known interest in the natural world helped to break down barriers preventing women from developing an interest in the sciences and her example was important for many well-to-do ladies.[11] At Richmond, where a

papers will be cited as WYW1352 and the shelf mark provided. 4 Festing, 'Menageries and the landscape garden', p. 104. 5 R.J. Hoage, Anne Roskell and Jane Mansour, 'Menageries and zoos to 1900' in Robert J. Hoage and William A. Deiss (eds), *New worlds, new animals: from menagerie to zoological park in the nineteenth century* (London, 1996), p. 13. See also Daniel Hahn, *The Tower menagerie* (New York, 2003). 6 Joanna Marschner, *Queen Caroline: cultural politics at the early eighteenth-century court* (London, 2014), pp 37, 39. 7 Mark Laird, 'An august domain: gardening in the princesses' Kew' in Joanna Marschner with David Bindman and Lisa L. Ford (eds), *Enlightened princesses: Caroline, Augusta, Charlotte, and the shaping of the modern world* (London, 2017), pp 136–7. 8 Laird, 'An august domain', p. 139; Tyler Griffith and Amy Meyers, 'The natures of Britain and empire' in Marschner et al. (eds), *Enlightened Princesses*, p. 476. 9 Laird, 'An august domain', pp 139, 147; Griffith and Meyers, 'The natures of Britain and empire', pp 346, 505. 10 Festing, 'Menageries and the landscape garden', p. 111. 11 Clarissa Campbell Orr, 'Queen Charlotte, "scientific queen"' in Clarissa Campbell Orr (ed.), *Queenship in Britain, 1660–1837: royal patronage, court culture and dynastic*

'New Menagerie' was built on the site where Queen Caroline's had stood, Charlotte and her family were able to admire cattle from Algeria and India, buffalo, a quagga, a nilgai and kangaroos.[12] Elephants and a zebra – the latter painted by George Stubbs and (in)famously known as 'the Queen's Ass' – were accommodated near Buckingham House.[13]

Although there is no archival evidence to suggest that the Winns of Nostell visited the royal collections, they were well known to anyone of fashion who visited the capital or read the periodical press. The same holds true for London's commercial menageries, pet shops and the wild animal shows that travelled throughout the British Isles. There were simply too many of them to go unnoticed.

Other celebrated collections of which the Winns would have been aware were those amassed by Charles Lennox, 2nd duke of Richmond, at Goodwood, West Sussex, and by Queen Charlotte's friend Margaret Cavendish-Holles-Harley-Bentinck, duchess of Portland, at Bulstrode Park, Buckinghamshire. The duke of Richmond owned one of the largest of eighteenth-century menageries. From 1725–6 (when a monkey appears in the accounts[14]) until his death in 1750, he acquired a veritable Noah's ark that included an armadillo; primates; black, brown and white bears; lions, tigers and a leopard; raccoons; wolves; birds of prey; ostriches and goldfish.[15] Apart from the fish, which resided indoors in Kanxi porcelain bowls,[16] the animals inhabited outdoor enclosures and cages. When the duke wished to view them, the cages were loaded onto carts and transported to the High Wood area of the park, where a network of tunnels made it possible for the animals to emerge in either a large brick chamber fronted by an iron grille or in an open-air run, much to the delight of onlookers.[17] In the 1760s, the 3rd duke modified the menagerie his father had built in a disused chalk pit so that he could house pheasants and rare birds, and constructed an obelisk-shaped chimney for the garden folly below.[18]

The duchess of Portland's collections of exotica were even larger. After a childhood spent at Wimpole Hall, Cambridgeshire, where her parents had an aviary and a menagerie, and a subsequent move to Welbeck Abbey, Nottinghamshire, with the remnants of their collections after her father's death

*politics* (Manchester, 2002), p. 238. Women 'were the motivating force behind more than a third of the menageries listed'; Festing, 'Menageries and the landscape garden', pp 108, 111–15. 12 Laird, 'An august domain', p. 147; Royal Botanic Gardens Kew, 'Royal Treasures', https://www.kew.org/kew-gardens/attractions/queen-charlottes-cottage, accessed 20 Sept. 2018. 13 Judy Egerton, *George Stubbs, painter: catalogue raisonné* (London, 2007), pp 50–1, 180–1; Florence Grant, 'Visual satire and caricature' in Marschner et al. (eds), *Enlightened princesses*, pp 269–72. See also Christopher Plumb, *The Georgian menagerie: exotic animals in eighteenth-century London* (London, 2015), pp 111, 172, 185–7; Griffith and Meyers, 'The natures of Britain and empire', pp 481, 512–13. 14 Festing, 'Menageries and the landscape garden', p. 105; Rosemary Baird, *Goodwood: art and architecture, sport and family* (London, 2007), p. 62. 15 Baird, *Goodwood*, pp 62–3. 16 Ibid., p. 63. 17 Ibid., p. 67; Festing, 'Menageries and the landscape garden', pp 106–7. 18 Baird, *Goodwood*, p. 66.

in 1740,[19] it was perhaps inevitable that the duchess would follow in their footsteps. At Bulstrode, her garden was planted with specimens from around the world; she commissioned nearly 800 paintings of foreign and native plants from the German-born George Ehret, and paid the Swedish botanist Daniel Solander to catalogue her collections.[20]

Bulstrode's botanical specimens have been described as second only in size to those in Sir Hans Sloane's collection – and his collection formed the nucleus of the British Museum.[21] However it is the duchess' exotic birds and animals that are most pertinent. Her close friend Mary Delany described breakfasting at Bulstrode in September 1768 alongside a 'little jonquil parrot … it is the prettiest good-humoured little creature I ever saw', and on other occasions remarked on the beauty and number of birds indoors and outside.[22] As described by the visiting Mrs Lybbe Powys in 1769, the duchess' menagerie housed larger birds such as storks, pheasants, bustards and albatrosses, while the aviary was home to smaller waxbills, parakeets and long-tailed widowbirds.[23] A decade later, Mrs Delany remarked on the

> beautiful deer, oxen, cows, sheep of all countries, bufalos, mouflons, horses, asses, all in their proper places. Then, *hares* and *squirrels at every step you take*, so confident of their security that they hardly run away! The great lawn before the house is the nursery of all sorts of pheasants, pea fowl and Guinea fowl, besides interlopers of Bantam pidgeons.[24]

Among the duchess' prized possessions was also a zebu bull.[25]

Few families could aspire to menageries of such scale and expense as these, but more realistically sized forerunners closer to home for the Winns could be found at Bretton Hall and Wentworth Castle, both in South Yorkshire. At the former, where Sir William Wentworth and his wife Diana Blackett built the present Bretton Hall *c.*1730, it may be of some relevance that their architect, Colonel James Moyser, was also responsible for the early designs of Nostell *c.*1731.[26] Sir Thomas Wentworth inherited Bretton in 1763 and further estates from Sir Walter Calverley Blackett in 1777, after which he added to Bretton Hall and continued work on the park and lakes.[27] The Bretton menagerie was located on an island,[28] although it is unclear whether it was created for Sir William or Sir Thomas.

**19** Michael Hall, *Treasures of the Portland Collection* (Welbeck, 2016), pp 46, 58. **20** Ibid., p. 59. **21** Huxley, 'Natural history collectors and their collections', p. 85. **22** Plumb, *Georgian menagerie*, p. 203. **23** Beth Fowkes Tobin, *The duchess's shells: natural history collecting in the age of Cook's voyages* (London, 2014), pp 48–9. **24** Mary Delany to Miss Port, 1 Aug. 1779, quoted in Fowkes Tobin, *The duchess's shells*, p. 48. **25** Festing, 'Menageries and the landscape garden', p. 105; Fowkes Tobin, *The duchess's shells*, p. 49. **26** Howard Colvin, *A biographical dictionary of British architects, 1600–1840* (4th ed. London, 2008), p. 713. **27** The Blacketts of North East England, 'Bretton Hall', https://www.theblacketts.com/articles/82-bretton-hall, accessed 13 Sept. 2018. **28** Festing, 'Menageries and the landscape

At Wentworth Castle in the late 1720s, Thomas Wentworth, 1st earl of Strafford, created a menagerie garden in a disused quarry and built a banqueting house to overlook it.[29] His son William, the 2nd earl, and daughter-in-law Lady Anne Campbell, added to the menagerie. That inveterate gossip Horace Walpole called Anne 'the lady of the menagerie' and she was well known for her love of animals.[30] According to Lady Louisa Stuart, the countess' epilepsy had left her isolated at Wentworth, where she

> delighted in animals of every sort and species; had favourite horses, dogs, cats, squirrels, parroquets, and singing-birds. Nay, I remember to this hour the pleasure it gave me … to see a couple of tame green lizards, which she kept in a box, let loose to sport and catch flies in the sunshine.[31]

Given that the mid-century Winns were deeply embedded in county society, they would almost certainly have been aware of these menageries, as well as those at Bawtry Hall, Harewood House, Temple Newsam, Wentworth Woodhouse and no doubt many other Yorkshire estates that await rediscovery.

## NOSTELL AND THE MENAGERIE HOUSE

The early plans for developing the park and gardens at Nostell coincide with plans for building a new house made shortly after Sir Rowland Winn, 4th baronet, returned from his Grand Tour in 1729. Around 1730, the Pontefract-based horticulturalist Joseph Perfect produced a scheme with a wilderness area behind the house, although only avenues of trees are depicted in the spot where the Menagerie Garden was created.[32] About the same time, a plan attributed to Stephen Switzer includes 'A Hermitage and Cascade out of the Old Quarry' and 'A Menagerie and a place for Fowls', suggesting that the 4th baronet was considering amassing a collection of exotica in the 1730s. For what may have been financial reasons, however, it was not until 1758 that William Perfect provided a list of plants for 'Ye hill in the menagerie',[33] and *c.*1759 that the area soon to be known as the Menagerie Garden was developed in an abandoned quarry at the same time as a new bridge was constructed for the road behind.[34]

garden', pp 108, 110. **29** Ibid., p. 110; Baird, *Goodwood*, pp 65–6. **30** Ingrid H. Tague, *Animal companions: pets and social change in eighteenth-century Britain* (University Park, PA, 2015), pp 227–8. **31** Ibid. **32** Perfect's plan is reproduced in Jacqueline Riding with Chris Blackburn, Roger Carr-Whitworth, Paul Dibb and Mark Purcell, *Nostell, West Yorkshire: a souvenir guide* (Swindon, 2016), p. 57. The Perfect family were active at Nostell throughout the century. William Perfect supplied plants to the 5th baronet and the 6th baronet paid John and G. Perfect £108 18*s.* 6*d.* for trees in 1793. **33** This document is quoted in Janette Ray Associates, Chris Burnett Associates and Northern Archaeological Associates, *Nostell Priory historic landscape management plan* (2000), p. 28, but no reference accompanies it. **34** A plan dating from *c.*1759 of part of the Nostell estate shows an area with what appear to be

The Menagerie House, most likely designed by James Paine, featured a green and white Gothick room with plasterwork of 1763 by Joseph Rose senior that looked out over a series of penned-in areas or cages.[35] The following year, evergreens were planted 'within the Neting for the Fowls to Bask under' and the garden was planted with more evergreens and a mind-bogglingly international array of flowering trees and shrubs such as rock rose (cistus), barberry (berberis), honeysuckle (diervilla), myrtle, laburnum, lilac, sea buckthorn, roses, spindle trees, spiraea or meadowsweet, tamarisk, syringa, laurel, box, juniper, viburnum, acacia and shrub cinquefoil.[36] Heady scents and bright flowers would have made the garden a charming retreat in summer and it is not difficult to imagine Sir Rowland, his children and their guests drinking tea in the Menagerie House while observing the exotic birds.

Later in 1764, while Charlotte Winn was staying at Bridlington, she wrote to offer her father a parrot that she described as able to 'talk extremely well'.[37] Because parrots were among the most popular exotics and could be seen in many middle-class homes, coffee houses, taverns and commercial menageries, as well as in aristocratic collections,[38] the presence of this parrot for sale at a northern seaside town is less surprising than one might imagine. It may have cost anywhere from £1 to twenty guineas, depending upon its coloration.[39] Although Miss Winn was not interested in the bird herself, she thought Sir Rowland might want it for his menagerie or, if not, wondered whether her brother Rowland would like it instead.

The following year, Mary Winn wrote to inform her father that 'The Pea fowl which layed upon the Ice House has forsook her Nest so leasd any Rain sho'd come, I have spoke to Mr Allen to send for the Thatcher' to repair the building.[40] As peafowl have an unfortunate tendency to wander, this suggests that the Nostell ostentation had been confined for several weeks to aid the birds' recognition of the Menagerie Garden as 'home'. They cannot have been confined permanently, however, as the icehouse is located behind the Menagerie House and would thus have been hidden from view.

enclosures, although the Menagerie House is not yet present. The plan is reproduced as illustration 4 in Ray et al., *Nostell Priory historic landscape management plan*, but the original document cannot be located. **35** Joseph Rose to Sir Rowland Winn, 15 Apr. 1765, with an account that includes a charge of £12 13*s.* ¼*d.* for work 'at the Gothick room in the Managerie' (WYW1352/1/4/114/43); Joseph Rose to Sir Rowland Winn, n.d. but after the 4th baronet's death on 23 Aug. 1765, notes that the work on the Menagerie House dated from 1763 and cost £12 13*s.* 1½*d.* (WYW1352/1/4/97/27). **36** William Perfect to Sir Rowland Winn, 11 Feb. 1764 (WYW1352/1/4/46/1), and list of plants and trees (WYW1352/1/4/46/2). **37** Charlotte Winn to Sir Rowland Winn, 4 Sept. 1764 (WYW1352/1/4/3/48). **38** Plumb, *Georgian menagerie, passim*. **39** For the difficulty of estimating the price of exotica, see Tague, *Animal companions*, p. 33; Plumb, *Georgian menagerie*, p. 196. **40** Mary Winn to Sir Rowland Winn, 23 May 1765 (WYW1352/1/4/1/36). As a peacock cost about half a crown, peafowl were expensive birds to acquire; Plumb, *Georgian menagerie*, p. 21.

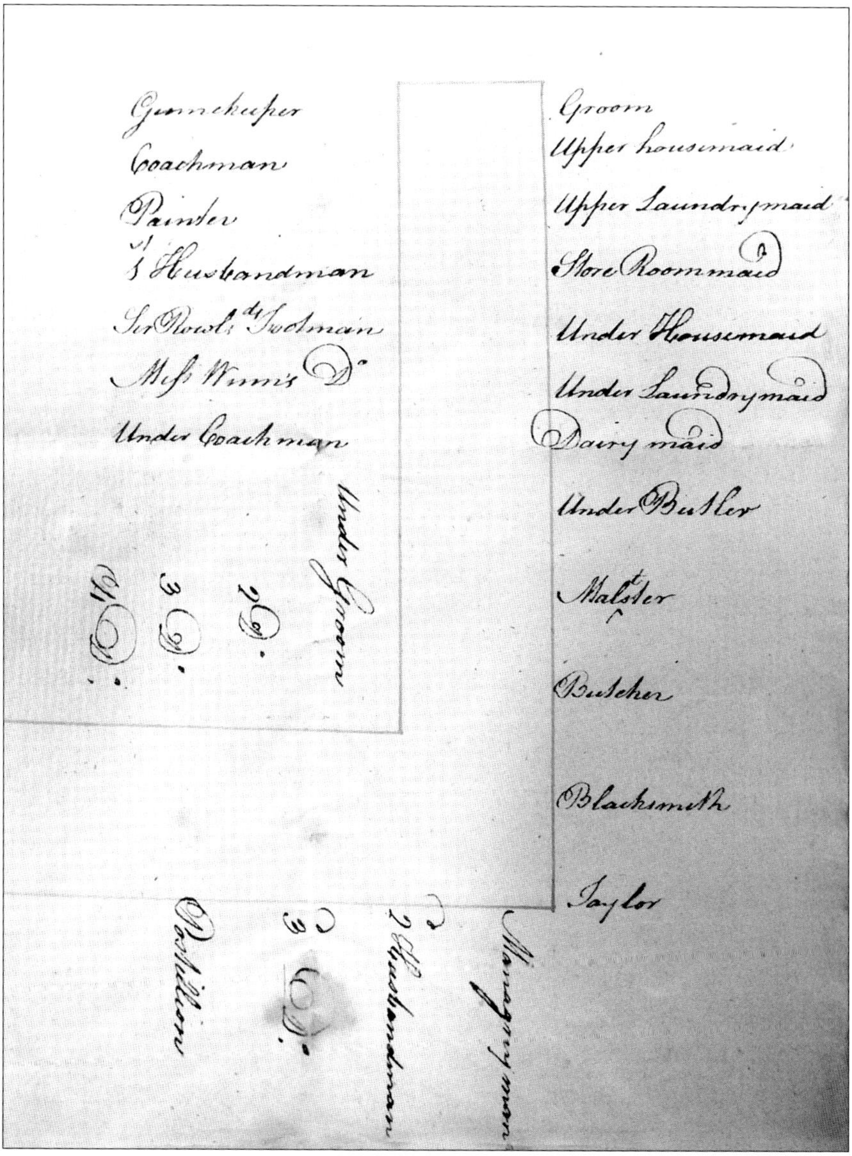

1.2 Servants' hall seating plan, coll. West Yorkshire Archive Service (Wakefield), Winn papers, WYW1352/3/4/2/2. Photo: author.

Although one presumes that the 4th baronet employed someone to look after his menagerie, it is only during the tenure of the 5th baronet that evidence survives. This Sir Rowland employed a 'Menagrey man', whose status in the service hierarchy is indicated by his seat at the bottom of the servants' dining table alongside the second and third husbandmen and postilion (fig. 1.2).[41] The 5th baronet also commissioned Robert Adam to add wings to the Menagerie House around 1776.[42]

## A CANINE INTERLUDE

Lady Winn's lapdogs were a frequent topic of discussion in letters between the couple, usually written when the 5th baronet was in London on business and his wife was at Nostell. This is one area where size mattered and, in the absence of the breed standards and specialist breeders that developed in the nineteenth century, much of the language Sir Rowland used is that of the trophy hunter in search of the tiniest dog he could find rather than that of the animal lover.[43]

In a century many historians have characterized as beset by 'anxiety', pet ownership, particularly by women, appears to have been an area of deep concern. In her study of the relationship between humans and animals, Ingrid Tague has suggested that it was only in Georgian Britain that the custom of allowing certain animals into spaces previously reserved for humans 'became possible on a broad scale'.[44] However, the special treatment lavished on parrots and lapdogs brought with it criticism of the threat posed by women who became so emotionally attached to their pets that they neglected their homes, husbands and children.[45] Diana Donald has made a similar point: excessive attention to animals on the part of women was seen as a 'dereliction of their stronger moral duty to care for fellow-humans, and was ruthlessly satirised as foolish or false sentimentality'.[46] This seems churlish, but many Georgian commentators bemoaned what they saw as immoral waste. In an era when even the middle classes could struggle to find enough to eat, pets were seen as consumers of food for which they gave nothing in return (by definition lapdogs were not working dogs and parrots

41 Servants' hall seating plan (WYW1352/3/4/2/2). Although the archive catalogue asserts that this document dates from the nineteenth century, it is annotated in French in Sabine Winn's hand. It dates from after 1768 when the Winns' daughter Esther was born (hence the seat for Miss Winn's footman) and before 1775 when their son Rowland was born, as there is no seat for a nursemaid or equivalent. 42 Joseph Rose Jnr billed the Winns £6 6*s*. 10*d*. for work done on the Menagerie House between August 1776 and August 1777 (WYW 1352/3/3/1/5/5/2). 43 An account from Mr Martinnant dated 25 Mar. 1785 includes an entry for 'a little dog (£4 4*s*. 0*d*.)' (Various receipts and accounts from traders and merchants, WYW1352/3/4/3/2); Mr Rosewell to Sir Rowland Winn, n.d. (WYW1352/3/4/3/1). See also Tague, *Animal companions*, pp 22–3, where she notes that: 'Extremely small dogs were apparently both much in demand and difficult to obtain.' That the Winns were not animal lovers in the modern sense is also suggested by the construction of a cockpit in 1783. Agreement from John Tattersell and William Heseltine, 28 Aug. 1786 (WYW1352/3/3/1/5/5/6). 44 Tague, *Animal companions*, p. 19. 45 Ibid., p. 106. See also Plumb, *Georgian menagerie*, p. 195 and Fowkes Tobin, *The duchess's shells*, pp 50–3 for a pithy discussion of similar beliefs about natural history collectors. 46 Diana Donald, *Picturing animals in Britain, 1750–1850* (London, 2007), p. 23. See also Plumb, *Georgian menagerie*, p. 198.

merely sat in cages) and their specialized accoutrements such as collars and feeding bowls suggested wasteful extravagance and 'luxury', another abiding anxiety in this most anxious of centuries.[47]

No such concerns appear to have troubled the Winns, however, whose correspondence contradicts much recent scholarship. Lady Winn was explicit in her need for a dog as a husband substitute and, far from fearing a diminution of his own importance at Nostell, Sir Rowland was an active agent in supplying his replacement(s).

The relevant correspondence begins on 22 January 1773, when he informed his wife: 'I have no news yet from this … man with his dog, therefore I intend to put an advertisement in all the daily papers for a very little dog of the Danish or Spanish breed, and this way I hope to at least succeed.'[48] The 'Danish' breed is unidentifiable, but the 'Spanish' dog was probably a papillon.[49] Sir Rowland's comment about the advertisement suggests that finding the right pet could be time consuming and points to a wider reality: the printed press was often the means by which animals changed hands.[50]

Within three weeks, the owner of a likely canine candidate had contacted Sir Rowland:

> I have news to announce … it is that I might have found you a little dog … but I haven't seen it yet, it is out of town and he [the owner] promised to show it to me in a week … I really hope that it will correspond to the description he gave me, but we cannot rely on this. Anyway, I will give you news about it as soon as I have seen it.[51]

Four days later, on 18 February 1773, the 5th baronet told his wife he had still not seen the man with the dog,[52] and by 20 February was becoming impatient:

> I do not understand why he loyally promised me to bring it back to me when he returned from the countryside thus I will wait for him at any moment because I sent for him but I was told that he wasn't back. You can be sure that I will inform you as soon as I get news from him.[53]

Perhaps the anticipation had been too great for Sir Rowland was crestfallen the next time the lapdog was mentioned:

47 Tague, *Animal companions*, pp 37–8, 92–4, 101. 48 Sir Rowland Winn to Sabine Winn, 22 Jan. 1773 (WYW1352/1/1/6/3). 49 For the identification of a 'Spanish' dog as a papillon, see Madeleine Pinault Sørensen, 'Portraits of animals, 1600–1800' in Matthew Senior (ed.), *A cultural history of animals in the Age of Enlightenment* (Oxford and New York, 2011), p. 181 and Egerton, *Stubbs*, p. 366. 50 Plumb, *Georgian menagerie*, p. 22; Tague, *Animal companions*, pp 22–4. 51 Sir Rowland Winn to Sabine Winn, 14 Feb. 1773 (WYW 1352/1/1/6/3). 52 Sir Rowland Winn to Sabine Winn, 18 Feb. 1773 (WYW1352/1/1/6/3). 53 Sir Rowland Winn to Sabine Winn, 20 Feb. 1773 (WYW1352/1/1/6/3).

> I have finally seen the man with the dog and who promised to show it to me on Sunday without fail but from what he told me this morning I am afraid that it is not as small as what he had described … I also put advertisements in the morning papers but without any effect until now. However I want to continue them for a few days … I assure you that I really wish to succeed in finding one like you want and you can count on me to not neglect any means for this.[54]

A month later, he was able to inform Lady Winn that 'Your little dog sleeps with me every night, I think you will like her, she is very lively.'[55]

Perhaps that particular dog was short-lived or Lady Winn decided to add to her canine family, because Sir Rowland returned to the subject of lapdogs in May 1774,[56] and again in April 1777 when he was able to report that he was about to see a dog she might like,[57] before recording:

> I must tell you that I haven't just seen the little dog I told you about, but I am actually in possession of it. According to me, it is the prettiest little animal I have ever seen, as white as snow and … so soft. If you are happy when you see it I'll be happy, and as you say that you need something to pass the time while I am gone I am determined to send this little miniature … I mustn't forget to give you the name of your little dog. She is called Mina … so my dear please write to me if you think when you've seen her that one guinea for the trouble of sourcing her is too much.[58]

Sir Rowland returned to the topic of little Mina on 14 April, 19 April and again on 22 April 1777, by which time she and other animals had been shipped north with instructions for their care.[59]

In 1783 Lady Winn was in possession of yet another lapdog, and had been combing the newspapers for dog-related advertisements. Unfortunately, when Sir Rowland went to inspect one that had caught her eye, he found it

> all mangy, almost dying and not even two months old. Never had I seen a beast so disgusting, it could make one vomit and, besides, it was already almost as big as your Jessy … I would not have taken it even if I had been offered twenty guineas to do so, and I am sure that if you had seen it, it would have disgusted you so much (even if it had been as small as the man

**54** Sir Rowland Winn to Sabine Winn, 25 Feb. 1773 (WYW1352/1/1/6/3). **55** Sir Rowland Winn to Sabine Winn, 20 Mar. 1773 (WYW1352/1/1/6/3). **56** Sir Rowland Winn to Sabine Winn, 25 May 1774 (WYW1352/1/1/6/3). **57** Sir Rowland Winn to Sabine Winn, 10 Apr. 1777 (WYW1352/1/1/6/3). **58** Sir Rowland Winn to Sabine Winn, 12 Apr. 1777 (WYW1352/1/1/6/3). **59** Sir Rowland Winn to Sabine Winn, 14 Apr. 1777; Sir Rowland Winn to Sabine Winn, 19 Apr. 1777; Sir Rowland Winn to Sabine Winn, 22 Apr. 1777 (all WYW1352/1/1/6/3).

> had maintained) that you would not have wanted to see it again … I am afraid, my dear, that regarding the advertisement you would have had the idea that this animal was one of nature's masterpieces … You can see from the description I'm giving you that one cannot rely on advertisements, and the one that I am enclosing here from the same man, is as false as the rest, because his Child of the Sun is nothing else but a big monkey.[60]

Two days later, the unfortunate puppy was dead.[61]

## INDOORS AND OUT: MARMOSETS AND OTHER EXOTICA

Sir Rowland's complaint about the false advertising of the size of the puppy, and the casual comment that the 'Child of the Sun' was only 'a big monkey', offers a glimpse into the global nature of the Winns' menagerie: in the late 1760s, they owned a small primate.

Primates were popular pets in most of Europe by the sixteenth century and, by happy coincidence, Rowland Lockey's copy of Hans Holbein's portrait of the family of Sir Thomas More – which passed by descent from More's daughter Margaret Roper to the Winns and is still on display at Nostell – depicts a monkey beside More's wife Alice.[62] By the eighteenth century, however, exotica from all over the world were arriving in European ports in increasing numbers. The wider the exposure to different primates, the deeper the moral and philosophical questions became. Given that they could not be tamed like dogs, the more humanoid primates were yet another cause of anxiety, largely because of their demonstrable human-like behaviours and emotions.[63] Some, such as Georges Louis Leclerc, comte de Buffon, author of the best-selling *Historie naturelle* (1749–88), asserted that primates only seemed to be intelligent because they could mimic humans, although this raised the enormous problem of accounting for the presence of a primate's brain.[64] For others, primates raised important questions about man's place at the apex of the Great Chain of Being, as well as the nature of 'savages' who possessed what were perceived to be simian characteristics.[65] Tague has also written persuasively on the questions raised by

**60** Sir Rowland Winn to Sabine Winn, 24 May 1783 (WYW1352/1/1/6/3). The newspaper advertisement has not been located. **61** Sir Rowland Winn to Sabine Winn, 26 May 1783 (WYW1352/1/1/6/3). **62** Pinault Sørensen, 'Portraits of animals; p. 188; Grigson, *Menagerie*, p. 9. This monkey is discussed in David R. Smith. 'Portrait and counter-portrait in Holbein's "The Family of Sir Thomas More"', *Art Bulletin*, 87:3 (Sept. 2005), pp 484–506. It was a family pet, but appears in the painting for reasons of 'art' rather than 'zoology'. **63** Tague, *Animal companions*, pp 50–1. **64** Donald, *Picturing animals*, pp 104–5. English and French editions of Buffon's *Historie naturelle* are in the collection at Nostell, but they appear to have been acquired in the nineteenth century. National Trust Collections, *Histoire naturelle, générale et particulière* …, http://www.nationaltrustcollections.org.uk/object/3089627, accessed 30 Sept. 2018. **65** Tague, *Animal companions*, p. 53.

primates, the ways in which eighteenth-century theorists and commentators discussed the trade in enslaved Africans and the contradictions posed by slaves who shared characteristics such as the ability to reason with other humans but not with animals.[66] The Winns shared no thoughts on such matters in their correspondence, and there is nothing to indicate that their primate prompted any moral dilemmas for the couple. In fact, the opposite may have been true. The recent discovery of three letters sent from Vevey in Switzerland by an unidentified Susette Pilgrim addressed to 'Monsieur Jan Philipe more chè Monsieur le Chevallier Winn a Nostel', to 'Monsieur Jan Philipe Negre chè Monsieur le Chevallier Winn a Nostel' and to 'Monsieur Jan Philipe Negre chè Miledi Winn a Nostel' reveal that the Winns had an enslaved (or formerly enslaved) African man in attendance; this is substantiated by several references to a personal servant named Jean in Sir Rowland's letters; and a charge of £1 3*s*. 0*d*. in a Chippendale account for '2 Blankets for the housekeepers & the blacks bed' at Nostell, together.[67] Added to this is a troubling letter from W. Pitney offering Sir Rowland a 'pretty little black Boy' who is

> to be disposed off he is about 13 Yr[s] Old think he will suit you for Miss [Sir Rowland's daughter Esther]. I have the refusal is the property of a Corn facter near Smithfield … his Mastr will sell a loaf of Bread for £30 & give the Boy in the bargain, not being allowed to sell the Boy by Act of Parlimt he has not been Christend as yet, is a smart boy bears a very good Charactr he is one of the rough headed ones …[68]

Although the Winns do not appear to have taken advantage of this special offer, it is not the sort of letter one sends unless one is very sure of its reception. The unpalatable reality may be that the Winns saw Jean Philipe in much the same light as they saw their primate – as a fashionably exotic accessory to an elite lifestyle that raised no moral questions.

Certainly the Winns' primate was prized enough to have its portrait painted by Hugh Douglas Hamilton at a cost of two guineas in 1768, the same year in which Thomas Chippendale provided 'A Mahogany House for a Monkey' (fig. 1.3).[69] The fact that Hamilton billed his work as a portrait rather than merely as a painting brings to light a paradox. On the one hand, he was not a zoological illustrator intent on capturing the exact appearance of an exotic

66 Ibid., pp 50–90. 67 Susette Pilgrim to Jan Philipe, 23 June 1769 (WYW1352/1/4/24/21), 21 Apr. 1771 (WYW1352/1/4/24/14) and 21 Aug. (WYW1352/1/4/24/29); Sir Rowland Winn to Sabine Winn, 11 Oct. 1774, 10 Apr. 1777, 14 Apr. 1777, 14 May 1783, 22 May 1783 (WYW1352/1/1/6/3); Thomas Chippendale Account 1766–72, entry for 20 Jan. 1770 (WYW1352/3/3/1/5/3/47). 68 W. Pitney to Sir Rowland Winn, 14 Sept. 1775 (WYW1352/1/4/88/17). 69 Bill from Hugh Douglas Hamilton (WYW1352/1/4/56/32); Sir Rowland Winn's account to Thomas Chippendale for work at the London townhouse, 1766–9, entry for 24 June 1767 (WYW1352/3/3/1/5/3/47).

1.3 Hugh Douglas Hamilton, portrait of Sir Rowland Winn's marmoset, private collection. Photo: author.

species for a natural history publication but, on the other, he had aimed to capture its 'likeness' in much the same way that he had with *Sir Rowland and Lady Winn in the library at Nostell*, as well as the untraced portrait of Sir Rowland's brother Edward that also appears on Hamilton's bill.

As the words 'marmoset' and 'monkey' were used interchangeably in the eighteenth century to describe any small primate, it is only with the very recent discovery of Hamilton's painting that it is now possible to confirm that the Winns owned a Geoffroy's marmoset, an arboreal species with characteristically tuffed ears and striped tail that is native to the Amazon rainforest.

An adult marmoset is approximately nineteen centimetres tall and a 'Mahogany House' that cost only eighteen shillings cannot have been particularly large. In common with most primates kept in captivity at this time,

70 Grigson, *Menagerie*, p. 267; Adam Bowett, 'Sir Rowland Winn's monkey house', *Furniture History Society Newsletter*, 213 (Feb. 2019), 14–15 at p. 14; https://nationalzoo.si. edu/ geoffroys-marmoset (accessed 15 Feb. 2019).

the little mammal probably also had a chain around its waist so that it could not escape when taken from its cage.[71] One can only hope that it did not misbehave in the same way that the marmoset belonging to the royal midwife Sidney Kennon did when it snacked on her prized Chinese goldfish,[72] but it must have been a lonely life for a gregarious animal that normally lives in the treetops in troops of a dozen or more.

Three further exotic species can be located at Nostell: goldfish, buffalo and mynah birds. While the 5th baronet's attitude to some of the animals in his ownership may be offensive to twenty-first-century sensibilities, it was nonetheless characteristic of him to send and keep instructions on their care, as in the case of the goldfish, which, depending on the season, appear to have spent their lives alternating between a pond in the grounds and a bowl in the house.[73] Goldfish were prized commodities, often displayed in expensive bowls that evoked their original habitat – China. However, they were relatively easy to come by in the 1780s, when the Winns acquired theirs, and by the end of the eighteenth century goldfish 'could be found swimming in London's ditches'.[74] This may explain why their presence at Nostell went otherwise unremarked.

The buffalo merited a mention in a letter of May 1774 from Sir Rowland to his wife, Sabine:

> I have found for you another rarity which I acquired for very good value, I don't know if I should tell you but I can't resist and I must say it: it is a buffalo bullock and cow, of a very small size and very soft. I also found a male and female [illegible] from Siberia, they are extraordinarily rare and you can please tell the dear little angel about it because they are for you and her. I plan on sending them to the country with the boys who brought the horses ...[75]

The description of the beasts as 'small' and 'soft' suggests that they may have been Mediterranean water buffalo; the kind that produce milk for bufala mozzarella. Frustratingly, there is no further reference to the buffalo in the archive, nor any means of identifying what the animals from Siberia might have been.

With the mynah bird, a native of India and parts of southern Asia, one is on surer ground. It most likely came from one of London's many specialist bird dealers and lived indoors with a number of other birds, some of which were breeding pairs, in Sir Rowland's twelve mahogany aviaries.[76]

71 Tague, *Animal companions*, pp 41–2. 72 Plumb, *Georgian menagerie*, p. 47. 73 Instructions on how to look after goldfish, 6 Nov. 1780 (WYW1352/3/4/3/1). For instructions on the care of small birds, see Sir Rowland Winn to Sabine Winn, 22 Apr. 1777 (WYW1352/1/1/6/3). 74 Plumb, *Georgian Menagerie*, p. 2. 75 Sir Rowland Winn to Sabine Winn, 25 May 1774 (WYW1352/1/1/6/3). The illegible word looks like 'Bribys'. 76 Inventory and valuation taken at Nostell Mansion ... July 1806 (WYW1352/3/4/1/30).

Because Lady Winn and her daughter Esther cared for the birds during Sir Rowland's frequent absences, reports were made on their health. In spite of the close association many believed existed between women and birds,[77] Lady Winn disliked the mynah and made disparaging comments about it:

> Madame Le Pecq and my little girl are taking particular care of the birds in your room who are all full of health and appetite. There is not one dead. The myna bird eats like a wolf, accompanied by a liberty of stomach that is not gracious to see. Peggy and the other birds are more decent. The very small ones are not so bald.[78]
>
> All the birds are well, but that myna is a disgusting character. He digests as quickly as he eats and he doesn't do anything else all day.[79]

While it is true that mynahs do have a short digestive tract in comparison with other birds, the real surprise is that Lady Winn never mentions why they were desirable in the first place: they are excellent mimics. As a result, mynahs had been highly collectable for over a century. In 1664 Samuel Pepys described one as able to talk and neigh like a horse, and Sir Hans Sloane presented one 'that spoke very prittily' to Queen Caroline.[80] They were brought to Europe in comparatively large numbers with the Dutch and the British East India Companies, and came via the same trade route that supplied the Chinese wallpaper for the Nostell state apartment. Like the primate, the mynah was an exotic predicated on an expanding empire and the desire to appear fashionable.

## PETS FOR THE CHILDREN

As this author has explored elsewhere, Lady Winn isolated herself at Nostell after the birth of the 6th baronet in 1775 and this had important ramifications for the way that she shopped.[81] Unable to visit her favourite purveyors in person, she relied on correspondence and proxy shopping. This explains the references to newspaper advertisements in surviving letters, a trade card advertising birds and animals for sale at a shop called The Parrot on London's Oxford Street (fig. 1.4),[82] and memoranda that the 5th baronet made to ensure that he

**77** Donald, *Picturing animals*, p. 23; Plumb, *Georgian menagerie*, p. 193. **78** Sabine Winn to Sir Rowland Winn, 4 July 1776 (WYW1352/1/4/29/12). **79** Sabine Winn to Sir Rowland Winn, 18 July 1776 (WYW1352/1/4/29/14). **80** Grigson, *Menagerie*, pp 37, 63. **81** Kerry Bristol, 'Between the exotic and the everyday: Sabine Winn at home 1765–1798' in Johanna Ilmakunnas and Jon Stobart (eds), *A taste for luxury in early modern Europe: display, acquisition and boundaries* (London, 2017), pp 161–78. **82** Various receipts and accounts from traders and merchants (WYW1352/3/4/3/1). Tague, *Animal companions*, p. 14 quotes from an advertisement in the *Public Advertiser*, 9 Jan. 1759, for a shop 'at the Sign of the Parrot', but parrots were so ubiquitous in eighteenth-century London that anyone with birds or animals for sale might call his establishment after them.

1.4 Trade card of a pet shop at the sign of The Parrot on Oxford Street, London, coll. West Yorkshire Archive Service (Wakefield), Winn papers, WYW1352/3/4/3/1. Photo: author.

remembered to fulfil his wife's commissions when he was away from home. Couched between notes on shoe buckles, snuff, vellum, children's clothing and a pianoforte is an entry for 'Some little small animals alive such as White Mice, DorMice, Squeralls, little Dog as are quite Tame for the Little Boy'.[83]

In fact, it was Esther Winn and not her brother who kept a pet squirrel. As such, the animal was a marker of class privilege for the 2-year-old child because it required accoutrements such as the 'Squirrells chain & collar' for which the Winns paid fifteen shillings to the silversmith Mark Cripps on 1 May 1770.[84] Presumably the rodent also had a cage, although there is no surviving evidence of such a purchase.

Squirrels were popular pets; hence they appear in many portraits, conversation pieces and still lifes where an image of a squirrel taking meat from a nut was sometimes used as an allegory 'of patience, diligence, and perseverance'.[85] As three portraits by John Singleton Copley suggest, pet squirrels seem to have been closely associated with young boys in America.[86] This may also have been

83 Memoranda (WYW1352/1/4/91/3). 84 Account of Sir Rowland Winn with Cripps & Co., 11 July 1766–19 Apr. 1770 (WYW1352/1/4/59/8). 85 Carrie Rebora, Paul Staiti, Erica E. Hirshler, Theodore E. Stebbins Jnr and Carol Troyen, *John Singleton Copley in America* (New York, 1995), p. 218. 86 *Boy with a squirrel (Henry Pelham)*, 1765, coll. Museum of Fine Arts, Boston; *John Bee Holmes*, 1765, private collection; and *Daniel Crommelin Verplanck*, 1771, coll. Metropolitan Museum of Art, New York, although it should be noted that Copley's portrait of Frances Deering Wentworth (Mrs Theodore Atkinson junior), n.d., coll. New York

1.5 Johan Zoffany, *Lady Anne, Lady Caroline and Lady Louisa Stuart, the three youngest daughters of John, third earl of Bute* (1763–4), oil on canvas, 101.2 x 126.5cm, coll. Tate, London.

the case in the Netherlands, as for example in Diderick Cuypers' *c.*1755 portrait of John Albert Bentinck with a pet squirrel sitting proudly on the young man's raised arm.[87] But British portraits that include squirrels are often depictions of young girls, and in several cases there are pendant portraits of brothers or fathers that have no squirrel present.

The allegories, symbolism and meanings of the British portraits have been discussed at length by Mary Webster in the case of Johan Zoffany's *Lady Anne, Lady Caroline and Lady Louisa Stuart, the three youngest daughters of John, third earl of Bute* of 1763–4 (fig. 1.5) and by Marcia Poynton with Philip Reinagle's *Mrs Congreve and her children* (1782). In the Zoffany, Lady Louisa is attempting to coax her pet squirrel down from the tree to which it has escaped, while Anne

Public Library, also includes a squirrel. 87 Illustrated in Hall, *Treasures of the Portland Collection*, pp 102–3.

holds her for steadiness and Caroline puts up a finger to encourage her youngest sister not to make a noise.[88] The Reinagle is a complex composition that speaks of dynastic continuity, domesticity, a presence through absence and an absence through presence.[89] In both cases, what we have are visible manifestations of the emphasis on care, restraint and learning advocated by eighteenth-century educational theorists.

Influenced by the writings of John Locke and his followers, this was a time when many parents believed that children were born a *tabula rasa* and needed to be educated to see, learn and perceive correctly.[90] Paul Staiti suggests that there was a growing link 'between the methods of training animals and the moral development of children'.[91] Encouraging a child to look after a pet and bring it from a wild into a civilized or domesticated state was widely believed to do much the same for the child by teaching him or her about the careful and correct use of power.[92] In many portraits of children with pet squirrels, the rodents 'like their masters, have been civilized. Yet the rodents are nevertheless held in check with … collars and chains.'[93] This can be read as an allegory of the freedom that comes with moral restraint. Donald has also suggested that, among the many roles for education expounded in Jean-Jacques Rousseau's *Émile* (1762, published in English in 1763), a key suggestion taken up by many parents was that

> To become sensitive and pitiful the child must know that he has fellow-creatures who suffer as he has suffered … indeed, how can we let ourselves be stirred by pity unless we go beyond ourselves and identify ourselves with the suffering animal, by leaving, so to speak, our own nature and taking his.[94]

Rousseau had been born in Geneva and spent much of his peripatetic life fleeing from and returning to the city of his birth. His works would have been well known to Lady Winn as her father was governor of the district of Vevey and she herself had been born on the shores of Lake Geneva. It is surely significant

88 Mary Webster, *Johan Zoffany, 1733–1810* (London, 2011), p. 127. See also Martin Postle (ed.), *Johan Zoffany RA: society observed* (London, 2011), p. 245. **89** Marcia Pointon, *Hanging the head: portraiture and social formation in eighteenth-century England* (London, 1993), pp 170–4. Although Pointon suggests that Ann Catherine Penelope Congreve is holding 'a toy squirrel on a string' (p. 170), it is more likely that the squirrel was the little girl's pet. See also Kate Retford, *The conversation piece: making modern art in eighteenth-century Britain* (London, 2017), pp 235–6. **90** Paul Staiti, 'Character and class' in Rebora et al., *John Singleton Copley*, p. 61. **91** Ibid., p. 65. **92** Ibid., 'Character and class', p. 64; Postle (ed.), *Johan Zoffany RA*, p. 244; Tague, *Animal companions,* p. 67. **93** Staiti, 'Character and class', p. 64. **94** Jean-Jacques Rousseau, *Émile, or on education*, trans. Barbara Foxley (London, 1911), pp 183–4, quoted in Donald, *Picturing animals*, p. 13. A 1761 edition of *Lettres de deux amans, habitans d'une petite ville au pied des Alpes: recueillies et publiées par J.J. Rousseau* is now in the library at Nostell but its provenance is uncertain. National Trust Collections, *Lettres de*

that a portrait of Rousseau, and one of Voltaire, who settled nearby, were among the works of art included in an inventory taken at the death of the Winns' grandson John Williamson in 1817.[95]

In much the same way that Esther was given a pet squirrel and later a pair of turtle doves,[96] her brother, the future 6th baronet, was presented with a dog. Sir Rowland's attempts to acquire the perfect canine for his son are recorded in the memorandum quoted above. A former retainer of the Winns, Mrs E. Nicholson, was also on the lookout for a small dog in June 1783,[97] as was the 5th baronet's sister Charlotte, who mentioned her search and that of her friend James Coxeter in letters of 23 June and 15 July 1783.[98] Although the evidence points towards a parental desire for a small dog for the 8-year-old Rowland, Coxeter secured a Newfoundland puppy named Neptune and the dog was duly sent to the Winns' townhouse in St James' Square.[99] Charlotte was dismayed to discover that the animal had then been dispatched north to Nostell without advance warning.[100] Alas Neptune did not live up to his advance billing,[101] and his subsequent history is unknown. It was the dog found by Mrs Nicholson that proved to be of the requisite size.

## SLAUGHTERED IN THE NAME OF SCIENCE?

No investigation of animals at Nostell can ignore the mention of mice in the 5th baronet's memorandum. As he recorded that they must be alive, were they intended as pets for his children or destined for a different fate? As Christopher Plumb notes: 'Animal merchants sold their animals as living commodities, but the consumption of exotic animals by the elite was also gustatory and cosmetic.'[102] Fostered by a boom in publications on natural history, that consumption could also be 'scientific'.

Evidence for the 4th baronet's interest in natural history comes in the form of a letter from the Revd Henry Zouch notifying him that a collection of fossils and shells about to be sold might be of interest because Sir Rowland 'seemed to have a taste for natural curiosities'.[103] There is more evidence of the 5th baronet's scientific interests preserved in the form of directions for using a microscope to view creatures such as a louse; objects such as fish scales, flies' wings and human

*deux amans* …, http://www.nationaltrustcollections.org.uk object/3090341, accessed 30 Sept. 2018. **95** Inventory of property taken after the death of the late John Winn esq., 17 Nov. 1817 (WYW1352/3/4/1/31). **96** Sir Rowland Winn to Sabine Winn, 22 Apr. 1777 (WYW 1352/1/1/6/3). **97** E. Nicholson to Sabine Winn, 2 June 1783 (WYW1352/1/1/6/5). **98** Charlotte Winn to Sir Rowland Winn, 23 June 1783 (WYW1352/1/4/37/4); Charlotte Winn to Sir Rowland Winn, 15 July 1783 (WYW1352/1/4/37/3). **99** James Coxeter to Sir Rowland Winn, 22 July 1783 (WYW1352/1/4/37/2). **100** Charlotte Winn to Sir Rowland Winn, 4 Sept. 1783 (WYW1352/1/4/1/43). **101** Charlotte Winn to Sir Rowland Winn, 14 Oct. 1783 (WYW1352/1/4/37/5). **102** Plumb, *Georgian menagerie*, p. 59. **103** Henry Zouch to Sir Rowland Winn, 13 Nov. 1763 (WYW1352/1/4/18/6/1).

hair; and processes such as the circulation of blood in a living frog.[104] Although they are not in the library at Nostell today, this list suggests that Sir Rowland was familiar with canonical texts such as Robert Hooke's *Micrographia: or some physiological descriptions of minute bodies made by magnifying glasses* (1665), which famously included an illustration of a louse; William Harvey's treatise on the motion of the heart, *Exercitatio anatomica de motu cordis et sanguinis in animalibus* (1628); and Marcello Malpighi's treatise *De viscerum structura exercitatio anatomica ... accedit dissertatio ... de polypo cordis* (1669). These last two publications were concerned with pulmonary action and blood circulation. Evidence of Lady Winn's interest is thinner, but in common with most elite women of her era, she was active in the still room. This explains the presence of a handwritten pro forma addressed to John Murray in London about purchasing books on 'officinal Botany'.[105] Although she informed him that she was 'not wishing to Spend more time in pursuing the Scientific knowledge of Vegetables' and was only interested in recipes for preparing various drugs, she also asked for:

> parts of the foreign Medical Review; Containing an Account with Extracts, of all the New Books published on Natural History
> Botany
> Materia Medica
> Chemistry
> Anatomy
> Surgery &c
> and the practice of physic in Every part of the Continent of Europe &c &c[106]

All of this suggests that the Winns had a fashionable interest in the new experimental science that had emerged in tandem with improvements in the manufacture and availability of scientific instruments. The collection that survives at Burton Constable Hall, East Yorkshire, is perhaps the best preserved of its type, but many country houses would have been home to similar items. They speak of a change in attitude towards scientific experimentation. As Silke Ackermann and Jane Wess have described, there were three classes of standardized instruments available in the latter half of the eighteenth century – philosophical, mathematical and optical.[107] As evidence of all three can be found

**104** Directions for using a microscope with a list of objects to view (WYW1352/1/4/18/2). **105** Several sheets of paper containing details of various products to be bought from different tradespeople in London, undated pro forma from Sabine Wynn to John Murray (WYW1352/1/4/32/17). **106** Ibid. Written on the reverse is Murray's response: 'Mr Murray is of opinion that the following books are those that will suit Lady Wynn/ Lewes's hist. of Materia Medica 4$^{to}$/ ____ New Dispensatory 8$^{vo}$/ Pomets hist. of Drugs 4$^{to}$'. **107** Silke Ackermann and Jane Wess, 'Between antiquarianism and experiment: Hans Sloane, at eighteenth-century Nostell, it is useful to define them here. Philosophical instruments were those used in experimental philosophy, i.e. those used for demonstration, which were usually divided into mechanics (including magnetism), pneumatics (air and gases), hydrostatics (water pressure, siphons), optics and astronomy. Sir Rowland's electrical machine and air pump discussed below fall into this category. Mathematical instruments were those used in astronomy, timekeeping, navigation, surveying, gunnery, carpentry, gauging and other trades. A theodolite is recorded in an 1806 inventory of Nostell,[108] although its acquisition may post-date the 5th baronet's lifetime. Finally, optical instruments included telescopes, microscopes and spectacles. Sir Rowland owned a microscope, as noted above, and a camera obscura was among the contents listed at Nostell when his son died.[109]

What distinguishes such instruments from their predecessors is the uses to which they were put in the quest to define the meaning of 'science', and the uses to which such knowledge was applied. It is the difference between the more passive collecting and observation of specimens and instruments by men such as Sir Hans Sloane and the active demonstration of physical processes that characterized the enquiries of Robert Boyle, Sir Isaac Newton and Francis Hauksbee: between treating knowledge as something acquired through the process of collecting or as something that happened only after a collection had been acquired and investigated, with the instruments put to work.[110] Joseph Priestley defined this distinction in 1761:

> Works of fiction resemble those machines which we contrive to illustrate the principles of philosophy, such as globes and orreries, the use of which extend no further than the views of human ingenuity; whereas real history resembles the experiments by the air pump, condensing engine and electrical machine, which exhibit the operations of nature, and the God of nature himself.[111]

For Sir Rowland and his contemporaries, whether orthodox believer or religious subversive, the 'natural world was interrogated through a series of experiments, not simply reflected by passive specimens',[112] and this spurred his acquisition of scientific instruments before the shocking of elderly ladies and slaughter of small animals at Nostell could begin. The 5th baronet's callous treatment of humans and animals in the name of science is laid bare in the

George III and collecting science' in Sloan with Burnett (eds), *Enlightenment*, pp 150–7.
**108** Inventory and valuation taken at Nostell Mansion … July 1806 (WYW1352/3/4/1/30).
**109** Ibid. **110** Ackermann and Wess, 'Between antiquarianism and experiment', pp 154–5.
**111** Quoted in Simon Schaffer, 'Natural philosophy and public spectacle in the eighteenth century', *History of Science*, 21:1 (1 Mar. 1983), pp 1–43 at p. 1. **112** Ackermann and Wess, 'Between antiquarianism and experiment', p. 156. See also Donald, *Picturing animals*, p. 6.

memoirs of his distant cousin Catharine Cappe, née Harrison. Miss Harrison found both Winns unbearable but reserved particular scorn for their treatment of an elderly widow whom they had invited to live at Nostell:

> The baronet had an electrical machine, and was continually making experiments, of which she was frequently the subject. She had a foolish antipathy to mice, and when he had obtained a few of these wretched little victims for his air pump, she was in agonies, lest he should set them at liberty, as he threatened, for her discomfiture and terror.[113]

The electrical machine was probably a hand-cranked electrostatic device 'that used friction to generate short bursts of electricity', possibly with an attached Leyden jar partially filled with water either 'wrapped inside and out with wires' or stopped with a cork in which a piece of metal such as a wire was attached.[114] By turning the crank and charging the phial, electric shocks could be created for the amusement of onlookers, although patently not for Sir Rowland's timid victim.

In the matter of Sir Rowland's air pump, the image that most readily springs to mind is that of Joseph Wright's *An experiment on a bird in the air pump* (1768) (fig. 1.6). Donald's masterful analysis of this work – one in which the human responses to the imminent death of an expensive cockatoo are varied, gendered and the real subject of the painting – has revealed the moral dilemma at its heart: is life disposable? The air pump had been developed (although not invented) by Robert Boyle in the mid-seventeenth century to test the physical nature of air and led to what later became known as Boyle's Law ('the volume of a gas varies inversely with pressure'[115]). Although there were those who advocated using a candle instead of a live animal to demonstrate what happened when air was withdrawn to create a vacuum,[116] the experiment was ultimately driven by a desire to explain the 'physiological processes of human respiration in relation to heart action and blood circulation' and that, of course, needed a living participant.[117]

113 Mary Cappe (ed.), *Memoirs of the life of the late Mrs Catharine Cappe, written by herself* (London, 1822), pp 98–9. 114 Alberta Culture and Tourism, 'Electricity and alternative energy', http://www.history.alberta.ca/energyheritage/energy/electricity/electricity-through-the-eighteenth-century.aspx, accessed 21 Sept. 2018. Good illustrations can be found at Spark Museum, 'Electric machines', http://www.sparkmuseum.com/FRICTION.HTM and Early Tech, 'Eighteenth-century Cavallo-type electric machine', https://www.earlytech.com/earlytech/item?id=242, both accessed 21 Sept. 2018. 115 Science History Institute, 'Robert Boyle', https://www.sciencehistory.org/historical-profile/robert-boyle, accessed 21 Sept. 2018. See also King's College London, 'Boyle's air-pump', http://www.kingscollections.org/exhibitions/specialcollections/to-scrutinize-nature/boyle-and-hooke/boyles-air-pump, accessed 21 Sept. 2018. 116 Donald, *Picturing animals*, p. 7, gives the examples of James Ferguson in *Lectures on select subjects in mechanics, hydrostatics, pneumatics, and optics* (London, 1760) and Benjamin Martin's *The description and use of a new, portable, table air-pump and condensing machine* (London, 1766). A copy of the latter is in the library at Nostell, but it bears the mid-nineteenth-century bookplate of William Robert Hay. 117 Donald, *Picturing*

1.6 Joseph Wright, *An experiment on a bird in the air pump* (1768), oil on canvas, 183 x 244cm, coll. National Gallery, London.

The 6th baronet inherited at the age of 10 and, like the children in Wright's painting, one wonders if he was enthralled or horrified by these experiments, or if he and his sister were even allowed to observe them. Because of his mother's estrangement from her in-laws, the bitter custody battle that had followed the death of the 5th baronet in 1785 and the elopement of Esther with the Nostell baker John Williamson in 1792, the 6th baronet received little education (scientific or otherwise) after he reached his early teenage years, and had no close family or correspondents with whom to share his thoughts.[118] Most of the scientific instruments disappeared at an unknown date during his lifetime, but the menagerie at Nostell was maintained since a contemporary 'List of poultry' mentions guinea fowl and peafowl, and a list of servants who were allowed board wages in 1797 includes an unnamed 'Menagery man & Woman' who, between them, had an allowance of twelve shillings per week.[119] The steward William

*animals*, p. 8. **118** Kerry Bristol, 'Families are "sometimes … the best at a distance": sisters and sisters-in-law at Nostell Priory, West Yorkshire' in Terence Dooley, Maeve O'Riordan and Christopher Ridgway (eds), *Women and the country house in Ireland and Britain* (Dublin, 2018), pp 33–56. Given the Huguenot interest in the sciences, it is surprising that Lady Winn showed little interest in her children's education. **119** List of poultry, 1798 (WYW1352/3/3/1/9/1); list of servants' names 1797 (WYW1352/3/4/2/9).

Dawson's account reveals that the menagerie man George Hall was paid £14 2*s*. 6*d*. in 1798, but by 1806 an estimate of servants' wages prepared for Sir Rowland's nephew and heir John Williamson reveals that the menagerie was no more.[120] Williamson also dispatched his grandfather's mahogany aviaries to London for immediate sale,[121] bringing the eighteenth-century Winns' relationship with exotic birds and animals to a close.

## CONCLUSION

From an initial consideration of the Menagerie House, further exploration of the family archive at Nostell has demonstrated that the Winns were neither obsessive collectors nor passionate zoologists, yet their house and gardens were populated by numerous birds, fish and animals. Some were companions at times of loneliness and isolation; others were tools of instruction, status symbols and objects of curiosity; and the fate of some may have been to die in the name of scientific entertainment. These creatures may be almost invisible to us today but they were an integral part of life at Nostell for more than five decades. Ranging from a fashionable engagement with the sciences to definitions of 'freedom' and the troublesome morality of enslavement, the Winns' menagerie has been revealed as much more than a simple collection of exotica. It is a microcosm of the contradictions inherent in Enlightenment attitudes towards life and living entities and, although it has only been possible to touch upon them here, it opens up rich new avenues of investigation for this archive and the menageries of other families in the region and beyond.[122]

**120** Mr William Dawson's account for 1798 and the select account for the same years (WYW1352/3/3/1/11/1); estimate of servants' wages 1806 (WYW1352/3/4/2/8). A gamekeeper and gardener are included in the list, but no one to look after the menagerie. An undated list of servants' wages prepared about the same time confirms this suggestion. (WYW1352/3/4/2/1). **121** Inventory and valuation taken at Nostell Mansion ... July 1806 (WYW1352/3/4/1/30). **122** I would like to thank the team at West Yorkshire Archive Service (Wakefield) for their support. I am also grateful to David Allott, Adam Bowett, Gail Day, Edna Green, Wendy Hamilton, Sarah Ledjmi, James Lomax and Conor Lucey. Staff at Special Collections, Brotherton Library, University of Leeds, waived the 48-hour advance-notice rule. Screwdriver to hand, Simon McCormack was a star in facilitating access to the Menagerie House and provided me with a copy of the *Historic landscape management plan* (2000).

# Edith Somerville and the West Carbery Hunt, 1903–19

LAURA SERVILAN BROWN

In the 1901 census of Ireland, Edith Somerville, at this time a relatively obscure painter and illustrator, listed her occupation as 'artist' and recorded herself as head of the family.[1] Her home was Drishane, a small landed estate in Castletownshend, County Cork. In the years that followed, she enjoyed sustained professional success, not only as a painter, but through her literary collaborations, most notably the Irish RM series of short stories, with her cousin Violet Martin. Set in the rural Irish landscape of hunting, horse coping and underlying political tensions, the stories enjoyed critical acclaim and popular success. Although neither became rich from their writing, both succeeded in obtaining financial freedom from their families, allowing them to travel around Europe and pay for their own art education. In the 1911 census return, despite, or possibly because of, this professional success, Somerville described herself not only as 'head of family' but as an 'author, artist and dairy farmer'.[2]

The life of Edith Somerville as a writer, artist, feminist and social reformer has been well-documented, not least because of the vast array of letters, diaries and other archival sources available to researchers interested in this aspect of her life. However, the relative paucity of material relating to her management of her family's farm and estate means that Somerville's involvement with the West Carbery Hunt, which consumed a significant amount of her time and energy, is under-studied and frequently misunderstood. Insights into her involvement in hunting, particularly her two tenures as master of fox hounds (MFH), have been coloured by either a feminist bias or a general sense of discomfort surrounding the hyperbolic nature of the Irish RM stories. These approaches have prevented the chance to view Edith Somerville through the prism through which she viewed herself, and any investigation of the practical, daily realities of life on landed estates in Edwardian Ireland. Somerville's tenure as MFH of the West Carbery Hunt coincided with a difficult decade not only for the landed class generally, but for the Somervilles as a family, in the main because of the absence of most male family members.

Edith's involvement in hunting, and specifically her stewardship of the West Carbery Hunt, undertaken as one of a wide variety of roles and responsibilities she assumed as de facto head of the family, poses many questions about the

1 Household return (form A), Somerville family, Drishane (Castlehaven North, Cork), 1901 Census of Ireland. 2 Household return (form A), Somerville family, Drishane (Castlehaven North, Cork), 1911 Census of Ireland.

nature of women's participation in the running of landed estates, the wider social responsibilities they assumed and the realities of the lives of unmarried daughters in gentry families. It also asks searching questions about the legitimacy of the long-held assumption that the outbreak of the First World War was the most significant problem to that point faced by Irish hunts, and that female participation was limited, rare, and solely linked to male wartime absences.

*Burke's Irish family records* states that the Somerville family was descended from the Cameron clan of Scotland, who fled the persecution of Anglicans, and who came to Ireland in 1692.[3] This lineage is dubious, described by Gifford Lewis, Somerville's most recent biographer, as little more than 'hopeful fiction'; no archival evidence exists to suggest that the Somervilles were any more high-born than the rest of the seventeenth-century influx.[4] By the mid-eighteenth century, however, the family had prospered considerably, and Edith Somerville's pride in an exaggerated family pedigree can be seen in her 1940 *Records of the Somerville family of Castlehaven and Drishane, from 1174–1904*, whose date range implies a noble, Norman lineage.[5]

In reality, the Somerville family fortune was based upon trade. Drishane House was built *c.*1790 by Edith Somerville's great-great-grandfather, financed from the highly lucrative trade route he established between Cork and the West Indies, which allowed him to export Irish butter and import mahogany and other high-value woods. This probably explains the family's social anxiety about its lineage, and that of Edith Somerville in particular, who is reported to have painted a series of 'ancestors' to hang at Drishane.[6]

Griffith's Valuation calculates the Drishane estate at a very modest 450 acres. The family also owned pockets of land elsewhere in west Cork, including substantial properties at Cosheen and Glenbarrahane, and several houses and cottages in Castletownshend village. However, rental income was low, and often in arrears, due to the poor quality of the west Cork land. Therefore, although the family had reasonably successfully navigated the difficult path from trade to gentrification, the estate's finances were constrained by both local circumstances and, increasingly, by the general political and economic problems of the late nineteenth century.

Edith was born in Corfu in 1858, when her father was serving as a lieutenant colonel with the Durham Light Infantry.[7] Although the family returned to Ireland when she was 3, her childhood and early years were punctuated by constant absences of the family's men as they undertook military or colonial service. Both her paternal uncles served in the British Army and as her five

3 *Burke's Irish family records* (London, 1970), p. 1041. 4 Gifford Lewis, *Edith Somerville: a biography* (Dublin, 2005), pp 13–14. 5 Edith Somerville and Boyle Somerville, *Records of the Somerville family of Castlehaven and Drishane, from 1174–1904* (Cork, 1940). 6 Gifford Lewis, *Edith Somerville, a biography* (Dublin, 2005), p. 55. 7 *Burke's Irish family records* (London, 1970), p. 1042.

2.1 Edith Somerville as master of the West Carbery Hunt, 1905.

brothers grew up four would make permanent careers in the army, navy or colonial service.[8] Three of them – Henry, Thomas and Hugh – joined the Royal Navy. John served in the British Army and even Aylmer, who lived at Drishane for most of his life, served in South Africa as a young man, and re-entered military service on the outbreak of war in 1914.[9]

Military and colonial service traditionally acted as a convenient entry point for younger sons from prominent families into the wide variety of senior diplomatic appointments that the British empire offered. This was especially true of the sons of the Somerville family who, conscious of the small scale of their land holdings, needed to make careers elsewhere. Indeed, all of Edith's brothers were educated at Clifton College, suggesting that any available family money was spent on their schooling, with a view to launching them into socially and financially advantageous careers abroad.[10] These careers were vital to the enhancement of the Somervilles' social standing, both within County Cork and in the wider world. Despite the family's aspirations to nobility, they were at best a relatively newly established modest gentry family. The Military Cross awarded to Desmond Somerville – son of Aylmer – after he was wounded at Gallipoli in

8 Ibid. 9 Ibid. 10 W.T. Pike, *Cork and County Cork in the twentieth century* (Cork, 1901), p. 286.

1916 was reported extensively in both the local and national media. Similarly, the military honours awarded to four members of the Somerville family in 1918 were described in the local press as 'upholding a fine family tradition'.[11] This was important in enhancing perceptions of the family's commitment and loyalty to the empire.

However, the near ubiquity of military service became problematic from 1898, which saw the death of Edith Somerville's father. Her eldest brother, Cameron Fitzgerald Somerville, now head of the family, was stationed in China. Letters written during this year suggest that Aylmer was the only male in residence, but despite being 33, he does not appear to have been trusted with management of the estate. This is illustrated by a letter written by Edith Somerville to her eldest brother in which she discusses the question of who should sit at the head of the table. Breaching traditional protocol, which dictated that Aylmer as the ranking and present son should have assumed this honour, Edith took this place as Cameron's 'representative', which, she stated, would provide evidence of her position as joint-head of the establishment.[12]

One of the most pressing problems created by the Somerville tradition of service was the absence of men to participate in the local social rituals that preserved the family's status in the area. The most obvious of these rituals was hunting, a sport revered almost to spiritual levels in the Somerville family and one that both forged positive community bonds and reinforced the stratified social order of the Irish countryside. The Somerville family's connection to their local hunt, the West Carbery, was long-standing. Almost all members of the Somerville family, male and female, hunted. Edith Somerville herself was said to have been blooded by her grandfather at the age of 5. While this is an unverified and possibly fanciful story, it nevertheless highlights the importance of hunting in the family and even to Edith's personal foundation myth and adult self-image. Hunting foxes in terrain described as 'a difficult one for both hounds and horses', which presented a challenge to riders by virtue of 'the Atlantic cliffs and the wild character of a good deal of the country', became one of Edith Somerville's most time-consuming, financially demanding and emotionally absorbing activities, even during her busy years as a successful writer, painter and illustrator.[13]

Like most hunting packs, the West Carbery Hunt started life as a private pack belonging to Colonel John Beecher of Hollybrook House near Skibbereen in 1760. Colonel Beecher's wealth allowed for the rapid development of the hunt, including the securing of kennels and the appointment of hunt servants. Richard Beecher, his eldest son, succeeded his father, followed by Henry Beecher, his grandson.[14] Both men continued Colonel Beecher's practice of investing heavily

11 *Skibbereen Eagle*, 29 June 1918. 12 Edith Somerville to Thomas Somerville, 20 Apr. 1898 (Drishane Archive, LA 251, a–d). 13 *British hunts and huntsmen* (London, 1909), p. 598. 14 Ibid., p. 596.

in the pack, building permanent kennels and increasing the number of subscriptions. The death of prominent members of the Beecher family from 1838, and the onset of the Great Famine in the following years (1845–51), saw the hunt fall into decline for several decades. A series of temporary masters, maintaining only a scratch pack, kept hunting barely alive for most of the remaining century.

However, in 1891, Aylmer Somerville established a committee of socially prominent local men hoping to revive the West Carbery Hunt.[15] Purchasing a pack of fourteen couples and establishing kennels at Drishane, Aylmer was a successful and well-liked MFH; this was reflected by a steady increase in subscriptions. Similarly, his successful cultivation of the local community is evident in the level of public subscriptions paid for replacement hounds and the building of new kennels when the pack was dissolved following an outbreak of rabies in 1897.[16] This is in stark contrast to the lack of initiative he demonstrated as the farm manager at Drishane, where sporadic interest in improving the estate gave way to long periods of disinterested inertia, much to the frustration of his sister.

Aylmer resigned in 1903 for unknown reasons, and in the absence of any other male Somerville, Edith became MFH from 1903 to 1908, and again from 1912 to 1919. In her early years, before the West Carbery Hunt was re-established, she had extensive experience of the hunting field, hunting with the Meath Hunt in Ireland and the Quorn, Cottesmore and Mr Fernie's hunts in England.[17] Edith is often described as the first female master of fox hounds in Britain or Ireland, a title she greatly relished. However, recent research into the levels of participation of nineteenth-century women in fox hunting suggest that this was not the case. In her examination of female stewardship of hunts in Britain and Ireland, Erica Munkwitz notes that a Mrs Cheape became MFH of the Linlithgow and Stirlingshire Foxhounds in 1889 when deputizing for her absent husband, and in 1891 established the Bentley Harriers.[18] Similarly, Miss Isa McClintock became master of the Tynan and Armagh Harriers in 1899, a position she held until 1952.[19] However, Edith Somerville's literary and artistic fame meant that she was undoubtedly the most famous of the 'lady masters' of the early twentieth century.

Edith's first actions as MFH were to buy the West Carbery pack, consisting of fourteen couples, from the hunt committee and to appoint a new huntsman and whip; this allowed her to run the hunt as she saw fit. While this was not an unusual action for incoming masters, her letters from this period indicate that she was highly motivated in developing the hunt rather than simply continuing what her brother had done in previous seasons. She also augmented the pack,

15 Ibid., p. 597. 16 Ibid. 17 Ibid., p. 598. 18 Erica Munkwitz, '"The master is the mistress": women and fox hunting as sports coaching in Britain', *Sport in History*, 37 (2017), p. 407. 19 Ibid.

improved the kennels and increased the number of subscriptions. Her efforts were noted in the local newspaper, the *Skibbereen Eagle*, which reported in December 1907 that 'fox-hunting in West Carbery was never in such a flourishing and prosperous condition as it is at present'.[20]

A key aspect of her responsibilities as MFH was the maintenance of positive relationships among the hunt, farmers and the wider local community. This was an undertaking that Somerville took seriously and she was unfailingly polite to those who supported or were otherwise involved in hunting, as is evident in her many letters to the editor of the *Skibbereen Eagle* thanking people for their support. Similarly, the establishment of a 'Fur and Feather fund' in 1906, which sought to 'compensate, as far as possible, those in the hunting area who lose poultry, etc., from the depredations of the foxes', suggests a level of engagement with the local community.[21] While none of Edith's papers link such initiatives to political change in rural Ireland, the impact of the Wyndham Land Purchase Act of 1903 was beginning to be felt around this time. Patrick Maume notes that under the act Munster saw the highest number of tenant purchases in Ireland, expertly organized by charismatic local nationalist leaders such as D.D. Sheehan. Therefore, it is likely that 'the Fur and Feather fund', a practice which does not appear to have been commonplace elsewhere, was a considered response to shifting social and political realities, or even a form of subtle bribery on the part of the West Carbery Hunt, ensuring continued local support for their activities.[22]

Despite her success as MFH, there is ample evidence to suggest that Somerville felt that her gender was a weakness rather than a strength, and that it was a duty borne simply out of family circumstances. An account of her life written by her niece, Moira Somerville,[23] illustrates how socially conventional Edith was – for example, she always rode side-saddle, even when other women were abandoning this style. Likewise, although immensely proud of her silver master's hunting horn, she never used it as she believed that doing so would be considered unladylike; instead, she relayed messages to her huntsman with a whistle. She also acted as her own secretary to avoid any awkwardness in issuing orders to a male subordinate. This would indicate that even when assuming predominately male roles, Somerville was reluctant to overthrow traditional gender hierarchies – her actions were prompted by pragmatism rather than personal rebellion.

In 1908, however, she resigned, probably because of the demands of her writing career as her publishers were exerting immense pressure on her to produce a new collection of RM stories. Her successor, Major Burns-Lindlow, does not appear to have been a success, and he resigned in 1909, citing among his reasons a lack of support and, indeed, a lack of foxes. Edith was reappointed

**20** *Skibbereen Eagle*, 7 Dec. 1907. **21** Ibid., 20 Oct. 1906. **22** Patrick Maume, *The long gestation: Irish nationalist life, 1891–1918* (Dublin, 1999), pp 74–5. **23** Moira Somerville, 'E. Œ Somerville: an intimate recollection' (Drishane archive, B.8. a-m).

shortly afterwards and held the position until the break-up of the pack. Despite Edith's efforts, and her continual augmentation of hunt finances with both Somerville family money and her personal earnings, she found it impossible to maintain the hunt, and the West Carbery pack was disbanded in 1919.

In determining the reasons for this course of action, Somerville's letter to the *Skibbereen Eagle* in August 1919, and its emotive editorial in response to her decision, offers us considerable insight into the chain of events that led to the hunt's disbandment. Edith's letter notes that a 'lack of support' (or subscriptions) left her with no alternative, noting also that the 'war took from the hunt its best and most faithful followers'.[24] While the outbreak of war in 1914 is known to have adversely impacted hunting in Ireland and Great Britain, most hunts survived the calamity by using any available female labour to run the hunt, reducing the number of days per week spent in the field, and even temporarily reducing the numbers of hounds kept in order to make hunting less costly. Therefore, while the outbreak of war, and the practical and financial difficulties created by the absence of the hunt's most valuable supporters was a considerable difficulty, it did not in itself mean automatic closure of a hunt.

Similarly, it is yet to be ascertained whether the deteriorating political situation played a part in Edith's inability to maintain the hunt after 1919. While an emerging body of research indicates that several Irish hunts fell into decline due to being actively interfered with as a means of political protest,[25] there is no evidence that this was the case for the West Carbery Hunt. While it is possible that some local farmers no longer wished to participate in hunting for political reasons, proof of this is scarce. Furthermore, Somerville herself believed that her mastership of the West Carbery Hunt allowed her to maintain a positive relationship with local republican figures, later relating that 'I was told that I was a nice lady always, with many allusions made to the hounds and the sport.'[26] Indeed, both Somerville and Drishane survived the War of Independence relatively unscathed. As Otto Rauchbauer has observed, Somerville 'realised how lucky she and her family had been' to have suffered only 'a few, relatively harmless raids on Drishane House and a few stolen horses'.[27]

This is in contrast to the 1936 murder of her brother Boyle Somerville, who came to the notice of a nearby IRA unit that opposed his habit of assisting local men with their applications to join the Royal Navy, a popular choice of livelihood in County Cork. In its report of the incident, the *Times* noted that a letter was placed beside Somerville's body, explaining that 'this English agent has sent 52 Irishmen to the English Forces during the last seven weeks'.[28] His murder

24 *Skibbereen Eagle*, 16 Aug. 1919. 25 See William Murphy, 'Sport in a time of revolution: Sinn Féin and the Hunt in Ireland', *Éire-Ireland*, 48:1–2 (2013), pp 112–47. 26 Quoted in Geraldine Cummins, *Dr E.OE. Somerville* (London, 1952), pp 204–5. 27 Otto Rauchbauer, *The Edith Œnone Somerville archive in Drishane: a catalogue and evaluative essay* (Dublin, 1995), p. 209. 28 *Times*, 26 Mar. 1936.

outraged public opinion within Cork and elsewhere in Ireland and Britain, where it was extensively reported upon in national newspapers. Even Eamon de Valera, who had previously been hostile to the Somerville family, condemned 'the cowardly murder of [an] old man, for doing what he thought was a friendly act'.[29] The decline of the West Carbery Hunt therefore seems largely unconnected to the deteriorating political situation; if anything its continuing presence was a means of maintaining reasonably stable local relationships and consequently its eventual demise after 1919 made the maintenance of these relationships increasingly difficult for the Somerville family.

A less-explored reason for Edith Somerville's inability to continue the maintenance of the hunt was the rapid post-war social change that occurred, even in outlying areas of rural west Cork. The *Skibbereen Eagle* editorial in response to the disbandment of the hunt was complimentary about Somerville's efforts, noting that her 'hounds have been a familiar attractive sight in our fields and among our roads' and that 'in keeping the hounds under circumstances of increasing difficulty, Miss Somerville displayed the fine spirit characteristic of her family'. However these comments can also be read as a sycophantic gesture of goodwill from a local unionist newspaper to a once-powerful local family.[30] In reality, the break-up of the West Carbery Hunt was indicative of the long demise of the Irish Big House, and the beginning of a world in which its inhabitants were increasingly marginalized with their social position weakened.

The nature of this social change was explicitly described in the *Skibbereen Eagle*, which complained that local farmers have 'grown flaccid in their prosperity, and bartered for the luxury of motor car or spring car, the fine daring and spirit that, in the days of their grand-fathers, gave Irish "packs" a European reputation'.[31] This echoes Somerville's letter, which had noted that members who left the hunt for the duration of the First World War 'have been caught in the tide of a wider life, and none have taken their places'.[32] These comments suggest a radically different rationale for the break-up of the hunt: rather than the usual reasons of political tensions, war and problems in the rural economy, instead personal economic prosperity, modernity, technology and the availability of new leisure pursuits may have been the defining factors. Even in the most remote corners of Europe, post-bellum social change was rapid and unstoppable. In his examination of the post-war social order around Europe, Modris Eksteins argues that in the years after 1918, traditional activities were rapidly displaced by the 'excitement and bustle' of 'cinema, motor cars, [and] aeroplanes'.[33]

The problems faced by the West Carbery Hunt after the First World War were ones familiar in hunts elsewhere in Ireland. The Kildare Hunt, which proudly noted that it had 'carried on hunting during the terrible war',

29 *Times*, 3 Apr. 1936. 30 *Skibbereen Eagle*, 16 Aug. 1919. 31 Ibid. 32 Ibid. 33 Modris Eksteins, 'Memory and the Great War' in Hew Strachan (ed.), *The Oxford illustrated history of the First World War* (Oxford, 2000), pp 305–19 at p. 310.

nevertheless struggled for subscriptions in 1919, to the extent that many of its activities were wound down.[34] By November of that year, the *Leinster Leader* reported that the Hunt Club was in 'deep water', and had undertaken a scheme of social and financial reform, including the appointment of the new class of 'farmer land owners' to the hunt committee, a move described as 'a very wise step'.[35] There was a political dimension to the difficulties faced by the Kildare Hunt as Sinn Féin is reported to have attended hunt committee meetings and handed around leaflets calling for the release or trial of 'untried prisoners in English jails'.[36] However, the principal difficulties faced by the Kildare Hunt were similar to those of the West Carbery Hunt, namely dwindling subscriptions and a lack of interest on the part of local farmers in hunting as a leisure activity. This is reflected in an admonition issued in a *Leinster Leader* editorial in November 1919, which contended that 'the farmers of Kildare are practical masters of the situation being now the owners of the land and if they desire the continuance of the Hunt it is up to them to take a practical interest in it.'[37] This demonstrates the extent to which social customs and leisure pursuits changed over the cataclysmic years of the First World War. Hunting, an expensive and time-consuming activity, no longer appealed to large numbers of people, even among prosperous farmers.

Writing after Edith Somerville's death in 1949, Moira Somerville recalled her aunt's vast energy and her ability to attend to both the estate and her dual career as a writer and painter, commenting that 'she contrived to do all these things, run the farm ... the house and garden ... continue her literary work and her painting is a mystery to anyone'.[38] Indeed, it can be difficult for a contemporary critic to determine which part of Edith Somerville's extraordinarily varied and busy life is the most significant. However, Somerville's successes and failures as a MFH, an overlooked part of her life, offer another insight into many aspects of Irish country-house life in the early years of the twentieth century, particularly in relation to gender, political identity, and relationships within rural communities. These insights offer challenges to the existing body of literature, not only in relation to Somerville herself, but the social and political world she represents.

Edith Somerville's self-image as head of family, de facto manager of Drishane and her mastership of the West Carbery Hunt has been linked by some of her biographers, most recently Gifford Lewis, to her feminist leanings, particularly her campaigns for female suffrage and the right of women to participate in the working world.[39] Indeed, her participation in the suffragette movement via the Munster Women's Franchise League and her appointment as a female master of fox hounds suggest that she was motivated, in part at least, by a sense of being a 'New Woman', or a post-Victorian proto-feminist. However, the evidence

34 *Leinster Leader*, 8 Mar. 1919. 35 Ibid., 1 Nov. 1919. 36 Ibid., 8 Mar. 1919. 37 *Leinster Leader*, 1 Nov. 1919. 38 Somerville, *E. Œ Somerville*. 39 Gifford Lewis, *Edith Somerville: a biography* (Dublin, 2005).

presented in this study suggests that Somerville's involvement in the West Carbery Hunt cannot be credibly interpreted as a political statement, but rather a rational response to the myriad political and social problems that weakened the status of Irish landed estates during her lifetime, which were amplified by tensions within the family and the near-continual absence of male family members. Evidence of her social conservatism can be seen elsewhere in her life, particularly in her personal relationships. She flatly rejected the attempts of the feminist composer Ethel Smith to turn their friendship into a physical relationship, explaining in a letter in 1923 that 'I'm inured now to my limitations and don't often feel they are hampering. But they are.'[40] Smith's letters to Somerville are often tinged with ill-concealed irritation at her conventionality, and on several occasions she accused her of being little more than a link in a chain of familial obligation. However, any attempt to understand Somerville's innermost feelings through her letters and diaries, which are largely non-confessional in tone, runs the risk of attempting to recreate too much from too little evidence.

Similarly, Gifford Lewis argues that Edith Somerville made a deliberate decision not to marry and to secure her financial independence through writing and painting, praising her apparent decision to 'find another way' as an artist and author in order to avoid both 'marriage or maiden aunthood in a brother's house'.[41] This argument can be challenged on two counts. Firstly, as discussed, Somerville's unconventional activities were a pragmatic reaction to the absence of male family members, who were occupied by prestigious postings around the British empire, rather than a deliberate attempt to avoid traditional female life. Secondly, for most of her adult life, Somerville committed far more time to hunting and other country pursuits connected to the management of Drishane than she did to her professional occupations. Therefore, it could be argued that her unmarried status freed her up, not necessarily to write, paint and participate in politics, but to contribute constructively to the survival of her family's estate and social reputation through time-consuming activities such as hunting and the assumption of responsibilities such as kennelling the hunting pack.

This conclusion points to another aspect of life on Irish landed estates in the early twentieth century, namely the status of unmarried women or 'daughters at home'. Popular perceptions of such women have been largely coloured by fiction, in the main written by female novelists including Edith Somerville herself. Somerville and Ross' depiction of Bobbie Bennett in the Irish RM stories links her unmarried status to her underhanded and duplicitous personality, and the eponymous main character of *The real Charlotte* is similarly scheming and dislikeable. More recently, Molly Keane's portrayals of unmarried

40 Edith Somerville to Ethel Smith, 7 Apr. 1923 (Drishane Archive, LA 251. a-d).
41 Gifford Lewis, 'Introduction' in Edith Somerville and Martin Ross, *The real Charlotte* (Dublin, 2003), p. x.

female residents of Irish landed estates were predominately negative, most notably Aroon St Charles, the unloved and unlovely narrator of Keane's landmark 1981 novel *Good behaviour*.[42] Many of the fictionalized accounts of 'daughters at home' descend into caricature, depicting them as isolated within their families, mocked by the wider community and often described as irritating or unconventional. However, Edith Somerville's relative success in preserving her family's social and material integrity through difficult times, and via the adoption of somewhat unconventional roles, including the mastership of a hunting pack, serves as a counterpoint to this clichéd view which surely requires further investigation.

Equally, the circumstances in which Edith Somerville disbanded the West Carbery Hunt suggest that in this case at least, conditions unfavourable to hunting such as economic problems, the effects of the First World War, the threat of political violence, and the weakening social status of the Irish country house, while all important, were less fatal to the hunt than changing social customs which saw prosperous young farmers purchasing motor cars for leisure purposes and gradually losing interest in traditional gentlemanly pursuits such as hunting. This dimension to the collapse of the West Carbery Hunt has been overlooked, as has the possibility that it may have been a contributory factor to the decline of hunts elsewhere in Britain and Ireland during the same period.

Edith Somerville, through her fame as the co-author of the Irish RM stories, is likely to be perpetually remembered by the public as a once-popular author whose Edwardian writing style and bawdy sense of humour is now considered out-dated and even offensive. The 1980s television adaptation of the stories, which replaced Somerville and Ross' talent for dark humour and irony with simplistic gags based on racial stereotypes, did much to damage her reputation as a serious writer. However, her recent literary rehabilitation has seen renewed academic interest in her other works, undoubtedly as part of the continued interest in the literature of the Irish Big House in general. Therefore, it is to be hoped that other aspects of Edith Somerville's extraordinary life will be reassessed in the coming years. This essay, exploring Somerville's championing of the West Carbery Hunt, provides an illuminating entry point into the long-neglected subject of women in landed families, and also into equally under-studied themes such as the impact of military and colonial service on Irish estates, relationships between the residents of country houses and local communities and the centrality of fox hunting as a means of preserving family status.

42 Molly Keane, *Good behaviour* (London, 1981).

# 'U is for Union, the name of our hunt': the South Union Hunt in the lives of the south Cork gentry

FERGAL BROWNE

> I is the inquest held after the run,
> The size of the fences you jumped with such fun,
> The falls you escaped with such wonderful skill
> And the very few in it when in at the knell
> The fences grow larger, the pace more appalling,
> When dancing to music entirely enthralling[1]

The above lines are an extract from a poem written in 1911 by Major Roderick McKenzie Knolles of Oatlands House, near Belgooly, County Cork, entitled 'The ABC of the South Union Hunt'. He was likely taking his lead from Edith Somerville's 'Slipper's ABC of Foxhunting', published a few years before, as he employed a similar acrostic technique providing a verse for each letter of the alphabet. The poem uses the names of many prominent families making up the gentry of south Cork at the time, such as Ashurst of Ravenswood, Newenham of Coolmore and Major Owens of Heathburn Hall, and indicates the role played by the South Union Foxhounds (later Hunt) in their lives. This essay examines that role, and aims to show how the hunt was used as a vehicle for social mobility, both by existing families – such as the Knolles – already well established in south Cork, and by new arrivals in the area. The essay also discusses the relationship between the hunt and the local branch of the National League, and demonstrates that relations between hunting gentry, farmers and labourers could be more complex than has been portrayed in the existing historiography around 'stopping the hunt' during the Land War in Ireland.[2] As this essay will demonstrate, labouring organizations often took the side of the hunt in disputes. Lastly, it looks at how the hunt survived the turmoil of the 1920s, remaining in existence and even thriving in the present day.

1 Roderick MacKenzie Knolles, 'The ABC of the South Union Hunt' (poem in possession of Lesley Roberts, Mount Rivers, Carrigaline, County Cork). 2 On this aspect of the Land War, see L.P. Curtis Jnr, 'Stopping the hunt, 1881–82' in C.H.E. Philpin, *Nationalism and popular protest in Ireland* (Cambridge, 1987), pp 349–402; and for a later period, William Murphy, 'Sport in a time of revolution: Sinn Féin and the hunt in Ireland, 1919', *Éire-Ireland*, 48:1–2 (Spring/Summer 2013), pp 112–47.

## THE DAUNT FAMILY

The story of the South Union begins a distance from Cork and, indeed, Ireland. It starts in Uley, a small village in south Gloucestershire, England. A short distance outside the village is the manor and church of Owlpen. The house, built in the thirteenth century, was the residence of the Daunt family. Walking through the church, many of the commemorative plaques refer to Gortigrenane, near Tracton, in south County Cork. Thomas Daunt II of Owlpen (d. 1621) acquired the lands of the former Cistercian Abbey of Tracton in 1588, and in 1595 expanded his holding by purchasing the nearby estate of Gortigrenane.[3] A later descendant, Thomas Daunt IV (1676–1749), built Gortigrenane House, near Minane Bridge, County Cork. Hunting was one of the main pastimes of the Daunt family – so much so that Robert Boyle, the 'great earl of Cork', was once asked why he did not keep hounds and hunt like Mr Daunt. He replied that he 'preferred to hunt in his own way', by which he was taken to mean that he preferred to hunt Irishmen rather than foxes.[4] Thomas IV brought over his own pack of hounds from his cousin Giles Daunt of Newark, Gloucestershire, and many hunting parties were subsequently held at Gortigrenane.

So connected were the wider Daunt family with hunting that when in 1755 Letitia Digby of Landenstown House, County Kildare, married Revd George Daunt of Fahalea House, Carrigaline, she brought with her a pack of hounds as a dowry. Letitia was herself an expert huntswoman and acted as master of her own pack of hounds. Thomas Daunt V (1702–77) of Gortigrenane held a meet of his hounds in Daunt's Square in Cork city in 1757, to which a large crowd of onlookers turned up. They were welcomed to the city by the mayor, George Hodder. Daunt used a special hunting horn, fashioned from the horn of a medieval ox (which is still in the possession of the family today). Thomas V of Gortigrenane died unmarried and so his estates and his hounds passed to his nephew, Thomas Daunt VI (1755–1803). As Thomas VI grew older and too ill to hunt, his cousin Thomas Knolles of Killeighy, near Belgooly, took over. When Daunt died in 1803, his daughter Mary presented the hounds to Knolles, who hunted the country until he died in 1829.[5] Mary was Thomas Daunt VI's only child. In 1815, she married Thomas Anthony Stoughton, a wealthy landowner from Ballyhorgan, near Listowel in County Kerry. The couple moved to the Daunt estates in Gloucestershire, as Stoughton had extensive family business interests in Britain, most notably in Monmouthshire coal mines. The Stoughtons lived in the newly constructed Owlpen House, which stood beside the original Owlpen Manor.[6]

3 John Daunt, *Some account of the family of Daunt* (London, 1899), p. 12. 4 Ibid., p. 15. 5 John Daunt, 'A short history of the South Union Hunt', *Carrigdhoun*, 25 Dec. 1999. 6 Owlpen Manor estate, 'History of Owlpen and its owners', https://owlpen.com/history/history, accessed 24 Sept. 2018.

3.1 Thomas Walton Knolles of Oatlands, Belgooly, County Cork.
Master of foxhounds for the South Union Hunt, 1829–89.
Collection of the late Vilma Ellis, now in the possession of the author.

The Knolles and Daunts were not the only families to keep hounds in the Kinsale district. At nearby Ballintober House, Revd Robert Meade, land steward of the earl of Clanwilliam's Ballintober estate, kept a diary for 1776 in which hunting trips were mentioned more often than church attendances.[7] Local lore tells how, late at night, after returning from a public house, the man employed by the Meades to look after the hounds climbed drunkenly into the loft in which he lived above the kennels, fell through the floor and was promptly killed and eaten by his charges.[8]

## THOMAS WALTON KNOLLES AND THE FOUNDING OF THE SOUTH UNION

Following Thomas Daunt VI's death, a meeting was held at the newly constructed Knolles residence of Oatlands House to decide on the future of the pack. It was attended by various members of the Knolles and Daunt families, together with other gentry families such as the Meades of Ballintober and Ballymartle, Newenhams of Coolmore and Hayeses of Crosshaven. It was decided to found a formal hunting club, known as the South Union Foxhounds. Captain Thomas Knolles (1784–1840), son of the previously mentioned Thomas Knolles, was elected master and Mary Daunt presented the medieval Daunt hunting horn to him as a 'badge of office'. However, it was Captain Knolles' son, Thomas Walton Knolles (1808–90), who would do the most to develop the hunt over the following years.[9]

In the nineteenth century, landed estates in County Cork ranged from roughly 30,000 acres downwards; the Knolles estate of Oatlands was comparatively small at 886 acres.[10] While the house was described in 1837 by Samuel Lewis as 'a handsome modern mansion', it was considerably smaller than some of its neighbours, such as that of the Hodders of Hoddersfield, the Newenhams of Coolmore or even the Daunt residence of Gortigrenane.[11] The Knolles' modest social and economic status was indicated by the fact that no member of the family served as county high sheriff, although members did occasionally serve on the Cork grand jury.[12] But it was his hunting exploits that would raise Thomas Walton Knolles' profile in county society well above what his modest acreage and house would indicate.

Muriel Bowen's *Irish hunting* states that

> Taking on the hounds was a difficult position for a young man to be faced with, as subscriptions were non-existent in the South Union in [the 1830s–1840s], which meant he had to meet all expenses himself. But the greatest

7 Rosemary ffolliott, *The Pooles of Mayfield* (Dublin, 1958), pp 171–90. 8 Conversation with Stephen Harte, current owner of Ballintober, 14 Sept. 2017. 9 Daunt, 'A short history of the South Union Hunt', p. 25. 10 U.H. Hussey De Burgh, *The landowners of Ireland* (Dublin, 1878), pp 211, 254, 325, 336–7. 11 Samuel Lewis, *A topographical dictionary of Ireland* (London, 1837), p. 182. 12 *Cork Constitution*, 20 July 1861, 18 July 1873.

> difficulty to be overcome was the lack of foxes. However dogged perseverance, personal popularity and tact triumphed over difficulties that would have forced another man to give up. He refused the luxury of a pony and trap, always riding to the meet and returning after the day, with his hounds. In this way, he got to know the country like a book and the locals had it that he could ride over it blindfolded.[13]

The South Union was a harrier club, hunting hares until 1866, when the changeover to foxes was made. At the time, there would have been a certain snobbery associated with hunting foxes as opposed to hunting hares; this is suggested in the disparaging remarks made about harriers and hare hunting in Somerville and Ross' Irish RM novels.[14] The Knolles, both father and son, kept up the old Irish breed of foxhounds, described as white, mottled blue and grey. They had much longer bodies than present-day foxhounds. While meeting most of the expenses of the hunt himself, Thomas Walton Knolles was also supported with large subscriptions by Marmeduke Coghill Cramer of Rathmore House, Kinsale, a man of considerable resources according to B.M. Fitzpatrick.[15]

Drafts of new foxhounds were produced regularly from some of the best kennels in the south, including Hedges Eyre of Macroom Castle, and Captain George Rye of Rye Court. It was believed these hounds could be traced back to an ancient breed found on both sides of the Irish Sea. In later years, Knolles also obtained drafts of hounds from the Duhallow United Hunt and Lord Doneraile's kennels. Knolles hunted hounds himself until 1864, when he fell from his horse onto the road and severely injured his knee.[16]

During the worst years of the Great Famine, the hunt did not meet, but it did recommence in 1849, hunting on Tuesdays and Fridays. From then on, the list of meet locations shows how integrated the hunt was in the social life of the gentry of south Cork. For example, in January 1865 it met at least eight times: 3 January at Heathburn Hall; 6 January at Castletreasure; 10 January at Tracton; 13 January again at Castletreasure; 20 January at Ballintober House; 24 January at Maryborough House; 27 January at Heathburn Hall; and 31 January at Ballinhassig.[17]

Knolles presided over some famous hunts, which were typically described in some detail in provincial and sometimes national newspapers, or remembered by enthusiasts later in their published memoirs. For example, Bernard Fitzpatrick recounted a hunt in the 1870s when a fox was 'put up' around Ballinhassig and the hounds hunted him almost to Skibbereen, a distance of over forty miles. The

13 Muriel Bowen, *Irish hunting* (Tralee, 1954), p. 152. 14 See, for example, E. Somerville and M. Ross, *Some experiences of an Irish RM* (New York, 1899), pp 23–4. 15 B.M. Fitzpatrick, *Irish sports and sportsmen* (Dublin, 1878), p. 212. 16 Sporting Life, *British hunts and huntsmen*, iv: *England North, Scotland and Ireland* (London, 1911), pp 580–5. 17 Daunt, 'A short history of the South Union Hunt', p. 25.

3.2 Oatlands House, Belgooly, County Cork. The South Union Hunt was founded here in 1829. Photo courtesy of Carmel Hayes, Oatlands.

fox eventually disappeared over the cliffs at Baltimore. It took three days to recapture all of the hounds. In the 1875–6 season, the South Union hunted fifty-three days, killed ten braces of foxes, ran to ground forty-four, had ten unaccounted for and only three blank days. The hunting district at that time extended along the seashore from the Bandon River to Cork, and was bounded on the north side by the hills of Ballincollig.[18] When Knolles died in May 1890, the *Cork Constitution* suggested that he was the longest serving master of fox hounds in the British Isles. He was compared to John Warde, an English master of fox hounds who had died in 1839, who had been known as the 'father of fox hunting' and who had served for fifty seven years. The *Constitution* commented that Knolles had started hunting in 1822 – before even the South Union had been founded – and did so continuously up to 1889, a total of seventy-seven years.[19] Knolles was held in high regard by the followers of the South Union; in September 1865 'two very handsome pieces of plate' were presented to him for his mastership by 'his many friends' as a testimonial to his service.[20]

Following Knolles' death, William Henry Moore-Hodder of Hoddersfield, near Crosshaven, took over as master. On the night following the day that the hounds were moved from their kennels at Oatlands to their new quarters at Hoddersfield, the hounds escaped and returned to bay outside the windows of their former master at Oatlands.[21] For the last decades of the nineteenth century

18 Fitzpatrick, *Irish sports and sportsmen*, pp 212–13. 19 *Cork Constitution*, 28 Oct. 1890. 20 *Dublin Evening Mail*, 26 Sept. 1865. 21 D & D, 'The South Union Foxhounds' (MS in author's possession).

3.3 Hoddersfield House, near Crosshaven. After sixty years at Oatlands, in 1890 the South Union Hounds moved to kennels at Hoddersfield when William Moore-Hodder took over as master. The house is now in ruins but the kennel yard still exists. Photo courtesy of Niall and Billy Nicholson.

and the early decades of the twentieth, masters of the hunt continued to come from the ranks of the gentry, including Richard Hayes of Bayview, Frederick George Hayes of Crosshaven House, Major Charles Lynch of Parkgarriffe House, near Monkstown and Captain Frank Hodder of Ballea Castle, Carrigaline.[22]

## CROSSING THE CLASS DIVIDE

While hunting was primarily organized and financially supported by the gentry, the relationships between individuals and classes in the hunting world were complex and interdependent. Hunting represented a way of life, and a way of looking at the world, which often led to the development of unexpected personal relationships among people of different social classes. An example of this was John Robert Allen (1837–93), who served as huntsman to Thomas Walton Knolles. John Allen had trained as a vet in Patrickswell in Limerick, but due to lack of funds was unable to attend university in Edinburgh in order to qualify. A Protestant, he was obliged to leave home when he eloped with a Catholic girl from Charleville, County Cork. Thomas Walton Knolles offered him a job as

22 Sporting Life, *British hunts and huntsmen*, iv, pp 580–5.

coachman and huntsman to the South Union at Oatlands. He was renowned for various 'cures' that he had for horses. When Allen died in 1893, such was the esteem and affection held for him, the Knolles family requested that he be buried in the family vault at Kinure Cemetery, near Oysterhaven. However, as Allen had converted to Catholicism on his marriage, the local Catholic clergy refused to allow him to be buried in a 'Protestant tomb'; he was therefore interred in a separate grave, close to the Knolles vault.[23] Another hunt servant was Jack Ahern, who acted as kennel man for Knolles. 'Jacky the Dogs', as he was known, had been bedridden before he died in 1894, but often asked to be propped up in his bed so that he could hear the 'sweet music of the hounds'. The *Cork Constitution* greatly exaggerated his place in life as 'the best friend' of Thomas Walton Knolles, but the esteem in which he was held was seen in the subscription raised to pay for his funeral expenses.[24]

Religion, class and politics usually created unbridgeable gaps between landlord and tenant. As early as 1887, the stopping of hunting over farmers' land was being used as a weapon by the Irish National League.[25] There is a reference to this strategy being supported by the Belgooly branch of the National League as early as 1888, but it seems only to have been used as a weapon in 1906 and then for specific land disputes.[26] One case in point concerned the eviction of William Murphy from his farm at Cramers Court, near Belgooly. The farm was eventually taken by another farmer by the name of Good, who had recently returned from America.[27] The Belgooly United Irish League called for a boycott of Good, and extended that boycott to cover any farmer that hired out Good's threshing machine. Good was a prominent member of the South Union Hunt, so it is understandable that the hunt was seen by the League as a means to strike at him and the other farmers and landowners under boycott.[28] On 23 January 1906, farmers blocked the hunt from entering lands at Heathburn Hall, as part of the boycott action against its resident, Colonel Shaw, who had hired Good's threshing machine. The UIL presented three demands: first, that the South Union Hunt would not meet at Heathburn Hall in future; second, that the hunt would not draw the Heathburn Hall coverts; and thirdly, that when the hunt was riding over the farms of members of the UIL, that they would prevent any farmer under boycott due to the dispute with Good from riding with them.

In a period when tenant purchase was gathering momentum in the aftermath of the passing of the 1903 Land Act, and the power of the gentry was visibly on the wane, it is perhaps understandable that the hunt committee was anxious to maintain their principal pastime, if nothing else. Thus, they agreed to no longer

23 Conversation with Gerard Allen, 7 Feb. 2018; Padraig Allen, 'Descendants of John Robert Allen 1837' (Allen family collection). 24 *Cork Constitution*, 22 Feb. 1894. 25 Irish Loyal and Patriotic Union, *Ireland in 1887*, ii: *extracts from proceedings of National League branches* (Dublin, 1887), p. 73; see also, Curtis, 'Stopping the hunt'. 26 *Freeman's Journal*, 22 Oct. 1888. 27 *Southern Star*, 25 July 1908; *Cork Examiner*, 21 July 1908. 28 *Cork Examiner*, 20 Jan. 1932.

meet at Heathburn Hall and to exclude one farmer (this was most likely Good himself). However, they stated that they could not agree to refrain from drawing the Heathburn Hall coverts, or to exclude any of the other people requested by the League, as they felt that this would lead to the break-up of the South Union Hunt.

This resulted in a stormy meeting of the Belgooly branch of the UIL on 28 January 1906, where some of the members stated that they did not wish to be responsible for the break-up of the South Union, while others demanded that the UIL carry through its business to the finish. The chairman, Fr Walsh, parish priest of Belgooly, proposed at the meeting that the League accept what the hunt was offering, but to warn the hunt that at the beginning of the next season, their demands regarding the other farmers still associating with Good would be renewed. Fr Walsh felt that this would give those people an opportunity to 'mend their ways'. This motion was carried, but with some members dissenting. It is not clear who the dissenting parties were, but they most likely comprised representatives of both sides of the argument: those who wanted to see all of the demands met, and those who did not wish to interfere with the hunt at all.[29] It is understandable that some farmers may have looked beyond the social aspect of the hunt. As recently as 2000, landowners and gamekeepers in England and Wales considered fox hunting necessary to manage fox populations in view of the damage to farming and game management.[30]

Demonstrating the complexities of economic interdependence that could finesse politics, the Belgooly UIL was heavily criticized by the Cork United Trades Association. It might have been expected that a labour association – one of Cork's first trade unions – would support the League against a hunt whose members consisted largely of the gentry and 'strong-farmer' class. However, this did not materialize, and it was not difficult to understand why. The trades that formed the organization included farriers, bootmakers, shoemakers, tailors, coachmakers and others likely to earn substantial income from a hunt club.[31] Following the meeting on 28 January, the secretary of the CUTA stated that there were certain members of the Belgooly UIL with 'sore heads', whose objective seemed to be the break-up of the South Union. He considered this unfair and unjust and criticized the 'strong farmers' for actions that could damage the incomes of the working classes of Cork city. The chairman of the CUTA, Michael Egan, was equally critical of a statement allegedly made at the Belgooly UIL meeting that the labourers of Cork city should 'take their eyes off of their bread and butter for the time being', presumably meaning that they should support the rural organization in its agrarian campaign against landlords. Egan hit back that the grandfathers of the Cork working classes had indeed

29 *Cork Examiner*, 8 Feb. 1906. 30 *Guardian*, 13 June 2000. 31 Maura J.B. Murphy, 'The role of organized labour in the political and economic life of Cork city, 1820–1899' (PhD, University of Leicester, 1979), pp 394–402.

3.4 Portrait of Michael Egan JP TC, chairman of Cork United Trades Association. Photo cropped from 'Ireland's National Pledge' (April 1918), Wikimedia Commons.

'taken their eyes off of their bread and butter' in order to help the people who were tilling the land at the time of the Famine, and 'if that was the return that the working classes were going to get from the farmers, it was time they should make a desperate effort to look to their own interests'.[32]

Recent studies of the Waterford landlord Henry Villiers Stuart have shown that the economic and social networks in this period were never clear-cut. Stuart's support for the agricultural labourers in the late 1870s was a source of frustration to nationalist larger farmers. Furthermore, there were several clashes between labourers and farmers throughout the 1870s and 1880s, including farm labourers' strikes in Cork in 1881 and 1882.[33] The CUTA-Belgooly UIL-South

32 *Cork Examiner*, 17 Mar. 1906. 33 Ian d'Alton, 'Before Molly Keane: image and reality in the lives of the nineteenth-century gentry of east Cork and west Waterford', *Decies*, 70 (2014), pp 85–101; *idem*, '"A first voice": Henry Windsor Villiers Stuart and the agricultural labourers'

Union Hunt imbroglio pointed to the nuances and intricacies of what we might call 'economic politics' in this period. Ireland was much more complicated than a simple political polarity of unionist and nationalist or landlord and tenant. This was not the first time that the CUTA had intervened in hunting matters. In April 1905, the master of the Muskerry Hunt, Mr H.W. Leader, announced his intention to resign, and in the absence of a successor it looked as if that hunt club would collapse. CUTA was concerned that this would mean the loss of between £4,000 and £5,000 a year to the various trades in Cork city who did business with the hunt clubs. They resolved to write to the master to ask him to reconsider. In the event, the Muskerry Hunt continued in existence.[34] The economic concerns raised by the CUTA in 1900 are still to the fore in the present day. The economic and social impact of hunting on rural communities was debated in the early twenty-first century, when a ban on fox hunting was mooted in the UK. The Burns Report into hunting with dogs in England and Wales (2000) estimated that between 6,000 and 8,000 jobs in the rural economy were dependent on fox hunting, with as many as 700 people being directly employed by hunts. While the belief was that initial job losses would be offset as the rural economy adjusted, the report acknowledged, similar to the CUTA a century before, that jobs involving some specialized skills would be difficult to secure elsewhere.[35]

The intervention from the CUTA, coupled with rumours circulating that the UIL was determined to break up the South Union Hunt at any cost, caused Fr Walsh and his curate, Fr Carmody, to announce their withdrawal from the League. The original agreement seems to have failed to command the support of all of the farmers. Once the priests withdrew from the League, the binding force which had held the agreement together was lost, and the farmers in the League withdrew from the agreement made with the South Union. A second meeting was held between the UIL and the hunt (without the priests), where the original demands were reiterated. This time, the hunt committee, led by the then master, Captain Frank Hodder, virtually capitulated. Besides agreeing to hold no further hunts at Heathburn Hall, the committee asked the secretary of the UIL to write to those people with whom the League had a dispute, asking them to withdraw voluntarily from the hunt. If they did not do so, the hunt committee undertook to warn them off. The negotiations ended amicably and at a follow-up meeting of the UIL, a vote of thanks was given by the members to Captain Hodder and the other members of the hunt committee.[36] The dispute demonstrated the complexities of socio-economic relations in this twilight period of landlordism.

in Brian Casey (ed.), *Defying the law of the land: agrarian radicals in Irish history* (Dublin, 2013), pp 164–75. 34 *Cork Examiner*, 3 Apr. 1905. 35 *Guardian*, 13 June 2000. 36 *Cork Examiner*, 24 Feb. 1906.

## A VEHICLE FOR SOCIAL MOBILITY AND CONNECTIVITY

Besides being a social and sporting outlet for the south Cork gentry, the South Union cemented them into the military nexus, through garrisons at Cork and Kinsale. Officers of the 13th Hussars are listed as hunting with the South Union in the 1880s.[37] The hunt even had a military race in its point-to-point race card, open to officers serving in the Cork command. A detailed account of the 1908 race appeared in the monthly chronicle of the Royal Highland Fusiliers, which had five starters out of a field of sixteen, though none finished in any of the winning or runner-up positions.[38]

The South Union had held its first steeplechase in 1888, with many of the local gentry serving as stewards, including Colonel Frederick Shaw of Heathburn Hall and Major Newenham of Coolmore. The hunt's point-to-points were originally held at Knocknagore, Crosshaven. These attracted entries from far and wide; at the race meeting there in 1889 a mare called Miss Bonny came from County Kilkenny to Cork by train and was stabled at Phelan's yard in Cork city overnight. The following day she walked from Cork to Knocknagore, won her race in great style and then walked back to Cork to catch the train to Kilkenny. The South Union point-to-point races were later moved to Cummeen, Carrigaline, which became known as the 'Fairyhouse of the South'. The races were usually held every Whit Monday and attracted large crowds.[39]

As well as integrating the military into social and marital manoeuvres, the hunt was also useful for newly arrived members of the gentry to establish a place for themselves in the local social scene. To take two examples: Lieutenant-Colonel William Stopford had married the 16-year-old daughter of Marmeduke Cramer, Wilhelmina, who inherited the Rathmore estate when her father died. Stopford became master of the South Union in 1895. It is possible he obtained the mastership out of deference to his father-in-law's contributions to the coffers of the hunt over the years. Whilemina Stopford was an accomplished horsewoman and at one stage had ninety-seven horses stabled at Rathmore. She exhibited horses, hunted with the South Union, and drove single and double paired carriages with great success at shows in both Ireland and England. Colonel Stopford only served for five years with the hunt as in 1900 he left to fight in the Boer War with the North Cork Rifles.[40] In 1909, Major Isaac William Burns-Lindow came to live at Pallastown House, Belgooly, leasing it from the Heard family. A long-serving military man, Major Lindow had commanded the massed bands of the Hussars' Brigade in Queen Victoria's diamond jubilee procession in London in 1897. He brought his own pack of sixty hounds with him to Pallastown, erecting kennels for them there. He was experienced, having

37 D & D, 'The South Union Foxhounds'. 38 *Royal Highland Fusiliers Chronicle*, Jan. 1908, pp 59–60. 39 Daunt, 'A short history of the South Union Hunt', p. 25. 40 Sporting Life, *British hunts and huntsmen*, p. 581; Terry Connolly, 'The Cramer family of Rathmore', *Kinsale*

previously served as master of the West Carbery Hunt from 1908 to 1909; and was prepared, bringing his huntsman, Fred Cooper, with him.[41] Lindow took on the job of master of the South Union in 1909. His secretaries were Major Ashurst of Ravenswood House, Carrigaline and Major F.G. Hayes of Crosshaven House. In 1914, hunt numbers declined as many of the followers went to fight in the First World War with the South Irish Horse. Major Burns-Lindow was later promoted to lieutenant-colonel and became commander of the South Irish Horse. In 1922, he was present, as the commander of the South Irish Horse, at the flag presentation ceremony at Windsor Castle, when the colours of the Irish regiments of the British Army were presented to King George V, following the disbandment of the regiments upon the establishment of the Irish Free State.[42]

## LATER HISTORY

In 1919, Clayton Austin Love became master of the South Union Hunt. This was a departure from the usual style of master as Love came from the 'strong farmer' class, rather than being a member of the gentry.[43] In an 1876 list of Irish landowners, the Love family are shown as owning 82 acres in their own right at Ballea, near Ballygarvan. By contrast, other masters of the South Union such as Knolles, Moore-Hodder and Hayes had owned estates of between 750 and 1,500 acres each.[44] Love was a superb horseman and huntsman, and served as master of the South Union up to 1930 before continuing as joint master with Major T.P. Morgan of Kilnagleary to 1947, and then with Commander Everett of Glanmire House to 1959, the year in which Love died.[45] The ranks of the gentry were significantly reduced by 1919–20, and the class would continue to thin in the following decades.[46] The Shaws and Owenses of Heathburn Hall and Moore-Hodders of Hoddersfield sold up in 1918, while the Knolles of Oatlands rented out Oatlands House and land from 1919 and eventually sold it in 1937. Lieutenant-Colonel Burns-Lindow did not return to Pallastown after the First World War and it was sold by the Heard family in 1920.[47]

There is a story told in north Cork of a businessman from the city who was out hunting with the Duhallow Hunt, sometime after Irish independence.

*Record*, 13 (2005), pp 19–24. 41 Sporting Life, *British hunts and huntsmen*, p. 583. 42 R.G. Harris, *The Irish regiments, a pictorial history, 1683–1987* (Kent, 1989), p. 242. 43 Daunt, 'A short history of the South Union Hunt', p. 25. 44 https://www.failteromhat.com/lo1876/cork.pdf, accessed 2 Jan. 2019. 45 Daunt, 'A short history of the South Union Hunt', p. 25. 46 See Terence Dooley, *The decline of the Big House in Ireland* (Dublin, 2001); Olwen Purdue, *The Big House in the north of Ireland: land, power and social elites, 1878–1960* (Dublin, 2009); Emer Crooke, *'White elephants': the country house and the state in independent Ireland* (Dublin, 2018). 47 *Irish Times*, 9 Feb. 1918; *Irish Times*, 15 Feb. 1937; Diarmuid O'Murchada, 'History of Crosshaven', *Cork Historical Guides Committee* (Cork, 1976), p. 37; *Cork Examiner*, 27 Nov. 1920.

3.5 Austin Love at the South Union Hunt meet at Ballea Castle, Carrigaline, County Cork, 20 Feb. 1934. Photo courtesy of the *Irish Examiner* archives.

Getting separated from the pack, and riding alone along a country road, he came across an aging countryman: 'When did the last gentleman go by?' the businessman asked the labourer. Without missing a beat, the labourer replied, '1922, sor'. It is a simple story that illustrates the changing nature of hunt membership in the mid- to late twentieth century, as, indeed, was reflected in the South Union, where during the 1970s and 1980s Denis J. Murphy, a Cork businessman, served as master of the hunt.[48] Other prominent members from the mercantile classes included the Crosbie family, owners of the *Cork Examiner* newspaper. The committee elected in 1974 is of particular significance because during the AGM of that year a debate was held as to whether the hunt should be wound up. New kennels were going to be required and this was going to impose a significant financial burden on the club. The chairman, Noel Horgan, asked members whether they felt that it would be worth continuing. Several members spoke enthusiastically in favour. The officers elected to the committee in 1974 consisted of two members of the old gentry families – William Worth

48 *Irish Times*, 27 July 2002.

**3.6** Presentation by members of the South Union Hunt to Tracton GAA Hall Committee. Included in photo is William Worth Newenham of Coolmore, Carrigaline (centre, holding hunting horn). Photo courtesy of *Tracton News Sheet*.

Newenham (master) and John Newenham (field master). The other fifteen members were of the farming and commercial classes.[49]

The South Union hunt is still in existence today and is best known for its meet on St Stephen's Day on the main street of Carrigaline. It also has a very active pony club with several junior members. And it still provides an irresistible atmosphere. In 1982, the hunt had the opportunity to relive its glory days when it was invited to take part in a BBC adaptation of Molly Keane's Anglo-Irish novel, *Good behaviour*. The members of the hunt appeared in many scenes filmed at Coolmore, which stood in for Temple Alice, the Big House featured in the novel, and they took part in a hunt ball filmed inside the house.[50] Like John Locke's sock, which despite being completely covered with patches remains the same sock, the genius of the Irish hunt scene has been its ability to adapt to circumstances and to remain both relevant and anachronistic at the same time. While the hunt may have had its origins among the landed gentry of south Cork, its tradition is maintained by members from a variety of classes and backgrounds today. And still, on occasion, the hunt harks back to its roots, when meets are held at the ruined mansions of its founders.

**49** *Southern Star*, 27 Apr. 1974. **50** Email correspondence with Gabi Keller, South Union Hunt member, 21 Jan. 2016.

# Travel, recreation and hospitality: the Richards and Orpen families, 1860–1960[1]

PHILIP BULL

Edward Richards-Orpen was a complex, highly intelligent and immensely creative Irishman who, although brought up in London, was deeply committed to the future of the new state within which he inherited Monksgrange in County Wexford on the death of his mother, Adela Orpen, in 1927. His initial venture was the establishment of the Grange Furniture Industry, producing furniture to the principles of the Arts and Crafts movement, using Irish timber and none of the mass production techniques that had taken over most furniture manufacture. While important in introducing new design concepts to Ireland, the late Nicola Gordon Bowe has shown in a perceptive and richly illustrated article that it was not a business success and ceased operation in 1933.[2] His lifelong commitment, however, was in the area of agricultural economics, where he combined his scientific skills with his understanding of economics and his day-to-day experience as a working farmer to encourage debate and research about Ireland's agricultural sector in an international context. To his agricultural research, he applied high intellectual analysis and played a significant role in the development of agricultural policy in the Fine Gael party, as well as contributing to the creation and general management of that party, particularly through his close working relationship with James Dillon. Edward served as a senator between 1948 and 1951.

The theme of sport and leisure in the country house presents something of a challenge in dealing with the family of Edward Richards-Orpen. His grandson, Jeremy Hill, recounts his experience as a child of dining with his grandparents accompanied by earnest discussion of significant intellectual or contemporary issues, often rather boring to children. Edward and his wife Margaret were committed to pursuing serious questions and important causes and most of what they did, even when it might fall broadly into the category of leisure, was done

1 This chapter was originally the 2018 Edward Richards-Orpen Memorial Lecture delivered at the Sixteenth Annual Historic Houses Conference at Maynooth University, 8–9 June 2018. I thank the Edward Richards-Orpen Memorial Trust for their invitation to give this lecture and their support for it, as well as to the Centre for the Study of Historic Irish Houses and Estates, Maynooth University, for its continued support of my research. 2 Nicola Gordon Bowe, 'A Cotswold-inspired venture towards Modernism in Ireland: Edward Richards Orpen (1884–1967) and the Grange Furniture Industry, 1927–1932', *Journal of the Decorative Arts Society* (2003), pp 95–111; see also her 'The Irishman who loved a chair', *Country Life*, 16 Jan. 2003, pp 58–60.

with ulterior purposes in mind. In Edward's childhood, on holiday with his father, Goddard Orpen, as a 14-year old, he spent an hour and a half at Amiens Street railway station observing steam engines, and then the afternoon at the railway workshops at Inchicore where his father took photographs of locomotives for him.[3] A year earlier, he had written to his grandfather for advice on a paper he could subscribe to, dedicated to locomotives, on condition that it would cost 'about 2d or not more than 6d a month'.[4] He also asked his grandfather to make a drawing of a 'little shunting engine named "Cambria"' when he next went to Rosslare.[5] This was a lifelong leisure pursuit for Edward and his papers are filled with drawings, highly skilled ones, of steam locomotives in Britain and Ireland. Indeed, it was an extension of this that provided a major leisure recreation for Edward in later years: the construction of a most impressive model railway in one of the out-buildings at Monksgrange.

As an undergraduate at Cambridge, sport and leisure were very much part of Edward's life; he was in much demand for tennis and other sports, for performing at musical events and for his presence at parties; all this perhaps part of the reason for his not getting the honours degree expected of him. Back in Wexford in 1901, at the age of 17, his mother noted how much he had enjoyed himself at a dance and observed how popular he was on the dance floor.[6] By 1908, he had acquired a more serious side and he cancelled going to a dance in Ferns because of a preoccupation with a machine he had bought,[7] and most of his recreational or leisure activities in later life had very serious purposes. In marrying Margaret Tomalin, the daughter of the founder of the Jaeger clothing company,[8] he was matching himself with someone with the same intense and serious approach to life. A sense of her youthful leisure activity is glimpsed, however, in the jocular remark of her father, Lewis Tomalin, who, when asked if she would miss him when she moved from London to Ireland, replied that he thought 'she would miss Harrods more'.[9]

Service in the British Army in France in the First World War may not seem the place to look for leisure activities, but Edward used his talents to create opportunities for his fellow officers to relax. He was put in charge of his unit's motor vehicles because of his engineering and general scientific skills, which he used to set up generators and lighting in tents, enabling officers to read and write at night; his improvements caused officers from another unit to express astonishment at this inventiveness as well as the other comforts that were enjoyed

3 Goddard Henry Orpen to Adela Elizabeth Orpen, 21 Apr. 1898, Monksgrange Archives (hereafter MGA) I/M(7b). 4 Edward Richards Orpen to Edward Moore Richards (hereafter EMR), 3 May [1897], MGA/I/K(22). 5 Edward Richards Orpen to EMR, 3 Jan. 1898, MGA/I/O(2a). 6 Adela Elizabeth Orpen (hereafter AEO), journal entry, 4 Jan. 1901, MGA/I/BB(5e). 7 AEO to EMR, 29 Jan. 1908, MGA/I/K(33). 8 Lewis Tomalin had established 'Dr Jaeger's Sanitary Woollen System Company' in 1884 under licence from the German originator of a concept of woollen clothes being healthier than cotton. 9 Lewis Tomalin to Friedrich Fick, 15 June 1914, MGA/VII/D(2).

in his mess.[10] He designed modifications to a tent to improve ventilation and reduce the threat of rain getting in. Music played on a turntable in the tent was a particular pleasure and Edward ensured that new records were secured. Margaret sent magazines and papers,[11] including *Country Life* with its articles and illustrations of architecture and furniture. This was a particular favourite for him and his fellow officers. Indeed, so much did he improve living conditions and opportunities for leisure that one of his colleagues jokingly suggested contributing an article, illustrating their mess tent and the furniture Edward had managed to buy or scavenge, to *Country Life*'s series on lesser country houses.[12] His fellow officers thus owed him a debt for the greater comfort and scope for leisure in what were otherwise unpleasant and stressful conditions.[13]

Once Edward had inherited Monksgrange in 1927, one begins to see the pattern of his and Margaret's leisure life developing in the form of hospitality. Margaret had suffered from separation from family and friends in London and her compensation took the form of frequent weekend house parties at Monksgrange, to which English friends and relatives were invited, together with the couple's Irish friends and acquaintances. But these events were also extremely important, as Margaret recognized, in bringing together people who were significant for Edward's political and intellectual pursuits; one of the most regular guests was the politician James Dillon (Minister for Agriculture, 1948–51 and 1954–57; leader of Fine Gael 1959–65). A popular pastime was tennis and Edward and Margaret, like most of the other members of their family, were keen players and tennis parties were a major feature of life at Monksgrange. These parties were frequent during the summer months and usually spontaneous, with anything between two and three dozen visitors turning up, the number never known in advance. Margaret ensured that catering for such numbers did not become a burden for her, as explained by her daughter, Charmian Hill:

> Mum kept a store of porter cakes to supplement the usual afternoon tea. These were rich fruit cakes softened with stout which, if kept in tins, improved with age so could be kept for any length of time. To slake the thirst when playing tennis she provided raspberry vinegar, a much pleasanter drink than the name suggests which we made during the raspberry season to keep in store for the rest of the year.[14]

10 Edward Richards Richards-Orpen (hereafter ERR-O) to Margaret Richards-Orpen (hereafter MR-O), 24 May 1917, MGA/VII/A(4d). Edward had changed his surname from Orpen to Richards-Orpen in 1914. 11 MR-O to ERR-O, 14 Mar. 1917, MGA/VII/A(4b). 12 Ibid., 9 June 1917, MGA/VII/A(4e). 13 For a fuller account of his wartime experiences, see Philip Bull, 'Behind the Front in France: the story of the heir to Monksgrange' in Terence Dooley and Christopher Ridgway (eds), *The country house and the Great War: Irish and British experiences* (Dublin, 2016), pp 40–52. 14 Charmian Hill, unpublished reminiscences of childhood, MGA/VII/D(19), p. 12.

Margaret knew how to plan efficiently and keep an eye on her commitments and her household finances while at the same time ensuring an important leisure and recreational dimension to their lives.

It was for financial reasons that the couple embarked on a hospitality project that met the leisure needs of others more than their own. In 1936 they became part of the Europe on Wheels venture organized from London and enabling wealthy Americans to stay in prestigious homes while they travelled. While Margaret took on the responsibility of providing for them in the house, Edward acted as chauffeur introducing them to historic and other sites around Ireland. Charmian Hill explained what was involved: 'They [the tourists] really did get their taste of family life because meals were eaten with us and consisted of good fresh country food with no extra frills.'[15] This scheme was brought to an end by the outbreak of war in 1939 but Edward and Margaret revived the concept in the 1950s with the Monksgrange private guest house venture.[16] This was part of the constant battle against the odds in keeping the property financially viable.

For Edward's grandfather, Edward Moore Richards, what others might have considered leisure activities were to be viewed very much in terms of usefulness. He once declared himself to be 'much opposed to competitive muscular exercise of all kinds',[17] and in response to an enquiry from an old friend coming to stay in 1881 as to the availability of a 'hunter' he wrote: 'I am not a sporting man at all, especially I am not in the hunting line,' but he went on to advise that as 'so many hunts are given up in Ireland … I should judge it a probable time to get hold of a good hunter'.[18] This was an impish comment on what was happening as a result of the Land League campaign.[19] In Anthony Trollope's novel *The Land Leaguers*, stopping the hunt by sending crowds of people over the land had become a source of leisure and fun for the Land League agitators, denying a popular pursuit for the landed gentry and their associates. As a young man Edward Moore Richards had lived in the United States, in Virginia and in Kansas, and in the latter in particular he had taken part in boar and deer hunting excursions, but these were organized to secure food supplies. He intensely disliked horse racing and avoided whenever possible going to the theatre.

What he liked, however, was walking. While in Virginia in 1859 he had walked for eight days through the region of the James River, and in Kansas he undertook a number of long walks, especially one from Mound City to Leavenworth from 17 to 20 June 1864, and returning between 20 and 23 June; this was a total of 100 miles, averaging 30 miles a day.[20] This pattern continued on his return to Europe, with a walk of a couple of weeks along the chain of the Vosges Mountains, and in 1871 a marathon walk through the English Lake District and northern Scotland lasting for almost four months. He justified walking as the key to good mental

**15** Ibid., p. 12; MGA/VII/H(29a–k). **16** MGA/VII/H(29j). **17** EMR to AEO, 2 Dec. 1897, MGA/I/K(22). **18** EMR to John Magrath, 19 Dec. 1881 (copy), EMR letter book, 1880–3, p. 281, MGA/I/BB(2c). **19** For further insights into the decline of hunting, see Laura Brown's essay in this volume. **20** MGA/V/H(2).

and physical health and he tended to do it at times of crisis or change in his personal life. He believed that walking was 'the King of all exercises for health'.[21] This was perhaps also true of ice skating, a recreation that was very important to him immediately after his return from America. This he pursued in Sweden, with an ulterior motive, as he was hoping to marry a Swedish woman, but this courtship proved unsuccessful. In the 1870s, both he and his daughter Adela were members of the Wexford archery club. This was an especially apposite choice of activity for him to share with his daughter for archery had since the late eighteenth century become a sport particularly open to women. One newspaper reported in 1864 that 'In archery the gentler sex have the superiority over the men. They beat them hollow.'[22] It would thus have fitted into both his commitment to equality of women and also his concern at this time about his daughter's physical health.

A major recreation for Edward Moore Richards for at least a decade from the mid-1870s was his obsession with astronomy and the construction of an observatory and a telescope at Monksgrange. Originally justified as an interest that Adela wished to pursue, his correspondence reveals that this went well beyond anything she aspired to.[23] For a man for whom a recreation had to have an ulterior dimension, the intensity of his work on a telescope made use of his talents as an able and sophisticated civil engineer who, by unexpectedly inheriting a landed estate on the death of his older brother, had been denied the opportunity of practising that profession.

Ever serious, one of Edward Moore Richards' abiding interests was his passion for reform of women's dress. The origins of this lay with his observation of indigenous women at Seven Islands Bay in the Gulf of St Lawrence in 1847, but his commitment to the cause intensified during his years in Virginia and Kansas. In writing to his mother from Virginia in 1859, he described stays as 'one of the greatest curses in the world',[24] and attributed to them a range of ailments including consumption and depression. For him, female modes of dress were not only injurious to health but symbolized women's lack of freedom in society. Over the years he 'lost all expectation that womankind as a whole will … have sense and independence enough to emancipate herself from the slavery of fashion',[25] but by the 1890s he was encouraged by the renewed vigour of the campaign for reform of women's dress stimulated as it was by the advent of cycling, although he was adamant that his only interest in cycling was as a means of granting

21 EMR to Miss L.C. Davidson, 1 Dec. 1893 (copy), EMR letter book, 92–7, p. 228, MGA/I/BB(2f). 22 *Nottinghamshire Guardian*, 16 Dec. 1864, quoted in Don Chapman, *Wearing the trousers: fashion, freedom and the rise of the modern woman* (Stroud, 2017), p. 105. 23 For his interest in astronomy, see Lesley Whiteside, 'Amateur astronomy in the nineteenth-century Irish country house: the observatory at Monksgrange, County Wexford', in this volume of essays. 24 EMR to Dorothea Sargent, 29 Mar. 1859, MGA/I/G(13). 25 EMR to Miss Lissy Reynolds (Brighton), 3 Jan. 1894 (copy), EMR letter book, 1892–7, p. 250, MGA/I/BB(2f).

4.1 EMR in rational dress and helmet looking more like a sportsman than he was.

women 'the right to dress as they please'.[26] This cause became once more a significant part of his recreational world in the later years of his life, involving him in extensive correspondence with people in Britain and Ireland who were active in the campaign, and led him to join in 1897 the Western Rational Dress Club based in Cheltenham.[27] He again began writing for papers and journals on

26 EMR to Lissy Reynolds, 24 Apr. 1894 (copy), EMR letter book, 1892–7, p. 343, MGA/I/BB(2f); EMR to Lillias Davidson, 25 Apr. 1894 (copy), EMR letter book, 1892–7, pp 344–5, MGA/I/BB(2f). For a comprehensive history of the women's dress reform movement see Chapman, *Wearing the trousers*. 27 EMR to Sydney Buckman, 19 July 1897 (copy), EMR letter book, 1892–7, p. 969, MGA/I/BB(2f); Chapman, *Wearing the trousers*, pp 202–3.

the subject, submitting a number of letters to the *Rational Dress Gazette* published by the Rational Dress League formed under the leadership of Lady Harberton in 1898;[28] the *Gazette* reprinted a substantial article of his from the *Wexford Independent*.[29] He also argued for reform of male dress and set an example himself.

When Edward Moore Richards' daughter, Adela, married Goddard Orpen she joined a family for whom pleasure for its own sake had a higher priority. While always allowing themselves to be educated by what they saw, the Orpens walked and travelled for enjoyment and recreation and, in the case of Goddard and his siblings, for the pleasure to be derived from each other's company. The pattern had been established already in the late eighteenth century by Goddard's grandfather, Thomas Herbert Orpen, who left accounts of journeys to Edinburgh in 1795, to England in 1797 and variously around Scotland, Wales and Ireland on other occasions.[30] His son and Goddard's father, the Dublin barrister John Herbert Orpen, was an inveterate traveller, although almost always within the British Isles. Like the other travellers in his family J.H. Orpen kept journals of his travels in England between 1843 and 1883,[31] and in Wales, England, Ireland and Scotland between 1863 and 1866.[32] We also know from letters he wrote to his wife that he visited Scotland in 1850 and 1854.[33] In 1862 he broke out of previous boundaries by travelling to Switzerland and Germany.[34] The journals he wrote took a distinctive character, comprising pre-illustrated pages on which he wrote up the events of the day.

In 1862 and 1863, John Herbert Orpen took his young sons on trips to England and the north of Ireland, with the journals written up by his son John Richards Orpen.[35] If his intention was to give his sons an apprenticeship in the art of travel it certainly worked, for by the time they were in their twenties they, together with their sisters Penelope and Ellen, were regular travellers in their own right. In particular, between August and October 1877, Goddard and Thomas Orpen, together with another cousin and his wife and an aunt, toured the Continent from the Netherlands to Venice, and in 1878 a similar party spent a month together in Switzerland. On both these trips Adela Richards, the daughter of Edward Moore Richards, accompanied them, and in his journal of the second tour Goddard recorded that it 'was big with the destiny of two human souls'.[36] There was certainly an ulterior motive for these two trips, for they facilitated the courtship of Goddard and Adela away from the eye of her father, who it transpired was opposed to the match but at the time believed them to be innocent cousinly ventures. Travel was also an opportunity for drawing and

28 See Chapman, *Wearing the trousers*, pp 207ff. 29 EMR, 'Bloomerism', *Rational Dress Gazette: Organ of the Rational Dress League*, 16 (Jan. 1900). 30 MGA/IV/B(1b). 31 MGA/IV/D(2b). 32 MGA/IV/ D(2c). 33 MGA/IV/D(2e). 34 MGA/IV/D(2f). 35 MGA/IV/D(2g). 36 Goddard Henry Orpen, 'Journal of a tour in Switzerland from August 21st to September 21st 1878', MGA/I/BB(7b).

4.2 Richard and Penelope Orpen and two friends on the Dolomites. Photo by Goddard Orpen.

painting, a recreation enjoyed particularly by Penelope Orpen who produced a very significant portfolio of paintings on her travels.

Travel for this younger generation was very different from that of Goddard's father, for this was now the height of the age of steam. There was the excitement of speed and with it opportunities to visit many more locations within a single trip, such as in the 1877 tour that took them from the Netherlands to Venice. There was also the Victorian fascination with scientific and technological achievement; not only was the train itself a relative novelty but the associated infrastructure was exciting to view – tunnels, bridges, grand railway stations and other features – not to mention the unprecedented comfort the train provided. What added to the enjoyment of these trips was the chance to become familiar with foreign places and to become known to the local people, to be greeted by hotel staff they knew from previous visits, and to be invited to local social events. For Adela Richards, importantly, the travel enabled her to meet up with friends and relatives from her American childhood who were travelling in Europe.

Even before her trips with the Orpens, Adela Richards had travelled to the Continent, initially at least for educational reasons. One trip in 1873 involved a thirty-six-hour train journey from Geneva to Florence. In 1876, accompanied by her 76-year-old grandmother, the intention had been to cross to Egypt, but her grandmother took ill in Paris en route. Rather than return home they persisted as far as Italy in the hope that the warmer climate would bring a recovery for her, as indeed it did. But Egypt was now out of the question. Such exploits as these would have been much more difficult, if not impossible, a decade earlier. Some of the pleasure of such journeys derived from the great sense of participating in modernity.

Modernity also marked the life of Goddard and Adela following their marriage in 1880, her father now reconciled to the match, for they went to live in Bedford Park, a newly established garden and artistic enclave in London. Here they lived what might be called an avant-garde life, and this was where their children grew up, including the young Edward. By this time Goddard had begun a new recreational activity that was to be a major preoccupation for the rest of his life: photography. In this, modernity was also the key, for he moved quickly with new innovations and became an extremely skilled photographer. Even by 1891 he was developing plates for others, many of them for his brother, although he was not yet entirely happy with his workmanship, predicting – incorrectly as it turned out – that 'I think I have finished with Photography.'[37] While some of what he did was recording historical and archaeological remains, much of it was of a more recreational character. Although Goddard Orpen was to become one of the most distinguished historians of his generation, the author of a four-volume history still acclaimed to this day,[38] he was never officially employed for this work. His research was undertaken first of all in Bedford Park as a hobby alongside his job as a barrister and then, after 1900, as a more-or-less full-time, but still voluntary, activity at Monksgrange. These scholarly pursuits in his leisure time gave him pleasure and fulfilment. Such pleasure bubbles up in his account of observing ancient artefacts on the Aran Islands in 1895 with the young archaeologist R.A.S. McAlister: 'We used to talk about inscriptions, hunt for them together, rub them & photograph them, & compare notes in the evening.'[39] His son Edward also records his father's excitement at finding particular archaeological remains exactly where he predicted they would be.[40] Goddard became a great professional historian but his enjoyment in research and writing constituted for him leisure at its best.

37 Goddard Henry Orpen to AEO, 10 Nov. 1891, MGA/I/M(6a). 38 G.H. Orpen, *Ireland under the Normans, 1169–1333*, 4 vols (Oxford, 1911–20). 39 Goddard Henry Orpen to AEO, 14 July 1895, MGA/I/M(6c). 40 Edward Richards Orpen, Diary, 15 July 1906, MGA/VII/D(7g). This discovery was of 'Poolcaum' on the River Slaney; G.H. Orpen, 'The castle of Raymond Le Gros at Fodredunolan', *Journal of the Royal Society of Antiquaries of Ireland*, 5th ser., 16 (31 Dec. 1906), pp 374–5. I am indebted to Seán Duffy for this reference.

While Goddard was occupying himself with his historical research and photography, Adela's leisure in Bedford Park was drawing and writing, undertaken with the same degree of professionalism that her husband was showing. Thus, she took classes in 'the School of Art',[41] published articles in journals and newspapers and eventually produced three novels and a travel book; she also left many unpublished manuscripts. But it was in Bedford Park that the passion for tennis is most evident. A tennis court had been built at Grange (as Monksgrange was then called) sometime in the 1870s, probably for Adela. But before she could make much use of it she was married and she and Goddard became members of the Bedford Park Tennis Club. They were not just casual club members, but regular and enthusiastic players. Goddard was intensely competitive, determined to win every game, which he usually did. Of the 1882 Bedford Park grand tennis tournament Adela recorded that 'Goddard won the challenge after a most exciting struggle,' and she had felt 'dreadfully anxious' for him to win.[42] In the 1883 tournament Adela won the Ladies Singles Handicap, for which she was awarded a silver sugar bowl and tongs; this sterling physical performance followed just four months after she had given birth to her daughter Iris.[43] This was one instance of committed sporting activity in these families. Another serious sportsman was Edward Moore Richards' half-brother, Harry Sargent, who was a keen hunter and a regular rider in horse races – a subject on which he published a book.[44]

One very important recreation that both the Richards and the Orpen families enjoyed in more or less equal measure was cycling, also an activity identified with modernity. Edward Moore Richards had been an enthusiastic cyclist in the early 1870s, often cycling for long distances. He would cycle from Grange to New Ross to meet people arriving on the Waterford boat and then cycle back, sometimes alongside the carriage bringing the passengers. He also followed cycling as an observer, fascinated by exploits such as that of a Mr Thorpe who cycled the 195 miles from London to York in 22½ hours, and he himself was tempted in 1876 to go to London for the Oxford-Cambridge bicycle race. Goddard Orpen was an enthusiastic cyclist; he had made a long cycle ride to Grange while courting Adela, and he cycled extensively with his brothers and his sister Penelope, and later with his young son Edward. Later in life Edward Moore Richards and his second wife Ellen did a modest amount of cycling, partly in the context of the movement for women's dress reform.

One of the commonest enthusiasms for the occupants of large country houses was gardening, and historically Monksgrange features very strongly in this

41 Probably the Chiswick School of Art, founded in Bedford Park in 1881, shortly after the Orpens moved there. 42 AEO, journal, 15 July 1882, MGA/I/BB(95d). 43 *Bedford Park Gazette*, 2 (Aug. 1883), MGA/I/AA(3q). 44 Harry R. Sargent, *Thoughts upon sport: a work dealing shortly with each branch of sport … to which are added, a complete history of the Curraghmore Hunt and memoirs of notable sportsmen* (London, 1895; facsimile, 2016).

4.3 Ellen Richards in rational dress and with her bicycle.

regard. The original eighteenth-century builder of the house, Goddard Richards, laid out an avenue of trees many years before the house was built to ensure a mature landscape once it was occupied. Successive occupants all placed a high priority on gardening – for landscaping, for flower ornamentation and for fruit and vegetable production – but the pinnacle of achievement was the work of Edward Richards-Orpen and his sister, Iris Orpen. After their mother assumed proprietorship of the property in 1900, Iris in particular set herself the task of redesigning and reconstructing the gardens. In line with the Arts and Crafts

4.4 Iris Orpen in the garden she created: photo by Goddard Orpen.

principles they removed the fussy garden beds from the front of the house replacing them with a sweep of grass held back by a stone retaining wall. The gardens to the rear of the house were completely redesigned in the style of Gertrude Jekyll and the architect Edwin Lutyens. While Edward designed and built the infrastructure of paths and steps, Iris was largely responsible for planting. Her garden remains an impressive feature of Monksgrange to this day.

Her other activities included music and drawing. Her mother once recorded that she had come home from a music lesson 'in great spirits as always with music',[45] and in art she was identified by Thomas McGreevy as one of a group of women artists whose names are 'guarantees of fine work'.[46] She was a consummate achiever.

45 AEO, journal, 4 Jan. 1901, MGA/I/BB(5e). 46 Thomas McGreevy, 'A lively exhibition',

'Achievers' is the appropriate word for the occupants of Monksgrange. This was what they did to occupy themselves. Very rarely was it done for monetary gain – Europe on Wheels the notable exception – but to give personal satisfaction. Purposeful leisure was how the Richards family passed their free time and Monksgrange provided a most appropriate site. The Orpens were different; they were professionals, lawyers, doctors, clerics, and for leisure they needed to get away from work and nothing satisfied that need so well as travel. Goddard Orpen was the cross-over figure. Hating the legal profession, he abandoned it to take advantage of his wife's inheritance, not to become a country gentleman – although that came with the territory – but to use his time to achieve, which he did with brilliant results. These two families had very different concepts of what constituted leisure: the Richardses were imbued with a sense of purpose and the need to justify their activities in terms of achievement and contributions to society or family and to the maintenance of their house and its history; the Orpens were altogether more relaxed with themselves, much less serious about who they were and eager to get away from day-to-day responsibilities and to enjoy themselves and the company of each other, as well as that of friends. The merger of the two families created far more of a balance between these two outlooks.

'Over the past century countless historic houses have continued to become more outward facing and have become attractive visitor destinations in their own right', appealing to a wider public 'whose idea of leisure and recreation includes cultural tourism'.[47] Under the auspices of Edward and Margaret Richards-Orpen's grandson, Jeremy Hill, and his wife, Rosemary, Monksgrange has played its part more recently in opening itself up to a public attracted to cultural offers. This has included presenting, in conjunction with the Kavanaghs at Borris, a series of open-air operas between 2001 and 2005 and, through the Norman Gallery, providing opportunities for artists, especially younger ones, to hold exhibitions of their work. Moreover Iris' Arts and Crafts garden is open to the public through the summer months and is one of the most impressive legacies of Monksgrange's history, while the operation by Ben Hill and his wife, Joyce, of the company Celtic Equine has given to the property an important new economic function. The availability of the Monksgrange archives – not only the documentary but also the photographic, music, map and art collections – provides yet another focus for outside engagement and scholarship. Although very different from his own tenure of the house, this continuing cultural, scholarly and business role for Monksgrange would be a cause of pleasure to Edward Richards-Orpen.

Finally, despite his commitment to very serious purposes, Edward Richards-Orpen was a man with a real sense of fun and engagement with people. His sense

*Irish Times*, 30 Mar. 1943. **47** Terence Dooley and Christopher Ridgway, 'Call for papers', 16th Annual Historic Houses Conference at Maynooth University, 8–9 June 2018.

4.5 'Officer-in-charge of officers' instruction': self-portrait by Edward Richards-Orpen drawn for his son John.

of fun is captured in this self-portrait drawn for his 3-year old son, John, to mark his promotion in the British Army in France to officer in charge of officers' instruction.

He had outstanding skills, as a mathematician, an engineer, a craftsman, a draughtsman, an intellectual, an educationalist and a visionary for the future of his country. But he was also devoted to his immediate family and determined to provide an environment in which his family's tradition of individual achievement was maintained. By teasing out the approaches to recreation a picture emerges of the diverse interests and achievements of members of the Richards and Orpen families.

# Horse racing and the country house

OLIVER COX

In April 1889, the American journalist Charles Pelham-Clinton published an account of his visit to the 6th duke of Portland's estate at Welbeck Abbey, Nottinghamshire. He observed that:

> Marvellous as is the Abbey and its immediate surroundings, I think these wonders are surpassed by the stables. I believe there is nothing in the world that approaches them … [The stables] occupy one acre of ground, and there is room for ninety-six horses … [The riding school] is the largest school in the world save one at Moscow and the tan gallop, covered with glass, of which the roof contains sixty four thousand feet – the total length of the ride is one thousand two hundred and eighty-four feet. It is so constructed that a horse going at a fair gallop can make the turn at either end without slackening speed.[1]

The extraordinary stable and training complex, inherited by the 6th duke a decade earlier, had been constructed and financed by his cousin, John Cavendish-Bentinck-Scott, 5th duke of Portland. The Tan Gallop at Welbeck, along with the stable complexes at Goodwood, Sussex and Wentworth Woodhouse, Yorkshire, from the century before, demonstrate in architecture the significance of the horse for the country house.

By the time Pelham-Clinton visited Welbeck, the 6th duke of Portland was already putting his inherited infrastructure to good use. In 1887, one of the most famous racehorses of the nineteenth century, St Simon, moved to the duke's stud at Welbeck where he was leading sire from 1890 to 1896 and from 1900 to 1901. Between 1888 and 1900, the duke won all three of the Classic races (the 2000 Guineas, Derby and St Leger) with horses he had bred at Welbeck. Many horses made their way onto the walls of Welbeck, some as paintings by artists including Emil Adam and Lynwood Palmer,[2] others as bijou bronze additions to the living space, or – in the case of St Simon and Portland's two Derby winners (Donovan and Ayrshire) – by having their hides preserved and mounted in vertical wood and glass display cases in the entrance hall.[3]

1 Charles S. Pelham-Clinton, 'A subterranean estate', *Cosmopolitan: A Monthly Illustrated Magazine*, 6:6 (New York, 1889), pp 594–5. 2 'The Welbeck Stud', *Country Life*, 78:2015 (1935), pp 216–17. 3 These hides were given to the Newmarket trainer Sir Mark Prescott by Lady Anne Cavendish-Bentinck, and they now hang in the tack room at Heath House stables

5.1 *Horse and groom in front of Welbeck Abbey* (*c.*1630).

Today, the remnants of this racing and breeding infrastructure have been repurposed. The Tan Gallop, for example, now anchors a new gallery for the Portland Collection by Hugh Broughton Architects completed in spring 2016.[4] In addition to the equine architectural fragments within which the new gallery sits, the historic collections on display articulate the centrality of the horse to Welbeck's story before the 6th duke, and the extent to which enthusiasm for, and interest in, horses was often a multi-generational phenomenon, with each successive generation altering and influencing the architecture and collections of the country house in different ways. Four paintings in the collection illustrate themes that are central to this essay.

In the 22-metre Long Gallery hang *Horse and groom in front of Welbeck Abbey* (*c.*1630) (fig. 5.1) and John Wootton's *Arabian horse sent from Aleppo by Mr Nathaniel Harley* (1724) (fig. 5.2). The former, one of a series of twelve huge paintings of horses, hints at the centrality and significance of horses and

in Newmarket, Suffolk. 4 Michael Hall, *Treasures of the Portland Collection* (Welbeck, 2016), p. 106. See also, Catherine Slessor, 'The Harley Gallery by Hugh Broughton Associates', *Architect's Journal*, 23 Mar. 2016, https://www.architectsjournal.co.uk/buildings/the-harley-gallery-by-hugh-broughton-architects/10003978.article, accessed 30 Sept. 2018.

5.2 *Arabian horse sent from Aleppo by Mr Nathaniel Harley* (1724).

horsemanship to William Cavendish, 1st duke of Newcastle, who built large stables and riding schools at both Welbeck and Bolsover Castle, laid out a five-mile racecourse at Welbeck, and published a hugely influential manual for a particular form of training and riding of horses known as *haute école*.[5] The painting's sheer scale denotes the importance of the horse, with Welbeck Abbey itself reduced to a cameo between the horse's legs.

Wootton's painting captures the obsession of the next generation of horsemen with the pedigrees and breeding that were to become an essential part of horse racing in the eighteenth century. The Bloody Shouldered Arabian was one of a number of horses imported from the Levant and Middle East in the late seventeenth century and early eighteenth century, which were selectively bred with English stock to produce the Thoroughbred racehorse.[6] Aristocratic families with younger sons in mercantile or consular positions in cities like Aleppo were most likely to be successful in the securing of Arabian horses.[7] The

5 On Cavendish's life and architectural patronage, see Lucy Worsley, *Cavalier: a tale of chivalry, passion and great houses* (London, 2007); and Lucy Worsley and Tom Addyman, 'Riding houses and horses: William Cavendish's architecture for the art of horsemanship', *Architectural History*, 45 (2002), pp 194–229. 6 Donna Landry, *Noble brutes: how eastern horses transformed English culture* (Baltimore, 2009), *passim*. 7 Philip Mansel, *Aleppo: the rise*

5.3 *William Henry Cavendish Bentinck, 3rd duke of Portland in front of Welbeck Abbey riding stables* (1766–7).

Harley family were particularly well placed thanks to Edward Harley, 2nd earl of Oxford's uncle, Nathaniel, who had lived in Aleppo since 1686, and exported at least nine Arabian horses using English men of war or Levant Company merchant ships before his death in 1720.[8] A number of these Arabians were held at stud at the Harley family seats of Welbeck and Wimpole Hall, Cambridgeshire.[9] Wootton painted the Bloody Shouldered Arabian nine times,[10] and as Donna Landry has demonstrated, the colt's significance lay in his value

*and fall of Syria's great merchant city* (London, 2016), pp 14, 19. 8 Donna Landry, 'Rewriting the sea from the desert shore: equine and equestrian perspectives on a new maritime history' in Mario Fusaro, Colin Heywood and Mohamed-Salah Omri (eds), *Trade and cultural exchange in the early modern Mediterranean: Braudel's maritime legacy* (London, 2010), p. 257. See also: Charles Matthew Prior, *Early records of the Thoroughbred horse: containing reproductions of some original stud-books, and other papers, of the eighteenth century* (London, 1924), pp 137–8; and British Library Add. MS 70143 for Nathaniel Harley's letters from Aleppo. 9 For further details of the equine genealogy of the 'Welbeck Arabians', and their links with other Harley family properties (for example, Wimpole Hall), see Thorougbred Bloodlines, 'Welbeck Orientals', http://www.bloodlines.net/TB/Bios/WelbeckArabians.htm, accessed 6 Oct. 2018. 10 Arline Meyer, *John Wootton, 1682–1764: landscapes and sporting art in early Georgian England* (London, 1984), p. 34.

5.4 *William Henry Cavendish Bentinck, 3rd duke of Portland and his younger brother, Lord Edward* (1767–8).

as a sire, with requests to have mares covered by him from the 4th earl of Berkshire and Sir Gervas Clinton among others.[11] The Bloody Shouldered Arabian sired Sir Nathaniel Curzon's horse Brisk, winner of several Royal Plates, and the duke of Bolton's horse Sweepstakes, who, in turn, sired Lord Rockingham's Whistlejacket. Wootton's painting simultaneously emphasizes the Englishness and the exoticism of the Bloody Shouldered Arabian. The horse is accompanied by a groom in Turkish or Arab dress and by a type of eastern greyhound known as a saluki, the landscape background includes a body of water – hinting at the horse's journey from Aleppo – and the classical architecture frames the horse within the signifiers of established good taste.[12] Wootton's painting reminds the viewer of the global reach of the country house.

Moving through into the Treasury Gallery of the Portland Collection, a pair of George Stubbs paintings combine ancestral lineage with an indication of the impact of the Thoroughbred racehorse on the English landscape. *William Henry*

11 Donna Landry, 'The Bloody Shouldered Arabian and early modern English culture', *Criticism*, 46:1 (2004), 41–69. 12 At Wimpole Hall, Wootton's *Arabian horse sent from Aleppo by Nathaniel Harley to his nephew, Edward Lord Harley* (1715), emphasizes the Arabian aspects even more forcefully with a pair of pyramids, a palm tree and a prominent Ottoman saddle in

*Cavendish Bentinck, 3rd duke of Portland in front of Welbeck Abbey riding stables* (1766–7) (fig. 5.3), Stubbs' first commission from Portland, was a statement of equine pedigree, showing the duke on horseback in front of the stables built by his grandmother and next to William Cavendish's Jacobean riding house, perhaps as a tribute to his celebrated ancestor.[13] *William Henry Cavendish Bentinck, 3rd duke of Portland and his younger brother, Lord Edward* (1767–8) (fig. 5.4), commissioned from Stubbs a year later, focuses attention on the breeding and training of horses.

As Judy Egerton argues, this was a new setting pioneered by Stubbs, which would become popular with his patrons, 'because the quiet, almost private nature of the subject showed their passion for horses in a gentler, more "polite" and less boastful light that the traditional portraiture of "winners".'[14] Stubbs' work at Welbeck was a direct result of Portland's political connection and personal friendship with the 2nd marquess of Rockingham. Horseflesh and the swirling aristocratic factional politics of the 1760s went hand-in-hand.

These four paintings hint at the centrality of the horse to country-house life. Sporting pictures, much like family pictures, emphasize dynastic connections and historical pedigree. Just as family portraits split across a range of locations can demonstrate the kinship networks vital to the maintenance of aristocratic sociability and political power, so can sporting paintings of thoroughbreds and their achievements on the racecourse. The exchange and breeding of racehorses could consolidate family connections and build political alliances.

The racehorse sits at the top of the vast, highly stratified pyramid of horseflesh that enabled and sustained life in the country house until the early decades of the twentieth century. Without the efficient breeding, training, exchange, stabling and management of horses, country houses could not perform the variety of functions that their owners required of them. The racehorse, in particular, could impact on the country house in a number of different ways. Yet, if racing does feature in accounts of country-house life, it is usually as a symbol of aristocratic dissolution and dissipation, as the first step on the way to ruin.[15]

This essay does not seek to argue otherwise – racing has always been an efficient way of turning a large fortune into a small one – but in taking horse racing as an important component of country-house life, one can open up new avenues of scholarly enquiry. Horse racing can provide insights into shifting patterns of aristocratic and gentry politicking and sociability; highlight the twin concerns of equine and human bloodstock; and explain artistic and architectural developments. The materiality of horse racing permeates through the country house yet is often overlooked by scholars and visitors.

the foreground. 13 Hall, *Treasures of the Portland Collection*, p. 68. See also, Judy Egerton, *George Stubbs, painter: catalogue raisonné* (London, 2007), p. 246. 14 Egerton, *George Stubbs, painter*, p. 46. 15 For the archetypical eighteenth-century portrayal, see the second painting in the sequence of Hogarth's *The rake's progress*, where a jockey crouches clasping a silver cup with running horses on it.

Racecourses, like the country house, have long provided an alternative venue to Westminster for conducting politics at a local, regional, national or international level. When politics is personal, proximity matters. Politics, the country house and horse racing have been closely entwined from the mid-seventeenth century. However, historians have tended to overlook the connections between politics and racing that participants in both activities understood so well. From entries in the *Oxford dictionary of national biography* it is clear that for many political historians there was a binary division between politics and racing, one reserved for public life, and the other for private. The entry for August Fitzroy, 3rd duke of Grafton, is instructive, noting of the political discussions surrounding a change of administration in 1765 that: 'Though Grafton and [the duke of] Cumberland had had several contacts in recent months, both in political matters and at Newmarket, Grafton was not one of the principal members of Newcastle's circle.'[16]

For contemporaries, there was no such division. In 1763, the *London Magazine* depicted runners and riders lined up for the King's Plate – otherwise known as the battle for the Treasury precipitated by Lord Bute's resignation from office – with each aristocrat, or aristocratic faction, anthropomorphized in equine form.

> Charles Townshend's horse, *Trimmer*, ran on the wrong side of the post.
>
> Mr Pitt's bay horse, *Guide*, was in training for this match, and expected to enter at the post, but went off.
>
> Great expectations from Lord Shelburne's Colt, but he ran resty; and 'tis supposed he will not start any more. Some knowing-ones, who had backed him for a considerable sum, were taken in deep.[17]

The factional aristocratic politics of the 1760s provided ample opportunity for satirists and commentators to reinforce the links between the turf and politics. Some were more sympathetic than others. Considering the marquess of Rockingham's potential elevation to first lord of the Treasury, a one-sheet broadside, *City Races*, observed:

> Lord Rockingham's wall-eyed horse MERCATOR: This Horse, tho' aged, is a Maiden one, having never started for a Plate; he bears training exceeding well, and comes thro' his exercise much to the satisfaction of those who have seen him; he was got by the famous Horse COMMERCE, well known for having won a great many Plates, but by unskilful Jockies is now scarce able to stand on his Legs: This Horse is in high favour with the Gentlemen of the Turf.[18]

16 P. Durrant, 'Fitzroy, Augustus Henry, third duke of Grafton', *ODNB*. 17 'Westminster Races', *London Magazine, or, Gentleman's Monthly Intelligencer*, 33 (1764), p. 253. 18 *City Races* (London, 1765). This is a one-page pamphlet.

It seems fitting then, that, as Sarah Bunbury (née Lennox) related, 'Ld Rockingham, the D. of Grafton, & Genl Conway kissed hands the day Gimcrack ran',[19] an action which confirmed George III's installation of Rockingham as first lord of the Treasury, Grafton as secretary of state for the Northern Department, Conway as secretary of state for the Southern Department, and therefore the start of the first Rockingham ministry.[20]

The duke of Grafton wasn't treated so favourably, with *Westminster Magazine* noting:

> It may be said, that he was called from the Stable to the Cabinet, and from the study of Horses to the management of Men. In the occupations and amusements of the Turf he had more knowledge than his groom; in the science of Government it was not possible he could have less.[21]

The duke, it seems, heartily embraced this characterization. Two years earlier in 1763 he had hosted a meeting at Euston Hall between October meetings at Newmarket, to which he invited Earl Gower among others for political talk 'made chiefly up of Jockeys'.[22] The country house and the racecourse appear as interchangeable venues for politicking and sociability in eighteenth-century correspondence. Writing of the same Newmarket meetings in 1763, Sarah Bunbury informed Lady Sarah Lennox how:

> Newmarket was charming, all the charming men were there. Dr Mr Meynell lost sums of money on a horse of my brother's, beat by the little mare Hermione of Mr Calvert; its name was Goodwood & got by Brilliant; but I hear he has made up all his losses again at cards at Euston, where the Duke [of Cumberland] & all the Newmarket folks are; he a *fat wretch*, has won everything on earth; poor dear Mr Greville has lost, Sir John Moore has lost near £5,000 between quinze & horses.[23]

The significance of gambling and betting in this political world cannot be overstated.

For Charles James Fox, politics was mostly an extension of friendships forged on the turf, and it was to his landed and estate-owning friends he turned to when taken in deep with gambling losses. The earl of Carlisle stood surety for £16,000 worth of Fox's debts, with the annual interest payments of £2,000 accounting for one-sixth of Carlisle's income. In 1807 after Fox's death, the dukes of Bedford

**19** Countess of Ilchester (ed.), *The life and letters of Lady Sarah Lennox, 1745–1826* (London, 1901), pp 172–3. **20** For the role of the kiss outside the confines of the court, see Elaine Chalus, 'Kisses for votes: the kiss and corruption in eighteenth-century English elections' in Karen Harvey (ed.), *The kiss in history* (Manchester, 2005), pp 122–47. **21** *Westminster Magazine* (July 1773), p. 418. **22** Carl B. Cone, 'Parliamenteering and racing', *Historian*, 37:3 (1975), p. 411. **23** Countess of Ilchester (ed.), *The life and letters of Lady Sarah Lennox*, p. 134.

and Devonshire, and Earl Fitzwilliam, collected another £10,000 to pay off even more creditors.[24] As Leslie Mitchell suggests, 'part of this willingness to subsidize must be put down to the fact that the careers and political aspirations of many of his friends would be realised if Fox triumphed, and would be ruined if he sank'.[25]

As this discussion of eighteenth-century politics has illustrated, to form a divide between horse racing and the practical business of politics can be both arbitrary and, at worst, anachronistic. Richard Nash has demonstrated the extent to which key events in the transition from Stuart to Hanoverian dynasties were mediated through the racecourse. The duke of Monmouth, for example, rode in a series of match races in 1680 and 1682 while the earl of Shaftesbury sought the passage of an exclusion bill, which signalled an impressive display of Protestant populism.[26] The Rye House Plot to assassinate Charles II and James, duke of York, hinged upon a country house on the road to Newmarket.[27] William III, Queen Anne and George I all understood the significance of the racecourse as an arena for politics. Indeed, George I's only royal progress was a visit to Newmarket, where this well-choreographed moment of political theatre was recorded in paintings by John Wootton and Peter Tillemans.[28] In Ireland, James Kelly has highlighted the importance of vice-regal patronage for the emergence of the Curragh as the centre of racing and political life.[29] Politicking was not just confined to Newmarket. Free boroughs that had races could expect their incumbent member of parliament and prospective candidates to subsidize the race prizes. At Beverley, for example, the local MPs made donations. Sir Charles Hotham regularly gave fifteen guineas, while Charles Pelham and Sir Charles Codrington contributed sums of up to £30 in well publicized donations during the election season of 1748 and 1749.[30] Race meetings could therefore shore up voting patterns at the entry level as well as at the summit of politics.

Even those families for whom racing was not a passion understood the importance of the racecourse. Ahead of the 1774 general election, for example, Lord Temple introduced his nephew, the younger George Grenville, to the political public at the 1773 Aylesbury races, and got him named steward for the following year's race meeting. The race meeting, as Edmund Burke reported to the marquess of Rockingham, suited Temple's political needs as there were

**24** Leslie Mitchell, *Charles James Fox* (London, 1997), pp 102–3, 106. **25** Ibid., p. 101. **26** Richard Nash, 'Sporting with kings' in Rebecca Cassidy (ed.), *The Cambridge companion to horse racing* (Cambridge, 2013), p. 16. **27** Doreen J. Milne, 'The results of the Rye House plot and their influence upon the revolution of 1688', *Transactions of the Royal Historical Society*, 1 (1951), p. 91. **28** Richard Nash, 'The Jockey Club before 1750: politics, art and sport in the early formation of the Jockey Club' in David Oldrey, Timothy Cox and Richard Nash, *The Heath and the horse: a history of racing and art on Newmarket Heath* (London, 2016), p. 277. **29** James Kelly, *Sport in Ireland, 1600–1840* (Dublin, 2014), p. 33. **30** I.M. Middleton, *The developing pattern of horse racing in Yorkshire 1700–1749: an analysis of the people and the places* (PhD, Leicester De Montfort University, 2000), p. 53.

present many of the landed class and political weight of the county in the nobility, gentry and other freeholders.[31] Twenty years earlier, Sir Roger Newdigate (MP for the University of Oxford) visited the races at Warwick, Rugby, Oxford and Nuneaton, and placed one guinea bets at each event, as part of a broader process of socializing with polite society.[32] Race meetings were especially useful to politicians as they normally fell between April and November, when parliament was not in session.

The stars of the turf could also play a significant role in aristocratic and gentry self-fashioning within the country house. Recent scholarship has emphasized the importance and attention given to dynastic considerations within the masculine identity of the landed elite, and the variety of means through which this could be expressed and signified.[33] Art historians have explored how family portraits could contribute to 'a carefully choreographed display of wealth power and/or political affiliation' through their positioning within country houses; they could emphasize the importance of the 'context of the sitter's linear and nuclear families', where 'the web of connections visually evident in such a display often extends outwards, as the constant process of intermarriage and complex arrangements of inheritance continually bound families together'.[34]

These considerations can be extended to the display of descriptive and documentary pictures of racehorses which, as Stephen Deuchar has noted, 'often included written information of the image itself about the particular occurrence or animal portrayed, leaving the viewer in no doubt of the "reality" of the scene portrayed'.[35] Judy Egerton likewise articulates the importance of identities in her catalogue raisonée for George Stubbs:

> More facts are known about most of the horses Stubbs painted than about the painter himself. Here the cataloguer is confronted with a dilemma – whether to record all the available information about a horse (and bore the art historians) or to condense it (and disappoint historians of racing). I have compromised. When horses depicted by Stubbs are identifiable, I have recorded by and out of whom they were bred, and when and where they were foaled; such facts are, after all, not essentially different from those establishing the identity of sitters in portraits by Reynolds or Gainsborough.[36]

31 Cone, 'Parliamenteering and racing', p. 407. 32 Jon Stobart and Mark Rothery, *Consumption and the country house* (Oxford, 2016), p. 32. 33 Henry French and Mark Rothery, *Man's estate: landed gentry masculinites, 1600–1900* (Oxford, 2012), p. 233. 34 Kate Retford, Gill Perry and Jordan Vibert, 'Introduction: placing faces in the country house' in Gill Perry, Kate Retford, Jordan Vibert and Hannah Lyons (eds), *Placing faces: the portrait and the English country house in the long eighteenth century* (Manchester, 2013), pp 4–7. 35 Stephen Deuchar, *Sporting art in eighteenth-century England: a social and political history* (London, 1988), p. 12. 36 Egerton, *George Stubbs, painter*, p. 7.

Equine heroes could, therefore, occupy prominent positions within the country house and provide visual signifiers of bloodstock connections to significant families and significant horses. Of most importance were those horses that were able to trace their bloodline back to one of the three foundation sires of the English Thoroughbred: the Byerley Turk, the Godolphin Arabian and the Darley Arabian. Some families placed their horses in more prominent positions than others, and like the family portraits that demonstrated networks of influence and control, so Arabian horses spoke to country-house owners' needs to create and display status.

At Grimsthorpe Castle, Lincolnshire, horses were as important as kings. Stubbs' painting of *The duke of Ancaster's bay stallion Blank* (*c.*1761) was listed in the Grimsthorpe inventory of 1812 as framed and hanging in the great hall, with eight other portraits of horses by unnamed artists. Importantly, Blank was sired by the Godolphin Arabian, and this direct link to a foundation sire was of huge significance to the Ancaster stud.[37] The pendant to *Blank, the duke of Ancaster's bay stallion Spectator, held by a groom*, likewise reinforced significant familial links. Spectator was bred by Thomas Panton, keeper of the king's running horses, whose daughter, Mary, Ancaster married in 1750. Ancaster bought Spectator in 1755 from his father-in-law thus emphasizing both equine and familial lineage and connections. The arcaded side walls on the south side are painted in grisaille with seven kings of England by Sir James Thornhill who had granted lands and titles to the Bertie clan – namely George I, William III, Henry VIII, Henry VII, William the Conqueror, Edward III and Henry V.[38] In a home so anxious about genealogy and the inheritance of title, the prominent position of horseflesh in the heart of the great hall is revealing of the status and importance of the racehorse to the Bertie family.

Displaying racehorses was not just a ducal activity. Lower down the aristocratic spectrum, these pictures functioned in similar ways, often to emphasize connections with more prominent families. *'Furiband' with his owner, Sir Harry Harpur, and a groom* is one of four racehorses painted by Sawrey Gilpin for Sir Harry in 1774. The picture hangs in the library at Calke Abbey in a celebration of horseflesh, with '*Furiband*' joined by Harpur's three other Gilpins.[39]

Prominent racing families also amassed significant collections of silver and silver-gilt race cups. These cups often, as in the case of the Doncaster Race Cup (1828) at Lotherton Hall, combined twin aristocratic passions of fidelity to antique design with a record of race victories.[40] Gold Cups provided an

37 Ibid., p. 190. 38 Vaughan Hart, *Sir John Vanbrugh: storyteller in stone* (London, 2008), pp 194–207; Jeremy Musson, *The country houses of Sir John Vanbrugh: from the archives of Country Life* (London, 2008), p. 149. 39 Alastair Laing, *In trust for the nation: paintings from National Trust houses* (London, 1995), p. 68. 40 Judy Egerton and Gervase Jackson-Stopps, *Treasure houses of Britain*, p. 526.

important opportunity for racing's patrons to express their connoisseurship. The races at Richmond, North Yorkshire, took place on part of the Dundas family's estate at Aske Hall, perhaps encouraging the family to commission Robert Adam to produce a design for a 'Vase for Thomas Dundas Esqr for a prize'. Adam took the form of a classical Greek urn and enriched it with a frieze of racehorses and jockeys between beaded borders below the rim. Oval medallions on each side of the cup depict horses in training, and the race itself.[41]

At Sandbeck Park, Yorkshire, the relationship between paint and silver-gilt is captured in Ben Marshall's portrait *The 6th earl of Scarborough with Catton, his jockey and trainer* (1816). Catton, owned and bred by Scarborough, won fourteen out of the twenty-two races in which he ran, and the four Gold Cups that he gained for Lord Scarborough are depicted by Marshall in the painting on an architectural monument that also records each of the horse's victories. Scarborough, clearly proud of the horse's achievements, turned to Marshall to celebrate the horse, but also to silversmiths Rebeccah Emes and Paul Storr, who made four silver-gilt cups.[42] Horses, like marriages, solidified links between families and dynasties, and ensured that the achievements of one generation were remembered by another.

Some country houses' associations with horse racing are more apparent than others'. Proximity to the races can explain particular acquisitions of houses and architectural developments. Newmarket, which still acts as the epicentre for purchasing, breeding and racing, was from the late seventeenth century progressively surrounded by a number of significant country houses, including Wimpole Hall, Euston Hall in Suffolk, Cheveley Park in Cambridgeshire, and Audley End in Essex. Some houses have even given their names to prominent races, with Lord Derby's country house near Epsom, The Oaks, giving its name to the fillies' equivalent of the Derby. As Giles Worsley has demonstrated, most stabling for thoroughbreds was concentrated around racing centres such as Newmarket and Epsom. Lord Rockingham is a case in point, for as he began work on the great stables at Wentworth Woodhouse, he was also rebuilding the stables on the house he bought at Newmarket.[43] The country-house landscape was more significantly altered by the demands of stud farms, rather than stable blocks designed primarily for hunters. At Goodwood, although the stables are now used for racehorses, the initial purpose from their construction in 1757 was to house the newly reformed Charlton Hunt.[44] Stud farms at Wentworth Woodhouse, Lydiard Tregoze in Wiltshire, Eaton Hall in Cheshire and Euston Hall were important aspects of the designed landscape of the country house, which have remained comparatively under-researched. Stubbs' paintings of stud farms provide some hints as to the significance of these spaces to aristocratic

41 Ibid., p. 521. 42 Ibid., pp 504–5. 43 Giles Worsley, *The British stable* (London, 2004), pp 195–6. 44 Rosemary Baird, *Goodwood: art and architecture, sport and family* (London, 2007), pp 99–100.

self-fashioning, for, as Deuchar suggests, these images 'forwarded the idea that sport was in some sense a science – an activity involving sportsmen's judicious breeding of impressive animals and painstaking monitoring of their ever-improving performances in the field'.[45] Such images also offered a carefully calibrated rebuttal to public perception of the social and moral irresponsibility of the behaviour of those at the heart of the sporting world.

Horses could also provide the reason for the dispersal of country-house collections. The 4th earl of Abingdon was plunged into debt through racing and died insolvent in 1799. His heirs demolished the ancestral seat at Rycote, Oxfordshire, to assuage their creditors. A similar story befell the 17th Lord Saye and Sele at Broughton Castle, Oxfordshire, whose enthusiasm for racing required the family to vacate the property for rental tenants. The 12th duke of Hamilton's excesses – 'a fondness for racehorses and expensive yachts' – precipitated one of the most significant country-house sales of the nineteenth century.[46] Over a seventeen-day sale, with more than 2,000 lots, the ancestral collections of the Hamiltons were sold at Christie's. The need to sell had little to do with the agricultural depression as the majority of the ducal revenue came from coal mining. There is a certain irony that the land on which Hamilton Palace once stood is now Hamilton Park Racecourse.

For the many millions of visitors to country houses in the UK and Ireland, discovering the impact of horses on these properties and their landscapes can often be an archaeological exercise. The enormous growth in visitor numbers means that those structures seen as peripheral to the main property and collection are re-purposed into gift-shops, cafes and toilets. More often than not these spaces are the stables. Within the house, sporting art is rarely given prominence. However, as this essay suggests, stables were far from peripheral. Horses underpinned the successful functioning of the country house, and the pursuit of victory on the racecourse led to innovations in architectural design and country-house technology; the development and consolidation of social and political networks; and, in some cases, to the sale and dispersal of significant country-house collections and even the demolition of the house itself.

45 Deuchar, *Sporting art*, p. 67. 46 Christopher Maxwell, '"Spurious articles": the purchases of the Department of Science and Art from the Hamilton Palace sale of 1882', *Journal of the History of Collections*, 28:1 (2016), p. 110.

# 'Aquatic gentlemen …': the sport and status of sailing in the gentry's world from the 1830s to the 1920s

IAN D'ALTON

Yachting was tailor-made for the Irish gentry. Like hunting, it allowed them to signal ostentatious wealth and conspicuous consumption as well as sporting prowess. A caste and team sport, it expressed individualism, too. It is tempting to downplay the sporting element, but the many detailed reports of races, regattas and cruises testify to the popularity of sailing with a readership outside those directly involved.[1] There was a great deal more to sailing than just getting saturated and salted. It was a socio-economic construct that cemented cultural connectivity to a particular variant of national identity. This essay argues that high-end yachting was much like the GAA in that it had additional purposes and aims that ran alongside its sporting objectives and leisure objectives and activities. If the GAA was innately bound up with a 'national objective', so too was yachting – except that *its* 'national objective' was the concept of the 'loyal Irishman' within the British imperial project. To illustrate this, the focus here will be on a representative cross-section of sailing and sociability in Cork, Kingstown (Dún Laoghaire) and the river Shannon, its lakes and its estuary.

Sailing for private pleasure started in early seventeenth-century Holland. Charles II, while in exile, picked up on this new pastime. After the restoration, the Dutch presented Charles with a yacht, which he sailed on the Thames. Several courtiers followed his example, one of whom was Murrough O'Brien, the 1st earl of Inchiquin, owner of the Rostellan estate on the eastern side of Cork harbour. In Cork, the geographical and the social came together in happy circumstance. It boasts one of the finest natural harbours in the world, guarded by two forts. The motto of Cork – '*Statio bene fide carinis*', 'A safe harbour for ships' – speaks to the geography that may have encouraged the development of sailing there.[2] Along its shores are numerous towns such as Monkstown, Cobh ('Cove', or 'Cove of Cork' to 1849, and then Queenstown until 1922) and Crosshaven, and large landed estates such as Fota, home to the Smith Barry family, and Cuskinny to the east of Cove where the French family's demesne spectacularly swept down to the water's edge. All these families were prominent

1 For cruising, see, as one example, W.T.P. (William Trumperant Potts), *Notes of the cruise of the 'Caprice' yacht: Royal St George's Yacht Club, to Iceland and Norway, in the summer and autumn of 1850* (Dublin, 1851). From 1846, the *Westmeath Independent* newspaper reported on nearly every yacht race and regatta held on Lough Ree. 2 The text is from Virgil's Aeneid (II, 23: *statio male fida carinis*, 'an unsafe harbour') but corrupted for unknown reasons to '*fide*'.

in Cork yachting circles. In 1720, Murrough's great-grandson William was instrumental in formalizing yachting in the Water Club of the Harbour of Cork.[3] It successively became Cork Harbour Water Club, and then, during the 1820s, Cork Harbour Yacht Club and Cork Yacht Club, finally acquiring the prefix 'Royal' in 1831, when William's son-in-law and nephew, Murrough O'Brien, who became marquess of Thomond in 1800, was prominent in the club. It is generally accepted as the world's oldest sailing club.

The Water Club's foundation in 1720 did not herald a general upsurge of interest in pleasure sailing during the eighteenth century; not until the early years of the nineteenth did yachting in the British Isles start to get the wind in its sails. The Yacht Club at Cowes on the Isle of Wight was established in 1815.[4] In 1820, that club was granted the prefix 'Royal'; and in 1833, courtesy of King William IV, the 'Sailor King', it became the Royal Yacht Squadron. It was, and remains, the premier yacht club in Britain.[5] Clubs entitled to the prefix 'Royal' were the most prestigious and by 1852 there were eighteen in the British Isles, four of which were in Ireland. Most received Admiralty warrants – a mark of official approval – in the period after 1829.[6] Cork Yacht Club had applied for the name of 'Royal Irish Yacht Club' in 1830 as 'the only yacht club exclusively composed of Irish members and consequently the only one qualified to adopt such a National appellation'.[7] But it was never granted the name. Instead, the name was eventually appropriated by another club set up in Kingstown in 1831, where yachting began to flourish with the construction of the harbour, which had commenced in 1817 (but was not completed until 1842).[8] That club was inspired by the formidable Lord Anglesey, a noted yachtsman in Britain, a prominent member of the Royal Yacht Club and thus eminently qualified to set the style. 'In Dublin Bay the Marquis of Anglesey organized sailing matches as early as 1829, and to these matches may be traced the formation of the original Royal Irish Yacht Club, which held its first regatta in 1832.'[9] Anglesey was the club's first commodore; he brought his yacht the *Pearl* to race at Kingstown when lord lieutenant of Ireland (1828–9, 1830–3).

3 NUIG, Landed Estates Database, 'O'Brien (Inchiquin Castle)', http://landedestates.nuigalway.ie /LandedEstates/jsp/estate-show.jsp?id=2094 (Inchiquin) and 'Rostellan', http://landedestates.nuigalway.ie/LandedEstates/jsp/property-show.jsp?id=3617, accessed 19 Sept. 2018. 4 National Maritime Museum Cornwall, 'The Royal Yacht Squadron', https://www.maritimeviews.co.uk/yacht-clubs/the-royal-yacht-squadron, accessed 19 Sep. 2018. 5 Royal Yacht Squadron, 'About RYS', https://www.rys.org.uk/about/history, accessed 19 Sept. 2018. 6 *Hunt's Universal Yacht List for 1852* (London, 1852), pp 17–21, 24. 7 Alicia St Leger, *A history of the Royal Cork Yacht Club* (Cork, 2005), p. 77. 8 Dun Laoghaire Harbour Company, *The construction of Dun Laoghaire Harbour* (n.p, n.d), pp 5–15, 17–18. 9 Royal Irish Yacht Club, 'The history of the RIYC', http://www.riyc.ie/Commodore_s_Welcome/The_History_of_the_Club.aspx; National Maritime Museum Cornwall, 'Maritime views: maritime history from the Bartlett Maritime Research Centre', http://maritimeviews.nmmc.co.uk/index.php?/british_yachts_and_yachtsmen/chapter_4_-_organisation_1815_-_1851-1, accessed 19 Sept. 2018.

There were two other prominent clubs in Kingstown. Socially elevated in the early nineteenth century was the Royal St George (known as 'the George'), although it had sprung from somewhat humble origins. It had been founded as Kingstown Boat Club in 1838 by members from Dublin of the Pembroke Boat Club who were anxious to escape the river Liffey – 'every year becoming fouler and less agreeable for aquatic pursuits'. The club received the prefix 'Royal' in May 1845 – patrons were the queen and Prince Albert – and quickly became colonized by the gentry: the first committee included Arthur Bushe of Kilkenny, James Hamilton of Dublin (later Lord Holmpatrick) and Richard Cooper of Markree Castle, County Sligo.[10] The first commodore was the Marquess Conyngham; a mark of the club's social status was that subsequent commodores up to the late 1950s were almost all from the peerage – the marquess of Drogheda, 1861–92, Earl Fitzwilliam 1910–42, and the earl of Iveagh from 1950 to 1959.[11]

The other club at Kingstown was founded later. Although there are references to an active 'club' prior to 1870, the Kingstown Royal Harbour Boat Club was registered with Lloyds in the same year. By 1872, the name had been changed to the Kingstown Harbour Boat Club. In 1881, a proprietary club called the Kingstown Harbour Yacht Club was founded. The lease of the clubhouse was purchased in 1901 by three trustees, who registered it as the Edward Yacht Club. It was more Catholic than the other clubs, which had predominantly Protestant memberships, and was rechristened the National Yacht Club in 1930.[12]

If the east coast had to await a built harbour, the river Shannon, with its lakes and estuary, was a magnificent natural cradle for yachting. Founded in 1770, Athlone Yacht Club, later Lough Ree Yacht Club from 1895, claims to be the second oldest sailing club in the world – its origins in the town were encapsulated in its burgee which contains the lion and roses from the arms of Athlone.[13] Foynes Union Yacht Club was established in the 1870s.[14] Lough Derg Yacht Club was formed in 1836.[15] Covering the Shannon estuary and the coasts of Clare and Kerry, the Royal Western Yacht Club of Ireland – an offshoot of the Royal Western Yacht Club in England – was originally established in Kilrush, County Clare in 1828 and received its 'Royal' designation in 1832.[16] This was a large club, with a membership of 201 and 82 yachts in 1837, located in a number of centres:

**10** Stella Archer and Peter Pearson, *The Royal St George Yacht Club: a history* (Dublin, 1988), pp 1–2. **11** Ibid., pp 5, 34, 46, 60. **12** National Yacht Club, 'History', http://www.nyc.ie/about/history, accessed 19 Sept. 2018. **13** E.F. McNally, *Irish yachting (1720–1946)* (Dublin, 1946), pp 16–20; A.S. Woulfe-Smyth, 'Lough Ree Y.C.', *Athlone Civic Week Brochure, 1950*, pp 23–7; N.W. English, *Lough Ree Yacht Club: a memoir* (Athlone, 1970), p. 4. **14** Yachting historian Adrian O'Connell to the author, email 24 Apr. 2018. **15** V.T.H. Delaney, *The Lough Derg Y.C.: a memoir* (Athlone, 1956), *passim*; Lough Derg Yacht Club, 'About LDYC', https://loughdergyachtclub.wildapricot.org/LDYC-Who-we-are, accessed 19 Sept. 2018. **16** Adrian O'Connell, 'The Royal Western Yacht Club of Ireland', *Afloat*, 9 July 2009; Royal Western Yacht Club of Ireland, 'History', http://www.westernyachtclub.com/history,

**Table 6.1 The Royal Western Yacht Club of Ireland**

| Centre | Members/Yachts |
|---|---|
| Shannon estuary/Limerick | 60 members, 18 yachts |
| Kerry | 10 members, 4 yachts |
| Cork | 14 members, 7 yachts |
| Westport | 4 members, 2 yachts |
| Galway | 3 members, 2 yachts |
| Dublin | 10 members, 6 yachts |

The remainder was based elsewhere in the British Isles.

## YACHT CLUBS AND ASSOCIATIONAL CULTURE

Few clubs were as upfront about their social function as the short-lived Killinure Yacht Club, founded in 1831 on Lough Ree, whose 'regulations have been drawn up for the sole purpose of establishing conviviality and sociability for the next Summer month'.[17] Nevertheless, in the more prestigious institutions, one can observe similar aims: often dressed in protocols and with a tightly controlled system for electing members, outsiders were kept at bay by the use of obscure symbols and internalized language. Yachting was particularly prone to this form of arcane behaviour, reflecting a society fixated upon lineage, indicators of status and set standards. In it was a concatenation of technical necessity, social rules derived from the manners and mores of the gentry on land and a distinct style of ritual. There was much of the colourful code of heraldry – dressing-up, ranks and degrees, ritualistic behaviour, special language and symbolic understanding, defined this nautical craft of freemasonry.

Thus, the ritual of gathering and sailing under the club flag was significant in how the in-group was held together, especially in the period up to the mid-nineteenth century (when the practice had largely died out). For instance, in June 1832 a summons was sent out to the Royal Cork's yacht owners:

> The attendance of your yacht is particularly requested at the outer Spit Buoy on Wednesday next, the 26th inst., at 12 noon, when the fleet will proceed to Rostellan, there to fire a *feu-de joie* in honour of the arrival of the Admiral of the Fleet [the marquess of Thomond].[18]

In 1845, as the history of the George records, it was resolved 'that the Yachts belonging to the Club shall sail in Fleet Convoy every Wednesday at 12.00 o'clock under the orders of the Commodore or Vice-Commodore'.[19]

accessed 19 Sept. 2018. **17** English, *Lough Ree*, pp 24–5. **18** Corinthia [H.P.F. Donegan], *History of yachting in the south of Ireland, 1720–1908* (Cork, 1909), p. 15. **19** Archer and

A uniform established recognition and communality. The Royal Cork Yacht Club's was a plain coat lined with buff and gilt buttons adorned with a crown and anchor, a blue waistcoat and blue trousers.[20] The members of Killinure Yacht Club were 'always to appear on board their boats in the blue uniform', viz., 'blue jacket with appropriate buttons, waistcoat white cashmere with the club buttons, trousers blue, white or chequered'.[21] This sort of behaviour would be mocked in Gilbert and Sullivan; sometimes the obsession with rules and form echoed the seventeenth-century poet George Herbert's aphorism 'Praise the sea, but keep on land'.[22]

Several gradations and degrees of membership established a pecking order. In 1858, a snapshot of the Royal Cork Yacht Club showed that, in addition to ordinary members, it had a plethora of honorary memberships. Connections with the armed forces were particularly emphasized. Privileges were extended to: all serving officers in the Royal Navy, from the rank of mate upwards; to lieutenants in the Coast Guard; as well as to the East India Company services; the army; and officers of the constabulary above sub-inspector rank. In addition, naval and army commanders of the Cork station had automatic *ex officio* honorary full membership. Below these categories came the use and privileges of the clubhouse at Queenstown for serving and visiting naval and army officers for a period not exceeding fourteen days. Reflecting status and standing, visiting members of 'royal' yacht clubs with their yachts could also use the clubhouse. Members of the Munster Bar not resident in Cork city or county, and judges visiting the assizes were admitted as honorary members without payment of subscription.[23]

Military personnel were prominent in many clubs – of the forty members of Lough Ree in 1895, twelve were military men;[24] at the club's regatta in 1846, of the six stewards, two were from the army regiment stationed at Athlone.[25] In 1853, 'the splendid bands of the 39th and 89th regiments performed' at the Royal Cork's regatta at Queenstown. In 1854 and 1858, Royal Navy ships were present at Kinsale regatta.[26] Regatta expenses for the George in 1862 included forty-two dinners for the band of the 12th Regiment, as well as a quantity of drink.[27]

Reflecting the availability of resources and time as well as appropriate social standing, yacht club membership in the early nineteenth century was principally

Pearson, *The Royal St George*, p. 103. **20** *General rules and regulations of the Royal Cork Yacht Club corrected to 1858* (Cork, 1858), pp 7–10 (NLI, E. McClintock Dix bequest); *General rules and regulations of the Royal Cork Yacht Club: corrected to 1st May, 1904* (Cork, 1904), p. 7. The 1858 rules specified a blue coat and a buff or blue waistcoat. **21** English, *Lough Ree*, p. 24. **22** George Herbert, 'Jacula Prudentum' in *The works of George Herbert in prose and verse* (London, 1846), vol. i, p. 318. **23** *General rules and regulations of the Royal Cork Yacht Club corrected to 1858*, pp 7–10; St Leger, *A history of the Royal Cork*, p. 129. **24** English, *Lough Ree*, pp 33–4. **25** *History of yachting in the south of Ireland,* p. 191; English, *Lough Ree*, p. 8. **26** *History of yachting in the south of Ireland*, pp 33, 191. **27** Archer and Pearson, *The Royal*

Protestant, with the gentry predominant. This is illustrated in a list of officers and committee of the Royal Western for 1828,[28] where the president was Lord Dunraven, and the committee was peppered with members of the gentry class – Crofton Vandeleur, the Knight of Glin, William Monsell and John Bindon Scott, among others. Yet there were some outliers, such as the Limerick merchant Francis Spaight; and a class of loyal Catholics (of suitable wealth and social standing, even if of dubious politics) was always welcome, with Maurice and John O'Connell, sons of the Liberator, serving as committee members. As in hunting, the clergy were noticeable by their presence, too: Killinure Yacht Club had two clergymen – Revd Thomas Caulfield and Revd William Battersby – as committee members, and the Royal Western had at least one clerical yacht owner, Revd Francis Longfield.[29]

Language and terminology discouraged outsiders, although it was often obscure and confusing for insiders, too. 'Setting the topsail', 'going about to avoid a lee shore', 'luffing to starboard', 'riding turns on the winch', are all terms that one wit has described as the language of 'yachtish'.[30] The widespread use and importance of such technical terminology was encapsulated in the following extracts from a sailing book issued by the Royal Irish Yacht Club in 1846:

> Thus, suppose the Commodore wanted the squadron to tack together, he would hoist the Preparative Flag and the Signal 'Tack together,' and when answered he would haul down the Preparative at the moment of putting his helm down, as a signal for all the Yachts to put theirs a-lee at the same time.
>
> The Burgee over a Blue Ensign at the Main Mast-head is to ascertain whether a distant stranger Vessel be a Yacht of the Club … The Burgee over a Wheft of the Ensign (stopped only at the head), [is] to request the stranger to close within signal difference …[31]

All these detailed instructions really meant, as the text went on to explain, was that 'This Flag, when hoisted alone (either at gaff-end or masthead), is to be understood to imply "look out, and follow the motions of the Commodore".'

The material iconography of yachting was decorative as well as utilitarian. Cups, salvers and plate were awarded as prizes, as were medals in precious metals, such as those of the Royal Cinque Ports Yacht Club in silver (fig. 6.1) awarded by the marquess of Dufferin and Ava, whose seat was at Clandeboye, County Down. These indicators of the high status of yachting reinforced the message of aristocratic ownership, participation and patronage.

*St George*, p. 89. **28** *Afloat*, 5 Oct. 2009, at https://afloat.ie/resources/irish-sailing-clubs/royal-irish-yacht-club/itemlist/tag/boats?start=110, accessed 19 Sept. 2018. **29** English, *Lough Ree*, p. 24; Corinthia, *History of yachting in the south of Ireland*, p. 45. **30** Captain Flashheart, 'Speaking yachtish', http://www.boogie-nights.org/2016/10/speaking-yachtish.html, accessed 19 Sept. 2018. **31** *Signals of the Royal Irish Yacht Club, 1846* (Dublin, 1847), p. 5.

**6.1** Yachting medals. Photos: author.

Flags, on the other hand, despite landlubbers thinking they were merely colourful bunting, were critical to communication, a form of utilitarian 'marine heraldry'. Most clubs produced a flag signals book – such as that by the Royal Western Yacht Club of Ireland in 1832. A colour-printed signals book allowed members to communicate at sea or at anchor about topics such as their health, and whether they had drink, food or women on board.[32] The Royal Irish Yacht

**32** O'Connell, 'Royal Western Yacht Club of Ireland', *Afloat*, 15 July 2009; also at https://afloat.ie/resources/irish-sailing-clubs/royal-western-yacht-club-of-ireland, accessed 19 Sept. 2018.

Club's similar signals book has over eighty pages of messages, consisting of nearly 3,800 words and phrases, covering every conceivable situation, as in number 530, 'Can you lend, Ale, a bottle of'; number 441, 'Bowsprit, I have sprung my'. The list covered geographical locations, lighthouses and ships, including Her Majesty's revenue cutters – this last always useful in an era of smuggling.[33]

Each member of the Royal Irish was allocated a private signal, which he used to identify his yacht. The club and its officers had their own flags, or burgees. The officers entitled to a flag would be the commodore and vice commodore (or, in the exalted case of the Royal Cork, its admiral and vice admiral). The flags of the club and its officers held significance beyond the merely utilitarian; here is where a brand of British national symbolism interconnected with the apparatus of the state, and anchored the clubs and their members firmly within an identity that was determinedly British, and mediated through a prism of a sort of honorary membership of the Royal Navy. Admiralty warrants that set out which ensign – white, blue or red – could be used as the basis for club flags were much prized, and usually reproduced in club literature, such as sailing instructions, rules and regulations and so on.

As with many aspects of aristocratic life, elite status (and sub-divisions thereof) were very important in a hierarchical world. Great significance was placed on the flags authorized, as in the case of the Royal Western Yacht Club of Ireland, where the tropes of status, standing, belonging and connectivity are in evidence. In January 1832, the Admiralty gave permission for the club to fly the white ensign (the most prestigious of the Royal Navy's flags) with a red cross, a crown in the centre with a wreath of shamrocks surrounding it and the Union flag at the head of the pennant. However, in 1842, the Admiralty decided that the white ensign could only be flown by the navy and the premier yachting club, the Royal Yacht Squadron. Leave to fly the ensign was withdrawn from all yacht clubs individually, but it seems that the Royal Western, possibly because of its remoteness, was simply overlooked. The Royal Yacht Squadron, ever mindful of its dignity (and possibly the fact that its subscription rate of a guinea was several orders of magnitude greater than that of the Royal Western), petitioned the Admiralty, which, however, decided that for the time being the Royal Western could continue to use the white ensign – a decision seemingly based also on the club's remoteness and small membership. However, the Royal Yacht Squadron continued to object, and the privilege was finally withdrawn in 1858. A memorial was drawn up by the club membership, threatening disbandment if it were removed. Subsequently, it is recorded that in 1860 the club had no secretary, commodore or vice commodore, and was insolvent.[34] The Admiralty warrant

33 *Signals of the Royal Irish Yacht Club 1846*, pp 14, 21, 23, 29. 34 Archer and Pearson, *The Royal St George*, p. 10; O'Connell, 'Royal Western Yacht Club of Ireland', *Afloat*, 15 July 2009.

was, according to this account, transferred to a new club at Queenstown.[35] One yachting historian has speculated that the dogged stubbornness of the Royal Western in hanging on to its white ensign was because several of its yachts were involved in smuggling drink from France and that it was useful if they were mistaken for revenue cutters flying the white ensign.[36]

A similar contretemps had occurred in Kingstown. In 1847, the club became the Royal St George Yacht Club – the title it holds today. On 4 May 1847, permission was given by the Admiralty for the club to fly the white ensign, only for that to be countermanded 24 hours later, presumably because the civil servant involved realized his social faux pas. Interestingly, the George then sought to have a green ensign; this was vetoed by the Admiralty, on the basis that 'their Lordships cannot sanction the introduction of a new colour to be worn by British ships'.[37] On 9 May, the Admiralty gave permission 'to wear the red ensign of her Majesty's fleet on board their vessels, with a white cross and crown in the centre of the burgee'.

The government-granted privilege of flying the ensigns continued to be an important marker of identity. In 1922, the George's management minutes recorded a request from the Provisional Government of the Irish Free State to cease flying its burgee, with its Union flag and crown presumably seen as a provocation.[38] In 1938, the Royal Cork had to be asked by Cobh urban district council to fly the Irish tricolour.[39] After Irish independence a warrant was issued to the National Yacht Club in 1950 by the government under the Merchant Shipping Act, authorizing members to hoist a club ensign in lieu of the national flag, the new ensign to include a representation of the harp. This privilege is unique and specific to members of the National Yacht Club.[40]

## ECONOMIC SOCIABILITY

Yachting has always been, and still is, an expensive pastime, likened to standing under an icy-cold shower while tearing up £50 notes. Early nineteenth-century yachts were big beasts, made of heavy materials (iron and wood), expensive to build, maintain and run. The George, at its foundation, boasted twenty-eight vessels that were in excess of 100 tons.[41] In 1852, Commodore Marquess Conyngham's schooner, *Constance*, weighed 218 tons, and the vice commodore, Sir James Stewart, Bt, had a cutter of 73 tons. Royal Cork Admiral J.H. Smith Barry's yacht was a yawl of 90 tons.[42] Even as late as 1907, sailing yachts of members of the Royal Cork ranged in size from 3 tons up to a staggering 278

35 Corinthia, *History of yachting in the south of Ireland*, pp 44, 47. 36 Personal information from Adrian O'Connell, 11 May 2018. 37 Archer and Pearson, *The Royal St George*, pp 4–5, 6, 8, 10. 38 Ibid., p. 117. 39 St Leger, *A history of the Royal Cork*, pp 201, 216. 40 National Yacht Club, 'History', http://www.nyc.ie/about/history, accessed 30 Apr. 2019. 41 Archer and Pearson, *The Royal St George*, p. 2. 42 *Hunt's universal yacht list for 1852* (London, 1852), pp 17, 19. 43 St Leger, *A history of the Royal Cork*, p. 181.

tons.[43] The earl of Dunraven's two attempts to capture the America's Cup in 1893 and 1895 would have cost a small fortune; Sir Thomas Lipton is reckoned to have spent over £1 million on his challenges.[44]

The sport was effectively professional in the early nineteenth century. The large yachts were crewed by 'paid hands', with the owners helming (steering). A mini-economy flourished around these clubs and yachts. As the historian of the Royal Cork has written: '[Y]acht building also gave much needed employment to shipwrights and suppliers of sails, rope and other necessary equipment.' In 1858, the club had an accredited apothecary, a marine painter, a nautical instrument maker, a chart seller, a flag maker and a printer and lithographer. By 1902, the club directly employed fifteen people, from a manageress to a quay man;[45] and in the 1860s, the newly opened Queen's Hotel at Queenstown benefited from club members' patronage.[46] Apart from these commercial activities, there was a betting economy and races took place for substantial wagers put up by the yacht owners.

Regattas – gatherings of yachts to race competitively in the midsummer months – were events where the worlds of betting, prize money and socializing met. Direct remuneration for sailing was not socially acceptable for gentlemen, and was only permitted for paid hands. But racing for wagers, silverware and substantial cash prizes was permitted.[47] These could be substantial. Cork Harbour regatta had £337 in prize money in 1829, and £313 in 1830 – around £30,000 sterling in 2018 values.[48] In June 1865, the first race at the Royal Western's regatta at Queenstown had £75 for the winner, and £25 for second place, and in 1866 the Queen's Cup was contested for £100.[49] In Dublin, the Royal Alfred Yacht Club in 1877 ranked number one on the list of total prize money offered by yacht clubs in the British Isles, with £712 in prizes for eleven races, equivalent to about £45,000 in 2018.[50] The lesser clubs also offered substantial prizes. Lough Derg Yacht Club's regatta in 1837 – under the commodoreship of Lord Avonmore – was held over three days. With entrance fees between one and two guineas, the yachts raced successively at Killaloe, Dromineer and Portumna for substantial cash prizes and a silver cup.[51]

44 See Patrick Maume, 'Quin, Windham Thomas Wyndham', *DIB*, viii, p. 353; for Lord Dunraven's controversial challenge in 1895, see ClassicSailboats.Org, 'The yacht race investigation', http://classicsailboats.org/on-this-day-december-8-americas-cup-withdrawal-of-valkyrie-iii, accessed 3 Jan. 2019; also XS Sailing, 'Lord Dunraven: America's Cup Hall of Fame 2016', http://www.xssailing.com/ news/lord-dunraven-americas-cup-hall-fame-2016, accessed 19 Sept. 2018. 45 St Leger, *A history of the Royal Cork*, pp 84, 127. 46 *General rules and regulations of the Royal Cork Yacht Club corrected to 1858*, p. 6; St Leger, *A history of the Royal Cork Yacht Club*, p. 157. 47 Each season between 1852 and 1887, *Hunt's Yachting Magazine* published a list of racing results for all the yacht races in the British Isles, and also the total value of the prizes awarded by the various clubs. 48 St Leger, *A history of the Royal Cork*, p. 86. 49 Corinthia, *History of yachting in the south of Ireland*, p. 64. 50 The Alfred regularly featured in the top three of such prestigious clubs; *Afloat*, 16 July 2009. 51 Waterways Ireland, *Classic boats on Lough Derg: 1835–2008* (Enniskillen, 2008), p. 2.

The Cork coast also witnessed this sort of travelling sailing circus. In July 1908 for instance, the crack yachts raced competitively in the Royal Cork regatta and then processed to events at Kinsale, Courtmacsherry, Glandore, Monkstown in Cork Harbour, Crosshaven and Queenstown, before finishing with an ocean race from Monkstown to Youghal. On shore regattas were lively social occasions, too; Lough Ree Yacht Club's in August 1852 was not untypical. One observer noted that

> Hither flock the fashion and beauty of the district for miles around and once more a fleet enlivens the aspect of the usually deserted lake. Gay vessels decorated with many-coloured streamers, accompanied by bands of music, and laden with gentlest ladies and gallant gentlemen glide tranquilly over the scene …[52]

The aristocracy were formal patrons of the Lough Ree regattas: in 1846, for instance, Lord Castlemaine and Hon. L.H. King-Harman.[53] Exoticism knew no bounds at Lough Ree; in 1853, it was reported that as the Club did not then possess premises of its own 'the aquatic gentlemen were most sumptuously entertained … at Madame De Ruyter's Railway Hotel' in Athlone.[54]

## DEMOCRATIZATION AND THE CORINTHIAN IDEAL

Irish yachting began to change from about the 1870s. It was still a high-status sport, for in 1904, the lord lieutenant, Lord Dudley, was sailing around the coast at Kingstown in his racing yacht *Fodhla* (fig. 6.2) much as his predecessor Lord Anglesey had done in *Pearl* in the 1830s.[55]

But yacht club membership, which had increased in the middle years of the century, began to decline – it is not clear why – and some clubs found themselves in financial difficulties.[56] Lough Ree had trouble collecting subscriptions, and effectively collapsed.[57] The Royal Alfred Yacht Club in Dublin Bay noted a decline in revenue in 1895, reporting that the number of new members was 'considerably under what was expected'.[58] Even the prestigious Royal St George felt the pinch – membership reached an all-time low in 1902 and reductions in staff numbers had to be made.[59]

Sir Thomas Lipton, dismissed by Kaiser William as that 'damned grocer', was an unsuccessful challenger for the America's Cup, and was barred from the

52 W.F. Wakeman, *Three days on the Shannon; from Limerick to Lough Key* (Dublin, 1852), p. 39. 53 *Westmeath Independent*, 8 Aug. 1846. 54 Ibid., 8 Aug. 1853; English, *Lough Ree*, p. 11. 55 W.M. Nixon, 'Sailing on Saturdays', *Afloat*, 25 Nov. 2016 (photo). 56 St Leger, *A history of the Royal Cork*, p. 201; Archer and Pearson, *The Royal St George*, p. 51. 57 English, *Lough Ree*, p. 12. 58 Royal Alfred Yacht Club, list of members and account of subscriptions received, 1885–95, especially the accounts for 1895 (NLI, Add. MS 773). 59 Archer and Pearson, *The Royal St George*, pp 51, 57.

**6.2** Lord Dudley's yacht *Fodhla* in Kingstown Harbour, 1904 (from a postcard).

Royal Yacht Squadron because of his being 'in trade'; as a consequence, his challenges were made under the burgee of the Royal Ulster Yacht Club.[60] But other clubs could not afford to be so picky. The gentry's dominance began to be supplanted by a wider establishment, based more on middle-class business and professional gentlemen, including well-off and well-connected Catholics. As early as 1862, the George's membership showed evidence of a creeping suburbanization.[61] Lough Ree Yacht Club's membership in 1895 still consisted predominantly of gentry, but with a very significant leavening of military officers and a couple of bank managers.[62] The gentry families of Penrose-Fitzgerald, French and Smith Barry remained prominent in the Royal Cork up to and beyond Irish independence, but Cork city professional and business families – Exham, Yelverton Pearson, Tanner, Nicholson, Julian – were also increasingly seen in the membership lists.[63]

Sailing as an amateur sport began to grow in popularity and affordability with the decrease in boat size and the rise of one-design classes, which popularized 'scratch', or non-handicapped, racing. This 'Corinthian', or amateur, ideal can be seen in the example of the Munster Model Yacht Club, founded in 1872 to promote the sailing of smaller vessels, and in Kingstown's the Prince Alfred, founded in 1857. The Alfred was noted for its lack of premises – it was what we

**60** Ian d'Alton, 'Lipton, Sir Thomas Johnstone', *DIB*, v, p. 514. **61** *Rules and regulations of the Royal St George Yacht Club*, pp 13–35. **62** English, *Lough Ree*, pp 30–2. **63** Corinthia, *History of yachting in the south of Ireland*, *passim*; St Leger, *A history of the Royal Cork*, pp 130, 137. A.H. Smith Barry of Fota (Lord Barrymore from 1902) was admiral from 1890 to his would now call a 'virtual' club, organized for purely sporting purposes. Its racing rules subsequently became the basis of the rules of the Yacht Racing Association, later the UK's Royal Yachting Association in 1870–1. This reflected its origins more in sailing than sociability – it had started out as the Irish Model Yacht Club, seen as 'a thorn in the flesh of the sailing establishment'.[64] But Victorian gentrification soon took hold of these clubs. The Munster Model Yacht Club became the Royal Munster Yacht Club in 1893.[65] The Alfred became the Royal Alfred Yacht Club in 1864; its commodore in 1907 was the duke of Connaught.[66] Members' yachts were permitted to have two 'paid hands' – not sailors, but a steward and a lady's maid. Its original spirit was taken up by Dublin Bay Sailing Club (DBSC) in 1884 and, while the Alfred continued to organize racing, the two clubs were eventually amalgamated in 2016 under the DBSC name.[67]

## WOMEN AND THEIR PLACE IN YACHTING

Women were not unknown on yachts. One of the 1846 Royal Irish flag codes was for 'woman'. They were often represented as decidedly tough. In the Somerville & Ross Irish RM sailing story 'The house of Fahy', the women come off best among the generally unwell guests on board. As Major Yeates says, they 'talked untiringly, with that singular indifference to their marine surroundings that I have often observed in ladies who are not sea-sick'.[68] Edith Somerville was an early enthusiast of women's sailing, writing of her and Violet Martin's 'happy lives' as children, 'boating on sea and lake' in the early 1860s.[69]

Edith sailed the river Shannon in convoy in 1879, and at Youghal in 1887, and she raced in small boats at Castletownshend (fig. 6.3).[70]

*The real Charlotte* published a decade later has several yachting episodes.[71] Lough Ree Yacht Club had two women members at the end of the nineteenth century,[72] when women's participation in racing started to become worthy of mention, reflecting wider changes in society at large. The Royal Munster YC in 1893 had a women's race contested by Mrs Crawford and Miss Gubbins. In

death in 1925. **64** 'Royal Alfred Yacht Club', *Afloat*, 16 July 2009; W.M. Nixon, 'Dublin Bay Sailing Club and Sherry Fitzgerald Launch Yacht Racing Alliance in the Capital', *Afloat*, 16 Apr. 2016. **65** National Maritime Museum Cornwall, 'Royal Munster Yacht Club', https://www. maritimeviews.co.uk/yacht-clubs/royal-munster-yacht-club, accessed 19 Sept. 2018. **66** National Maritime Museum Cornwall, 'Royal Alfred Yacht Club', https://www. maritimeviews.co.uk/yacht-clubs/royal-alfred-yacht-club, accessed 19 Sept. 2018. **67** W.M. Nixon, 'Sailing on Saturdays', https://afloat.ie/item/31909-dublin-bay-sailing-club-sherry-fitzgerald-launch-2016, accessed 19 Sept. 2018. **68** E.Œ Somerville and Martin Ross, *Experiences of an Irish R.M.* (London, 1970), p. 135. **69** Edith Somerville, 'Introduction' in Somerville and Ross, *Experiences of an Irish R.M.*, p. vi. **70** Gifford Lewis, *Edith Somerville: a biography* (Dublin, 2005), pp 55, 115. **71** E. Œ Somerville and Martin Ross, *The real Charlotte* [1894] (Nashville, 1999), pp 101–5; Lewis, *Edith Somerville*, pp 53, 81. **72** English, *Lough Ree*, pp 33–4.

6.3 'West Carbery', an Edith Somerville sketch from E. Somerville and M. Ross, *All our yesterdays* (London, 1906), facing p. 217.

1908, at Courtmacsherry regatta the yacht *Geraldine* was crewed by Mrs Rowan and Miss McKenzie, who, it was reported, were cheered by the crowd.[73]

## YACHTING AND IDENTITY

The 1988 history of the Royal St George Yacht Club captures the spirit of nineteenth-century yachting, and what the clubs meant to the world of aristocracy and gentry. The Royal St George YC claimed in 1843 that 'it was composed of some four hundred Irish noblemen and gentlemen'; in 1870 the club objected to a member's guest on the basis that he was a 'native Irishman'; and the following year a member was expelled for entertaining, it was said, a Catholic priest as his guest.[74] Somerville and Ross, writing of autumnal Kingstown in *The real Charlotte*, encapsulated that exclusivity, still present at the end of the century, although now more a manifestation of Victorian respectability and snobbery than religious or political prejudice:

> [T]he Dublin people come down to snatch what they can of the sea before the short afternoon darkens, and the hour arrives when they look out for members of the Royal St George Yacht Club to take them in to tea.[75]

73 Corinthia, *History of yachting in the south of Ireland*, pp 105, 176. 74 Archer and Pearson, *The Royal St George*, pp 19, 55, 57–9. 75 Ibid., p. 39.

What the 'noblemen and gentlemen' wanted – and got – was a gentleman's club. The yachting variety was not easy to distinguish from, say, the Kildare Street or University clubs in Dublin, or the County Club in Cork – or indeed the Royal Western's landlocked premises in Dublin's Grafton Street, far away from its original sailing grounds.[76] The historiography of the yacht clubs often reflect this. One example is the 1988 history of the Royal St George YC. Of its 147 pages and 14 chapters, only 46 pages and 2 chapters are devoted to sailing. The rest is about the clubhouse, the dining, the billiards and smoking rooms, cards, chess, backgammon and the idiosyncratic staff.[77] Alicia St Leger's 2005 history of the Royal Cork YC has more balance from the sporting point of view, but one is still left in little doubt as to the essentially social function of the club, and its important position as a marker of status and wealth.

If, in the words of Thomas French, admiral of the Royal Cork from 1857 to 1866, 'yachting shall be to the amusement of the gentry of Ireland',[78] the 'noblemen and gentlemen' were supplemented with, and eventually supplanted by, a carefully self-selecting class of Protestant and loyal Catholic bourgeoisie – a key shift that was common to most high-status, expensive sports and leisure activities. That influx was vital in sustaining the clubs when the aristocracy and gentry began to be etiolated in the revolutionary period from the 1870s. 'Loyal Irishness', essentially military and imperial, was an identity expressed in high-end yachting, from the Royal Navy-related burgees, through welcoming royal visitors at their point of embarkation, to membership of clubs containing 'many Army and Navy personnel'.[79] Demonstrations of loyalty to the crown had to be conspicuous; a fracas occurred at Cork regatta in 1869 when many yachts failed to dress for the anniversary of Queen Victoria's coronation, and a furious naval officer 'declared his belief that half the members of the RCYC were Fenians'.[80] That was unlikely. Even after Irish independence, royalism – if not loyalism – continued to be a mark of the yacht clubs. In 1926, the Royal St George YC attempted to find some *modus vivendi* with the new dispensation by inviting both the Garda band and the governor general to a regatta.[81] But the Club's letter-headings bore the address 'Kingstown' well into the 1930s; and 'Queenstown' took a long time to be supplanted by 'Cobh' in the Royal Cork's lexicography.[82]

After 1922, in the provost of Trinity College Dublin's phrase, 'The King's Government in Ireland' did strictly exist, at least in constitutional and legal

76 O'Connell, 'Royal Western Yacht Club of Ireland', *Afloat*, 15 July 2009. 77 Archer and Pearson, *The Royal St George*, p. 25. 78 Thomas G. French to John Daunt, 12, 15 Nov. 1860, in minutes, 1853–67 (Royal Cork Yacht Club archives, unnumbered). 79 Archer and Pearson, *The Royal St George*, p. 38. 80 St Leger, *A history of the Royal Cork*, p. 162. 81 Ian d'Alton, 'Remembering the future, imagining the past: how southern Irish Protestants survived' in Felix M. Larkin (ed.), *Librarians, poets and scholars: a festschrift for Dónall Ó Luanaigh* (Dublin, 2007), pp 212–30; *idem*, '"A vestigial population"? Perspectives on southern Irish Protestants in the twentieth century' in *Éire-Ireland*, 44 (Winter 2009–10), pp 9–42; Archer and Pearson, *The Royal St George*, p. 117. 82 Archer and Pearson, *The Royal St George*, p. 117.

terms, but it was not a political concept that Saorstát Éireann, the Irish Free State, particularly acknowledged.[83] However, for loyalists and ex-unionists its existence facilitated the fancy that change was minimal. Yacht clubs provided one of the spaces within which loyal Irishmen and Irishwomen could congregate, in which class and culture could transcend (or just ignore) politics. The Irish, the George, the Royal Cork – holding tenaciously onto their 'royal' appellations – were symbols of an *ancien régime* that lasted into the new Ireland for all those who wanted to see and hear it. This raises a final question. Yachting was a frontier activity, physical as well as cultural; the clubs were on the transition between land and wave. Every voyage involved leaving the land and heading out on the neutral sea. Perched on the edge of the island, facing outward, might sailing cliques have always been congenial to those members of the aristocracy and gentry for whom Ireland had always been, in essence, alien and 'other'?

83 J.H. Bernard to Col. Mitchell, 28 Sept. 1923 (TCD, J.H. Bernard papers, MS 2388–93/440).

# The Big House, aristocracy, and golf in Ireland, *c.*1890–1921*

TERENCE DOOLEY

> That the Royal and Ancient game has taken a firm and permanent hold on this country is plainly evidenced by the frequency with which new links are being opened in different parts. With the natural advantages with which we are fortunate in possessing in this country, it would be ungrateful did we not exercise to the full our opportunities for developing to the utmost a game which is adapted to indulgence by both sexes, and to the young and old in each.

Thus reported the *Belfast News-Letter* on 10 August 1896, referring to the rapid spread of golf in Ireland during the previous decade, particularly in north-east Ulster. This, of course, was not a phenomenon unique to Ireland; in Britain by 1898 there were 1,460 golf clubs, over half of which were in England, where a decade before there had been only twenty.[1] In roughly the same period, ninety-seven clubs were established in Ireland.[2] The reporter was right that golf's popularity stemmed from the fact that it could be enjoyed by men and women and by young and old. Therein lay some of its attraction to those male members of the Irish aristocracy, the focus of this essay, who had the time but perhaps not the robust masculine constitution or the finances required for hunting, the pre-eminent landlord sport.[3] Maybe some were like David Lloyd George – certainly no friend of the aristocracy – who observed that 'for middle-aged people pursuing a sedentary life like himself, golf was the greatest discovery of the age'.[4]

But there were, of course, many other reasons why golf appealed to the aristocracy. Rather than regarding it as a sedentary leisure pursuit, there were aristocrats who relished golf's inherent competitiveness, and the challenges and

* This paper is chiefly concerned with members of the Irish landed class who were titled noblemen, though reference will on occasion be made to members of the gentry. I would like to thank Vincent Comerford, Tom Hunt and Tony McCarthy for reading earlier drafts. 1 On this 'golf boom', see D.M. Cameron, *The golf boom in Victorian Britain* (Bodmin, Cornwall, 2010). 2 Daniel Mulhall, '"A gift from Scotland": golf's early days in Ireland', *History Ireland*, 14:5 (2006), p. 32; as a corollary, landlords who hunted could enjoy golf outside the hunting season, see Tom Hunt, *Sport and society in Victorian Ireland: the case of Westmeath* (Cork, 2007), p. 39. 3 On women and golf in Ireland, see Ivan Morris, *A history of women's golf in Ireland* (Dublin, 2018). 4 Quoted in Roland Quinault, 'Golf and Edwardian politics' in Negry Harte and Roland Quinault (eds), *Land and society in Britain, 1700–1914* (Manchester, 1996), pp 196–7.

opportunities of a varied nature it provided. In the past, aristocrats hunted across untamed landscapes, jumped open ditches with abandon, and came into conflict with aggrieved tenant farmers. With golf, they had first to tame the landscape in order to play, and that represented a fresh challenge, they had to overcome barriers – bunkers, trees, water – but these presented much less danger to life and limb, and golfers came into conflict with no one but themselves. Both hunting and golf appealed to physicality (at different levels), but golf was a sport that challenged the intellect too.

Therefore, it may not be a coincidence that the emergence of golf coincided with an era when a number of British and Irish aristocratic families – including prominent politicians – formed a country-house coterie who valued competitiveness and 'intellectual dexterity'.[5] The Souls were dominated by the Charteris, Tennant, Wyndham and Balfour families, all united by political and social ambition, and the common aim to advance each other's family interests. They also had a fascination with golf. The Wyndham estate at Clouds in Wiltshire had its own golf course (where they gave the names of political figures to the holes, rather than numbers).[6] Wyndham's sister Mary was married to Hugo Charteris (later earl of Wemyss) whose Gosford House estate had a number of private golf courses including Craigielow. In fact, Gosford's association with golf went as far back as the early fifteenth century when James V frequented it to play the ancient version of the game.[7] To the present day, leading amateurs play for the Tennant Cup, first presented to the Glasgow Golf Club (founded in 1787). No aristocrat made golf more popular than Arthur Balfour (1848–1930). In 1897, an article in the *Irish Times* claimed that while golf had been played for centuries in Scotland: 'It became epidemic in England through the efforts of Mr Arthur Balfour.'[8]

Balfour was the Souls' 'chief adornment'.[9] Often referred to as 'Arthur Golfour', he first became a golf enthusiast following his appointment as minister in charge of Scottish affairs in 1885. Balfour was also an intellectual; metaphysical research captivated him and he saw in golf the ideal pastime, combining a leisurely walk that allowed for quiet contemplation with the sophisticated challenge of mapping the flight of a small ball from tee to green by the shortest distance possible.[10] (His contemporary Sir Winston Churchill famously described the game as being akin to 'chasing a quinine pill around a cow pasture'.) In one of his existentialist pieces in praise of the sport, Balfour wrote: 'With a fine sea view, and a clear course in front of him, the golfer should find no difficulty in dismissing all worries from his mind and regarding golf …

5 Alvin Jackson, 'George Wyndham', *ODNB*. 6 *Irish Times*, 26 Apr. 1900. 7 Gosford House, 'Craigielaw Golf Club', http://www.gosfordhouse. co.uk/craigielaw-golf-club, 27 Sept. 2018. 8 *Irish Times*, 20 Feb. 1897. 9 Ruddock Mackay and H.C.G. Matthew, 'Balfour, Arthur James, first earl of Balfour, *ODNB*; see Angela Lambert, *Unquiet Souls: the Indian summer of the British aristocracy, 1880–1918* (London, 1984). 10 See Max Egremont, *Balfour: a life of Arthur James Balfour* (London, 1980).

as the true and adequate end of man's existence.'[11] There is some evidence that his philosophy gained currency with Irish aristocrats; Lord Greville of Westmeath told his audience at the opening of a new golf course in Mullingar in April 1895 that 'golfing was an amusement as healthy as it was innocent … Cricket, football and even hockey, debar people from engaging in them after they have passed a certain age; but such was not the case with golf'.[12]

Before examining Balfour's time in Ireland as chief secretary, it is worth considering his viewpoint of the golfing idyll in the context of what the *Belfast News-Letter* considered 'the natural advantages' which Ireland possessed. Some of the earliest course architects such as H.S. Colt believed, like Balfour, that golf was about 'enjoying the relaxation which delightful natural surroundings always give'.[13] This was the very reason why the aristocracy and their landscape architects created luxuriant parklands and ornamental gardens in the eighteenth century: the contours, undulating landscapes, open ground, trees and water features appealed to the visual senses of the leisured classes. In Britain, in the eighteenth-century landscape, architects such as Lancelot 'Capability' Brown worked for some of the wealthiest aristocrats, sweeping away formal gardens in favour of rolling parkland, decorous clumps of trees and water features, and working landscapes into a more natural state than had previously been fashionable. To some, Brown was a landscape genius but to others he was 'a destructive force' because of the revolutionary change he brought to landscape design.[14] Brown simply did what he was handsomely paid to do by the aristocracy who, at all times, did what they wanted to do with their landscape whenever it pleased them. In doing so, Brown (and others, of course) created landscapes that in the future would be highly conducive to golf courses.[15] In his 1989 study of sport geography, John Bale went as far as to contend that from the 1890s the golf architect in Britain 'emerged as a kind of sub-Capability Brown'.[16]

By the end of the nineteenth century, it was inevitable that change in the historic environment would happen again when demesnes were contemplated as golf courses. Some of the Irish aristocracy imitated their British counterparts – such as the Wyndham family at Clouds, the duke of Devonshire at Chatsworth

11 Quoted in Quinault, 'Golf and Edwardian politics', p. 192. 12 *Westmeath Guardian*, 5 Apr. 1895; quoted in Hunt, *Sport and society in Victorian Ireland*, p. 90. 13 Holt, *Golf architecture*, pp 2, 5. 14 Hannah Stephenson, 'Celebrating three centuries of Capability Brown', https://www.irishtimes.com/life-and-style/homes-and-property/gardens/celebrating-three-centuries-of-capability-brown-1.2532419, 22 Aug. 2018. See also David Brown and Tom Williamson, *Lancelot Brown and the capability men: landscape revolution in eighteenth-century England* (London, 2016); and John Phibbs, *Place-making: the art of Capability Brown* (Swindon, 2017). 15 In 2007, the European Institute of Golf Course Architects (EIGCA) published a report for English Heritage which found that almost 10 per cent of registered historic parks and gardens in Britain included golf courses, and of these 9 per cent had been designed by Brown (including Bowood in Wiltshire and Stowe in Buckinghamshire); European Institute of Golf Course Architects, *Golf courses as designed landscapes of historic interest* (2007), p. 12. 16 John Bale, *Sports geography* (London, 1989), p. 140.

and Compton Place and the Hope family at Deepdene – and redesigned their demesnes.[17] In 1895, Lord Massereene, one of Ulster's leading aristocrats, employed G.L. Baillie, an early pioneer of golf course design, to create an eighteen-hole course on his demesne in County Antrim.[18] The aesthetic was already there, a 'picturesque parkland course with panoramic views over Lough Neagh'. As well as adding bunkers, Baillie used the existing natural hazards of water (holes five and six were close enough to Lough Neagh 'to cause worry' to even the most experienced golfer), 'stately firs' and hedges to create a challenging course.[19] There was no public outcry that an historic landscape had been compromised.

Massereene built the course for his own pleasure. However, the membership of the club was drawn mainly from the industrialist and middle classes of Belfast and its hinterlands.[20] No golf club was representative of a locality's wider demography. The aristocracy and gentry were never likely to have it any other way; they had never favoured the democratization of the clubs they patronized. Subscription fees were the preferred method of keeping clubs socially exclusive. Moreover, as Wray Vamplew points out:

> Golf was a character-building 'respectable' pastime in which players practiced sportsmanship and fair play. Golf placed responsibility for policing on the players themselves and maintained notions of honor and chivalry. Breaches of behavioural norms – such as driving into those in front, counting an opponent's strokes in a bunker or leaving divots – led not to the forfeit of a hole but to loss of social status and possible ostracism within the club.[21]

Thus, golf club rules conformed to the strictest etiquette of conduct characteristic of gentlemen's clubs such as the Kildare Street in Dublin or the Carlton in London.

In the same way that aristocrats hunted in uniform, or went out to shoot dressed to the highest standards of respectability, so too those who went to play golf had to be fashionably attired. Moreover, the hunt was not merely about a chase across wide expanses of countryside in pursuit of a fox; there also was the initial meet, the hunt dinners or balls, the essential club sociability. When the earl of Dartrey established a links course on his Monaghan estate, he built a

17 Richard Holt, 'Golf and the English suburb: class and gender in a London club, *ca.*1890–*ca.*1960', *Sports Historian* 1:18 (May 1998), p. 79. 18 *Belfast News-Letter*, 2 Sept. 1895. 19 *Belfast News-Letter*, 2 Sept. 1895; Massereene Golf Club, www.massereenegc.co.uk, 23 Aug. 2018. 20 The prominent role of the middle class in the popularization of golf in Ireland is discussed in Roisin Higgins, '"The hallmark of pluperfect respectability": the early development of golf in Irish society', *Éire-Ireland*, 48:1–2, (Spring/Summer, 2013). 21 Wray Vamplew, 'Concepts of capital: an approach shot to the history of the British golf club before 1914', *Journal of Sport History*, 39:2 (Sept. 2012), p. 310.

'handsome club house' and furnished it at his own expense so that the committee and members could socialize.[22] The clubhouse became the inner sanctuary. It excluded even the greatest amateur and professional players of the age because they did not have the required social credentials.

The exciting thing for aristocrats was that they had the wealth (even if it was in decline), the time as the leisured class and the physical space to develop their private lands into courses, if they so desired, as Massereene did. The urban upper and middle classes had the wealth, and increasingly more leisure time, but they did not have access to land. Land was, therefore, the common denominator that brought urban elites and the aristocracy together to create golf courses. Other areas of commonality would follow. It had been the same with sports in the past such as hunting, horse racing, shooting and cricket. The aristocracy were deeply implicated in the introduction, development and administration of all of these sports, and, by extension, they were involved in the shaping of the physical and cultural landscapes that were associated with them, from creating racecourses such as Punchestown and Fairyhouse, to facilitating demesne cricket pitches. However, other classes had to be taken on board. For example, the estate cricket club was comprised of employees; and by the late nineteenth century, strong farmers were part of the local hunt. Golf was the quintessential sport where there was a mutual dependency between aristocracy and the middle classes that went beyond basic participation. The aristocracy had the land; the middle classes had the numbers and the money for subscriptions.

The late nineteenth century was also a time of emulation. The middle and upper classes imitated the aristocracy: they sent their children to private schools, they built suburban villas, and their participation in political life was ever more significant. However, they did not have aristocratic gravitas, and despite their declining financial circumstances, the aristocracy were still the models of behaviour that many aspired to. Newspaper and journal reportage on their movements between Ireland, Britain and further afield, on who they married, how they dressed, the social functions they attended and so on had a captive audience and filled more newspaper columns than ever before. Thus, the urban elites looked to them to provide prestige to local clubs. In return for their patronage – particularly the provision of lands – and the social prestige their titles gave to clubs, aristocrats were invited to become club presidents. For donating lands to create the Dufferin course in County Down, the marquess of Dufferin and Ava was made president in 1897; similarly the 5th viscount de Vesci was elected president of Monkstown in Cork after renting Monkstown Castle and demesne as course and club house.[23] In 1913, the first president of the Ardee club was Sir Henry Bellingham of Castlebellingham, and the captain was Capt George Taafe of Smarmore Castle; that same year they were both influential in securing land on the Ruxton demesne to lay out a new course.[24] In 1891, when

22 *Anglo-Celt*, 22 Nov. 1913. 23 Gibson, *Early Irish golf*, pp 160, 211. 24 *Irish Field*, 8 Feb. 1913; Gibson, *Early Irish golf*, p. 177; *Irish Times*, 5 July 1896; *Belfast News-Letter*, 9 July 1896.

7.1 Uchter John Mark Knox, 5th earl of Ranfurly, played golf simply because he enjoyed the game.

the middle-class-dominated Golfing Union of Ireland was established, Uchter John Mark Knox, 5th earl of Ranfurly, was chosen as one of its chief officers. W.A. Menton has argued that this was a shrewd move as Ranfurly was 'clearly a royal favourite as from 1895 to 1897 he was lord-in-waiting to Queen Victoria, and was Governor of New Zealand from 1897 to 1904'.[25]

But, first and foremost, Ranfurly played golf simply because he enjoyed the game. He constructed a twelve-hole course on his own demesne. Another avid golfer was Francis 6th earl of Annesley, captain of Royal County Down in 1909 and 1910, who played in the final of the Irish Close Championship, losing only to amateur legend Lionel Munn.[26] Charles Burke of Ballinahor House was 'an enthusiastic golfer' and reputedly the first to introduce golf to County Armagh when he built a private links on his demesne.[27] By 1909, the earl of Kenmare had provided land for the Killarney Club because his son, Lord Castlerosse, was 'already a young player of much promise'.[28] Similarly, in 1909, it was said of Walter MacMurrough Kavanagh, president of the Borris Club in Carlow, that he 'originally started golf in his park chiefly for the benefit of his sons.'[29] In the Edwardian era, the Leslies at Ballybay House, Lord Rosmore at Rosmore Park and Lord Francis Hope at Hope Castle in Castleblayney (who also had a course at Deepdene in Surrey) all constructed demesne courses in County Monaghan. The trend was similar further south where, for example, Lord Donoughmore established a course at Knocklofty in Tipperary; Lindsey Talbot Crosbie on his Ardfert demesne in Kerry; Lord Bandon at Castle Bernard in Cork; and the O'Conor Don at Clonalis in Roscommon. All were golfing enthusiasts. They also had recently sold the bulk of their lands under the Wyndham Land Act of 1903. It might be argued, therefore, that the development of courses on their demesnes was a signal that they intended to remain resident in Ireland and engage with the wider community. Certainly, none of these (former) landlords left Ireland directly after the sale of their estates.

There were also financial considerations. As aristocratic fortunes diminished in the late nineteenth century, golf became more affordable than hunting. In her oft-quoted memoirs, Lady Elizabeth ('Daisy') Fingall noted Lord Dudley's passion for golf when he was lord lieutenant of Ireland between 1902 and 1905. She also referred to her husband becoming almost bankrupt around this time as a result of being master of foxhounds to the Meath Hunt: 'It was no wonder', she wrote, 'that our fortunes – or what was left of them – went blazing up the chimney cheerfully … as cheerfully as they were eaten by the horses in the stables, and by the endless grooms and retainers outside'.[30] Golf was by no means cheap to play, but it was not as expensive as keeping a stable of horses and a pack of hounds. On the other hand, the prescience of Ulster aristocrats such as Lord Annesley and Lord Antrim in establishing courses on their lands should not be underestimated; in time these clubs became the Royal Portrush and Royal County Down, not only prestigious and commercially successful in their own

**25** W.A. Menton, *The Golfing Union of Ireland, 1891–1991* (Dublin, 1991), p. 14. **26** Gibson, *Early Irish golf*, p. 87. **27** Ibid., p. 150. **28** *Irish Field*, 2 Oct. 1909. **29** Gibson, *Early Irish golf*, p. 135. **30** Fingall, *Seventy years young*, pp 186, 280. **31** *Irish Times*, 8 Oct 1910.

right but also very important to the local economy. In 1910, the earl of Antrim raised the rent on Royal Portrush to £500 per annum.[31] If the average course at the time was around seventy-five acres then this equated to a rental value of £6.6 per acre, which would have been a very decent return even compared to agricultural rents. Moreover, the golf course also enhanced the value of Antrim's real estate around Portrush. It was just a picturesque fishing village until it became a popular tourist resort with the Belfast middle classes when a railway line was built in 1855; hotels such as the Northern Counties were constructed to provide accommodation, and the golf club was founded in 1888. In 1896, the *Freeman's Journal* reported that golf had 'done wonders' for Portrush.

This was part of a much wider trend. By the early 1890s, financially beleaguered landlords and middle-class speculators had begun to take note of the tourism potential that golf offered, especially if golf clubs could work in collaboration with railways and hoteliers.[32] In 1891, at the first meeting of the Golfing Union of Ireland, one of its specified aims was 'to treat with different railway companies with the view to obtaining railway facilities for golfers'.[33] That same year, Arthur Balfour's Land Act made provision for the establishment of the Congested Districts Board, which over time invested in the construction of light railway lines connecting peripheral counties such as Galway, Donegal, Kerry and Clare to the centre. New golf resorts such as Portsalon (Donegal) and Ennis (Clare) became popular tourist attractions.[34] In 1891, the same year that the GUI was founded, the 4th earl of Leitrim saw an opportunity, through golf, to improve the tourist potential of the Rosapenna area in Donegal. He mortgaged his estates and employed the famous golf-course architect Tom Morris (then employed at St Andrew's in Scotland) to design a links course, and in 1892, just before his death, Leitrim began the construction of a hotel.[35] In the summer of 1896, the *Irish Times* reported that 'Cork was not short of entrepreneurs', and that a number of them had approached Lord Fermoy to lease lands on his Trabolgan demesne to develop a course. They then approached the earl of Bandon, who consented to be president. The plan was that 'when membership justifies the expenditure, a suitable clubhouse with bedrooms attached will be built'.[36] That same year, Lord Rathmore (president), Lord Kilmorey and Lord Russell of Killowen (vice presidents) were part of the group who planned a twelve-hole golf course and clubhouse at Greenore in County Louth, a collaborative project between the London and North Western Railway and the local Greenore Hotel.[37] The most authoritative work on the history of Irish tourism to date points out that the Great Southern, the first railway hotel

32 Andrew Carpenter et al. (eds), *Art and architecture of Ireland* (New Haven, 2015), iv, p. 481. 33 Menton, *Golfing Union of Ireland*, p. 6. 34 Quoted in Higgins, 'The hallmark of pluperfect respectability', p. 30. 35 Brigid Clesham, 'Catalogue of Leitrim papers' (NLI, collection list, no. 49). 36 *Irish Times*, 5 July 1896; *Belfast News-Letter*, 9 July 1896. 37 *Irish Times*, 23 Oct. 1896; Greenore Golf Club, 'History', http://www.greenoregolfclub.com/about/history, 22 Aug. 2018.

built in Ireland, was built on land owned by the earl of Kenmare because he was 'keen to promote tourism to cover ever-increasing costs of maintaining his estate'.[38] Around the same time, Lord Lansdowne provided the land for the development of the local golf club.[39] These were all commercial enterprises. The importance of profit came to the fore during the Great War when demand created a boom in agriculture. In August 1916, the *Irish Times* condemned attempts to 'extort more money' from golf club members up and down the country and complained that rents were 'ridiculously high'.[40] Landlords could not resist the lure of higher profits as the demand for grazing lands meant farmers were willing to pay more for conacre than golfers were for greens, and so the *Irish Times* lamented: 'The increased value of land for grazing has been the reason for bringing more than one club to its end.'[41]

In Ireland, as well as in Britain, in an age of radical political reform, it was inevitable that golf clubs would draw men of shared political ideologies together. Golf and politics were like bread and jam. In 1894, Lord Rosebery (1847–1929), briefly Liberal prime minister 1894–5, made a revealing speech at the Dornoch links course in Scotland – the development of which he put down to the efforts of 'a great statesman, although a great political opponent of his own, Mr Arthur James Balfour' – in which he remarked that future historians

> might record that a statesman looking around with an eagle eye for some new means of spreading his political creed had, under the guise of spreading a game with a bag of instruments – (laughter) – managed to form a great secret society which had extended all over England, and by which the principles of the party to which he belonged could be promulgated.[42]

At the time, the remark may have sounded tongue-in-cheek, but Rosebery had articulated what many believed to be the very *raison d'être* of a golf club, or any club for that matter: to foster a political identity among its members. This was the age of associational culture when clubs and societies in Ireland and elsewhere stimulated local, regional and political identity in an unprecedented manner.[43] Roland Quinault has convincingly argued that golf and Edwardian high politics were inextricably entwined in Britain. He pays little attention to Ireland, but he acknowledges that 'there were many golf links in the strongly unionist county of Antrim' as well as the unionist belt along the coast of Dublin.[44] He was, therefore, equating golf with unionist politics. Certainly,

38 Irene Furlong, *Irish tourism, 1880–1980* (Dublin, 2009), p. 15; on railways, hotels and golf clubs, see Higgins, 'The hallmark of pluperfect respectability', p. 29. 39 Kenmare Golf Club, 'History of the club', https://www.kenmaregolfclub.com/the-club/history, 26 Sept. 2018. 40 *Irish Times*, 19 Aug. 1916. 41 Ibid., 14 Oct. 1916. 42 Ibid., 27 Sept. 1894. 43 See R.V. Comerford and Jennifer Kelly (eds), *Associational culture in Ireland and the wider world* (Newbridge, 2010). 44 Quinault, 'Golf and Edwardian politics', pp 191, 204; he also

7.2 One of many cartoon-type images of Arthur 'Golfour' Balfour. Conservative chief secretary of Ireland, 1887–91.

anyone with a loyalist mentality could look at the Dublin Castle administration and feel that golf was an integral part of Castle politics. From the mid-1880s, most lord lieutenants were avid golfers who played in the Phoenix Park. In 1885, Lord Carnarvon was patron of the Dublin Golf Club. He was succeeded in office in 1886 by the earl of Aberdeen, 'an active golfer'. Lord Dudley, who arrived in 1902, had his own private golf course at Witley Court in Worcestershire. In 1902, he played with the duke and duchess of Connaught and Lady Cadogan in the Phoenix Park.[45] As he was departing Ireland, the *Irish Independent* could at least claim that Dudley 'did so much for Irish golf while resident at the Viceregal lodge'.[46]

quotes Roy Jenkins that 'golf was an almost essential accompaniment to Edwardian politics', ibid., p. 191. **45** Gibson, *Early Irish golf*, pp 79–82; For Dudley's obsession with golf, see Elizabeth Fingall, *Seventy years young* (London, 1937), pp 279–80; *Irish Golfer*, 5 Feb. 1902; see also *Irish Times*, 18 Apr. 1903. **46** *Irish Independent*, 12 Dec. 1905.

Even in the midst of parliamentary sessions, Irish peers and nationalist MPs indulged their golfing interests. In 1892, Sir Henry Mallaby Deeley (who would go on to own Carton House in Kildare in the 1920s[47]) founded Prince's Golf Club at Mitcham as the playground of the members of parliament.[48] In May 1901, there was 'an unusually large entry of peers' in the parliamentary tournament played there, including the earl of Donoughmore and the earl of Dunraven (both of whom had golf courses on their Irish demesnes).[49] In 1914, home rule MPs including Joe Devlin, Willie Redmond and at least ten others played a team from the London Irish Golfing Society in a challenge tournament on Walton Heath.[50] Michael Benton has contended that Walton became 'a surrogate parliament in the pre-war years'.[51] It had at least four prime ministers as members: David Lloyd George, Andrew Bonar Law, Winston Churchill and Arthur Balfour, of whom it has been said also that his 'rapid political rise boosted golf's profile at Westminster'.[52] Before he became prime minister, he was the British administrator in Ireland who had the most profound influence on the spread of golf.

Balfour arrived in Ireland as Conservative chief secretary in 1887 (staying in the post until 1892). At the time, he was an accomplished golfer but a relatively inexperienced politician and there were those, even within his own party, who doubted his resolve to administer Ireland during a very turbulent period of agrarian and political tensions.[53] He brought George Wyndham (1855–1929) with him as his private secretary. Shortly after their arrival, Wyndham wrote to his wife, Sibell Grosvenor, in typical Souls' fashion, that he and the chief secretary talked about 'Shakespeare, Shelley, the story of Hero and Leander, the difference of accent, quantity and numbering of syllables in English, Latin and French territory, politics, principles, warfare etc. etc.'. He also noted that Balfour was introducing him to the rudiments of golf.[54] Rosebery was right: Balfour understood how golf could be used to his political advantage, an impression certainly given by his dealings with Ulster unionists.

As chief secretary, Balfour took to his task with a steely resolve not expected of him. He introduced a draconian Crimes Act in 1887 granting the Irish executive emergency powers to deal with rural crime associated with the Plan of Campaign (a strategy adopted by the Irish National League from 1886 to aid tenants in their struggle for fair rents and to prevent evictions). Between July and August virtually all of Ireland was proclaimed as was the National League. On 9 September the RIC opened fire on League demonstrators in Mitchelstown,

47 Terence Dooley, *The decline and fall of the dukes of Leinster: love, war, debt, and madness* (Dublin, 2014). 48 *Leitrim Observer*, 13 Sept. 1913. 49 *Irish Times*, 4 May 1901. 50 Quinault, 'Golf and Edwardian politics', p. 204. 51 Michael Bentley, *Politics without democracy, 1815–1914* (Oxford, 1984), p. 245. 52 Quinault, 'Golf and Edwardian politics', p. 193. 53 See Max Egremont, *A life of Arthur James Balfour* (London, 1980). 54 George Wyndham to Countess (Sibell) Grosvenor, 12–13 Jan. 1888 (PRONI, Wyndham papers, T3221/1/2A).

killing three people, and Balfour resolutely defended the actions of the police, subsequently acquiring the sobriquet 'Bloody Balfour'. Nationalists despised him as he worked relentlessly to break the Plan. Landlords were more relieved: by the end of 1889 his coercion and conciliation policies had halved the crime rate from its 1886 level, and he could unproclaim most of the country. Rural Ireland became much less violent and home rule politics went into a decade of decline following Parnell's death in 1892. Balfour's Irish policies appealed to Ulster unionists who feted him time and again, and subsequently showed their appreciation by inviting him to the province to play golf. For example, in November 1890, a deputation of the West Belfast Unionist Association met Balfour in Liverpool. He thanked them for the message they had brought from 'the loyal population of Ulster ... The people of the most prosperous part of Ireland.'[55] Thus, Balfour cleverly equated loyalism with economic prosperity in full knowledge that Ulster unionists strongly protested that home rule would be detrimental to their economic future. In return, the deputation invited him to the industrial heartland of Ireland to play golf: 'Nothing could give me greater pleasure', he replied, 'than to add to my political engagements the less onerous engagement of playing a game of golf with you'.[56]

The 1890s and the Edwardian period became a time of social stability and improved prosperity for the middle classes of Belfast and Dublin, conducive to an increased interest in leisure pursuits that, in turn, stimulated the spread of golf. In 1887, when Balfour first came to Ireland, there were only a dozen clubs. A decade later, there were almost 130 and another forty were founded between 1898 and 1905.[57] It was no mere coincidence. More than anyone, Balfour made golf fashionable. It is also notable that this spurt of growth coincided with a period of almost uninterrupted Conservative power in Britain from 1886 to 1905 (Liberals held power only in the period from 1892 to 1895). Liberals did, of course, play golf. However, as society and politics underwent revolutionary change in Ireland both urban and rural Protestant middle-class elites, Conservative and unionist in their politics, had reason to find common cause with the aristocracy.[58] The example of Belfast merchant Thomas Sinclair, local Antrim landlord John Harrison and the founding of the Belfast Golf Club is instructive in this respect. Sinclair was former president of the Ulster chamber of commerce. In 1881, he returned from a holiday in Scotland where he had been 'smitten' by the game of golf. He approached Harrison, who agreed to provide part of his estate for the development of a course and the Belfast Golf Club was established with, typically, Harrison as the first president.

Sinclair was an enthusiastic golfer but he was also a very influential political player. In 1881, he had been a member of the Ulster Liberal party, a supporter

55 *Irish Times*, 20 Nov. 1890. 56 Ibid., 20 Nov. 1890; his brother Gerald was also an avid golfer; ibid., 26 Sept. 1900. 57 Quinault, 'Golf and Edwardian politics', pp 191, 204. 58 For the wider British case, see Huggins, 'Sport and the upper classes', p. 354.

of W.E. Gladstone, and of his Land Act of that year. Protestant liberals may have supported land reform but when Gladstone introduced his first home rule bill in 1886 that was an entirely different political matter. In the intervening five years, there had been significant developments. Parliamentary reforms in 1884–5 had resulted in the redrawing of constituency boundaries and the expansion of the electorate. The Catholic nationalist middle classes usurped the political power of Protestant landlords, who were routed in the general election of 1885 in most of the country outside the north-east. These developments gave rise to a counter movement – unionism – that depended for its leadership on landlords in the south and the wealthy Belfast industrialists and merchants in the north. In 1885 the Irish Loyal and Patriotic Union was founded, which would evolve into the Irish Unionist Alliance in 1891. In 1886, Gladstone's home rule bill provoked Sinclair into action, and in April that year he convened an anti-home rule meeting in the Ulster Hall. He then set up the Ulster Liberal Unionist Association and in June 1892 organized the Ulster Convention, the first mass anti-home rule movement (of around 12,000 unionists) called in Ireland. Sinclair remained a dedicated unionist for the rest of his life: he became a founding member of the Ulster Unionist Council in 1904, which would shape the course of Ulster unionism from that date, and in 1912, he drafted the Ulster Solemn League and Covenant, which pledged unionists to oppose home rule by force of arms if necessary.[59] Given Sinclair's political ideology, and undoubtedly that of his fellow Belfast Golf Club members, it was no surprise that in 1885 the club invited the Prince of Wales, later King Edward VII, to be its patron. He accepted and the club became 'Royal'. From the club's perspective this designation was highly sought after as it provided the most distinguished degree of prestige and respectability; for loyalists the designation was of immense political and symbolic significance.

Undoubtedly, Sinclair and others had established the Belfast Golf Club because they enjoyed the game, but, in the early years, the club assumed a political dimension that was strictly unionist in character.[60] This was a typical example of how political movers and their associations networked into other local bodies. They probably did likewise with the local tennis club, the Orange Order and church vestries. This also created social and career networks. To take but one prominent example: Vincent Craig, brother of James Craig, who along with Edward Carson led the Ulster unionist movement, designed the clubhouse at the Belfast Club (as he did at the Royal Down club).

The close links between golf and organized unionism were evident throughout the province of Ulster (and the same was true for increasingly popular sports such as tennis and rugby.) Unfortunately, there are no surviving records of the Dartrey Golf Links Club founded by the earl of Dartrey on his

**59** Bridget Hourican, 'Sinclair, Thomas', *DIB*. **60** Roisín Higgins points out that many Ulster golf clubs became predominantly unionist in character; Higgins, 'The hallmark of

Rockcorry demesne in County Monaghan in 1912. However, there are some newspaper reports, including one of the second annual meeting of the committee in November 1913, which clearly indicates the club's exclusive unionist outlook. The president was the earl of Dartrey, a leading light in the Ulster unionist movement whose residence, five months later, was used to store guns and ammunition taken into the county from Larne to arm the local battalions of the Ulster Volunteer Force. His wife, the countess of Dartrey, was also on the committee, and she was active in the Ulster Women's Unionist Council. Army officers (past and present) included Colonel John Leslie of Glaslough, then commanding officer of the 1st Battalion of the Monaghan UVF. Other local unionists, drawn from the professional and clergy classes, joined them, including Dr Fred Smith, Revd Skuse and Dartrey's estate agent, H.K. Leslie.[61] Neither the political nor sectarian nature of clubs was unique to place or time. Jarvie and Reid's 1999 study pointed out that 'There are still golf clubs in the west of Scotland where one would be hard pressed to find a Catholic member.'[62] Jews had to form their own club at Edmondstown in Dublin in 1944.[63] However, it would be wrong to generalize that all clubs discriminated along religious lines; in Monaghan, there were other clubs founded on demesnes – such as Rosmore Park, Hilton Park, and Ballybay – where the Protestant aristocracy and gentry mixed easily with the Catholic elites. Religion was not a discriminating factor, but social class was.

Social class issues, politics, religion, and revolution very often are entangled, and sport can become manipulated and politicized for all the wrong reasons. In their 1995 study of sport, society and sectarianism, Bairner and Sugden contended: 'Even those people who argue that sport and politics should not mix are forced to admit that in various circumstances the playing of sport can be adversely affected by external political considerations.' They concluded that 'sport can be an integral element in the creation and exacerbation of political conflict'.[64] Similarly, in the Irish context, R.V. Comerford argues that 'developments in Irish sport in the 1880s cannot be understood in terms of individual initiatives divorced from political and ideological pressures'.[65] The Land War, as already noted, created political and social chasms that affected hunting. Similarly, golf was a sport that could attract odium for both political and social reasons and sometimes it is difficult to separate one from the other.

The attacks by suffragettes on golf clubs and sometimes golfers in Britain and Ireland were politically motivated. Because golf clubs were so closely associated with the political fraternity, the Women's Social and Political Union (WSPU)

pluperfect respectability', pp 20, 22. **61** *Anglo-Celt*, 22 Nov. 1913; on this period in Monaghan history, see Terence Dooley, *The Irish revolution: Monaghan* (Dublin, 2017). **62** Grant Jarvie and I.A. Reid, 'Sport, nationalism and culture in Scotland', *Sports History*, 19:1 (1999), p. 119. **63** David White and Howard Jacobs, *Portrait of a golf club: Edmondstown 1944–2014* (Dublin, 2014). **64** Alan Bairner and John Sugden, *Sport, sectarianism and society in a divided Ireland* (London, 1995), p. 1.

regarded them as strategic targets to gain public attention in their struggle for votes for women.[66] In September 1912, when prime minister H.H. Asquith was playing the links course at Dornoch, he was interrupted by two suffragettes who warned him that 'You will be answerable for what happens to Mrs Leigh', a reference to the suffragette Mary Leigh, who was on hunger strike in a Dublin prison. In 1913, the wife of the Irish chief secretary (Augustine Birrell) 'hit a male suffragette (who was pouncing on her Augustine) with an umbrella on the head'.[67] In 1913, members of the WSPU burned down Killarney golf pavilion. The following year, the unionist editor of the *Belfast News-Letter* 'was assaulted by a suffragette' after he 'had urged golfers to take the law into their own hands if they were attacked by suffragettes'.[68] In May 1914, five greens on the Knock golf club near Belfast were damaged: up to eleven holes were crudely dug on them by someone using a large table knife. Weed killer was used on the grass. Suffragette material, including postcards calling for the vote for women, were found in the vicinity.

Golf and the preeminent nationalist sports organization, the Gaelic Athletic Association, took root and flowered during the extended revolutionary period in Ireland, 1879–1923. For different reasons, revolution impacted upon them in different ways. Historians have long argued that the GAA was pivotal to the revolutionary movement.[69] On several occasions, it banned its members from playing 'foreign games' including rugby, soccer and cricket. Golf was not one of them. Ronald Quinault makes the point that 'Golf was not favoured by the Gaelic revivalists because it was not an ancient Irish game.'[70] However, neither was cricket an ancient Irish game. Indeed, it was enjoyed by very many 'Gaels', including one of the founding fathers of the GAA, Michael Cusack. In Tipperary in the 1870s, it was even regarded as 'a republican sport'.[71] Yet, it was banned, and golf was not, probably because cricket facilitated the working-class man in Ireland in a way golf did not and the latter was, therefore, not seen as a threat to the anglicization of GAA membership. When the first Tailteann Games – 'Ireland's most significant contribution to nationalist invention in the area of sport …, inspired by the *Aonach Tailten* of medieval times'[72] – went ahead in independent Ireland in 1924, golf was one of the games included despite the misgivings of some GAA officials about 'shoneen games'.[73]

However, during the revolutionary period, the IRA, on occasion, singled out golf clubs or members for attention. There were political motivations in that

**65** Comerford, *Ireland*, p. 217; on the wider history of sport in Ireland, see Hunt, *Sport and society in Victorian Ireland*; William Murphy, 'Associational life, leisure and identity since 1740', Eugenio Biagini and Mary E. Daly (eds), *The Cambridge social history of modern Ireland* (Cambridge, 2017), pp 383–402; Paul Rousse, *Sport and Ireland: a history* (Oxford, 2015). **66** Quinault, 'Golf and Edwardian politics', pp 203–4. **67** Ibid., p. 204. **68** Ibid. **69** Recent publications include, Gearóid Ó Tuathaigh (ed.), *The GAA and revolution in Ireland, 1913–1923* (Cork, 2015). **70** Quinault, 'Golf and Edwardian politics', p. 204. **71** Comerford, *Ireland*, p. 214. **72** Ibid., p. 225. **73** Marcus de Búrca, *The GAA: a history* clubs were regarded as bastions of the old establishment and their members incurred some suspicion, but there may also have been class reasons, spurred by the resentment of those who were disappointed in what the revolution failed to deliver. There were some separatists who denounced golfers as 'snobocrats', men and women of 'alien tendencies'.[74] In November 1921, during the Anglo-Irish treaty negotiations, a report in the *Donegal Democrat* concluded: 'It is a poor excuse when smarting under criticism to say that golf is a Scottish game of Irish extraction'; the 'democracy of the game exists only in the imagination; not a game associated with patriotic values'.[75] Certainly, as Roisín Higgins points out, holders of office under the British administration were all 'very heavily represented in the golf clubs in Ireland'.[76] She also could have added the remnants of the Irish aristocracy and gentry. In the pre-war and war years, the blatantly unionist political activities of northern golf clubs alienated nationalists. In 1914, an attempt to raise a 'Sports Battalion' from the UVF received an enthusiastic welcome from the GUI.[77] During the Great War, several northern golf clubs organized fundraisers for the UVF Patriotic Fund to support prisoners of war.[78] In the period from July to October 1915, sixteen clubs provided around thirty days entertainment to wounded soldiers.[79] Further south, the grounds of the Royal Dublin Golf Club were temporarily commandeered and used for training young recruits. Over twenty fundraising events relating to the war effort were organized there between 1915 and 1918.[80] Many golf clubs, therefore, aligned their sympathies with the empire.

This meant that with the outbreak of the War of Independence social and political chasms were thrown into sharp relief. In May 1921, the pavilion of the Douglas Golf Club in Cork was destroyed during a period of intense destruction of property belonging to loyalists.[81] Michael Murphy, IRA leader in Cork, claimed that the burning of Douglas was because it was 'a regular den of imperialists'.[82] Willie Walsh, an IRA farm labourer from Clare, assisted in the burning of the golf pavilion at Athenry, 'which the military were using'.[83] (Pointing out that he was a farm labourer may be revealing.) In July 1921, Con Leddy 'decided to stage an attack on any British officers found on the golf links at Fermoy' in Cork.[84] In Tralee, on 15 April 1921, Major McKinnon of the Auxiliaries, blamed for the deaths of two local IRA men, was shot dead in the local golf club.[85] Peter Graham, a suspected spy, was executed on Killiney golf

(Dublin, 1999), p. 132. 74 *Donegal Democrat*, 11 Nov. 1921. 75 Ibid. 76 Higgins, 'The hallmark of pluperfect respectability'. 77 Neal Garnham, *Association football and society in pre-partition Ireland* (Belfast, 2004), p. 188. 78 *Belfast News-Letter*, 12 June 1916, 3 Apr. 1917; *Irish Times*, 19 Aug. 1916. 79 *Irish Times*, 18 Oct. 1915. 80 *The Times history* (London, 1917), xii, p. 427. 81 *Southern Star*, 25 May 1921; James S. Donnelly Jnr, 'Big house burnings in County Cork during the Irish revolution, 1920–21', *Éire-Ireland*, 47:3–4 (Fall/Winter 2012), pp 141–97. 82 Statement of Michael Murphy, Bureau of Military History, WS 1547. 83 IRA pension application of Willie Walshe, WMSP34REF9731 williamwalsh.pdf, 11 July 2018. 84 Con Leddy, WS 756. 85 Michael O'Leary, WS 1167.

links.[86] William Keane spent a month at a golf club in Waterford waiting for 'one of the worst blackguards', an officer in the Devonshires named Veo. He never turned up and Keane wondered afterwards who had 'tipped him off', his obvious insinuation being that the informer was a member of the club.[87] In Kilkenny, the IRA instructed Daniel Stapleton 'to take on intelligence work' in the golf club in which he worked since some of the locally stationed military officers played there, and it was thought that 'in the course of conversation at any time in the clubhouse, they might drop a hint as to intended operations'.[88] There was by no means any co-ordinated IRA policy to attack golf courses or players, and it would be foolish to exaggerate otherwise; but there were enough isolated incidents to suggest that there existed a variety of resentments – social, political and cultural – towards golf clubs and their members.

## CONCLUSION

In 1902, the player J.H. Taylor, who, along with Harry Vardon and James Braid, dominated British golf in the 1890s (and between them designed several golf courses in Ireland including Howth in Dublin, Mullingar in Westmeath and Dunfanaghy in Donegal), wrote: 'Irish turf is like velvet in its texture and the very finest putting greens in the world are to be found there. This is only what one might expect from the great climactic influences that are at work all the year round.'[89] Taylor prophetically saw the day when 'tourists will cross the Irish Sea – not for the mountains, the lsles or the fishing, but for the golf'.[90] Over a century later, in 2013, Fáilte Ireland estimated that 163,000 golf visitors would come to Ireland that year and spend in the region of €200 million.[91] In 2013, Ireland's preeminent golf tournament, the Irish Open, was played at Carton House in Kildare, on a controversially modified eighteenth-century demesne, which preservationists regarded as a desecration of an historic landscape.[92] The Mallaghan family, who then owned Carton, saw it differently; the development was part of the historical evolution of a country-house landscape.

In 1762, James, 1st duke of Leinster, is alleged to have invited Capability Brown to design the demesne at Carton, but the latter refused because, he said, 'he had not yet finished England'.[93] The duke and his wife, Emily, proceeded

**86** P.J. Brennan, WS 1773. **87** William Keane, WS 1023. **88** Daniel Stapleton, WS 1208. **89** John Redmond, *The book of Irish golf* (Dublin, 1997), p. 50. **90** Ibid., p. 50. **91** *Irish Examiner*, 13 May 2013; Fáilte Ireland, 'New Fáilte Ireland research shows golf to the fore in delivering tourism revenue', http://www.failteireland.ie/Footer/ Media-Centre/New-Failte-Ireland-research-shows-golf-to-the-fore.aspx, 20 Aug. 2018. **92** Robert O'Byrne, 'Not just glorified villas', *Irish Times*, 16 July 2011; Terence Dooley, 'The FitzGeralds: a survey history' in Terence Dooley et al. (eds), *Aspects of Irish aristocratic life: essays on the FitzGeralds and Carton House* (Dublin, 2014), pp 29–31. **93** Robert O'Byrne, 'Capability Brown, garden genius', *Irish Times*, 21 May 2011; Jane Brown Chatto Eindus, *The omnipotent magician:*

7.3 Eighteenth hole on Montgomerie course at Carton, with boathouse in the background. Courtesy of Conor Mallaghan.

with their own design, which resulted in the obliteration of any remnants of the sixteenth-century formal Italianate landscape, in favour of the 'Brownification' of the demesne. Changing trends and fashions had resulted in this evolution of the landscape. In the twentieth century, after Carton was lost to the Leinsters, evidence of the eighteenth-century landscape was almost erased by the encroachment and suffocation of nature during decades of neglect. One of Ireland's leading landscape historians, Arnold Horner, has argued that the installation of the golf courses actually brought back 'the great vistas' that had been lost.[94] Interestingly, at the height of the Carton controversy, no one pointed out that in the early days of golf in Ireland many of the aristocracy had volunteered their demesnes as golf courses.

*Lancelot 'Capability' Brown, 1716–1783* (London, 2011); Terence Dooley and Conor Mallaghan, *Carton: an illustrated history* (Celbridge, 2006). 94 Arnold Horner, 'Creating a landscape: Carton and its setting' in Dooley et al. (eds), *Aspects of Irish aristocratic life*, pp 90–1.

The courses at Carton would undoubtedly have appealed to J.H. Taylor, as well as to the earliest golf architects and playing enthusiasts, such as Arthur Balfour, who had craved such 'a classic parkland experience which meanders through acres of glorious pastures, ancient woodland and skirts the banks of the River Rye', in an environment where nature was in unison with the golfer.[95] Carton is just one of many great demesnes that have gone the same way; others include Adare, Ashford, Castlemartyr, Dromoland, Farnham, the K Club (Straffan), Lough Erne, Massereene and Mount Juliet. Christopher Ridgway points out that 'For many people the words "Golf Course", "hotel" and "country house" spark an almost irrational (although in many cases sadly justifiable) degree of fear and loathing.'[96] But, he argues, this need not always be the case; at Carton, for example: 'These courses did not require extensive excavation and reshaping of the parkland, which had always been characterised by vales and slopes of varying steepness – ideal terrain for golfers.'[97] In all of the above cases, the motivation for redesigning these demesnes was no different to that which stirred Irish aristocrats a hundred years and more before: the prospect that some financial advantage might accrue to help in the sustainability of their Big Houses.[98]

**95** Northumbria Golf Breaks, 'Carton House, O'Meara and Montgomerie golf courses', http://www.golfnorthumbria.com/hotels-courses/ireland/carton-house-omeara-montgomerie-golf-courses, accessed on 19 Sept. 2018. **96** Christopher Ridgway, 'The FitzGerald legacy' in Dooley et al. (eds), *Aspects of Irish aristocratic life*, p. 225. **97** Ibid. **98** On the subject of decline, see Terence Dooley, *The decline of the Big House in Ireland* (Dublin, 2001); and Olwen Purdue, *The Big House in the north of Ireland: land, power and social elites* (Dublin, 2009).

# Harry Worcester Smith and the Westmeath Hunt: a curious experiment

EUGENE DUNNE

On Friday 16 August 1912, Harry Worcester Smith, aged 46, of Worcester, Massachusetts, disembarked from the City of Dublin Steam Packet Company ship *Carlow*, which had arrived at the North Wall, Dublin from Liverpool. His arrival created quite a scene.[1] Smith had sailed from New York to Liverpool on the *Lusitania*, while his 19-year-old son Crompton, named after his wife's family – she was Mildred Mary Crompton (1870–1954) – and a personal staff of seven African-Americans had sailed on another ship.[2] In addition to seven tons of luggage, Smith also brought seventeen horses, seven ponies, a gamecock, three American-type buggies, a small trap and a yellow motor car. When everything had been loaded onto a specially requisitioned train to convey them to Mullingar, it was reported that the spectacle could easily have been mistaken for a travelling circus.[3] Prior to leaving the United States, Smith had shipped his pack of foxhounds, known as 'the Grafton Hounds', to England. The pack had been named after the town in Worcester County, Massachusetts, where Smith resided.[4] They had already spent six months quarantined in America and on arrival in England had again been placed in quarantine, where they would remain for a further three months.[5]

In June 1911, when Smith had been chosen as master of the Westmeath Hunt it was agreed that he would hold the position for two years.[6] The Westmeath Hunt had previously appointed English gentlemen, most of whom had some form of connection with the county, but this was the first time an American had been appointed to the position of master of a hunt anywhere in the United Kingdom.[7] Unfortunately, no records seem to survive showing why the Westmeath Hunt went to the extreme of appointing Smith, nor do local newspapers enlighten. However, Smith had wealthy credentials and American social respectability and he was an avid and, in many respects, pioneering enthusiast of fox hunting in the USA. For years, Smith had advocated the American-bred hound and championed the breed at every opportunity. In

1 *Freeman's Journal*, 17 Aug. 1912. 2 Harry Worcester Smith, *A sporting tour through Ireland, England, Wales and France* (Columbia, 1925), i, p. 1. 3 *Freeman's Journal*, 17 Aug. 1912. 4 A. Henry Higginson and Julian Ingersoll Chamberlain, *The hunts of the United States and Canada* (Boston, 1908), pp 43–7. 5 *Irish Independent*, 26 Aug. 1912. 6 *Connacht Telegraph*, 24 Aug. 1912. 7 Samuel A. Eliot, *Biographical history of Massachusetts* (Boston,

January 1905, Henry Higginson, an MFH in America, in a letter to a sporting publication, disparaged American-bred hounds as being inferior to the English breed. Higginson was prepared to put his money where his mouth was, and challenged Smith to dispute his claim. Each man agreed to put up $1,000 for a winner-take-all prize for a contest to determine which breed of hound was best equipped to hunt the fox in America. Sporting magazines such as the *Rider and Driver* and the *Sportsmen's Review* reported on the contest, as did the *New York Tribune* and the wider American press.[8] At the end of the contest, which began on 1 November 1905 and lasted a week, the judges declared Smith's hounds the winner. Smith took this as complete vindication of his opinion that the American hound was the best animal for hunting the red fox in America.[9] The contest had the effect of raising the profile of fox hunting in Virginia. It is likely that coming to Ireland provided Smith with an opportunity to further vindicate his claims.

Harry Worcester Smith had been born on Elm Street, Worcester, on 19 November 1865 to Charles (1828–83) and Josephine (née McCurdy) Worcester Smith. He was educated at Worcester High School, Lowell School of Design, Chemnitz Technical School in Germany, Glasgow School of Design in Scotland and Bradford Technical School in England.[10] Smith began his business career at the Crompton Loom Works. After he left that company he founded the Wachusett Mills and was its president for eighteen years. He perfected more than thirty patents on 'automatic colour weaving, which revolutionized the manufacture of ginghams, or drop box fabrics, in the United States and Europe'. Smith brought about the merger of Crompton Loom Works and the L.J. Knowles and Brother Company to form Crompton and Knowles Loom Works, which became the foremost manufacturers of weaving machinery in the world. As a result, Smith became an extremely wealthy man.[11]

Smith took up business and sport with equal success. He became an expert horseman, winning many competitions, and was regarded as one of the leading persons in American fox hunting; he had served as master of most of the leading hunts in the eastern United States, had established the Grafton Country Club and was master of the Grafton Hounds in Massachusetts, and master of the American Foxhounds Association. He was also a well-known horse and foxhound breeder and a leading judge at all the major shows in the eastern United States and Canada. Smith also won numerous cups and trophies for steeplechasing. As a gentleman rider who raced against leading amateur and professional jockeys, Smith never had a wager on himself or allowed his stable connections to do so.[12]

1917), vii, pp 383–8. 8 See, for example, *Times Dispatch*, 8 Mar. 1905; the full story has been told in Martha Wolfe, *The great hound match of 1905: Alexander Henry Higginson, Harry Worcester Smith and the rise of Virginia Hunt country* (Guilford, CT, 2016). 9 *Times Despatch*, 15 Nov. 1905. 10 Ibid. 11 *Irish Times*, 28 Sept. 1912. 12 Eliot, *Massachusetts*, pp 383–8.

8.1 and 8.2 Harry Worcester Smith.

So how did this gentleman end up in County Westmeath? In a newspaper interview in 1912, Smith stated that he had been looking forward for many years to coming to Ireland to hunt, having heard glowing reports from other Americans.[13] He had hunted in England in the past, particularly in Leicestershire, but this was his first visit to Ireland.

In his largely forgotten memoirs, first published in 1925, Smith stated that he had accepted the position of master on the understanding that he could hunt his American hounds in those parts of the county not being hunted by the Westmeath pack.[14] In 1912, Westmeath had large tracts of land that were ideal for fox hunting.[15] The west of the county had open pastures, stone walls, narrow banks and gorse cover with almost no woodland, while the north-west was wilder with extensive woodland. The east of the county was largely unsuitable for hunting containing large areas of bog.[16]

The Westmeath Hunt was one of the oldest in Ireland, with records dating back to 1738. The leading aristocratic and landed families in the county had been involved in hunting for generations, initially with each family supporting its own pack of hounds. In 1854, the hunting fraternity formed a committee, raised funds and formally established the Westmeath Hunt Club.[17] At various times, members of all the leading families in the county had held the position of master, including lords Longford and Greville, as well as baronets Levinge, Chapman and Nugent. The hunt ball held every spring was one of the social highlights of the landed elite's social calendar. Smith succeeded Frank Barbour, who had been master from 1908 to 1912. Barbour, an Englishman, had moved to Ireland in the early 1900s, where he made a significant contribution to local point-to-point horse racing. The Barbour Cup, which he donated to the Westmeath Hunt, is still competed for today.

On Tuesday 20 August, four days after his arrival, Smith began to test his horses and groomsmen over the Westmeath countryside. Under the guidance of two local huntsmen and with his son acting as whipper-in, Smith set out at the head of six of his string of horses, four of which were ridden by his African-American servants, much to the curiosity of the local people. Unfortunately the outing did not quite go to plan. Smith rode in front, successfully negotiating the many and varied jumping obstacles, but it was not long before two of the African-American riders came to grief, with one of them being unceremoniously dumped in a ditch. However, despite these mishaps the general opinion was that the American horses managed to cope with the fences and it was felt they would be able to hold their own with Irish hunters once they had got used to the terrain.[18] When asked how his American hunters were coping with the Westmeath ditches, Smith answered:

13 *Sunday Independent*, 15 Sept. 1912. 14 Smith, *A sporting tour*, i, pp vi–ix. 15 Dease, *Westmeath hunt*, i, pp 2–3. 16 Smith, *A sporting tour*, i, p. 85. 17 Dease, *Westmeath hunt*, i, p. 15. 18 *Westmeath Guardian*, 23 Aug. 1912.

8.3 Smith and the Westmeath Hounds at Knockdrin Castle.

8.4 Five of Smith's African-American servants: Norman Brooks, Dolph Wheeler, Sam Webster, Wiley Thrash, Joe Thomas.

> Right well, as I find my coloured servants have no difficulty in getting over them, and are all fine horsemen. These niggers are exceptionally light-handed in guiding a horse and possess a wonderful love for their mounts.[19]

Following his arrival in Mullingar, Smith stayed in temporary accommodation for a number of weeks before taking up residence in Portloman House, an eighteenth-century mansion on the shores of Lough Owel, about two miles north-west of Mullingar. The house, unoccupied for the previous twenty years, was formerly the home of the De Blaquiere baronets and had once hosted the duke of Wellington.[20] Smith negotiated an agreement with the agent that in return for carrying out some minor repairs to make the house habitable he could reside in it rent-free. The walled garden was also an ideal place to keep his hounds.[21]

From the outset, Smith began to interact with the aristocratic and gentry families of the county, dining during his first week with George Arthur Boyd-Rochfort (who would later win a VC in the First World War) and his wife Olivia, in their mansion at Middleton Park, near Castletowngeoghegan. A few days later, he met Sir Richard Levinge and Lord Longford and was invited to visit both their homes at Knockdrin and Pakenham Hall (now Tullynally), anytime he was hunting in the area.[22] A short time later, when visiting the Dublin Horse Show, he met another Westmeath aristocrat, Lord Castlemaine of Moydrum Castle, who welcomed him to Ireland and wished him an enjoyable season.[23] Smith was acutely aware of the social connections his new position promised, a major bonus to an American seeking gentrification; he later noted in his memoirs: 'A Master of Hounds is looked upon as a leader of sport in the community, and his social position is one which affords him every opportunity to mingle with the nobles and gentry.'[24]

Each year, prior to the commencement of the fox-hunting season in Westmeath, cub-hunting was practised. The purpose was threefold: to train the hounds to hunt and kill; to teach the hounds to hunt foxes only; and to cull weaker young foxes. On 16 September 1912, the opening event took place at Knockdrin Castle, the home of Sir Richard Levinge. On the first hunt, a cub gave Smith and his fellow hunters a merry chase for thirty minutes across the Knockdrin estate before it successfully went to ground. There followed hunts at Ballinagall, adjacent to Knockdrin, where a number of cubs were not so fortunate; Lord Longford's Pakenham Hall; Donore, the home of Sir Walter Nugent;[25] and Clonhugh, the residence of Lord Greville, where it was reported

**19** *Irish Times*, 30 Sept. 1912. **20** John Charles Lyons, *The grand juries of the county of Westmeath from the year 1727 to the year 1853* (Mullingar, 1853), ii, pp 60–4; see also *Westmeath Guardian*, 25 Oct. 1912; and *Westmeath Examiner*, 2 Nov. 1912. **21** Smith, *A sporting tour*, i, pp 37–8. **22** Ibid., pp 6–16. **23** Ibid., pp 18–23. **24** Ibid., p. 47. **25** Ibid., pp 42–7.

that cubs were in plentiful supply and good runs enjoyed.[26] It was not long before Smith had hunted on every landed estate in north Westmeath and dined in most of the surviving Big Houses. At one hunt on the Smythe estate at Barbavilla near the village of Drumcree, Smith was drawn in admiration to the similarity between himself and Lord Longford: both of them had a reputation as hard riders who feared nothing. Smith was also particularly taken by the number of ladies who partook in hunting in Ireland.[27]

Cub hunting continued until the hunting season opened in Westmeath around 12 November, lasting until the hunt races at Mullingar the following April.[28] During the season, the hunt usually met between four and six days each week. Prior to a hunt, it was customary for the master to write to the owner of an estate to ascertain when it would be convenient for him to facilitate the hunt on his property. The proprietor would reply offering a date, so that when the hunt arrived his cattle and horses would be penned and stabled.[29] However, Smith was largely unfortunate in that the summer of 1912 saw a series of unforeseen events that jeopardized his tenure as master. On 30 June 1912, an outbreak of foot-and-mouth disease was reported at Swords in County Dublin. It was the first case of the disease in Ireland for more than twenty-eight years.[30] It soon spread, with further outbreaks in Meath, Fermanagh, Kildare and Wicklow during August and September. However, the most serious outbreak occurred in Westmeath, at Mullingar. Between 18 October and 7 November there were 37 reported cases in the rural environs of the town. This resulted in the slaughter of 769 animals.[31] The government placed an immediate ban on the movement of animals in the affected areas. On 23 October, in an effort to curtail the spread of the disease, Smith suspended all hunting activities for the duration of the government restrictions.[32] Ironically, within days of the announcement he received notification that his hounds had been released from quarantine in England.

Not to be deterred, Smith sought sport further afield. Many of the masters of neighbouring packs took pity on him having come from America and invited him to hunt with them. His first invitation came from the Limerick Hunt and this was soon followed by one from Tipperary. Limerick was his first experience of hunting a fox in Ireland as he had only hunted cubs in Westmeath. While in Limerick he was invited to hunt with the Kerry Beagles and following his visit to Tipperary he went on to hunt with the Kilkenny, East Kilkenny and Queen's County hunts.[33] While the hunting in Limerick was good, Tipperary proved less enjoyable, not least because a fall while jumping a stream resulted in him injuring

**26** *Irish Times*, 30 Sept. 1912. **27** Smith, *A sporting tour*, i, pp 87–96. **28** *Westmeath Examiner*, 6 Feb. 1926. **29** Smith, *A sporting tour*, i, p. 49. **30** *Department of Agriculture and Technical Instruction for Ireland: report on foot and mouth disease in Ireland in the year 1912* [Cd.7103], HC 1914, xii, 793. **31** Ibid. **32** *Irish Independent*, 23 Oct. 1912; *Department of Agriculture and Technical Instruction for Ireland: report on foot and mouth disease in Ireland in the year 1912* [Cd.7103] HC 1914, xii, 793. **33** Smith, *A sporting tour*, i, pp 83–97.

his ankle.[34] After a short recuperation period, two further falls on the same day while hunting in Kilkenny resulted in a number of cracked ribs, as well as an aggravation of the ankle injury. After five weeks travelling from hunt to hunt, the foot-and-mouth restrictions were reduced to a five-mile radius around Mullingar, and Smith returned to Westmeath.[35] Even if it had not been ideal, Smith had still socialized with the leading landed families of the midlands, and had stayed as a guest in some of the grandest mansions of the area, such as Rockbarton House in Limerick, Rochestown, Lakefield and Grove House in Tipperary, and Birchfield, New Park, Castlecomer, Woodstock and Uppercourt in Kilkenny. Furthermore, during this time he also visited Truro in Cornwall and spent a few days hunting with the Four Burrow Hounds.[36]

Upon his return to Westmeath in early December 1912, Smith called a meeting of the hunt committee, where it was decided to resume hunting outside the Mullingar area of restriction.[37] It was not until 27 January 1913 that the final order lifting all restrictions came to an end.[38] In the meantime, the committee also decided that the American and Westmeath packs would not hunt together, thus confirming the original decision that the American hounds could not hunt in the Mullingar area unless by invitation of a landowner. This dismayed Smith, who considered his American hounds to be as good, if not better, than the Westmeath hounds; he considered the countryside around Moate to be an 'impossible district'.[39] Later in December, Smith received an invitation from a sympathetic Lord Longford to hunt in the Mullingar area, which would give the American hounds their first hunt in Ireland. Unfortunately, it and a subsequent second hunt proved to be abject failures as the inexperienced hounds seemed more interested in chasing rabbits.[40] Further catastrophe was to follow: on 23 December, while driving near Moate, Smith ran into a herd of cattle that was being driven on the road, injuring one heifer so badly that it had to be put down. It was alleged that Smith had been driving on the wrong side of the road (an obvious claim that he had been careless in forgetting where he was), and even though he refuted this, a decree for £9 with £1 expenses was awarded against him in January 1913 at the Mullingar quarter sessions.[41]

Smith spent the rest of the Christmas of 1912 at Middleton Park, home of the Boyd-Rochfort family, where he engaged in that other popular pastime of the landed gentry: shooting.[42] Fox hunting resumed on 26 December, and continued with several meets each week during January 1913 in various parts of the county, which brought Smith on visits to other country houses including Jamestown Court and Baronston House.[43] The end of January saw the beginning of the Hunt Ball season and Smith, in his role as master of the Westmeath, attended

34 Ibid., p. 134. 35 Ibid., pp 174–5. 36 Ibid., p. 293. 37 Ibid., p. 176. 38 *Times*, 25 Jan. 1913. 39 Smith, *A sporting tour*, i, p. ix. 40 Ibid., i, pp 196–7. 41 *Irish Independent*, 31 Jan. 1913. 42 Smith, *A sporting tour*, i, p. 204. 43 Ibid., ii, pp 219, 224.

the ball of the neighbouring hunt, the Ballymacads in County Meath, which was held in Loughcrew House, the home of the Naper family.[44]

In early February 1913, Smith tendered his resignation as master, to take effect from the end of the hunting season, and this was accepted by the committee.[45] However, tragedy struck the hunt on 24 February with the accidental death of the second whip, Alfred Curtis of Crompton, Somerset, who was killed when he fell from his horse on the road near Mullingar. He died in Smith's motor car without regaining consciousness, while being driven to the county infirmary.[46]

In mid-March, Smith took a break from Ireland and travelled to Itton Court near Chepstow, Monmouthshire, home of Edward Curre, where he hunted for several days.[47] Following a few days in London, he returned to Mullingar. As the hunting season was reaching its conclusion, a series of point-to-point races organized by the hunt committee were held. They were officiated over by stewards who included Lord Longford, his brother the Hon. Edward Pakenham, Sir Walter Nugent and Smith himself.[48] Despite their waning fortunes and the sales of their estates that had been taking place under the 1903 and 1909 Land Acts, the old gentry and aristocracy retained a grip on local and national horse racing.

Harry Worcester Smith's term as master of the Westmeath Hunt ended on Monday 31 March, three days after he had dined with the Levinges at Knockdrin and then attended the Westmeath Hunt Ball held in the newly built County Hall in Mullingar.[49] The season closed with a meeting at Castletown-geoghegan.[50] Smith did not bring his American hounds back home; instead he gifted them to an American friend who was master of the Pau Hunt in France.[51] He also sold the contents of Portloman House at auction, as well as two of the buggies and some of his horses.[52]

Why did Smith step down after only one season as master? In his letter of resignation, he stated that his reasons were entirely related to the dreadful Irish climatic conditions, pointing out that it had rained on eighty-seven out of ninety-one days during the season.[53] It does not seem to have been an exaggeration: the records confirm that the summer of 1912 was the third wettest since 1850, while the spring of 1913 was the wettest on record.[54] However, it is clear that there were other factors involved in his decision. Undoubtedly, the outbreak of foot-and-mouth disease had played a major part, with hunting suspended, resulting in the loss of three months at the height of the season. The

44 Ibid., p. 270. 45 *Evening Herald*, 8 Feb. 1913. 46 *Irish Times*, 26 Feb. 1913. 47 Smith, *A sporting tour*, ii, p. 312. 48 Ibid., p. 329. 49 *Westmeath Examiner*, 5 Apr. 1913. 50 *Freeman's Journal*, 31 Mar. 1913. 51 Smith, *A sporting tour*, ii, p. 348. 52 *Irish Times*, 19 Mar., 25 Apr. 1913. 53 Smith, *A sporting tour*, ii, p. 398. 54 Simon Noone, 'Development and analysis of a homogeneous long-term precipitation network (1850–2015) and assessment of historic droughts for the island of Ireland' (PhD, NUI Maynooth, 2016), p. 66.

decision of the hunt committee to restrict his American hounds, who clearly struggled to adjust to Irish hunting conditions, must also have influenced his decision. Perhaps the Irish terrain did not suit his style of riding, as by his own admission he had fallen more than thirty times during his time in Ireland.[55] His dominant and excessively competitive personality, and aggressive style of riding, may not have endeared him to the hunting fraternity; pointedly, there was no going-away party or formal presentation to mark his tenure. In assessing his term as master, the *Telegraph* newspaper remarked: 'Harry Worcester Smith, Master of the Westmeath, came over with the reputation as a hard rider. That puts it mildly; he is an abnormally hard rider.'[56] The local *Westmeath Guardian* newspaper was no less forgiving: 'Mr H.W. Smith had come over with a reputation of being a hard rider and an experienced master of hounds. The former qualification was abnormally borne out, as his idea seemed to be to compete with any rider, irrespective of the position of the pack, and to take little interest in the many matters which fall within the duty of the Master of Foxhounds in the British Isles.'[57] In relation to the Grafton Hounds, the same newspaper commented: 'Whatever successes may have attended his American hounds in pursuit of large game in their own country, their attempt to hunt a fox in Ireland was a complete failure.'[58] Smith excused their poor performance on the fact that they had been kept in quarantine for six months in the United States and a further three months in London, which meant the younger dogs had spent half their lives in quarantine.[59]

Smith had possibly arrived in Ireland with pre-conceived ideas of what the role of master would entail. It soon became apparent that these perceptions were in contrast to the expectations of the hunt committee. This is borne out to some extent by the *Westmeath Guardian*'s remarks. Other than actively participating in hunting, Smith took little interest in the other responsibilities and duties that were expected of the master of the hunt. In other words, he failed to give of the time and energy, and possibly even the finances, that had been expected of him in an administrative capacity. He may have regarded these duties as being beneath his standing, or perhaps the difference between being master in America and Ireland had not been explicitly and sufficiently explained to him.

However, the opportunity of playing the part of a self-styled country squire or 'lord of the manor', which entailed socializing and interacting with members of the local gentry and aristocracy, was clearly something that appealed to Smith. There are some similarities between Smith and other wealthy Americans who purchased large country houses and estates in Ireland: examples include Henry Laughlin, an American millionaire businessman who purchased Castle Hyde, a large country house near Fermoy in County Cork in 1931; Professor Arthur

55 Smith, *A sporting tour*, i, p. 210. 56 Eliot, *Massachusetts*, vii, pp 383–8. 57 *Westmeath Guardian*, 9 May 1913. 58 Ibid. 59 Smith, *A sporting tour*, i, p. ix.

Kingsley Porter of Harvard University, who purchased Glenveagh Castle in County Donegal in 1929; and Henry McIlhenny, who acquired the same house in 1933 following Porter's death.[60] According to Henry Laughlin's daughter, he liked to think of himself as a 'lord of the manor', which, despite his wealth, was something he could never achieve in the United States. In performing the role, Laughlin and his family entertained leading members of Boston and east coast American society for decades.[61] The desire to emulate members of the landed gentry was a craving that many could not resist.

In the spring of 1913, Harry Worcester Smith returned to his Lordvale estate in Grafton, Massachusetts, where he and his wife Mildred lived until 1940 (entertaining guests such as former US President Theodore Roosevelt in 1916), when the mansion was destroyed by fire. Smith died on 21 April 1945 aged 79. He never returned to Ireland.[62]

**60** Terence Dooley, *Castle Hyde: the changing fortunes of an Irish country house* (Dublin, 2017), p. 39. **61** Ibid., pp 42–6. **62** *Times*, 23 Apr. 1945. Smith's tenure as master of the Westmeath Hunt did not end the family's sporting connections with Europe. In 1965, his grandson Crompton 'Tommy' Smith (1937–2013) rode Jay Trump to victory in the Aintree Grand National, the first time an American-bred horse or an American jockey had won the famous race; *Irish Times*, 29 Mar. 1982.

# Banishing ennui, blue devils and thoughts of bad potatoes: the country house and sport and leisure during the Great Famine

BRIAN GRIFFIN

In the summer of 1858, two English tourists – Reverend Samuel Reynolds Hole, the vicar of Caunton, in Nottinghamshire, and John Leech, one of *Punch* magazine's illustrators – went on a holiday visit to Ireland. Hole and Leech's experiences and impressions formed the basis of a book about their Irish holiday, which Hole wrote and Leech illustrated. During their stay in Galway, a waiter gave the tourists a distressing account of the impact of the Great Famine on the peasantry of the surrounding countryside a decade earlier, when many had crawled into the city in search of food, their green and yellow faces swollen with hunger. The waiter often found their corpses in a nearby square at morning, with grass stuffed into their mouths in a futile attempt to nourish their starving bodies. Hole wrote movingly that

> In the beautiful land of the merry-hearted, 'all joy was darkened – the mirth of the land was gone'. In the country of song, and dance, and laughter, there was not heard, wherever that Famine came, one note of music, nor one cheerful sound – only the gasp of dying men, and the mourners' melancholy wail.[1]

Hole's characterization of Ireland during the Famine as a land engulfed by a tidal wave of grief, with the sounds of merriment replaced by the sounds of the dying and the wail of those mourning them, speaks volumes about his compassion, but it was, at best, an exaggeration. To Hole, who was not present in Ireland during the catastrophe in the 1840s, it made sense that the prevailing emotion during the Famine should have been one of grief, and that thoughts of amusement should have been far from people's minds. However, it is likely that most contemporaries would have been aware that much of Ireland had been *en fête* for at least one sustained period during the Famine – the visit of Queen Victoria and her husband, Prince Albert, in 1849.

During the visit, thousands of people, rich and poor alike, gave highly enthusiastic receptions to the queen as she passed through the cities of Cork,

1 'An Oxonian' [Samuel Reynolds Hole], *A little tour in Ireland* (London, 1859), p. 47. The internal quotation is based on a passage from the book of Isaiah.

Dublin and Belfast.[2] This instance of widespread public rejoicing during the Famine was neither an exception nor an aberration, but is merely the best-known example of an underexplored subject, that of large numbers of Irish people enjoying themselves at festive or recreational gatherings throughout the catastrophe that overwhelmed the poorest sections of the population.[3] It is estimated that during the course of the Famine around 1 million people died of hunger and diseases such as relapsing fever, typhus, dysentery and cholera, and that another million emigrated from Ireland. Although the Famine affected all areas of the country in varying degrees of severity, its impact was felt most severely by those on the bottom rungs of rural society – the landless labourers and cottier class, whose dependence on the potato was near total. Famine mortality was heaviest to the west of an imaginary line from the cities of Derry to Cork, but no part of the country escaped completely from deaths caused by the Famine.[4] Throughout the course of the disaster, sports and other recreations continued to be enjoyed by considerable numbers of people. In the countryside, the landed estate was the locus of much of this recreational activity. Throughout the Famine, sports that were confined mainly to the landed elite, such as hunting (especially fox hunting), greyhound coursing, archery and sailing regattas enlivened the social round of the upper echelons of rural society.[5] However, those lower down the social scale were not entirely excluded from these sports – this was particularly the case with sailing regattas, which proved a popular attraction to a much wider section of Irish society than just its landed elite. Landlords and tenants also engaged in joint celebrations to mark important milestones in the lives of landed estates, such as the coming of age of a landlord's son, marriages of landlords or members of their immediate family and harvest home festivities. While the Great Famine was undoubtedly a period of great suffering for a large proportion of Ireland's population, there is evidence that points to a vibrant recreational life on many landed estates.

2 James H. Murphy, *Abject loyalty: nationalism and monarchy in Ireland during the reign of Queen Victoria* (Cork, 2001), pp 87–99; James Loughlin, 'Allegiance and illusion: Queen Victoria's Irish visit of 1849', *History*, 87:288 (Oct. 2002), pp 491–513. 3 Edmund O'Riordan, '"Every delicacy of the season": conspicuous consumption during the Great Hunger', *History Ireland*, 26:3 (May–June 2018), pp 26–9. 4 There is a sizeable literature on the Famine's national and regional impact. Particularly recommended for detailed discussions of the subject are: James S. Donnelly Jnr, *The land and the people of nineteenth-century Cork: the rural economy and the land question* (London, 1975); Christine Kinealy, *This great calamity: the Irish Famine, 1845–52* (Dublin, 1994); Christine Kinealy and Trevor Parkhill (eds), *The Famine in Ulster* (Belfast, 1997); William Henry, *Famine: Galway's darkest years* (Cork, 2011); Gerard Macatasney, *The dead buried by the dying: the Great Famine in Leitrim* (Dublin, 2014); Ciarán Ó Murchadha, *Figures in a Famine landscape* (London, 2016); and John Crowley, William J. Smyth and Mike Murphy (eds), *Atlas of the Great Irish Famine, 1845–52* (Cork, 2012). 5 Although the focus of this essay is on the sports of the landed elite, it is important to bear in mind that all sections of Irish society, including the very poorest, participated in, or attended, sports events during the Famine years. On this, see Brian Griffin, '"The more sport the merrier, say we": sport in Ireland during the Great Famine', *Irish*

I

In May 1846, a convivial dinner was held in the former music room of Phillip's Hotel, Monaghan, to mark the retirement of A.A. Murray of Loughoona, master of the Monaghan Fox Hounds. In a speech to his fellow huntsmen, Murray acknowledged 'the soothing, care-banishing, entrancing raptures, which may be imagined, but not described, and which music will alone create', before contrasting the respective pleasures to be derived from music and from hunting foxes:

> But what are the inspiring strains of an organ – the martial tone of a military band, or the dulcet tones of a cultivated orchestra, in comparison with the huntsman's horn – the cheer, the heartfelt cheer of excitement and delight, and the thrilling cry of the hounds – (great cheers). They were all well in their way, but I fear will not bear the comparison – (laughter). For look at the effect – mark the maddening influence in both man and beast: – the game once in motion – the hounds settled to their work, and in full cry – what yawning gulf, or what double ditch – what wall, fence, or river can stop the huntsman and his steed's career. Away he dashes – thinking of nothing – fearing nothing, and stopping at nothing. *Ennui*, cares, and blue devils are banished – debts, unpaid bills, and bad potatoes, all forgotten. Could Jul[l]ien and all his band effect this?[6]

According to Murray, the cornopœan of Herman Louis Koenig, the famous contemporary cornetist, could not compare with the horn of Denny Grehan, the Monaghan Hounds' huntsman, while the voices of two of the hunt's dogs, Windsor and Pilot, were more tuneful than those of the Italian tenor Giovanni Battista Rubini, or the bass opera singer Luigi Lablache. Murray's words offer an invaluable insight into fox hunting's appeal for many of the male members of Ireland's landed elite. Edmund O'Riordan suggests that the elite's sports activity during the Famine constituted a form of conspicuous consumption,[7] lavish expenditure designed to maintain or enhance their social prestige. While this is correct to a degree, there was also much more involved. As Murray's speech suggests, hunting was both adventurous and a form of escapism for its devotees. Not only was hunting exciting, it was also addictive,[8] which helps to explain why the dozens of Irish hunts (fox hunts, stag hunts and harriers) held thousands of

*Economic and Social History*, 45:1 (2018), pp 90–114. 6 *Northern Standard*, 23 May 1846. Louis-Antoine Jullien (1812–60), who often performed in Ireland, was an internationally famous composer and conductor. 7 See O'Riordan, 'Conspicuous consumption'. 8 Asenath Nicholson gives a vivid description of hunting's fanatical appeal: 'There is a kind of enchantment, a witchery, hung around an open-air exercise like this, which the more it is practised the more it is loved, till all that tends to elevate the mind and cultivate the best principles of the heart are effaced' in Maureen Murphy (ed.), *Annals of the Famine in Ireland* (Dublin, 1998), p. 123.

meets throughout the Famine. Table 10.1 enumerates the advertised meets of two of these hunts, the County of Galway Hunt, who hunted foxes in south County Galway, and the Ward Union Stag Hounds, who hunted in the east County Dublin and south County Meath region. These two hunts clocked up more than 400 meets between them; although we will never know the true figure of hunt meets for the dozens of other hunts that operated throughout the country, it must surely number several thousand. Such was hunting's apparent ubiquity that, according to O'Riordan, 'during the hunting season it may well have been impossible for paupers to crawl their way to a workhouse or soup kitchen without encountering members of the local hunt on the way to a meet'.[9]

**Table 10.1. Number of advertised meets of two hunts, 1845–50**

| County of Galway Hunt | | Ward Union Stag Hounds | |
|---|---|---|---|
| October 1845–April 1846 | 47 | January–March 1846 | 20[10] |
| October 1846–April 1847 | 44 | November 1846–April 1847 | 40 |
| October 1847–April 1848 | 51 | November 1847–April 1848 | 39 |
| October 1848–April 1849 | 47 | November 1848–March 1849 | 38 |
| October 1849–April 1850 | 50 | November 1849–April 1850 | 43 |
| **Total** | **239** | **Total** | **180** |

*Source*: The 'hunting appointments' sections of the Irish Newspaper Archive online database, October 1845–April 1850.

Hunters documented their enthusiasm for their sport by writing stirring accounts of hunts in the newspapers. One of the most evocative pieces of writing attesting to this enthusiasm was a poem, 'Michaelmas Day, 1847', written by 'A Pink Jacket':

> Hurra! hurra! for the season that's here again,
> Men, horses, hounds are all in prime order.
> Hurra! hurra! Welcome the cheer again,
> When pink jackets sport o'er Tyrawly's gay borders.
> Oh! What are life's pleasures,
> Her joys or her treasures,
> Like sunbeams they pass in worthless disorder –
> Not so with fond 'Tally',
> That cheers through each valley,
> When pink jackets sport o'er Tyrawly's gay borders.
>
> Come, see, mark, all those jovial boys,
> Rushing like tempests, in sportsmanlike order;
> And say, then – where are life's cares, alloys! –

9 O'Riordan, 'Conspicuous consumption', p. 28. 10 No meets advertised October–December 1845.

When pink jackets sport o'er Tyrawly's gay borders.
Then bless me this hunting day,
Jovious and ever gay,
Our men, horses, hounds, turned out in prime order;
Long may they merry be
Happy, and ever free,
And long may pink jackets sport o'er our borders.[11]

Participating in hunts helped to sustain a collective sense of identity among enthusiasts of the chase, which helps to explain hunting's continued popularity throughout the Famine years. The convivial consumption of alcohol was an important aspect of the hunting experience,[12] a feature which William Carleton exaggerated to the point of caricature in his depiction of the profligate sportsman Squire Squander and his hunting friends in *The Squanders of Castle Squander*.[13] Dining together also helped to strengthen hunters' collective bonds,[14] as did annual balls that many hunts held towards the end of the hunting season. The hunt ball was a glittering and exclusive occasion, one of the most important social events of the year,[15] at which hunters and a wide circle of families from the rural elite gathered to socialize, to enjoy a lavish dinner and to dance into the small hours.[16] Although hunting and its ancillary leisure activities were primarily for the enjoyment of the rural elite, several hunts organized popular steeple-chases, some of which featured contests for horses owned by farmers over whose lands the hunts had ridden in the previous season, or horses owned by farmers resident in the same county in which the huntsmen hunted.[17]

11 *Westmeath Independent*, 9 Oct. 1847. 12 An intoxicated horse trainer named Goggin was killed by a fall when riding with the marquis of Waterford's hunt in December 1845. A witness reported that Goggin 'was not, apparently, a Mathewite, as I noticed him early in the hunt a perfect case': *Tipperary Free Press*, 24 Dec. 1845. 13 William Carleton, *The Squanders of Castle Squander*, 2 vols (London, 1852), i, pp 26, 39, 43, 48, 134–5, 210. I would like to thank Dr Melissa Fegan for bringing this source to my attention. 14 *Tipperary Free Press*, 5 Nov. 1845; *Wexford Independent*, 27 Feb. 1847, 28 Mar. 1849; David Thomson and Moyra McGusty (eds), *The Irish journals of Elizabeth Smith, 1850–1850* (Oxford, 1980), p. 246; David Butler, 'The landed classes during the Great Famine' in John Crowley, William J. Smyth and Mike Murphy (eds), *Atlas of the Great Irish Famine* (Cork, 2012), p. 273. The intimate link between hunting and sociability in the pre-Famine and post-Famine periods is discussed by Martyn J. Powell, 'Hunting clubs and societies' in James Kelly and Martyn J. Powell (eds), *Clubs and societies in eighteenth-century Ireland* (Dublin, 2010), pp 399–402; James Kelly, *Sport in Ireland 1600–1840* (Dublin, 2014), pp 146–7; and Tom Hunt, *Sport and society in Victorian Ireland: the case of Westmeath* (Cork, 2007), pp 29–32. 15 Edmund Mahony, *The Galway Blazers: memoirs* (Galway, 1979), p. 6. 16 *King's County Chronicle*, 22 Apr. 1846; *Connaught Telegraph*, 7 Oct. 1846; *Tipperary Free Press*, 2 Dec. 1846; *Waterford News*, 11 May 1849; Pat Bracken, *The growth and development of sport in County Tipperary, 1840–1880* (Cork, 2018), p. 109. 17 Prizes varied from cash to new ploughs. For the examples of the Killultagh (County Antrim), Kilkenny, Limerick, Emo (Queen's Co.) and Waterford Hunt races, see *Northern Whig*, 5 Mar. 1846; *Kilkenny Journal*, 1 Apr. 1848; *Limerick and Clare Chronicle*, 29 Apr. 1848; *Dublin Evening Mail*, 23 Mar. 1849; *Waterford News*, 11 May 1849.

Sailing regattas and archery meets were other country-house sporting activities that provided opportunities for members of the landed elite to engage in competitive sport and friendly social intercourse. Regattas were held on several lakes during the Famine, with the most popular being those that were held on Lough Ree and Lough Derg on the Shannon, Lough Ramor in County Cavan and Lough Erne, County Fermanagh. The races at these regattas consisted of a mixture of rowing contests between gentlemen, other races between professional boatmen and yacht races.[18] The regattas attracted the leading landed families from the surrounding counties, both as spectators and competitors, as well as large numbers of spectators from lower down the social scale. For example, the Lough Derg regatta at Killaloe, County Tipperary, in July 1846, featured a race between six yachts that enthralled rich and poor alike:

> The race, throughout, was well contested, and most exciting, each change in their position being hailed by the cheers of thousands of the country people, whom the regatta had attracted to the beautiful shores of Derry; and the last round, the boats were accompanied all the way from Castle Lough, by crowds running along the lake.

James Spaight's victory received a 'deafening welcome' from his spectating tenantry.[19] The Lough Erne regattas during the Famine also attracted a diverse range of spectators. The regattas may have been organized mainly for the amusement of the landed elite, but clearly they were not the only people present. According to one account of the August 1846 regatta:

> The weather was favourable, warm and pleasant for lookers-on, and innumerable picnic parties availed themselves of it and whirled in countless vehicles to Rossclare, the rendezvous of the boats. This beautiful locality had somewhat the appearance of Donnybrook fair. Pleasant parties squatted here, bivouacked there, and strolled yonder. The shores were lined with crowds and booths – music at every turn, to which the rustics danced and strove to tire each other down.[20]

The highlight of the September 1849 meeting, which was attended by an immense crowd of spectators from all classes of society, was a yacht race between *Wizard*, owned by the regatta commodore, Lord Erne, and *Kelpie*, owned by Paul Dane of Killyhevlin, high sheriff of Fermanagh. When news of *Kelpie*'s victory reached Enniskillen, many of its houses were illuminated and forty or fifty tar barrels were lit in celebration. Another nine or ten were lit at Deane's Killyhevlin seat, 'and fireworks were let off in splendid style. Bonfires blazed on

18 See Ian d'Alton's essay in this volume. 19 *Westmeath Independent*, 1 Aug. 1846. 20 *Saunders's News-Letter*, 8 Aug. 1846.

every hill, and bugles sounded in all directions.'[21] Although regattas attracted interest from a wide spectrum of society, nevertheless it is clear that these events were staged primarily for the enjoyment of the landed elite, as is made apparent by the fact that they always ended with sumptuous dinners and balls that were attended by hundreds of aristocratic and gentry families from the surrounding counties.[22]

Archery was a sport with a more limited appeal during the Famine, being contested or attended on a regular basis mainly by landed families in Meath and Wexford.[23] The Meath Archers, established in 1832, was Ireland's leading archery club. They conducted their sport along what were already well-established lines during the Famine, holding several meets during each season on a rotational basis at members' country estates. At each meet, men and women competed in separate competitions, the men competing for trophies or sweepstake prizes, the women for prizes such as jewellery or ornamental arrows. Competitors and guests were treated to a picnic dinner, and the proceedings were always rounded off with a ball (attended by leading landed families from Meath and neighbouring counties) that ended in the small hours, the music sometimes being provided by a military band.[24] The Wexford Archers were founded in 1845 and held their first competition in 1846. Their activities and membership social profile were similar to those of their fellow toxophilites in Meath.[25] It is possible that the female archers in Wexford were better than their male colleagues, judging from a *Wexford Independent* report of their meeting at Carrigmenan cricket ground in June 1848, which stated that 'Robin Hood and William Tell have disciples among the gentry, and *they* have rivals among the fairer sex, who are keener shots, and beat them hollow.'[26] Archery provided almost the only outlet for women to engage in sport in this period,[27] and it is clear that many women of Meath and Wexford's landed families thoroughly enjoyed this activity during the Famine.

A crucial part of archery's appeal was the sociable mingling of the sexes, but the world of greyhound coursing was thoroughly male. Coursing was practised over a much wider geographical area than archery during the Famine. Its strongholds were in the counties of Cork, Waterford, Tipperary, Kilkenny and

21 *Westmeath Independent*, 8 Sept. 1849. 22 For just some of the many accounts of these exclusive post-regatta entertainments, see *Anglo-Celt*, 11 Sept. 1846; *Westmeath Independent*, 7 Aug. 1847; *Tyrone Constitution*, 25 Aug. 1848; *Enniskillen Chronicle*, 6 Sept. 1849. 23 There is also patchy evidence of landed families engaging in archery in counties Dublin, Down, Sligo and Tipperary: *Dublin Evening Packet*, 27 June 1846; *Downpatrick Recorder*, 17 July 1847; *Sligo Journal*, 4 Aug. 1848; *Tipperary Vindicator*, 11 July 1849. 24 Summary of details from *Dublin Evening Packet*, 22 Aug. 1846; *Anglo-Celt*, 20 Aug. 1847, 26 May 1848, 6 Oct. 1848, 27 July 1849; *Drogheda Argus*, 1 Sept. 1849. 25 As ascertained from reports of their proceedings in *Wexford Independent*, 16 Sept. 1846, 29 July 1848, 21 July 1849. 26 *Wexford Independent*, 10 June 1848. Italics in original. 27 There is a small number of newspaper references to women participating in fox hunts during the Famine period. The most noted of these was an 'Irish Diana', Mrs Alloway, wife of the manager of the Emo Hunt; *King's County Chronicle*, 22 Apr.

Meath, where the most successful clubs were based, and there were also coursing clubs active in Kildare, Cavan and Fermanagh.[28] As was the case with fox and stag hunts, coursing club dinners promoted a sense of fellowship and sociability among the elite membership,[29] but winning cash prizes and gambling on the results of courses were the sport's main attraction. An examination of the details of some representative coursing meets illustrates how large amounts of money could be won by successful greyhound owners. At the Waterford, Tipperary and Kilkenny Coursing Club's meet held on the lands of Sir John Power, near Kilfane, in County Kilkenny, on 22 and 23 March 1848, the stakes were £1 10*s*. for each dog, with £10 added by the club: the winner's prize was £28, with £8 for second place and £5 10*s*. for third.[30] At the same club's meet at Colligan, near Dungarvan, on 27 and 28 March 1849, the stakes for each dog were £3 5*s*., for a winner's prize of £32 and a runner-up prize of £16. There were also several matches between pairs of hounds for prizes of £1 per match.[31]

II

The peasantry mainly played a secondary role as spectators at country-house sports during the Famine. This was not the case at various festivities that were held to mark important milestones in estate life in the same period. When these are examined in conjunction with country-house sports such as hunting, regattas, archery and coursing, it is clear that during the Famine many parts of rural Ireland rang with the sounds of merrymaking as well as the sounds of mourning that Hole referred to in his *Little tour*.

A frequent trigger for these estate celebrations was the arrival of landlords at their property for the first time, or after a lengthy absence. When Edward Litton QC travelled from Dublin to his Altmore estate in County Tyrone, with a barrister friend from Belfast, in October 1845 in order to enjoy a week's grouse shooting and coursing, as well as to inspect the progress of draining and other improvements, he received an affectionate welcome from some 1,500 to 2,000 of his tenants. Litton responded by inviting all of his tenants some days later to an open-air dance and day of general amusement, which included sack races, foot races, comic singing, dancing and fireworks, with ale, baps and sixpenny loaves being provided for the 'vast number' of merrymakers, who 'separated in the highest possible spirits'.[32] When Mrs Foster left her 'town mansion' to reside instead on her Newbliss estate in August 1846, her arrival in the Monaghan village was greeted with the lighting of numerous tar barrels, and the windows in every dwelling 'from the splendid manse to the veryest cabin' were

1846; *Dublin Evening Post*, 23 Apr. 1846. **28** Griffin, 'More sport the merrier', 104–5. **29** *Cork Examiner*, 19 Nov. 1847, 5 May 1848, 21 Mar. 1849. **30** *Tipperary Free Press*, 1 Apr. 1848. **31** *Waterford News*, 6 Apr. 1849. **32** *Coleraine Chronicle*, 18 Oct. 1845, 25 Oct. 1845.

illuminated, 'while the surrounding valleys were heard to re-echo with the deafening cheers of long life and prosperity to Mrs and Miss Foster'. Several of 'the stalwart sons of the tenantry' drew the Fosters' carriage down Newbliss' main street. On the following evening, Mrs Foster ordered that barrels of ale and other refreshments be liberally served to her tenants, and celebratory bonfires were lit throughout the village.[33] Charles Bianconi's tenants at his newly purchased Longfield estate in County Tipperary greeted him on his first appearance at his property in September 1846 by lighting a bonfire at the avenue gate and erecting a triumphal arch in his honour. The Cashel amateur band, 'dressed in their splendid uniforms', played several 'national airs'. The thronged space in front of the mansion was then the scene of a dance that began at 8 p.m. and continued until late, to the music of pipes, violin and tabor.[34] Similar scenes ensued when the tenants of Kilcoan, County Wexford, learned of the arrival of their landlord, Joseph Swan, on a visit with his brother. When Swan proceeded to the seat of John Rowe at Ballycross, 'tar barrels were collected, and bonfires lighted, around which thousands flocked to make merry and celebrate the advent of their benefactor to his paternal estates'. Swan's visit was the catalyst for two nights of drinking and dancing by his tenants.[35] Similarly, when William Monsell MP returned from parliament to his estate at Tervoe, County Limerick in October 1849, accompanied by his wife and lords Arundel and Surrey, Monsell's tenants lit several celebratory bonfires and tar barrels. Some of the tenants danced 'the Irish jig' for Arundel and Surrey, at Monsell's request. There was also a general dance in which the elite visitors participated.[36]

Although the Famine hit Tyrone less severely than it did most other Irish counties, nevertheless Tyrone's population in 1851 was some 18.3% lower than in 1841. There were local variations in the Famine's impact, with the Omagh and Clogher poor law unions, in the south of the county, having relatively higher numbers of destitute people receiving public relief than the other poor law unions in the county: Jim Grant, 'The Famine in County Tyrone' in Kinealy and Parkhill (eds), *Famine in Ulster*, pp 198–9. 33 *Northern Standard*, 29 Aug. 1846. Monaghan's population fell by almost 60,000 – some 29.2% – between 1841 and 1851. As was the case with Tyrone, there were marked local variations in the Famine's impact in Monaghan: some 25 of its 65 electoral divisions had population losses of more than 35%, with 11 of these losing more than 40% of their populations in this decade: Patrick Duffy, 'The Famine in County Monaghan' in Kinealy and Parkhill (eds), *Famine in Ulster*, p. 185. 34 *Tipperary Vindicator*, 19 Sept. 1846. According to James O'Shea, Tipperary's Catholic parishes saw a population loss of around 30% during the Famine, with some parishes recording higher losses: James O'Shea, *Priest, politics and society in post-Famine Ireland: a study of County Tipperary, 1850–1891* (Dublin, 1983), pp 58–9. 35 *Wexford Independent*, 30 Sept. 1848. Wexford experienced one of the smallest population declines in the 1841–51 period, which reflects the Famine's relatively slight impact on the county. Its population fell from a recorded 202,033 in 1841 to 179,790 in 1851, a decrease of 11%: Anna Kinsella, *County Wexford in the Famine years, 1845–1849* (Enniscorthy, 1995), p. 75. 36 *Limerick and Clare Examiner*, 6 Oct. 1849. This incident calls to mind the peasants dancing for the amusement of Queen Victoria and Prince Albert when they visited the duke of Leinster's Carton estate in 1849: Terence Dooley, *The decline and fall of the dukes of Leinster: love, war, debt and madness* (Dublin, 2014), pp 33–4.

9.1 'An Irish harvest home', *Illustrated London News*, 15 Sept. 1849, © The British Library Board, shelf mark 4367.150000.

Landlords' marriages, or marriages of their children, were also occasions of public rejoicing by the tenants on their estates. In January 1846 Lord Dunsandle's tenants on his Kilconnell estate marked the marriage of his son to Cecilia-Maria A'Court, daughter of Baron Heytesbury, the lord lieutenant, by illuminating Kilconnell and lighting a large bonfire opposite the ballroom of Dunsandle's mansion, where the tenants assembled for refreshments and a celebratory dance which lasted for several hours.[37] Henry Osborne Seward's tenants on his Douglas estate marked his son's nuptials the following month with numerous bonfires that illuminated the village; their happy mood was no doubt heightened the next day when Seward instructed his agent to remit altogether the next March gale of rent.[38] In September 1846, the inhabitants of Gorey and the surrounding area were 'agreeably excited' when their landlord's heir, Lord Stopford, got married. When Stopford travelled to Gorey with his bride, they were stopped some miles from the town and a banner-wielding procession was formed of 'the principal gentry and tenantry', the Gorey band, and the coastguard stationed at Courtown. A female tenant, 'being adequately attired, and mounted on a charger, headed the cavalcade in true amazon style, but without any departure from that propriety so peculiar to the Wexford ladies'.

37 *Dublin Evening Packet*, 17 Jan. 1846. 38 *Southern Reporter*, 19 Feb. 1846.

Gorey town and harbour were 'brilliantly illuminated, and the arms of the family might be seen frequently in beautiful transparency'. Nearly 300 of 'the leading gentry and respectable persons on the Courtown estate' then partook of 'a splendid dejeuner' in a large marquee.

On the next day, Stopford treated his workmen and cottiers, with their wives and daughters, to a harvest home dinner 'on a princely scale – roast beef and pudding, with a profusion of ale were in great abundance'. This was followed by a dance, which 'was kept up with unabated spirit till an advanced hour, in which all ranks joined'. A tenant named Turlough Brien, aged more than 90 years, presided over the event and danced a jig in the evening. On the following evening another dance was held, attended by more than 1,000 people, 'chiefly of the farmers, tenants and families', who received liberal amounts of refreshments.[39] The fireworks and illuminations with which the people of Maynooth had intended to celebrate the marriage of the marquess of Kildare did not go ahead as planned (at the request of the marquess and his father, the duke of Leinster) when the marquess arrived at the Carton estate with his new bride in October 1847, as a 'respectable' lady in Maynooth was ill and the fireworks and illuminations would disturb her. Nevertheless, an impressive celebration was still held at nearby Carton. More than 200 tenants and their wives and families were treated to 'an excellent dinner', which was followed by such sports as 'running in sacks, rolling in barrels, climbing of poles, and a variety of other rustic amusements'. A 'merry jig and reel' followed in the evening, which lasted until dusk, the music being provided by the Maynooth temperance band. The town of Maynooth and the seminary of St Patrick's College were eventually illuminated in celebration some days after these festivities.[40]

Similar scenes occurred in Ballinrobe in September 1848 when Alexander Clendining Lambert and his new bride passed through the Mayo town on their way to taking up residence at Lambert's Cranmore Park demesne. A 'monster bonfire' was lit and an 'enormous' crowd, 'composed of all classes, gentle and simple, old and young, soldiers and civilians' turned out to greet the newly-weds, whose carriage was pulled by the crowd through the gaily decorated streets. Most of Ballinrobe's houses were illuminated, and it was claimed that every window was decorated with laurels of roses. Ballinrobe's temperance band played and, rather incongruously, the revellers were also provided with twenty-five barrels of 'Figlies malt'; according to one observer, 'Many a fine half-starved Irish lad went home that night as tipsy, if not so happy, as a lord.'[41] When the earl of Bessborough married Lady Caroline Gordon Lennox in October 1849, the couple's arrival at Bessborough and Piltown, in County Kilkenny, was the occasion of two days of enthusiastic celebration, organized by the earl's agent, Mr Blackett. Some 700 pupils at the schools on Bessborough's estate 'were

39 *Dublin Evening Packet*, 3 Oct. 1846. 40 Details from *Dublin Evening Post*, 2 Nov. 1847; *Pilot*, 12 Nov. 1847; Dooley, *Dukes of Leinster*, pp 32–3. 41 *Pilot*, 2 Oct. 1848.

plentifully regaled with roast beef, sweet-loaf, plum-pudding, &c., and afterwards cheered with music and dancing, sportive exercises, and divers other amusements, which rendered it a truly exhilarating scene to behold'. Bessborough's workers and tenants were also 'sumptuously feasted' over two days, while bonfires blazed 'on hill and dale around', and the crowds enjoyed the free ale that was supplied to them in generous amounts. Every house in Piltown was 'brilliantly illuminated' and casks of beer were supplied to the thousands of revellers there. Several bands played music, with the Piltown village band playing a succession of English, Scottish and Irish airs. The local Irish Constabulary contingent, commanded by Sub-Inspector William Lavelle, added to the entertainment by firing a *feu de joie*.[42]

Another important milestone in the life of the country-house family – the coming of age of a landlord's son – was also commonly celebrated publicly by tenants in many areas of the country.[43] There are too many instances to describe individually here, but it is clear from newspaper descriptions that these followed a general pattern, in which deferential tenants congratulated their landlord's son, and were treated to a celebratory dinner and dance on the landlord's demesne. These were often lavish affairs. The marquess of Drogheda's majority was celebrated over several days at Moore Abbey, County Kildare, in August 1846. On his birthday, Lady Henry Moore presented over 400 frocks and bonnets to girls who had been in constant attendance at the Monasterevin schools for the preceding six months, and the boy pupils received new caps; between 600 and 700 children were 'regaled with a plentiful feast of tea, coffee, and cake' in a large pavilion erected for the occasion. The schoolchildren of Fontstown were feasted in a similar fashion, and the girls there received over 150 frocks. On the next day, the people of Monasterevin put on a 'general illumination, in which were displayed various mottoes and devices in coloured lamps'; this was accompanied by a 'very effective pyrotechnic exhibition'. Four days later, about 1,200 of Drogheda's tenants and workmen assembled outside Monasterevin wearing their 'holiday attire' and also scarfs, sashes and 'gaudy ribbons', carrying various banners and flags and preceded by several bands, and paraded four deep through and about the town before proceeding to Moore Abbey, where they were welcomed by their landlord's family. A dance was held, with music provided by 'the busy fiddle' as well as the band of the 70th Regiment, before the crowd was treated to a 'sumptuous dinner'.[44]

The coming of age of the second son of Robert Borrowes of Gilltown, County Kildare, was celebrated in September 1847. Triumphal arches were erected on

42 *Freeman's Journal*, 25 Oct. 1849; undated extract from *Dublin Evening Herald* in *Downpatrick Recorder*, 27 Oct. 1849. 43 For an account of such celebrations in King's Co., see Ciarán Reilly, *John Plunket Joly and the Great Famine in King's County* (Dublin, 2012), pp 34–5. For the Clonbrock estate in the post-Famine decades, see Kevin McKenna, 'Elites, ritual and legitimation of power on an Irish landed estate, 1855–90' in Ciaran O'Neill (ed.), *Irish elites in the nineteenth century* (Dublin, 2013), pp 68–82. 44 *Dublin Evening Packet*, 22 Aug. 1846.

the several approaches to Borrowes' estate, under which marched the Huntstown band, and Borrowes' 'numerous tenantry [...] four deep, wearing breast knots of blue and red, and equipped in their Sunday toggery', followed by their wives and daughters. A dinner – 'sumptuous as it was substantial' – was provided in two large marquees that were decorated with ormolu lamps, and, when it was over, 'the punch bowl was freely circulated'. Guests of a higher social standing were treated to 'a dinner on a most magnificent scale' in Borrowes' mansion. The celebratory meal was followed by a dance, which Borrowes led off by dancing with one of his tenants' daughters, and the day's entertainment was brought to a close by an elaborate fireworks display:

> On the lake in the lawn, Mr Bruce, the pyrotechnist, from Portobello Gardens, raised his throne like a fire-king, and summoned to his levee 'flaming ministers of light' of every size and order, from the water rocket that dived like some amphibious animal, to the sky rocket, that shot upwards, irradiating the gloom of night. Roman candles and artificial moonlight next diffused their splendour and brilliancy over the animated scene.[45]

In August 1848, Thomas Kavanagh of Borris House, County Carlow, gave a dinner 'on a scale of feudal magnificence' to some 500 to 600 of his tenants to mark his son's coming of age. This was followed by a 'grand ball, to which all the nobility and gentry of Carlow and the surrounding counties were invited', and a fireworks display 'on a most magnificent scale' which was overseen by William Drewett of Portobello Gardens.[46]

The most common festive occasion shared by families of the country house and their tenants during the Famine was the harvest home celebration. On 15 September 1849, the *Illustrated London News* published an account with images of what it considered to be the typical Irish harvest home of this period. It explained that a barn would be converted into a 'ball-room' for the festivities:

> From roof to floor it is decorated with laurels and other evergreens, through which some dozen lights gleam from rustic chandeliers, which are generally composed of a sheaf of corn lined with yellow clay, and fastened to the leafy drapery with wreaths of flowers. At one end of the barn is placed the threshing-machine, decorated after the same fashion. Forms are arranged to accommodate the various groups apart from the dancers. The rustic beaux and belles, neatly and simply attired, dance with an animation that would astonish a citizen; and, when the mirth grows 'fast and furious', pipers, fiddlers, and dancers display an energy that might rival the glories of Kirk-Alloway! Tea and coffee, with piles of slices of bread and cake, are

**45** *Dublin Evening Mail*, 4 Oct. 1847. **46** *Dublin Evening Packet*, 12, 15 Aug. 1848.

> handed about in capacious sieves and riddles; and later in the evening a plentiful supper is prepared, with the exhilarating addition of the 'mountain dew'.

The newspaper added that:

> 'The master' and his family always visit the scene of enjoyment, and by their presence ensure the good order as well as the good cheer of the labourers. Between the dances the song and jest go round briskly, with encounters of wit, in which the Irish, generally speaking, excel; by which we mean, not the heart-broken peasant, out seeking for labour in another land, but the hearty, hilarious Irishman in all his glory at home.

Although this is a generic account, rather than a description of a specific harvest home, its general gist is broadly borne out by other contemporary newspaper evidence. At St Ernan's, County Donegal, around 100 of John Hamilton's workers and their families enjoyed a harvest home dinner, tea and dance, and were entertained by Hamilton's children's magic lantern,[47] while at the earl of Clare's Mountshannon seat in Limerick, over 200 of Clare's 'tenantry, tradespeople, labourers, and their wives' were treated to a dinner of roast and boiled beef and plum and rice puddings, which was followed by a dance that was 'kept up with great animation'.[48] At Mervyn Pratt's residence at Enniscoe, near Crossmolina, 150 of his tenants and labourers celebrated their annual harvest home with festivities that included 'a most substantial dinner'; a series of amusements included 'several feats of strength and activity', and an 'exhilarating dance' that was 'kept up with spirit until a late hour' in a ballroom 'tastefully fitted up and decorated with evergreens and festoons of flowers'.[49] The earl of Mayo presided over similar events at Palmerstown House in County Kildare, hosting a harvest home 'feast not to be forgotten', which was followed by a dance and the singing of 'some choice melodies, joined in chorus by lords, ladies, masters, servants, bachelors, and maids, the effect of which seemed to linger in the air, as if magic horns were sounded upon enchanted land'.[50] A distinct pattern emerges in these newspaper reports. The harvest home is presented as a harmonious occasion, in which paternalistic and benevolent landlords mingle on easy terms with their deferential, grateful tenants and labourers. The landlord's common touch is frequently highlighted in these descriptions, as he wholeheartedly joins in the merrymaking, especially the dancing.

While harvest homes generally followed the same broad pattern, they included distinctive touches in some localities. For instance, the celebration at

47 *Armagh Guardian*, 9 Nov. 1847. 48 *Dublin Evening Packet*, 7 Oct. 1847. 49 Ibid., 9 Oct. 1847. 50 *Dublin Evening Mail*, 16 Oct. 1848.

Lord Newry's Mourne Park estate in September 1846 included the common 'substantial dinner of good beef, pudding, and ale', after which 'Due homage was paid to Terpsichore in the evening, in the maze of rustic dance'. But Newry added to the amusements by sending up a small balloon, which remained afloat 'for a considerable time', and some large guns on the surrounding hills discharged around forty rounds 'in superior military fashion'. At the festivities' conclusion, each family was presented with a large loaf of bread and 'a solid piece of beef'.[51] St John Jeffreyes' harvest home at Blarney in September 1847 was unusual in that 'no spiritous or fermented liquor' was provided, out of respect to the feelings of the large number of teetotallers among the more than 500 merrymakers – instead, 'best new milk' was served. This doesn't appear to have dampened people's spirits, to judge by the enthusiasm shown in the evening dance, which took place in part of the farmyard that was specially boarded for the occasion. Three fiddlers and a piper provided the music, and 'Reels, jigs, country dances and quadrilles were kept up for several hours with great spirit, in the dancing of which, the country girls exhibited a proficiency which would have done credit to the most fashionable drawing room'.[52] Lord Farnham's own band played the music at the Farnham harvest homes; another distinctive feature at the Farnham celebration in October 1849 was the presence of some merry Andrews (i.e. clowns), 'who delighted the young folk by their amusing grimaces'.[53]

## III

What should one make of these accounts of merrymaking by apparently contented and grateful tenants and labourers at harvest homes, coming-of-age celebrations and visits by long-absent landlords? The newspaper sources do not permit us to hear their unmediated voices, but one should nevertheless be cautious about accepting at face value the newspapers' versions of events.[54] This is clear when one reads of the joyous welcome given to Marcus Keane of Beech

51 *Newry Examiner*, 30 Sept. 1846. 52 *Limerick Reporter*, 21 Sept. 1847; *Tipperary Free Press*, 22 Sept. 1847. 53 *Anglo-Celt*, 20 Oct. 1848, 12 Oct. 1849. 54 For example, although the topic of the Irish press during the Famine is a relatively underexplored subject, it is clear from the work that has been completed that editors' and journalists' biases and political views coloured the contents of their publications: Michael O'Dwyer, 'The Famine in Kilkenny, as reported in the "Kilkenny Journal" newspaper, September 1845 to March 1848', *Old Kilkenny Review*, 47 (1995), pp 114–26; Eugene Broderick, 'The Famine in Waterford as reported in the local newspapers' in Des Cowman and Donald Brady (eds), *The Famine in Waterford, 1845–1850: teacht na bprátaí dubha* (Dublin, 1995), pp 153–214; Michael Foley, *Death in every paragraph: journalism and the Great Famine* (Hamden, CT, 2015), pp 24, 26–30. Some newspapers dwelt at length on the suffering of the poorer classes during the Famine, while others glossed over this and concentrated on other topics instead, as commented upon by the *Londonderry Journal* on 7 Apr. 1847, when it observed that 'Some of the Irish newspapers, after regretting that their space is inadequate to individualize the deaths by destitution,

Park, County Clare, by the tenants on his estate when he returned from his honeymoon in December 1847. As happened on similar occasions on other estates elsewhere in Ireland, Keane's tenants lit bonfires 'and every other means in their power were resorted to by the tenants to manifest their gratification and delight', including an offer – which Keane declined – to draw their landlord's carriage to Beech Park. However, when one considers the fact that Keane was a notorious evictor of tenants from his lands during the Famine, the apparent joy shown by his tenants takes on a different complexion. As Ciarán Ó Murchadha explains of Keane and his tenants, 'given the enormous power wielded by him, it would have been an unwise tenant indeed who would have failed to simulate the required level of joyous enthusiasm' on his return from his honeymoon.[55] Terence Dooley makes a similar general point regarding tenant participation at various country-house celebrations in the post-Famine decades when he notes that 'It was what today might be termed "good PR" for the tenants to present a decorative and illuminated address to a new landlord or to express congratulations to an existing one on his son's coming of age or getting married.'[56] The same observation may be made regarding tenants in the Famine period. Such examples of apparent rejoicing reveal as much about the power dynamics on landed estates as they do about the true state of mind of the tenants and labourers who participated in them. Doubtless those who were regaled at William Flood's harvest home at Farmley, County Kilkenny, in October 1848 and were treated to 'a comfortable and substantial dinner, which was done ample justice to, and which was washed down by copious potations of Sullivan's best pale butt', were pleased with the meal that they received, as well as the tea, coffee and punch served 'in abundance' during the subsequent dance, which was 'kept up until a late hour'. The newspaper reporter who described the Farmley festivities probably revealed more than he realized when he described how pleasing it was 'to see so many of the children of toil and labour, their faces glowing with gratitude and delight, *forgetting for the moment their drudgery*, and starting forth to join the merry dance'.[57]

Harvest homes and other country-house celebrations often involved landlords or their agents using these occasions to impress on what were essentially captive audiences the importance of industriousness or other qualities that they deemed it important for their social inferiors to possess. It seems reasonable to suppose that, for some of those present at least, these messages were not entirely welcome or, at the very least, that they jarred with what were ostensibly carefree occasions of leisure and enjoyment. The content of these didactic messages varied. At the coming-of-age celebrations for W. Mills Molony of Kiltannon, County Clare, in July 1846, James Molony told his tenants that they would, in effect, have to work

chronicle the meetings of the fox hounds.' 55 Ó Murchadha, *Famine landscape*, pp 101–2. 56 Dooley, *The decline of the Big House in Ireland*, p. 51. 57 *Kilkenny Journal*, 1 Nov. 1848. Author's italics.

harder in future by increasing the fertility of the soil to meet the challenge of the forthcoming repeal of the corn laws, which would throw British markets open to European competition.[58] Charles Bianconi told his Longfield estate tenants in September 1846 that they should 'Above all things avoid secret and illegal societies'. Cautioning them that 'There are still a few lurking vagabonds in Tipperary' he added:

> Therefore if any one asks you to violate the law, seize him, grapple with him, and drag him before a magistrate or your clergyman, for depend upon it, he is your enemy, and the enemy of your country [...] Follow the advice of O'Connell and your beloved clergy: be temperate, moral, peaceable, and you will advance your country, ameliorate your condition, and the blessing of God will attend you.[59]

At the Lanesborough Lodge harvest home, near Belturbet, in August 1847, Lord Lanesborough exhorted an audience of some 300 tenants and labourers 'to arouse themselves from their former lethargy and idleness; and to exert themselves to acts of industry and perseverance in tilling their farms'; while their wives and daughters should keep their cottages 'neat and clean, and every article well arranged', which he would check when he next visited them.[60] John Temple Reilly's harvest home at Scarva House, County Down, in the following month included a speech by Reverend Darcy of Galway, in which the clergyman told his audience that the 'harrowing' scenes that he had witnessed in the west would occur occasionally in Ireland 'until a reciprocal feeling sprung up between landlord and tenant – until their interests became identical – until they ceased to watch each other with jealousy, and until they studied that what benefitted the one would benefit the other'.[61] One can only speculate about the thoughts that went through the revellers' heads at St John Jeffreyes' harvest home at Blarney when, after their evening tea, they were treated to an address by Sir George Colthurst of Ardrum 'on the benefits arising from a proper and judicious system of agriculture, and on the profits to be derived from green cropping and feeding'.[62] When the marquess of Ormonde gave a harvest home dinner 'on a very grand scale' to 180 of his workmen at his Dunmore estate in County Kilkenny in October 1847, the diners ate their meal in a hall that was decorated with various mottoes, including one that stated that 'Honest and industrious men expect their reward.'[63]

58 *Clare Journal*, 3 Aug. 1846. 59 *Tipperary Vindicator*, 19 Sept. 1846. 60 *Anglo-Celt*, 20 Aug. 1847. 61 *Newry Telegraph*, 14 Sept. 1847. 62 *Tipperary Free Press*, 22 Sept. 1847. 63 *Dublin Evening Post*, 12 Oct. 1847.

## IV

These accounts show that Samuel Reynolds Hole's view of rural Ireland during the Famine as a world overwhelmed by grief and devoid of the sound of enjoyment was not an entirely accurate one. Although an estimated 1 million people died and a further 1 million emigrated during the Famine, even counties that were relatively severely hit by the catastrophe, such as Galway, Mayo and Cork, were often the scenes of pleasurable sporting activity such as fox hunting, and celebrations connected with the life of the country house, in which tenants and labourers played a central role. It is true that tenants and labourers may not always have been entirely free agents when it came to such scenes of celebration, but nevertheless the idea that 'the mirth of the land was gone' during the Famine needs to be modified. Many landlords suffered drastic falls in their incomes in these years, but the country house remained the source of much sporting and recreational pleasure, both for the landed elite and those further down the rural social scale.

# Cricket, Gaelic football and the Big House: the Avondale perspective

TOM HUNT

## I

Foundation myths form a central part of sporting folklore, and the match between a Garrison XI and an All-Ireland XI played on the Fifteen Acres in the Phoenix Park in August 1792 provides Irish cricket with its mythical point of origin. Plenty of cricket had been played in Ireland prior to this date; for example, the *Dublin Journal* reported that Lord Essex and his brother Lord John Sackville, the sons of the lord lieutenant, the duke of Dorset, attended by several persons of distinction, 'played at cricket' in the Phoenix Park on Wednesday 3 October 1733.[1] However, 1792 provides an appropriate point of reference from which to measure the progress of the sport, as less than a century later cricket was the most important and popular field game in Ireland and one that appealed to all social classes.

Initially, the game progressed slowly and seems to have remained restricted to the military.[2] Ballinasloe Cricket Club, the first formally established club in Ireland, was founded in 1825 by Lord Dunlo (eldest son and heir to the earl of Clancarty of Garbally House); in 1828 the club travelled to Dublin and achieved a notable victory against the City of Dublin with Dunlo and his brother playing starring roles in a match played in the Phoenix Park on 1 August.[3] The 1830s was the decade when cricket was diffused more widely in social and geographic terms. The Phoenix Club was founded in 1830, followed by the Trinity College Club in 1835, and the Leinster Cricket Club in 1845. Centres of the game outside Dublin in the 1830s included Ballinasloe, Kilkenny city, Carlow and Wicklow.[4]

Although military involvement was pivotal to the early development of Irish cricket, the sport became a central part of landed-gentry culture, and residents of the Big House were instrumental in popularizing it, particularly from the

1 Maighréad Ní Mhurchada, 'Two hundred men in tennis, sport in north Dublin 1600–1760', *Dublin Historical Record*, 61:1 (2008), p. 100. 2 Neal Garnham, 'The roles of cricket in Victorian and Edwardian Ireland', *Sporting Traditions: the Journal of the Australian Society for Sports History*, 19:2 (May 2003), p. 28. 3 Stephen Dolan, *The birth, growth and decline of cricket in Co. Galway, 1825–1925* (Galway, 2016), pp 6–7. 4 W.P. Hone, *Cricket in Ireland* (Tralee, 1956), pp 6–15; Trevor West, *Bold collegians: the development of sport in Trinity College Dublin* (Dublin, 1991), p. 14; N.D. McMillan, *One hundred and fifty years of cricket in County Carlow: an illustrated social history of conflict and sport, 1823–1981* (Dublin, 1983), p. 5; T.M. Pryal, 'The history of the club' in *The Phoenix Club, 1830–1980* (Dublin, 1980), unpaginated.

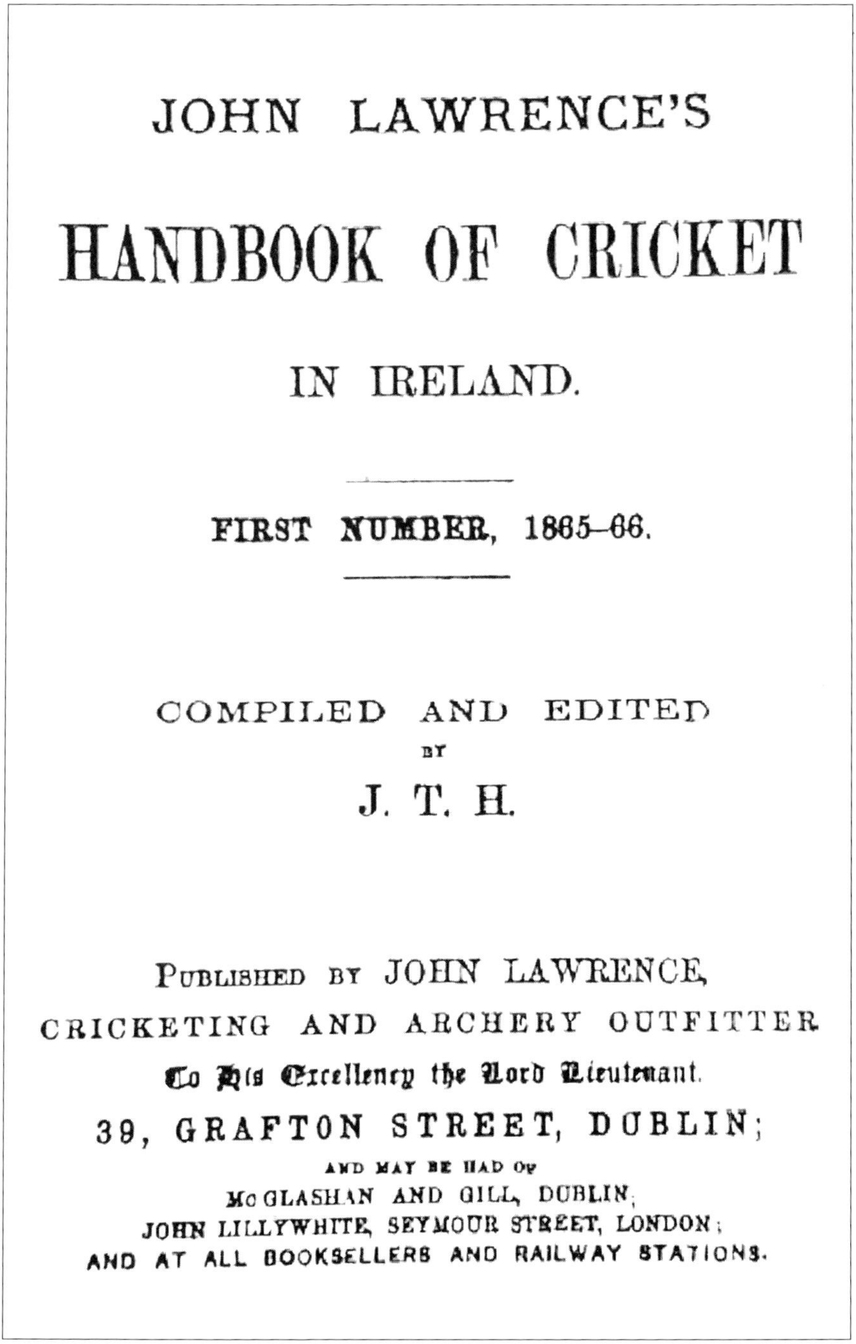

JOHN LAWRENCE'S

HANDBOOK OF CRICKET

IN IRELAND.

FIRST NUMBER, 1865–66.

COMPILED AND EDITED
BY
J. T. H.

PUBLISHED BY JOHN LAWRENCE,
CRICKETING AND ARCHERY OUTFITTER
To His Excellency the Lord Lieutenant.
39, GRAFTON STREET, DUBLIN;
AND MAY BE HAD OF
McGLASHAN AND GILL, DUBLIN;
JOHN LILLYWHITE, SEYMOUR STREET, LONDON;
AND AT ALL BOOKSELLERS AND RAILWAY STATIONS.

**10.1** John Lawrence's *Handbook of cricket in Ireland.*

mid-1850s to the mid-1870s. Members of the landed gentry introduced the sport to their estates, developed cricket creases, encouraged their tenants to form teams, hired professionals to manage the grounds, facilitated practice, played on teams themselves and provided the social prestige for the sport that encouraged emulation.[5] They even procured the playing equipment and other necessary paraphernalia (among the items auctioned following the death of John Henry Parnell was 'a good cricket-ground tent, in perfect order').[6]

The most spectacular growth took place during the 1860s and the sport was popular enough in Ireland in 1865 to encourage John Lawrence to publish his first *Handbook of cricket in Ireland*, an annual publication that continued to document the sport until 1881. The *Irish Times* reported in 1866 that there was 'scarcely a district in Ireland that has not its own cricket club'; the sport had replaced former pastimes among the middle classes. According to the report, it was possible to observe 'groups of artisans and labourers after working hours proceeding to some field in the localities in which they earn livelihood for the purpose of enjoying themselves in this excellent pastime'.[7] The *Freeman's Journal* reported a similar phenomenon in the mid-1860s: 'All classes, high, middle and low, now take an interest in cricket, and a game which was once exclusively English has now taken such deep root among us that cricket may fairly be considered one of our great pastimes.'[8] This popularity was reflected in Lawrence's publications, which reported on the activities of cricket clubs in every county in Ireland in 1871 and 1872; in 1875, the *Freeman's Journal* was confident that the future of the sport was secure: 'At present it is no exaggeration to say, cricket is known and played all over the island. We may take it for granted that the youth … will establish it permanently.'[9] Michael Cusack, one of the founding fathers of the Gaelic Athletic Association (GAA), was a believer in the value of the sport and as late as July 1882 advocated the establishment of a cricket club in every parish in Ireland; he even offered advice to boys on how to clean a cricket bat using linseed oil and how to store it for the winter. In Cusack's world, it was the ideal character-building sport for boys; in July 1882, Cusack wrote in the *Shamrock*: 'You may be certain that the boy who can play cricket well will not, in after years, lose his head and get flurried in the face of danger.'[10]

The values associated with the sport made it an attractive proposition for the elites of society and an activity worthy of promotion. The concern of the time with manliness made the sport an ideal vehicle for encouragement. Cricket was one of the 'most manly and athletic of all games' the *Irish Times* reported.[11] It was 'an exhilarating and manly game, tending to encourage that muscular

5 See Pat Bracken, *The growth and development of sport in County Tipperary, 1840–1880* (Cork, 2018); for information on the payments made by Viscount Ashbrook of Castle Durrow to his cricket players in the 1840s, see pp 44–6. 6 R.F. Foster, *Charles Stewart Parnell: the man and his family* (Sussex, 1979), p. 315. 7 *Irish Times*, 29 Aug. 1866. 8 *Freeman's Journal*, 12 May 1865. 9 Garnham, 'The roles of cricket', pp 28–9; *Freeman's Journal*, 26 Apr. 1875. 10 *Shamrock*, 8 July 1882. 11 *Irish Times*, 22 Apr. 1861.

development which has lately been too much neglected'.[12] The sport was also a valuable health-promoting exercise: there is 'none which more strengthens the limbs and increases the speed and vigour of youth'.[13] Cricket's supposed value in encouraging friendly feeling between the classes was also lauded. In Westmeath, Mr Fetherstonhaugh promoted cricket 'among the young men in his extensive employment', with 'a hope that it would tend to promote friendly feelings amongst all grades'.[14] Similar sentiments were expressed in the nationalist *Nation* newspaper in 1843 when it was claimed that the 'man who, while he plays cricket, is on a footing of equality with his labourer on a Monday is very unlikely to be other than a kind master and considerable patron to the same individual on Tuesday.'[15]

Despite the philosophizing about the high-order values of cricket and its role in encouraging manliness and other desirable personal qualities, the sport's central attraction lay in the opportunity it provided for sociability and socialization. Cricket matches at the homes of the landed gentry provided occasions when the land-owning class and their social equals could gather and socialize in their natural environment.[16] Hospitality and entertainment lay at the core of the demesne-based cricket event, which was as much about the social interaction as it was about the cricket. A cricket match was an acceptable way of entertaining friends, locally based army officers, neighbours, tenants and visitors, of engaging in a bout of conspicuous consumption, and of introducing eligible young men to marriageable daughters. It provided the summer's equivalent to winter hunting. John Lawrence's claim that the sport formed 'a bond of union between the country gentlemen of the day; and the same sportsmen who met in winter by the covert side, hailed each other joyfully in summer' at the crease is perceptive.[17]

Accounts of the entertainment associated with the sport are a standard feature of match reports. The opening match between County Wicklow and the 8th Regiment at the new ground at Mount Kennedy attracted a 'large number of the county families' who, together with the players, were 'hospitably entertained' by Major and Mrs Cunninghame.[18] At the interval in the match, 'the players retired to Casino House [Avondale] where a sumptuous *dejeuner* was served to them by Mr Hunter of the Woodenbridge Hotel, which certainly reflected great credit on Mr Hunter's establishment, everything being served in first style'.[19] In June 1874, 'after the first innings both clubs were entertained with a sumptuous repast underneath a spacious marquee', when Coolattin and Tinahely played, what was essentially an intra-estate match.[20] Lady Alice Howard attended a cricket match at Avondale with Lord and Lady Wicklow on 6 September 1874, and recorded in her diary that 'it was very pleasant – all the county were there – but we were

12 Ibid., 4 Sept. 1860. 13 Ibid., 22 Apr. 1861. 14 John Lawrence (ed.), *John Lawrence's handbook of cricket in Ireland, 1866–67* (Dublin, 1867), p. 90. 15 *Nation*, 12 Aug. 1843. 16 Garnham, 'The roles of cricket', pp 40–1. 17 J.T.H., *Handbook, 1877–78*, p. 19. 18 *Wicklow Newsletter*, 2 Sept. 1865. 19 *Freeman's Journal*, 11 July 1864. 20 *Wicklow Newsletter*, 27 June 1874.

nearly consumed by midges'.[21] However, as Roy Foster has pointed out all the county denoted a very narrow compass.[22]

A sensationalized account of the cricket-centred socializing that took place to celebrate Charles Stewart Parnell's twenty-first birthday is included in the sometimes fanciful recollections of his sister, Emily Monroe Dickinson.[23] Robert Kee identifies this occasion as the match between Mr Parnell's XI and Mr Crossdale's XI that took place on 20 July 1867, when Parnell was 'unavoidably absent' from the festivities organized to celebrate his coming of age, as he was 'required for important legal business in the Court of Chancery'.[24]

Emily's husband, Arthur Dickinson, had suggested 'a real spree' to celebrate Parnell's twenty-first birthday. The party was organized around a three-day cricket match between officers of the Dublin garrison and the Wicklow county side.[25] Emily's account relates how the county gentry were invited, the military band was organized, tents and marquees were erected, luncheon was served after the first innings at which champagne and wine flowed freely, brilliant and eloquent speeches were delivered, dinner was a great success and dancing was kept in full swing to a late hour. On the first day, the players, especially the army officers, 'fought bravely' and resisted the 'disturbing influence' of the 'presence of so many of the fair sex, which included several very pretty girls and still prettier young matrons'.[26] The sound of music hall songs accompanied by much riotous laughter and clapping of hands was heard late into the night.[27] On the second day, however, temptation was too great to resist and during the second innings players 'threw down their bats and joining the ladies, the whole party paired off into the woods'. Dickinson recorded:

> Now commenced a scene of fun and flirtation which surpassed description and which had probably never before been equalled in the old haunts of Avondale. In every shady nook and corner were to be seen an isolated couple engaged in the pleasant pastime of love-making, the young widow notwithstanding her robes of black, being foremost in the practice of the art.[28]

An attempt to finish the match on the third day was abandoned in favour of the rival and 'superior attractions of the ladies, more roaming, spooning and loitering under the trees in the woods, more eating and drinking, more dancing and flirting'.[29] The account may be excessively colourful in its detail but no doubt it represents a reasonable reconstruction of what might have taken place

**21** Diary Lady Alice Howard, 6 Sept. 1874, NLI (Wicklow papers, MS 3600). **22** Foster, *Parnell family*, p. 116. **23** Emily Monroe Dickinson, *A patriot's mistake, being personal recollections of the Parnell family* (Dublin, 1905), pp 63–78. **24** Robert Kee, *The laurel and the ivy, the story of Charles Stewart Parnell and Irish nationalism* (London, 1993), p. 41. **25** Dickinson, *A patriot's mistake*, p. 66. **26** Ibid., p. 69. **27** Ibid., pp 69–70. **28** Ibid., p. 71. **29** Ibid., p. 76.

at a coming-of-age party for a man about to inherit a landed estate, who was also a cricket enthusiast.

The social dimension was not confined to the landed gentry. All classes availed of the opportunity to organize a party in association with a match. The social life of rural Ireland was considerably enhanced by participation in the sport, as can be seen from several examples from County Westmeath. In July 1893, members of the Ringtown Club assembled on the shores of Lough Derravaragh to make the journey across the lake to play Stonehall. Thirty-two members of the club climbed on board a 'large boat, kindly placed at their disposal by a local turf merchant'. After what was described as a joyful half-hour's sail, 'during which songs were sung and music rendered,' the members arrived at Stonehall and disposed of the challenge presented by the host team. This image of a turf boat full of singing and dancing young men from rural Westmeath on their way to a pre-arranged cricket match is not one normally associated with the sport.[30] The social jamboree was an integral part of the sport regardless of the social class involved. There was, however, some concern that the associated costs were having a negative impact on the playing of matches. A pragmatic solution, which preserved one of the sport's traditional aspects, was proposed by 'Short Stop' in a letter to the *Westmeath Guardian*:

> It has hitherto been the custom with country clubs to provide luncheon and a half-barrel of porter for the visitors; which entailed expense to such a degree, as to deter clubs from engaging in more than a few matches during a season. Now as a good many matches is what most players desire, I would suggest that the luncheon be left out, and a half-barrel of porter alone be supplied: each player supplying his luncheon; which would be equally as satisfactory and a great deal cheaper than the other way.[31]

II

John Henry Parnell, Charles Stewart Parnell's father, was a pioneer of cricket in rural Ireland.[32] He was educated in Eton, entered Trinity College, Cambridge in April 1831, and matriculated at the end of that year. During his time in England, he played in at least two matches that might be considered first class. On 31 July 1828, he represented Eton College against Harrow School at Lord's. He managed one run in the first innings of the match but with Eton winning by six wickets was not again required to bat. Almost three years later, on 19 May 1831, he represented Cambridge University against the Cambridge Town Club, scoring two runs and three runs in his two appearances at bat.[33] John Henry returned from England as an evangelist for the sport. It is a familiar pattern of

30 *Westmeath Examiner*, 29 July 1893. 31 *Westmeath Guardian*, 8 June 1888. 32 McMillan, *Cricket in County Carlow*, p. 4. 33 Cricket Archive, www.cricketarchive.com, accessed 27

behaviour that was responsible for the diffusion of many sports: the son of a member of the landed gentry attended public school and returned home as an evangelist for a sport he had encountered while in England. He played for the Phoenix Club and introduced cricket to County Wicklow, where he founded the county club in 1835.[34] The withdrawal symptoms he experienced on his short-term separation from the sport are expressed in a diary he kept while travelling in Canada, the USA and Mexico between October 1834 and April 1835.[35] This is the only surviving first-hand account of any period of John Henry Parnell's life, and its opening page conveys his disappointment at failing to play cricket at Frederickton, Newfoundland; he attempted to organize a 'sort of a game of cricket' aboard ship en route to Vera Cruz and, in Mexico, he was relieved that he could again enjoy 'my old well beloved game'.[36] On his return, he established the County Wicklow Cricket Club, with its headquarters at Avondale, where the 'ground was well kept'. According to Arthur Samuels, the Wicklow Club was the second after Carlow to send a team to Dublin; Samuels frequently played at Avondale with the Phoenix, University and Roebuck clubs, where they were 'always well and hospitably entertained by Mr Parnell'.[37]

John Henry Parnell was also a leading member of the Phoenix Club in its early days. In 1838, the club was reorganized and a piece of land in the Phoenix Park close to the Wellington Monument was taken and railed at a cost of £50. A limited number of life memberships were made available to fund this development work and John Henry was one of the takers for this scheme.[38] According to the memoir of his son John Howard Parnell, his cricket obsession contributed directly to his untimely death in 1859, when he defied medical advice and travelled to Dublin to represent Phoenix against the Leinster Club. He had been under doctor's care for some time, suffering from 'rheumatism of the stomach'. Sir Frederick Marsh ordered him not to engage in violent exercise and 'although in a high fever' he insisted on playing. He became severely ill after the game and he died the following day in the Shelbourne Hotel.[39] Roy Foster provides a more laconic version of Parnell's death, stating simply that he died after attending a match between Wicklow and the 16th (Bedfordshire) Regiment while suffering rheumatic fever.[40]

## III

The memoirs of John Howard Parnell also provide evidence of the early cricketing days of his younger brother Charles. He was introduced to the game during his nursery days, when he toddled down to the Avondale demesne's

Aug. 2018. **34** Pryal, *The history of the club*, unpaginated. **35** Foster, *Parnell*, p. 35. **36** Ibid., p. 40. **37** Arthur Samuels, *Early cricket in Ireland* (Dublin, 1888), p. 100. **38** J.T.H., *Handbook, 1865–66*, p. 5. **39** John Parnell, *Charles Stewart Parnell: a memoir by his brother John Howard Parnell* (London, 1916), p. 38. **40** Foster, *Parnell*, p. 40.

private cricket ground 'hand in hand with Mrs Twopenny', the Parnell family nurse, and watched with 'keenest interest every phase of the game' as it was played on the 'celebrated' cricket ground at Avondale, located at the top of the lawn in front of the house.[41] John and Charles practised cricket 'assiduously' with their father on this ground and John, the older and stronger of the siblings, bowled while Charles acted as wicket-keeper.[42] In the evenings, the Parnell brothers further developed their skills playing with the working boys of the demesne on the slope that stretched from the cricket ground to the Casino, the dower house adjacent to Avondale.[43] Early match experience was gained in the young boys' matches played against Ballyarthur, which were generally held in conjunction with the adult games played between the estates, and Charles was 'invariably chosen to replace any player who did not turn up'.[44] Cricket was his main recreational activity but he also engaged in donkey races on the lawn in front of Avondale House, and the boys went fishing and shooting with their father. Following the death of the 15-year-old Hayes Parnell in a riding accident in 1855, his father John Henry Parnell retired as master of the hunt and sold his hounds; consequently hunting played no part in the life of the young Charles Stewart Parnell. Driving in a donkey and cart to Aughrim and panning for gold in the river there was a far more important pastime to him.[45]

This idyllic lifestyle ended in 1859 with the sudden death of John Henry Parnell. Charles, who inherited the estate, was the only member of the family in Ireland at the time, and was the only member who attended the funeral. Shortly afterwards, Avondale was vacated and Parnell began a decade of dislocation that characterized his teenage years. The family initially moved to Dalkey, then to Kingstown the following year, before finally settling at 14 Upper Temple Street in Dublin city in 1862. The Parnell children were wards of the court of chancery and the Avondale estate was leased until 1867 to Thomas Edwards, chief engineer with the Dublin, Wicklow and Wexford Railway Company, who continued to make the cricket lawn available for matches. The family connection with the district was maintained as the Parnell children had access to the Casino house for the entire 1860–7 period and regularly spent time there.

Charles Stewart Parnell's relationship with schooling and education was difficult and after periods in Yeovil as a 6-year-old and Kirk Langley when he was 8, Charles was educated at home from 1856 to 1859 by a succession of tutors, without any obvious success. In the words of Roy Foster, 'It is unlikely that he learnt much.'[46] In 1863, the brothers enrolled at Chipping Norton in Oxfordshire where, as boarders, they attended the private cramming school of Reverend Wishaw. The numbers attending the school were small. John and Charles had their own classroom, and lodged in a cottage opposite the rectory.[47] In October 1865, Charles Parnell entered Magdalene College in Cambridge, a

41 John Parnell, *Memoir*, pp 22, 15. 42 Ibid., p. 31. 43 Ibid., pp 14–15. 44 Ibid., p. 31. 45 Ibid., p. 75. 46 Foster, *Parnell*, pp 75–6. 47 Ibid., p. 107.

college that was notorious for its low academic standards. He remained registered as a student until May 1869 but he was present for only six of the twelve terms. He was absent for almost all of 1868 and only returned for the final seven weeks of April and May of 1869. A refusal to pay a subscription to the Boat Club earned him a degree of unpopularity with some of his fellow students. The story of his exit from Cambridge is well known: he was convicted for his part in a drunken brawl at the town's railway station and on 26 May was rusticated for the remainder of the term.[48] That was his final encounter with formal education; he abandoned what had been 'a negative and intellectually fruitless experience' and returned to Avondale without graduating.[49]

It is likely that during this peripatetic period of existence cricket provided one of the few meaningful activities to the teenage Parnell. The first newspaper reference to the Parnell brothers' participation in a cricket match dates from 1860, when the *Irish Times* carried a report on a match between Dalkey and the Eagle Club in which the brothers batted in both innings of the match without scoring a run.[50] The cricket apprenticeship continued between 1863 and 1865 when they were based at Chipping Norton. They regularly travelled to play cricket at the nearby village of Churchill, where Charles got a 'high reputation as a bat, wicket-keeper and catch'.[51] Despite telling T.P. O'Connor that he thought more about cricket than his studies, he did not get a freshman's trial and never represented the university. He seems to have played only twice for Magdalene College, failing to score against Peterhouse, but hitting nineteen runs against Trinity Hall in a match that took place two days after the incident for which he was later rusticated.[52]

An examination of John Lawrence's *Handbook of Irish cricket*, the *Wicklow Newsletter*, the *Irish Times*, the *Dublin Evening Post* and other sources has identified thirty-six cricket matches in which Parnell was a player. Of his enthusiasm for the game there can be little doubt. In one period of nine days in September 1865, he played cricket on no less than seven days, making the most of any opportunity to play before departing for Cambridge.[53]

This analysis reveals that Charles Stewart Parnell played for fifteen different teams in Ireland. He represented Dalkey, Avondale, County Wicklow, South Wicklow, Rathdrum, All-Comers, Na Shuler, the Phoenix Club, the 22 of Lord Fitzwilliam, the 18 of Dublin City, Bray Cricket Club, Dublin County, Mr Hobart's XI, Omnium Gatherum and a Wicklow-Wexford-Carlow combination. The bulk of his playing activity was confined to his teenage years. He played ten matches in 1864 and eight each in the 1862 and 1865 seasons. The variety of

48 Ged Martin, 'Parnell and Cambridge: some new evidence', *Magdalene College Magazine and Record*, 36 (1992), pp 37–41, accessed at www.gedmartin.net, 14 Sept. 2018. 49 Paul Bew, *Enigma: a new life of Charles Stewart Parnell* (Dublin, 2011), p. 12. 50 *Irish Times*, 3 Aug. 1860. 51 Parnell, *Memoir*, p. 51. 52 Martin, 'Parnell at Cambridge', p. 77; Kee, *The laurel and the ivy*, p. 37. 53 Kee, *The laurel and the ivy*, p. 25.

# CRICKET.

## EAGLE CRICKET CLUB v. DALKEY

This match was played in the Phœnix Park on Saturday last, and ended in favour of the Eagle by 118 runs, a result which was mainly attributable to the brilliant batting of Messrs. T. Phillips and Johnstone; and the excellent bowling of Mr. Nowlan. For Dalkey, Mr. A. Carpenter batted well, and the round-hand bowling of Mr. Goddard was difficult to play. The score was as follows:—

DALKEY.

| First Innings. | | Second Innings. | |
|---|---|---|---|
| — White, Esq, c Kennedy, b Nolan, | 7 | c Gartlan, b Williams, | 3 |
| —Goddard, Esq, c Kennedy, b Williams | 4 | c Gartlan, b Williams, | 8 |
| — Ellis, Esq, b Nolan, | 1 | c Gartlan, b Williams, | 7 |
| H Carpenter, Esq, b Nowlan, | 4 | c and b Williams, | 4 |
| J Preston, Esq, c Welland, b Williams | 0 | b Williams, | 2 |
| A Carpenter, Esq, l b w, b May, | 18 | b Nowlan, | 0 |
| J White, Esq, b Nowlan, | 2 | Not out, | 5 |
| — Hunt, Esq, b Nowlan, | 0 | c Gartlan, b Nowlan, | 1 |
| J Parnell, Esq, b Nowlan, | 0 | c Kennedy, b Williams, | 0 |
| W Preston, Esq, b Nowlan, | 0 | b Williams, | 0 |
| A Parnell, Esq, not out, | 0 | b Williams, | 0 |
| Byes, | 1 | | 2 |
| Total, | 37 | Total, | 29 |

EAGLE.

| 1st Innings. | | 2nd Innings. | |
|---|---|---|---|
| T Phillips, Esq, not out, | 0 | c Parnell, b Carpenter, | 52 |
| E Johnstone, Esq, b Preston, | 0 | l b w, b Goddard, | 30 |
| S Williams, Esq, b Goddard, | 4 | b Goddard, | 17 |
| J Kennedy, Esq, b Goddard, | 11 | b Goddard, | 2 |
| C Welland, Esq, b Goddard, | 5 | b Preston, | 2 |
| E Nolan, Esq, c Ellis, b Preston, | 6 | c Carpenter, b Goddard, | 0 |
| J Beaty, Esq, run out, | 3 | not out, | 0 |
| H Doran, Esq, run out, | 0 | b Preston, | 5 |

**10.2** First newspaper reference to Parnell brothers playing cricket, *Irish Times*, 3 Aug. 1860.

teams involved illustrates another aspect of how the sport developed in Ireland: the majority of these were transient combinations assembled for special occasions and challenges; however with the possible exception of the Phoenix Club, Parnell was playing with members of the landed gentry.

Parnell's career with the Phoenix Club, where he also served on the club committee, was rather short. In July and August 1865, he represented the club against Leinster and Westmeath.[54] However, at a committee meeting held in November 1866, it was reported that he had not paid his annual subscription. He did not play for Phoenix again and from that time his cricketing interests were mainly centred on County Wicklow.[55]

As a 17-year-old, Charles Stewart Parnell played in the Na Shuler Club's first match against the Vice-Regal Lodge, scoring twelve runs in the first innings and eighteen in the second, described by the *Irish Times* as 'a fluky 18, having been missed repeatedly'.[56] A close relationship existed between the massive Fitzwilliam estate at Coolattin and the members of the County Carlow Cricket Club. It was from this link that the Na Shuler Club, a nomadic landed-gentry conglomerate, emerged. In April 1863, several gentlemen lunched at Coolattin Park, where they founded a club for the 'encouragement of cricket in Ireland'. Membership was confined to Irish gentlemen 'by birth, family or residence'. The members were responsible for paying their own expenses on match days and consequently no membership fees were payable.[57] Na Shuler was intended to be an Irish version of the touring English I Zingari team founded in 1845 by a group of old Harrovians. This team owned no ground of their own but were available to play at any country house that offered suitable hospitality and entertainment, and the members combined playing cricket with attendance at elite balls and banquets. They hired no professionals and part of their mission was to end the dependency of gentlemen cricketers on professional bowlers.[58]

Cricket is a sport that lends itself to statistical analysis as a means of measuring a player's ability. In the thirty-six different matches involving Parnell where teams and scorers were listed, Parnell played a total of fifty innings, in which he accumulated a total of 410 runs giving him an average of 8.2 runs per innings. His highest score was forty-nine, scored for County Wicklow on his second visit to the crease against the team of the 12th Regiment in July 1864 where, according to the *Freeman's Journal*, 'he handled the willow in true cricketing style';[59] on seventeen occasions, he was dismissed without scoring. On twenty-seven occasions, he scored five runs or less, and he scored more than thirty runs in only three games. These batting statistics suggest that Parnell was a player of limited ability within his social circle but given his personal circumstances at the time and the semi-nomadic nature of his existence this is

54 *Dublin Evening Post*, 29, 31 July 1865; *Westmeath Guardian*, 10 Aug. 1865. 55 Payal, *Phoenix Club*, p. 8. 56 *Irish Times*, 1 Aug. 1863. 57 Ibid. 58 Derek Birley, *A social history of English cricket* (London, 1999), pp 82–3. 59 *Freeman's Journal*, 9 July 1864.

hardly surprising. Parnell's primary reputation was as a batsman, although he seldom featured as the opening batsman. His participation as a bowler was inconsistent and he rarely bowled against the better-quality sides. His best performances with ball in hand came against the local Wicklow teams. For example, in July 1863, he played for Avondale against Ballyarthur and bowled out seven of the opposition for a loss of twenty runs.[60]

Parnell's biographers have characterized him as an 'autocratic captain' who played just within the rules and often outside them. Contemporary sources make no reference to Parnell as a captain but no doubt when Avondale took to the crease the master of the estate donned the mantle of captaincy. He reputedly always insisted on the implementation of the two-minute law for batsmen, as defined in the Marylebone Cricket Club laws of the day, to the annoyance of the opposing team and umpires.[61] This wasn't unusual for the time and the great W.G. Grace wasn't averse to invoking it when the occasion demanded. Parnell's reputation as an autocratic captain is based on a passage in Barry O'Brien's *Life of Parnell*.[62] In this account, provided 'by one who knew him', the parallels between Parnell as a cricketer and as a politician are clearly implicit. A dispute between Parnell and the Phoenix captain ended with a stubborn Parnell refusing to concede on the point at issue, so he withdrew his team and 'marched his growling eleven' from the ground, ignoring the fact that many of the players had made long journeys to the venue. According to O'Brien 'the captain [Parnell] did not care. In later years Mr Parnell used to use the Irish party much as he used the Wicklow eleven'.[63] However, the story about Parnell withdrawing his Wicklow eleven following a dispute with the Phoenix captain lacks credibility. The story contains too many parallels with Parnell's later political career and has Parnell conveniently displaying many of the characteristics he later displayed as a politician. Given the history of the Wicklow county XI, the suggestion that 'In later years Mr Parnell used the Irish party much as he used the Wicklow eleven' is fanciful and almost certainly without foundation. Significantly, Arthur Samuels, who was a contemporary of Parnell and a member of the Phoenix Club, and very familiar with the cricket scene makes no reference to this incident.[64]

## IV

The Wicklow County Club should have been the primary vehicle available to Parnell to display his cricket prowess but the club was relatively inactive during

60 *Wicklow Newsletter*, 25 July 1863. Despite Parnell's best efforts Avondale were beaten by 36 runs. 61 Pryall, *The history of the club*, unpaginated. The two-minute rule is the time allowed for a new batsman to come to the crease; failure to do so in time constituted a legitimate method of dismissal. 62 R. Barry O'Brien, *The life of Charles Stewart Parnell* (London, 1910), i, p. 52. 63 Ibid. 64 Samuels, *Early cricket in Ireland*, pp 28–9.

**10.3** Avondale.

the 1860s. It was revived in 1862 and a new constitution adopted. Mondays and Fridays were the designated practice days and were initially held at Avondale.[65]

A standard white uniform was adopted, with a purple and gold riband adding a note of spectacle. A £1 10*s*. entrance subscription was required and honorary members also paid a 10*s*. fee. It would be wrong to think of the county team as in any way equating to a modern-day GAA representative team, or one that was composed of the outstanding players in a county. Family pedigree and social status determined membership rather than an individual's ability with ball or bat. Membership was confined to those connected to the county of Wicklow by birth, residence and property.[66] This was reflected in the composition of the county club committee in this period. The president of the club was the Honourable Frederick Ponsonby of Coolattin, a founder member of both the I Zingari and Na Shuler clubs, whose Wicklow property included almost 90,000 acres of land with a valuation of £46,440, which he managed in absentia. Major Gun Cunninghame of Mount Kennedy was the county club's vice president. Parnell was a committee member and was joined by other members of Wicklow landed-gentry society including Henry Hodgson (Ballyraine, Arklow),

**65** *Wicklow Newsletter*, 18 June 1864. **66** J.T.H., *Handbook, 1869–70*, p. 152; ibid., *1870–1*, p. 192.

O.B. Simpson (Carnew), F.G. Wright (Milltown Lodge), Christopher Barton (Glendalough), Capt. Posnett (Enniskerry), George Booth (Lara), Capt. Bayly (Ballyarthur) and the Honourable Henry Monck (Charleville).[67] Major Gun Cunninghame was the most proactive member of the committee. This was recognized in 1866, when he was presented with 'a splendid bat purchased from Mr John Lawrence' with the end of the handle mounted 'in silver and a suitable inscription engraved on it.' The presentation recognized Gun Cunninghame's 'exertions to promote cricket in the county, and his liberality in preparing a portion of the lawn of Mount Kennedy Demesne, on which he established weekly practice meetings.'[68]

Despite its proximity to Dublin, and the availability of three fine cricket grounds in different parts of the county at Coolattin, Avondale and Mount Kennedy, each in close proximity to a railway station, the involvement of the Wicklow gentry in the game was fitful at best during the 1860s and 1870s. (Glendalough was added to the list of county grounds available in 1870.[69]) The 1864 season was something of a disaster for the county side and included a debacle against Sandymount, who hit the record score of 524 runs against the 5 put up by the Wicklow team in their twenty minutes of playing time.[70] James Gilligan hammered the Wicklow bowling for 200, and was the first player to make a double-century in Irish cricket. The club's busiest season was 1865, when seven matches were played. The activity of any season was mediated by the presence or absence of the county families' cricketing enthusiasts. Only three matches – one in Avondale against St Columba's College and two in Coolattin against Na Shuler and County Carlow – were played in the 1866 season, 'owing to the absence of some of the leading members'.

In addition, a north v. south Wicklow match and return game were played at Mount Kennedy. Parnell was involved in only one of these matches.[71] In the 1867 season, 'no challenges were issued' and only matches against Na Shuler and Holyville Park School were played, both at Mount Kennedy; Parnell was one of the players who featured on both occasions. Two members had departed for the Cape of Good Hope and Canada, while O.B. Simpson suffered a severe injury following an accident. Consequently, the club was deprived of its best batsmen, fielders and most promising bowlers.[72] In 1869, Lawrence noted that no county match had been played at Avondale during the previous two seasons as Mount Kennedy again hosted the two county games played in the 1868 season, in contrast to their Westmeath and Meath equivalents, who engaged in fifteen and ten matches, respectively.[73] No matches were reported for the 1869 season. In 1870 and 1871 only two county matches were played in each season.[74] In 1870, the club lost the services of H. Hodgson, G. Sherwood and O. Simpson but

67 Ibid., *1865–66*, p. 67. 68 Ibid., *1866–67*, p. 6. 69 Ibid., *1870–71*, p. 192. 70 *Wicklow Newsletter*, 23 July 1864. 71 J.T.H., *Handbook, 1866–67*, pp 91–2. 72 Ibid., p. 102. 73 Ibid., *1868–69*, pp 153, 131. 74 Ibid., *1870–71*, p. 192; ibid., *1871–72*, p. 220.

gained the services of Capt. E. Bayly, who had returned to the Ballyarthur demesne from abroad, and 'showed that he had not lost any of his batting powers'. The captain's return added Ballyarthur as a venue for inter-estate matches and social gatherings and Colonel and Mrs Bayly 'entertained a large circle of friends in that beautiful and charming demesne' with a match between Mr Parnell's XI and Mr Bayly's XI the central attraction.[75] A combination of circumstances conspired in 1872 to prevent the county club from engaging in any matches. According to the report in the Lawrence handbook, the club's finest bowler, H. Hackett, was beguiled by 'the classic and scientific region of Trinity College'; H. Hodgson explored the 'sunny regions of Spain'; 'Captain Posnett was nowhere having surrendered to the regret of all to the gentle influences of the Misses Hippo, Squill and Tolu'; and the 'active Parnell had migrated to the American Continent', while 'the rainy season completed the disasters' of the County Wicklow Club. No cricket was played at Mount Kennedy because of family illness.[76]

Parnell had travelled to America, an odyssey inspired partly by his unrequited love of Miss Woods, partly to examine his coal-mining investments and also to visit his brother John, who had moved to Alabama a year or so earlier to plant cotton and grow fruit.[77] John Parnell considered Miss Woods' rejection to be a defining moment in his brother's life and wrote: 'His jilting undoubtedly helped to drive his energies into politics, for he was deeply hurt at the idea of being considered a country gentleman without any special abilities.'[78] The 1871 season was the last for which the Wicklow County Club made any returns of matches to the *Lawrence handbook*. It was also the last season for which any reference to Parnell's cricket-playing activities is to be found. Only one more reference to Avondale appears in *Lawrence*, and that relates to two matches played against Mr Tombe's XI in July 1876.[79] At this stage, Parnell's parliamentary career was in its embryonic stage as an elected home rule MP for the Meath constituency. He had successfully contested the Meath by-election in April 1875 after a failed attempt in a County Dublin by-election in 1874. His visits to Avondale remained regular up to 1882, but from 1883 became more and more infrequent, and during his later years the visits were primarily concerned with overseeing the estate mines and sawmills. The days when Avondale was a centre of hospitality and socializing, including the staging of inter-estate cricket occasions, were long gone by 1880. His active involvement in sport at this time was confined to his regular grouse-shooting expeditions to his mountain retreat at Aughavannagh during the month of August, where he could dispense with formality and unnecessary conversation. This was where he was happiest and most at ease. His companions on these shoots were generally his political colleagues.[80] These consistent

75 Ibid., *1870–71*, pp 191–3. 76 Ibid., *1872–73*, p. 198. 77 F.S.L. Lyons, *Charles Stewart Parnell* (London, 1977), p. 38. 78 Parnell, *Memoir*, p. 26; Bew, *Parnell*, p. 12. 79 J.H.T., *Handbook, 1876–77*, p. 123. 80 Foster, *Parnell*, pp 150, 185–8.

shooting expeditions represented the one part of the country gentleman tradition Parnell never abandoned.[81] According to Katherine O'Shea, Parnell ceased to attend cricket matches after his election to parliament but his enthusiasm for the game remained and she had a private ground laid out for him at her Eltham home.[82] However, Avondale was made available for another form of recreation and this has been largely ignored by historians.

## V

The GAA was founded at Hayes' Hotel, Thurles, on 1 November 1884 and Charles Stewart Parnell was invited to be one of the three patrons of the association, along with Archbishop Croke of Cashel, and Land League campaigner Michael Davitt. A high-profile patron was essential for any ambitious organization at the time, whether at a local or national level. The acceptance of an invitation provided a vote of approval or a type of character reference for the organization involved. The invitation by the officers of the GAA to the leaders of Catholic Ireland, nationalist Ireland and agrarian Ireland was particularly astute and their acceptance of the offer provided the opportunity for the new association to secure the support of politicians, land agitators and clergy at local level. According to Cusack, the invitation to Parnell was issued because 'The GAA, from the manner in which it would have to be worked, might appear to be slightly antagonistic to the National League. The patronage would remove that suspicion.'[83]

Parnell replied from the Irish parliamentary offices on 17 December 1884, accepting the position, and offered to do 'anything I can to render the working of the movement a success'.[84] He paid little attention to the GAA after his appointment, having, as W.F. Mandle points out, 'much else on his mind in the second half of the 1880s, both politically and personally'.[85] This may be so, but the appointment had practical implications for the GAA as the grounds at Avondale were made available for staging GAA events very different to the genteel cricket events previously held there.[86] Avondale, once famed as a venue for elites' sports events, now, on occasion, became a venue for mass participation and spectating. On these occasions, 'all the county' was represented in the broadest democratic sense.

Tournaments were very important promotional events in the spread of hurling and football as the public at large became familiar with the new GAA sports and their attendant rules. The spread of these tournaments became an

81 Ibid., p. 189. 82 Katherine O'Shea, *The uncrowned king of Ireland: Charles Stewart Parnell: his love story and political life* (London, 1973), p. 209. 83 *Celtic Times*, 19 Mar. 1887. 84 *Freeman's Journal*, 24 Dec. 1884. 85 W.F. Mandle, 'Parnell and sport', *Studia Hibernica*, 28 (1994), p. 106. 86 For more on the country house and the GAA, see Ciarán Reilly's essay

extraordinary cultural phenomenon that provided Irish people with a day out with a difference – in the words of Paul Rouse, 'a unique cocktail of sport and drink and music and pageantry which mixed the local with the national'.[87] The tournament hosted at Avondale on 31 October 1886, one of the first of its kind, was a logistical and athletic triumph as six football matches were played between teams from Wexford and Wicklow. Clubs from Wicklow town, Avondale, Togher (Roundwood), Ashford, Barndarraig and Rathnew represented the host county against clubs representing Wexford town, Rosslare, Crossabeg, Ballyore, Piercestown and Castlebridge. The event was a model of sound organization and planning. A programme of events was printed in advance that included the schedule for the day, and referees, umpires and timekeepers were appointed to manage the day's play. Two excursion trains travelled from Wexford to Rathdrum as well as a special train from Dublin. Some 12,000 people reportedly attended. Enough bands were present to provide an added air of musical festivity. These were the St Kevin's National Temperance Brass and Reed Band, Bray; the Arklow Irish Volunteers Band; the band of St Kieran's industrial school, Rathdrum; and the Ashford, Kilcoole and Wicklow fife and drum band.[88] The football field was located about a quarter of a mile inside the entrance to Avondale demesne 'and within view of the Parnell mansion'. Its suitability as a football pitch was lessened by an incline on one side and, as reported by the *Wexford People*, 'near the middle [stood] a small tree'.[89]

The Wexford clubs were better prepared for the tournament since the county committee had organized a qualifying tournament before the Avondale event. As often happened on these occasions, the size of the football pitch contracted as excitement heightened and the crowds encroached on the playing area. This was the only negative aspect of the day's event and was the subject of some criticism in *Sport* (though not featured in the *Wexford People* report). *Sport*'s reporter praised 'the order of the people', but felt that

> the arrangements for so big an affair were altogether incomplete. The sidelines were so badly roped that the people had burst in through them before play had properly commenced, while the end lines were apparently without even this fragile protection. Naturally the people crushed into the field for the purpose of getting, as they imagine, a better view.[90]

Although Parnell himself was not in attendance, the presence of other family members provided the Parnell stamp of approval to the occasion. His mother, Mrs Delia Parnell, was present, as were John Parnell and his sister Emily Dickinson. Michael Cusack also attended, along with officials of the Wicklow

in this volume. **87** Paul Rouse, *The hurlers: the first All-Ireland championship and the making of modern hurling* (Dublin, 2018), p. 64. **88** *Wexford People*, 3 Nov. 1886. **89** Ibid. **90** *Sport*, 6 Nov. 1886.

county committee.[91] Delia Parnell expressed herself delighted with the play, and remarked to the *Sport* reporter that the costumes were very handsome, and she was impressed with the athletic ability of the players. The play reminded her of what an American general once told her about 'How the Irish ran into battle – in fact they did not run, but they rushed'.[92] The Parnell family party remained in attendance until the last match concluded, and when they returned to Avondale House they were accompanied by some of the 'representative nationalists' in attendance, who were introduced to Delia and listened to her as she set out her democratic and republican principles:

> I don't care about any monarchy. I believe in a republic … if anybody offered me a crown I would not take it. It is better that the people should be ruled through the Congress or Parliament that has been returned by the people, than they should be governed by persons who have not their confidence, and who cannot then rule for their benefit …[93]

This was the type of high-profile occasion where Delia used to deliver what Roy Foster has termed 'inconsequential speeches', and it is probably fair to conclude that she had little understanding of the cultural significance of the occasion she had just witnessed. The staging of the tournament coincided with her return to Avondale in September 1886, where she remained until late 1887. She had spent very little time in Ireland over the previous twelve years, having moved to America in the early 1870s, where she resided in Bordenstown, New Jersey. She occasionally featured in news reports for her political dabbling, her eccentricity and the instability of her personal fortune.[94] Her return to Avondale followed well-publicized reports of her financial distress in her then base of New York.

Following the success of this tournament, Avondale hosted several Wicklow championship games in 1887. On 20 March, three championship games were played there, followed by three more on 3 April 1887. Four games were played on 17 April, and on 8 May five games attracted an attendance of over 8,000 spectators.[95] The *Celtic Times* reporter, undoubtedly Michael Cusack himself, was so impressed by what he witnessed on 17 April that he could scarcely bring himself to believe he was 'not in the heart of gallant Tipperary, so enthusiastic were the crowds, so charming were the girls and so thoroughly Gaelic did everything look. The field was well enclosed and excellent order was preserved throughout the contest.'[96]

Events were not so smooth during the next championship games staged in Avondale on 8 May, when the difficulties facing a sport attempting to make the transition from an unregulated traditional form to a modern codified form were

91 G.M. Byrne and P.J. Noonan, *50 years of Wicklow football* (Wicklow, 1935), pp 35–6. 92 *Sport*, 6 Nov. 1886. 93 *Wexford People*, 3 Nov. 1886. 94 Foster, *Parnell*, pp 226–8. 95 Jim Brophy, *The leather's echo* (Wicklow, 1984), pp 15–16. 96 *Celtic Times*, 23 Apr. 1887.

in evidence. This was an eventful day that brought the world of the early GAA, with all its pageantry, excitement, sporting endeavour, confusions and violence to Avondale. Parnell was present on this occasion and 'followed the play with great interest but he looked very pale and careworn'.[97] The *Celtic Times* reporter, Michael Cusack, 'saw Parnell on horseback, looking like a part of the horse, as the pair appeared to be worked by one controlling will'. This presumably was intended as a tribute to Parnell's horsemanship. Crowd encroachment onto the pitch proved to be a problem; the reporter saw 'the spectators, when no man of influence put in an appearance, steadily advancing on the field of play, and squatting on the grounds as the day advanced'. He saw a 'few ill-conditioned youths running round with a pole, and exciting the people … and stewards and spectators freely using ash saplings on one another's heads, in a manner worthy of the halcyon days of faction-fighting.' The Annacurra and Churches (Glendalough) match was abandoned after thirty minutes when 'a disgraceful boxing tournament took place instead of a football match'. The last scheduled game between Avoca and Togher saw 'forty-two men taking the field against the Avoca twenty-two'. The Delgany men had also reported for duty despite the fact that the county committee had previously disqualified them for using illegal players.[98] Despite the crowd trouble, the day was not without its characteristic pageantry. The Bray Emmet Club was accompanied to Avondale by the band of the Phoenix Brewery, and prior to their departure they stopped at Avondale House and performed 'God Save Ireland'. According to the *Belfast News-Letter*: 'a new song entitled "The New Campaign", making special reference to recent events in Ireland, was also sung and played in the hearing of Mr Parnell.'[99]

The promotion of athletics was part of the GAA's initial agenda, and on 16 August 1887 an athletics meeting under the rules of the association was held at Avondale.[100] This was the concluding event of a bazaar that was held for the purpose of paying off a debt on the Rathdrum industrial schools. On this occasion the appearance of Mrs Parnell 'was the signal for a tremendous outburst of cheering, and a forest of hats immediately began to wave'.[101]

## CONCLUSION

It is surprising how the use of Avondale as a venue for staging Gaelic football matches is largely ignored in the standard Parnell biographies. In general, the role of the aristocracy and gentry in promoting, or at least facilitating the early GAA has been a neglected topic in the history of the association, though this has now begun to be addressed by historians including Ciarán Reilly in this volume, and Paul Rouse in his history of the development of hurling.[102] Support for the

**97** *Belfast News-Letter*, 10 May 1887. **98** *Celtic Times*, 14 May 1887. **99** *Belfast News-Letter*, 10 May 1887. **100** Ibid., 13 Aug. 1887. **101** *Celtic Times*, 20 Aug. 1887. **102** Rouse, *Hurlers*,

GAA from the gentry and aristocracy was more widespread than previously imagined. The Pakenham family of Tullynally were one of the leading aristocratic unionist families in Westmeath, but this did not prevent them from supporting the Castlepollard hurling club, including providing a playing field, and in appreciation of this the members presented the countess of Longford with 'an Irish camán made from ash grown in Pakenham Hall'.[103]

The staging of tournament and championship Gaelic football matches at Avondale in the 1880s marked the return of sporting events to the Parnell estate for the first time in many years. Avondale's reputation as a cricket stronghold had belonged to the era of John Henry Parnell and this ended in 1859. Despite Charles Stewart Parnell's love of the sport, his involvement in matches took place for the most part outside of Avondale, and games of any significance were rarely staged there during his lifetime. He was absent from Avondale during the 1860s and from the early 1870s his interests lay elsewhere. This was also a time when the interests and involvement of the Wicklow landed gentry in the sport declined. The staging of the newly codified games of nationalist Ireland on the Avondale estate after Parnell, the leader of nationalist Ireland, had been nominated one of the patrons of the GAA was timely and appropriate to his political position. But his participation in the GAA was not unique to his class. The politico-religious demarcation lines that later became such a prominent feature of Irish sport had yet to be drawn.

Charles Stewart Parnell's prowess as a cricket player has been acknowledged by various biographers and historians. Roy Foster has described him as 'a good cricketer'. For F.S.L. Lyons, he was 'that valuable commodity, a good wicket-keeper-batsman' who carried 'gamesmanship to positively indecent extremes'.[104] Cricket historian Gerard Siggins has claimed that worse players than Parnell have represented Ireland,[105] a comment that perhaps tells us as much about the quality of the Irish cricket player as it does about Parnell's ability. Robert Kee's verdict was that Parnell 'seems to have been a fair all-rounder at the game'.[106] These observations are essentially based on the memoirs of John Howard Parnell, although both Kee and Foster also examined the *Wicklow Newsletter* for information on his cricket career. W.F. Mandle's summation of Parnell's sporting life, that 'it was conventional for his caste, not prolonged much beyond adolescence, varied indeed but not intensely pursued', is an appropriate one.[107] There was nothing unusual about someone from his social class and background being an active cricketer, and one must remember that when he began to play cricket it was the most popular field sport in Ireland. At that time, cricket was devoid of political baggage, and any suggestion that Parnell disassociated himself from the sport to further his political career is clearly untrue. The depiction of

pp 95, 102. **103** *Westmeath Guardian*, 6 July 1906. **104** Foster, *Parnell*, p. 75; Lyons, *Parnell*, pp 31, 37. **105** Gerard Siggins, *Green days: cricket in Ireland, 1792–2005* (Stroud, 2005), p. 17. **106** Kee, *The laurel and the ivy*, p. 23. **107** Mandle, 'Parnell and sport', p. 104.

cricket as an anti-national activity was an 1890s–1900s invention when cultural nationalism, in its various manifestations, targeted cricket and other 'alien' sports such as soccer and rugby as anti-national activities.[108] In the case of Charles Stewart Parnell, playing cricket was the ordinary in what was a truly extraordinary career.

**108** Tom Hunt, 'Classless cricket? Westmeath 1880–1905', *History Ireland*, 12:2 (Summer 2004), p. 29.

# Hill of Tarvit

ANTONIA LAURENCE-ALLEN

Hill of Tarvit mansion house is a family home designed by the prominent Scottish Arts and Crafts architect Robert Lorimer. Habitable by 1906, Tarvit is one of the most complete Edwardian houses in Scotland today, with its architecture, gardens, interiors and collections remaining largely intact.[1] It was commissioned by Frederick Sharp, a financier whose fortunes spun from his family's jute industry in Dundee, and his wife Beatrice White, just after the birth of their first child.

In his seminal study of French society, *Distinction*, Pierre Bourdieu showed how social order is created and legitimized. People's behaviours and tendencies are led by the 'cultural products' given to them – products like language, education, values and everyday activities like sport.[2] These products provide the individual with a sense of their place in a social group. Crucially, this sense is dominated by an unconscious feeling that something feels right, that one is 'in the right place'. This in turn reinforces social difference and ensures that class and hierarchy are legitimized. This essay argues that the design of Hill of Tarvit illustrates the Sharps' desire to be recognized and to feel 'at home' in the gentry class because their choices reflected both traditional values and modern fashions of the day. There are no letters, diaries or other archival materials to provide any personal insight into Frederick and Beatrice's decision to buy and develop Hill of Tarvit. However, their selected location, choice of house and pleasure grounds reveal the couple's disposition towards a certain set of societal norms, which would have guided their behaviour and thinking.

Lorimer created a new home filled with light and modern conveniences. Elements that both Beatrice and Frederick would have insisted upon. The couple married in 1896. Beatrice was at the relatively late age of 32 and came from a family interested in new technologies. Her father James and brother Martin had remodelled and modernized Balruddery House, where the family lived from 1881. It was one of the first houses in Scotland to run fully on electricity. By April 1881, Martin had installed a new oil-fired dynamo alongside a hydroelectric system that was powered by a dam located on the estate. Living with this technology meant that Beatrice had the knowledge and experience to

1 Interventions in the 1950s by the Marie Curie organization and in the 1990s by the National Trust for Scotland have meant that interiors and collections have been altered and added.
2 Pierre Bourdieu, *Distinction: a social critique of the judgement of taste*, trans. Richard Nice (6th ed., Cambridge, 1996).

11.1 Frederick Bower Sharp, n.d.

work with her husband to ensure their new home could take on new fashions. For example, the bathroom had running hot water and Tarvit was fully wired for electricity. The couple also abandoned the traditional 'below stairs' and placed the kitchen only 50 yards from the dining room, so food only had to travel

11.2 Beatrice White (pictured lying at the front) before she was married to Frederick Sharp. The group is made up of the Ogilvie, Sharp and White families, all of whom had businesses in Dundee and often gathered for sports and leisure activities, *c.*1880s.

through a small pantry and servery. The latter was fitted with an internal telephone system that connected to the dining room, to ensure immediate table service when a course had ended. The back of the house had a servants' hall, rooms for maids and storage cupboards for linen and modern appliances, such as the vacuum cleaner. The couple also ordered traditional features for the estate, such as the laundry house. This was located in the grounds and built on a grand scale with the same heated rolling racks that were only to be found in public wash houses.[3] It is a laundry fit for a Scottish country estate where changing for sports, entertaining and multiple activities would have generated a constant demand for clean, dry clothing and linen. As Sian Evans has pointed out, it was only country estates that tended to have these independent laundry houses: many other wealthy modern families sent their laundry off site.[4] Beatrice and Frederick were disposed to follow certain traditions as they constructed their new estate but they also availed themselves of new developments in convenience and comfort.

The design of Hill of Tarvit was largely driven by Frederick and Beatrice's generation, who were reacting to the dark and cluttered Victorian interiors of their childhoods. Frederick grew up on the banks of the Tay several miles east of Dundee in his father's Victorian house, Fernhall. The interiors were laden with dark furniture, and had richly patterned walls, heavy curtains and thick wall-to-wall carpets. Hill of Tarvit was therefore a reflection of the later nineteenth-

3 Annette Carruthers, 'The kitchen' in A. Carruthers (ed.), *The Scottish home* (Edinburgh, 1996), p. 95. 4 Sian Evans, *Life below stairs* (London, 2015), pp 72–5.

11.3 Hill of Tarvit laundry.

century 'cult of simplicity', following the more progressive and fashionable concept of blending the old and new while paring down ornament and furniture.[5] This is presumably why the Sharps hired Robert Lorimer, whose architectural practice was renowned for using Scottish craftsmen – like William Scott Morton and George Reid, of Whytock and Reid – to create Arts and Crafts buildings that paid homage to traditional crafts while making spaces more efficient.[6] All the rooms at Tarvit were designed to have a distinct purpose – from the French reception room (familiarly known to the family as the 'drawing room') to a baronial hall and the Chippendale-inspired dining room. Moreover, everything had a place, in order to avoid old-fashioned clutter. The pantry had a wooden sink to prevent damage to china and glass during washing. There was a bank-vault sized safe for the silver (as no butler was employed to guard it). A walk-in cupboard was added to the vestibule especially for muddy boots, croquet mallets, tennis racquets and umbrellas.

Beatrice and Frederick bought the estate of Wemyss Hall (as it was then known) in 1904, moving their nascent family to the rolling hills of Fife. Very aware of the dangers of city life, Sharp was one of three sons who continued their father John's jute business in Dundee, a city with over-crowded factory streets and some of the poorest air quality in Scotland. In 1896 life expectancy was low and large numbers of men were dying before the age of 40. Around a third of

5 Juliet Kinchin, 'The drawing room' in ibid., p. 178. 6 For more on Robert Lorimer's working methods, see Peter Savage, *Lorimer and the Edinburgh craft designers* (Edinburgh, 2005).

11.4 Hill of Tarvit library, with light coming from the floor-to-ceiling door that leads onto the terrace.

deaths were caused by bronchitis, tuberculosis and pneumonia.[7] The young couple's move to Fife was a calculated choice and it was not simply for the fresh air. Wemyss Hall was woven with Scottish heritage in a way that would have been invaluable to a couple with 'new' money. The landscape of Fife had all the hallmarks that would imbue an estate with signifiers of the gentry class, including ties to religion, royalty and history.

The estate lay just over a mile south of the station at Cupar, a Victorian commuter town on the Edinburgh-to-Dundee rail line that had been operating successfully since 1887.[8] Cupar was well known as one of the oldest country market centres in the region, dating back to the medieval period. In the mid-eighth century Fife had become a place of pilgrimage to visit the shrine of

7 City of Dundee report of the medical officer of health for the year ending 31 December 1896, Dundee City Archives, pp 1–15. 8 A rail bridge had opened in 1878 but collapsed the following year during a storm.

St Andrew's apostle, St Regulus. By the reign of David I in the twelfth century, monasteries were being built across Fife, from Culross in the west, to Dunfermline in the centre, Balmarino and Lindores in the north and St Andrews in the east. One of the main routes well-trodden by Christian pilgrims was through Cupar, an hour's walk from the grounds at Hill of Tarvit. As the county town for Fife, Cupar was very well placed to service travellers heading in all directions, and property in the area was coveted by nobles and merchants alike. During the fifteenth and sixteenth centuries this hive of activity increased as royal residences flourished, including the abbey and palace in Dunfermline and the hunting retreat at Falkland Palace.

Hill of Tarvit's land was first built upon by Sir John Scot, who had been a geographer and director of the chancel. Scot built a single tower in 1627 that he named Scotstarvit; the ruins can still be seen today. In 1904 the Sharps integrated this history into their new house by asking for the Scotstarvit fireplace to be installed into their new smoking room. After Scot's death the land remained in his family and a new house was built in 1697. The Wemyss family took over the estate in 1776 and renamed it Wemyss Hall, selling the mansion house to Frederick and Beatrice in 1904. The Wemyss family was regarded as one of the oldest noble families in Scotland, being directly descended from Celtic nobility through the clan MacDuff, the earls of Fife, who had owned the hunting grounds of nearby Falkland before James II confiscated them in the early fifteenth century. This rich history in and around Wemyss estate was the dynamic force that helped mould the new owners' social and subjective identities.[9] Being at the centre of Christian history, royalty and the clans of ancient Scotland were all things that added value to the land. Sport was also a primary contributor to Fife's attraction for a businessman like Frederick. The Wemyss estate was used for the Fife foxhound meet and the family knew 'Fife was considered a "swanky" place to live because of the hunt'.[10] As a keen hunter, the Wemyss Hall land ensured Frederick's place at the heart of an exclusive set.

Many Scottish industrialists were purchasing aristocratic estates as a means of elevating their status. The Sharps were not unusual in this. What is unique is their timing, for Frederick and Beatrice were designing the estate at the cusp of a new era. Hill of Tarvit illustrates how both Victorian values and Edwardian fashions were important social markers for a couple like the Sharps positioning themselves as gentry. It is well established that the Queen and Albert had successfully turned Scotland into a fashionable destination in the nineteenth century. Popularly known as 'North Britain', Scotland was embraced with a new interest. It was an area characterized by its opposition to the tame south. The north was wild, with sublime hills and mountains, and the perfect place for the

9 W.J.T. Mitchell (ed.), *Landscape and power* (2nd ed., Chicago, 2002), p. 2. 10 Joan Bentley (née Walker) was the granddaughter of Frederick's eldest brother John. She was interviewed by the property manager in 1997.

11.5 Hill of Tarvit mansion and gardens.

sports of hunting, shooting and fishing. In contrast to England's feminized picturesque landscapes, Scotland was a masculine space where the stag and the hunt were to be found. Edwin Landseer's 1851 painting, *Monarch of the Glen*, was a product and consequence of this stereotype, a painting commissioned to hang in the refreshment room of the House of Lords, where an English gentleman might be inspired to take up arms against the wilderness in Scotland.

Northern landscapes fascinated the Victorian public as they were representations of the 'sublime', as defined in the eighteenth century by the philosopher Edmund Burke to denote the expansive spaces that were to be feared and admired for their representation of divine intervention.[11] There was an admiration and fear of those people who lived in these spaces, and Victorian literature and culture is littered with perceptions of Highlanders as curios or 'savages' who seem happy with their lot living on the edge of the 'civilized' world. Scotland tended to be perceived in contrast to the civil, genteel and picturesque landscapes of England.[12] By the mid-nineteenth century photography was helping to increase the circulation of images that reinforced this idea.

11 Edward Burke, *A philosophical enquiry into the origin of our ideas of the sublime and beautiful* (London, 1757). 12 These concepts are discussed by many writers, for example, Murray

One photographer, contributing to a journal in the 1850s, had travelled through Scotland in despair, suggesting that Scottish hills were found wanting because they lacked the green and pleasant hedgerows, soft hills and glades of old England.[13]

Hill of Tarvit's landscape was shaped to reflect this old English ideal, with just the right mix of soft glades, pleasant rolling hills, abundant hedgerows and ancient trees. In the same way as Victoria and Albert had gentrified the estate of Balmoral in Aberdeenshire, Beatrice and Frederick could tame the old Wemyss lands. During the Victorian period the Scottish elite had fostered a national identity for themselves that was born from a loyalty and affection for British patriotism. Thus, to identify with the gentry class, Frederick and his wife would have clearly seen themselves as both British and Scottish, picturing themselves at the heart of the empire and thus firmly within a 'civilized' and genteel world, which could only be defined by an English landscape.[14]

The few accounts we have of Frederick and Beatrice suggest they were mild-mannered individuals with conservative attitudes, both growing up in wealthy families involved in the jute industry in Dundee and directly benefitting from the profits of empire.[15] This suggests they would have been guided by the social conventions of tradition. Beatrice's father was in a similar line of business to Frederick's family, having made his fortune exporting linen and jute products to New York. Frederick had met Beatrice at a family gathering; the Whites and Sharps often met for tennis or croquet afternoons at Balruddery.

Sport and leisure were the social habits that brought these families together, and women were encouraged to participate alongside their male counterparts. Healthy activity was very much a Victorian value and stemmed from increased leisure time for many middling classes combined with an anxiety about idleness.[16] This message was well known. A Bovril advertisement from 1890 depicts a woman striking a golf ball and has the tag line 'For Health, Strength and Beauty'. As well as overtly stating that a healthy diet (of which Bovril plays a key part) will make a woman strong and attractive, this advert also suggests that a woman of good repute should use her leisure time by taking an active interest in sports. Victorian etiquette dictated which sports and how much exertion were suitable for a lady, as the anxiety over idleness was coupled with a concern for gentility. When it came to dressing for golf or cycling, magazines like *Woman at Home* published 'how to' guides on proper attire and attitude. And, by the turn

Pittock, *The invention of Scotland: the Stuart myth and the Scottish identity, 1638 to the present* (London, 1991); Marjorie Morgan, *National identities and travel in Victorian Britain* (Hampshire, 2001); K.H. Grenier, *Tourism and identity in Scotland, 1770–1914: creating Caledonia* (Aldershot, 2005). **13** John Gutch, 'Recollections and jottings of a photographic tour, undertaken during the years 1856–1857', *Photographic Notes*, 3:51 (1858), p. 127. **14** For the growth of this idea, see: Graeme Morton, *Unionist nationalism: governing urban Scotland, 1830–1860* (East Linton, 1999). **15** Hill of Tarvit has no family records, but oral history has been documented from several family descendants. **16** K.E. McCrone, *Playing the game:*

**11.6** The garden terrace descends to a large lawn and the hedges are carved like buttresses.

of the century, debates in journals and newspapers suggested that certain types of exercise were wholly inappropriate for a lady. A (male) writer in the *Scottish Review* in 1900, for example, was anxious that 'boisterous bodily exertion is enshrined in the modern young lady's creed and ambitions' – so much so that sports, such as hockey, cricket and football, are considered too 'mannish' and unsuited to the sweetness and refinement of a woman's 'genuine nature'.[17] There were no such sports at Hill of Tarvit for women. Golf, tennis and croquet were the predominant games pursued on the estate.

Sport and leisure lay at the heart of the house's design. Lawrence Weaver writing in *Country Life* in 1912 suggested that Robert Lorimer was asked to 'make the ground-floor rooms lofty and well windowed to admit plentiful sunlight'.[18] The Sharps clearly wished their interiors to remain in direct conversation with the gardens. The entire front of the house was for the family and faced south; the services were all laid out at the back where sunlight was a rarer commodity. Beatrice adopted the more modern concept of hiring staff

*sport and the physical emancipation of English women, 1870–1914* (London, 1998). **17** Both anonymous articles from *Woman at Home* (1893–5) and T.P.W., 'The redundancy of spinster gentlewomen', *Scottish Review* (1900) are quoted by Linda Fleming, 'Bodies, sexuality and health' in E. Breitenbach, L. Fleming, S. Karly Kehoe and L. Orr (eds), *Scottish women: a documentary history, 1780–1914* (Edinburgh, 2013), pp 44–7. **18** L. Weaver, 'Hill of Tarvit, Fife: the seat of Mr. F.B. Sharp', *Country Life*, 834 (Dec. 1912), pp 926–31.

when she required them, so there was little need for a large servants' wing. At either end of the ground floor, two high rooms – each with paired sash windows – have doors leading onto the terrace, providing direct access to the gardens from the dining room and the drawing room. This new terrace ensured outside living was on par with inside life.

Sharp's 140-yard-long terrace ran the length of the south façade and fell in tiers down to a croquet and tennis lawn fourteen feet below. The lawn itself is lined by immaculate formal hedges, running like cathedral buttresses along the terrace wall, which metaphorically connect the garden and estate to the Gothic churches at the heart of local ecclesiastical architecture. The exterior of the house was also an important statement of place, being harled and painted white in the Fife coastal tradition by Robert Graham of Edinburgh. Below all this is a nine-hole golf course, spreading out to the boundaries of the walled estate.[19]

Frederick came from a family involved in the professionalization of golf. He, his brothers (John, Robert and William) and his son Hugh were all involved in the St Andrews Royal and Ancient Golf Club rules committee, at a time when people were flocking to public links courses, and Americans were starting to modify the game. It was only in the nineteenth century that leisure became an option for the new middle classes and it was a mark of success to take time off work. By the 1900s, however, Scottish working classes were also starting to enjoy 'half days' and scores of people boarded ferries at docks in Leith and Edinburgh for days out up the coast. As more ranks gained access to leisure time, the upper classes started to use their affluence to privatize their entertainment. The game of golf is a good example of this. A leisure activity for many years in various forms, golf had been accessible to all who had the time and inclination to play the game. The first golf clubs started formalizing in the mid-eighteenth century and by the 1850s there were sixteen clubs in Scotland. In the first decade of the twentieth century, eight new clubs opened in Fife alone. Many new clubs were also opening for women. The first women's club was founded at St Andrews in 1867, followed by one in Leven (1891) and one in Lundin (1910).[20]

As well as formalizing the professional game, the Sharp brothers were some of the key players in developing the first private courses in Scotland. They were all involved in the operations and management of Panmure Golf Club, east of Dundee, near Carnoustie. Robert administered the first Scottish Professional Championships at Panmure; he was also an avid collector of ceramics, clearly inspiring his younger brother Frederick to appreciate fine arts. Frederick's love of the game also dovetailed with the more elite pastime of collecting fine art. His first pictures were Dutch paintings of 'kolf', a nascent version of golf that was played on ice. Robert Lorimer had been specifically tasked with creating a home

**19** Statement of costs for Wemyss Hall (Papers of Sir Robert Stodart Lorimer, Edinburgh University Special Collections, 6a–27.Gen.1963/19/152). **20** Neil Tranter, *Sport, economy and society in Britain, 1750–1914* (Cambridge, 1998), pp 15, 84–5.

11.7 One of Frederick Sharp's 'kolf' paintings; attributed to Barent Avercamp. *Winter landscape with skaters on a river*, c.*1620–30*.

that could showcase Frederick's growing art collection. He designed the first-floor corridor in the tradition of a picture gallery especially for Frederick's kolf paintings, while the large central stairwell accommodated three sizeable Dutch oil paintings, all illustrating the spoils of the hunt.

The Sharps' golf course and art collection denoted taste as well as refined estate management, and exemplified Victorian etiquette by showing how 'new' money was spent wisely in acquiring and taming aristocratic land, as well as investing in the fine arts. The course also reflects a new Edwardian era, as it was only when the craze for golf took off in mid-Victorian Scotland, and municipal clubs were catering to the masses, that the ability to play in peace and in privacy became a signifier of wealth.[21] It was a very modern concept to have a golf course on your country estate. By installing a nine-hole course (as well as a tennis lawn), Frederick and Beatrice could avoid the general public and personalize their experience in an exclusive setting; such privacy had always been the privilege of the gentry class.

Hill of Tarvit estate's design emerged from habits nurtured by two people who identified with a particular way of life. Hill of Tarvit was specifically remembered as a home for entertaining and relaxing among family and friends.[22]

21 F.M.L. Thompson, *Gentrification and the enterprise culture: Britain, 1780–1980* (Oxford, 2001), p. 110. 22 John Bentley, interview with Hill of Tarvit property manager (Hill of Tarvit archives, uncatalogued, n.d.).

11.8 Hugh Sharp playing golf. According to the family, Hugh was a much finer golf player than his father Frederick, *c.*1930s.

It is therefore a direct reflection of, and a monument to, the habits Frederick and Beatrice gleaned from their family lives and their social circle. The house itself, with its modern conveniences and decluttered rooms, its large windows, south-facing terrace, paintings of landscapes, hunting and golf, reveal Frederick and Beatrice's culturally constructed tastes, all of which were clearly influenced by their education and family experiences. The couple created a modern house bedded in a traditional country estate and, in doing so, would have felt at home within the Scottish gentry class at the turn of the century. As Simon Ryan has pointed out, in the nineteenth century, the 'non-instrumental landscape garden' was a signifier for the 'luxury of being able to possess un-productive land'.[23] Tarvit projected this wealth and status, while also radiating a new idea that using land for sport and leisure was highly productive. Underpinning all this activity was the old Wemyss estate and the history of Fife. Tradition and modernity therefore enabled Frederick and Beatrice to feel a part of the heritage of Scotland and, therefore, 'natural' members of the landowning class.

23 S. Ryan, *The cartographic eye: how explorers saw Australia* (Cambridge, 1996), p. 73.

# A sporting politician: George Wyndham (1863–1913)

TONY McCARTHY

> The history of societies is more widely reflected in the way they spend their leisure time than by their work or politics.[1]

From an Irish perspective, George Wyndham is best known for having introduced the Land Act of 1903 that carries his name, while he was chief secretary of Ireland.[2] This highly ambitious, complex, and creative piece of legislation is credited by many historians as having solved what was long held to be the intractable Irish land question. Under the terms of the act, and its subsequent amending legislation, over 9.2 million acres were transferred from landlords to 257,000 tenant-farmers at a cost of £82.2 million.[3]

The description of the 1903 Land Act as 'highly ambitious, complex and creative' could just as easily be used to describe George Wyndham himself. A member of one of Britain's best connected and most prominent landed families, his father, Percy, was the second son of Lord Leconfield of Petworth House in Sussex. On his mother's side, George was related to Ireland's foremost aristocratic family, the dukes of Leinster; his maternal great-grandfather, Lord Edward Fitzgerald, was a leader of the United Irishmen rebellion of 1798. In 1887, George's marriage to Lady Sibell Grosvenor, the widow of Victor Grosvenor, heir to the dukedom of Westminster, meant that he married into another of Britain's premier elite families. George himself was a child prodigy. Educated at Eton, he then moved to the Royal Military College at Sandhurst and in 1883 was commissioned into his father's regiment, the Coldstream Guards (fig. 12.1).

After a brief military career, he entered politics and was elected Conservative MP for Dover in 1889 (fig. 12.2).[4] Articulate, well-read, and extremely handsome and charismatic, he would in time be spoken of as a future leader of the party and, indeed, prime minister. His first political position was as private secretary to Arthur Balfour when he was chief secretary of Ireland, 1887–91.

This essay is not concerned with George Wyndham the politician but rather Wyndham the sportsman.[5] Outside of politics he can best be described as a man

1 Harold Perkin, 'Teaching the nations how to play: sport and society in the British empire and Commonwealth', *International Journal of the History of Sport*, 6:2 (1989), p. 145. 2 The Irish Land Act 1903 (3 Edw. 7, c. 37, 14 Aug. 1903). 3 Tony Mc Carthy, 'From landlord to rentier: the Wyndham land Act 1903 and its economic consequences for Irish landlords 1903–1933' (PhD, Maynooth University, 2017), p. 247; see also Patrick J. Cosgrave, 'The Wyndham Land Act 1903: the final solution to the Irish land question?' (PhD, Maynooth University, 2008). 4 Alvin Jackson, 'George Wyndham', *ODNB*. 5 It is probably fair to say that

12.1 George Wyndham in the Coldstream Guards, 1885.

of strong passions: for life, the arts and sport. For a man who achieved high political office, and, indeed, significant literary acclaim, he considered the winning of his 'Eton colours' for the college equivalent of football as one of his greatest achievements.[6] He participated in a wide range of elite sports such as hunting, shooting, polo and tennis. In keeping with his class mores, he regarded sport as not simply a recreational pursuit but also as an important means of developing character, cultural identity and 'appropriate values'. He summarized his philosophy for a happy and successful life: 'Hunting all day and reading all night is the way to be healthy, wealthy and bright.'[7]

George was also a prolific letter writer and his private correspondence provides a penetrating insight into his own and, indeed, his class' attitude to, and engagement with, sport. His letters highlight the perceived importance of sport in projecting class and cultural distinctions, and in developing militaristic and imperialistic senses of superiority. They illustrate that the values taught in the English public-school system meant that the sports played by the ruling elites were intended to do more than develop athleticism and provide enjoyment; they were regarded as critical in developing character, social and political networks and propagating elite culture.

As J.A. Mangan has argued, sport should always be set within a cultural context and for much of history these contexts were fissured along class lines.[8] This essay will argue that sport provides a unique prism through which to understand how the social, cultural, political and economic worlds of aristocrats such as Wyndham interacted in late nineteenth- and early twentieth-century Britain and Ireland. Sport was used to uphold rural values and inculcate patriotism and militarism, all designed to advance the moral, economic and physical strength of those upon whom the British empire then depended.[9] In this context sport was central to 'British high culture'.[10] Indeed, class as defined by culture was very distinct from class as defined by economic circumstance. Over time, sporting activities became battlegrounds for many of the class tensions that arose between the newly emerging political and *nouveau riche* power brokers, and the once omnipotent landed classes.

Wyndham's Irish achievements were not matched by his wider British achievements. Moreover, despite his political prominence he still awaits a comprehensive biography. The most scholarly analysis of his life to date is Alvin Jackson, 'George Wyndham', *ODNB*. But see also J.W. Mackail and Guy Wyndham, *The life and letters of George Wyndham*, 2 vols (London, 1918); Charles Gatty, *Recognita* (London, 1917); John Biggs-Davison, *George Wyndham: a study in Toryism* (London, 1951); and Max Egremont, *The cousins* (London, 1977). **6** Egremont, *The cousins*, p. 30. **7** John Biggs-Davison, *George Wyndham, a study in toryism* (London, 1951), p. 52. **8** Mike Huggins, 'Direct and indirect influence: J.A. Mangan and the Victorian middle classes: major revisionist in the history of sport', *International Journal of the History of Sport*, 20:4 (2003), p. 27. **9** Mike Huggins, 'Sport and the British upper classes 1500–2000: a historic overview', *Sport in History*, 28:3 (2008), p. 366. **10** Ibid.

**12.2** The Rt Hon. George Wyndham, *c.*1900.

In Ireland, as the nineteenth century progressed, the aristocracy and gentry found themselves politically and socially isolated by home rulers and agrarian agitators, and under extreme financial pressure, particularly during the extended agricultural depression from the late 1870s. Wyndham's tenures in Ireland, firstly as private secretary to Balfour (1887–91), and secondly when he himself served as chief secretary (1900–5), coincided with a period characterized by significant change in the fortunes of the Irish landed gentry.

In this social and political climate, sport in its various manifestations provided the landed classes with an important means of social intercourse. And participation in sport among the elites was politically ecumenical. Three of the great Victorian prime ministers – Palmerston, Derby and Rosebery – were all prominent racehorse owners. Even Lord Salisbury, who was prime minister on three occasions in the closing decades of the nineteenth century, while having no great interest in horses himself, allowed his Liberal-Unionist minister, the duke of Devonshire, to dictate the dates of cabinet meetings in order to facilitate his attendance at various race meetings in Britain, earning these days the sobriquet 'Devonshire's Holy Days'.[11]

## I

George Wyndham's two-volume collection of letters, published posthumously by his brother Guy, contains hundreds of references to his participation in hunts, polo, shooting parties, race meetings and tennis.[12] Even while a serving government minister and in office as chief secretary in Ireland, his level of involvement in sport was significant. When he first arrived in Ireland with his political patron, Balfour, Wyndham clearly came prepared for sport in that he brought with him his hunting horses; in January 1890 he wrote to his father that 'I have Solyman and Dick with me and hunt once a week on Saturday.'[13] His letters make numerous references to buying horses in Ireland and sending them back to his home in Saighton, Cheshire, where he kept a small stable (fig. 12.3).

Wyndham was a regular participant in many of the hunts around Dublin (such as the Kildare, the Meath, the Ward Union) and further afield (the Ormonde in Kilkenny).[14] His friend and biographer, Charles Gatty, described Wyndham's conduct when hunting as

> brave, bordering on reckless. What he always enlarged upon to me when he got home was the physical joy of the thing, the swift movement, and the extraordinary exhilaration which comes from an ample oxygenation of the blood. To him all this was a real recreation and set up a physical and mental glow.[15]

And hunting was not just a weekend pastime to George Wyndham. His letters contain multiple references to 'ten-day hunts in Chester', or 'fourteen days riding in Tarporley'.[16] Even as an MP and minister, he often rode out for days on end with the Cheshire Regiment. In September 1898, he wrote from London to his cousin Wilfred Scawen Blunt: 'I attended the manoeuvres here [Blandford, north Dorset] attached to a Cavalry Regiment. It was divine to ride for 10 days'[17] (fig. 12.4).

11 John Pinfold, 'Horse racing and the upper classes in the nineteenth century', *Sport in History*, 28:3 (Sept. 2008), p. 414. 12 Guy Wyndham (ed.), *The letters of George Wyndham, 1877–1913*, vol. 1 (Edinburgh, 1915); J.W. Mackail and Guy Wyndham (eds), *The life and letters of George Wyndham*, vol. 2 (London, 1918). 13 George Wyndham (hereafter GW) to his father, 12 Jan. 1890; Mackail and Wyndham (eds), *The life and letters of George Wyndham*, vol. 2 (London, 1918). 14 GW to his father, 26 Nov. 1885; GW to his father, 14 Dec. 1885; GW to his sister Mary, 26 Mar. 1886; all in ibid., pp 101, 102, 105. 15 Charles Gatty, *Recognita* (London, 1917), p. 22. 16 GW to his mother, 2 Dec. 1893, and 10 Mar. 1892, *Letters of George Wyndham*, i, pp 266–8, 307. 17 GW to W.S. Blunt, 19 Sept. 1896, ibid., p. 417.

12.3 Saighton Grange, Chester, home to George Wyndham and his wife, Lady Sibell Grosvenor, 1887–1911.

12.4 A meet of the Wiltshire Hounds at Clouds, East Knoyle, during the celebrations for the coming of age of Percy Wyndham, 1908.

Of course, equestrian pleasures were not the only sporting preoccupation of members of the elite such as Wyndham. Shooting enjoyed an increase in popularity in the second half of the nineteenth century. The number of gamekeepers in Britain increased from 9,000 in 1851 to 23,000 in 1911.[18] In his correspondence, Wyndham noted three-day partridge and grouse shooting parties in Scotland, and other locations further south such as Sandeek Park near Rotherham.[19] While in Africa, he did not miss an opportunity to shoot; in 1896, he wrote to Scawen Blunt: 'I shot for the pot six pheasants, a partridge and a Koran (sort of bustard). My horse let me canter into the bush to shoot from his back.'[20] Emphasizing the importance of shooting, Wyndham wrote to his father in September 1889: 'All my plans (and, indeed, all Arthur B's [Balfour] too) have been made to hinge upon the Clouds shooting party. That is the sun of my political and social firmament round which all other dates revolve and take their chance of clashing.'[21]

Wyndham's references to shooting parties provide an insight into the tensions between old and new money. In a letter to his father in December 1897, he described a shooting party he attended in Wynyard Hall in Durham, also attended by many 'professional types':

> They live for shooting and 'record' bags on their several estates. And, in order to secure these bags, they have abandoned most of the precepts, shooting at everything near and far, taking the best places at their own shooting, being rude to their guests who shoot badly and generally destroying the amenities of what was a pretty sport by turning it into a vulgar and arduous competition.[22]

Wyndham held similar views about horse racing. In August 1898, he wrote to Scawen Blunt regarding the Chester races: 'I only went twice to the races and confirmed my conclusion that racing, as at present practised, combines the maximum vulgarity with the minimum of sport.'[23] This remark confirms the contention by historian John Pinfold that 'There is thus a sense that towards the end of the [nineteenth] century flat racing was changing from comprising contests between horses owned and bred by knowledgeable men into an entertainment industry, funded to a large extent by "new" money.'[24]

Wyndham was also a keen tennis player. He used it as a welcome break from the affairs of state; in 1898 Wyndham wrote to Blunt: 'I have discovered a new amusement. [Charles Wellington] Furse the painter lives in Abbey Gardens, opposite the House of Lords and hard by Marks' house. So I pop across and play a four of lawn tennis with them when the business is slack at the House.'[25] A

**18** Neil Tranter, *Sport, economy and society in Britain, 1750–1914* (Cambridge, 1998), p. 21. **19** GW to his father, 3 Oct. 1892, *Letters of George Wyndham*, i, p. 280. **20** GW to W.S. Blunt, 12 Oct. 1896, ibid., p. 358. **21** GW to his father, 26 Sept. 1880, ibid., p. 217. **22** GW to his father, 26 Dec. 1897, ibid., pp 381–2. **23** GW to W.S. Blunt, 8 Aug. 1898, ibid., p. 413. **24** Pinfold, 'Horse racing in the nineteenth century', p. 428. **25** GW to W.S. Blunt, member of the highly elite Crabbet Club, founded by Scawen Blunt, Wyndham described it as 'not literary but lawn-tennisy'. There he mixed with prominent politicians and socialites such as Lord Morpeth, Edward Hamilton (Gladstone's private secretary), Button Bourke (editor of the *Times*), George Curzon (future viceroy of India), Lord Alfred Douglas (lover of Oscar Wilde) and Harry Cust (editor of the *Pall Mall Gazette*). In fact, Wyndham did mix tennis with his literary talents. In 1892, Blunt recorded in his diary that 'George Wyndham performed a wonderful feat, writing a long poem in a most complicated metre, and full of excellent things in hardly more than an hour, between sets of lawn tennis.'[26] Wyndham and his friends provided other entertainments; Max Egremont recorded in *The cousins* how 'Early one morning one could see Harry Cust and Curzon defeating Blunt and Wyndham at lawn tennis – all four playing stark naked.'[27] However, sartorial decorum was more the norm. In 1910, Wyndham wrote to Mary Drew, the daughter of William Gladstone: 'On Sunday I played lawn tennis in a grey suit, as a concession to the Sabbath.'[28]

If it were not for the fact that Wyndham achieved so much during his time in Ireland, that he worked so hard as to drive himself to a nervous breakdown, one could be forgiven for thinking that the life of the chief secretary in Ireland was one devoted to leisure. Indeed, it is a conclusion one might draw from a letter written to his mother in August 1901:

> After breakfast, I have up the undersecretary, or vice-president of Local Government Board etc. and we put in two or three hours of easy-going work. Then Percy [his son] takes me to cricket matches, polo, Leopardstown [horse racing] etc. etc. And we wind up with frantic lawn tennis till 7.30 pm. Dinner at 8.00 pm. What with the Horse-show, cricket, polo, racing, hospitals, Congested Districts [Board], lawn tennis, croquet, billiards and pin-pong we manage to keep the tambourine a rowlin.[29]

For Wyndham, sport obviously provided an antidote to the pressures of life, including during election campaigns. In 1900, he wrote to his brother Guy:

> By the time this reaches you we shall, I believe, be in the midst of a General Election. I dislike the thought of the senseless chatter … I shall be trotted out every night for three weeks, and do not relish the prospect. I have been training for it here with one of my secretaries – a run around the garden and three sets of tennis in the evening.[30]

16 June 1898, *Letters of George Wyndham*, i, p. 410. **26** Wilfred Scawen Blunt, *My diaries: being a personal narrative of events, 1888–1914* (New York, 1923), i, p. 68. See also Nancy Ellenberge, *Balfour's world: aristocracy and political culture at the fin de siècle*. (Woodbridge, 2015), and the review by Tom Crewe, 'Aubade before breakfast', *London Review of Books*, 31 Mar. 2016. **27** Egremont, *The cousins*, p. 159. **28** GW to Mary Drew, 1 Nov. 1910, *Letters of George Wyndham*, ii, p. 673. **29** GW to his mother, 8 Aug. 1901, ibid., p. 418. **30** GW to Guy Wyndham, 14 Sept. 1900, *Letters of George Wyndham*, i, p. 520.

II

While Wyndham revelled in the physical exhilaration of sport, it was also a means of developing and maintaining social networks. His letters contain multiple references to trips to Ascot, hunting and shooting parties in country houses and other sporting occasions where the social composition of the assemblies was as important as the sporting event itself. For example, in a letter to his mother in June 1896, he told her that he had been to Ascot, where 'the party included the Londonderrys, Randolph Churchill, Lord Hastings, Houghtons, the duke of Portland, the Vyners, the Durhams and the Zetlands – they rode out each morning at 7.30 and played lawn tennis every evening.'[31] At a stag hunt and point-to-point race meeting near Mountstewart in January 1891, he told his father he had been joined by a mix of Irish and British aristocrats including the 'Talbots, Zetlands, Cloncurrys, Charteris and the Balfours' (Arthur and George).[32] Clearly, his parents liked to hear of the social circles in which he was moving in the early days of his political career, and he understood the importance of letting them know (fig. 12.5).

And yet this was at a time when the social base involved in the once elite sports of fox hunting and shooting was beginning to widen. Some years later, in a letter to his father in 1905, Wyndham noted that at a shooting party at the home of Sir William Eden, 'We shot three days and hunted Friday. It was a mixed party and amused me when I got used to it.'[33] His social snobbery was clear, as was the realization that change was imminent. As Huggins has argued, such views were widely held among the traditional elites and extended beyond the playing fields. The new wealthy and/or Jewish families such as the Sassoons (Trent Park House in London, Heytesbury House in Wiltshire) and the Rothchilds (Ascott House, Waddeston Manor and Halton House, all in Buckinghamshire), who emulated the aristocracy by building magnificent country houses, were scorned by many of the landed grandees, who dismissed their homes as being 'tasteless, vulgar, ostentatious and un English'.[34] This was a time of great change; the aristocracy on the decline had to meet the new wealthy on the rise; they faced financial constraints brought on by agricultural depression from the 1870s, and a gradual withdrawal from local and national politics in what Cannadine described as a shift 'from rootedness to restlessness, and from service to sport.'

Sporting gatherings became ever more critical in maintaining social networks.[35] In Ireland, Elizabeth, countess of Fingall, recalled in her memoirs the importance of fox hunting in the social life of County Meath at the turn of

31 GW to his mother, June 1886, ibid., p. 114. 32 GW to his father, 14 Dec. 1885, ibid., p. 102. 33 GW to his father, 26 Nov. 1905, *Letters of George Wyndham*, ii, p. 524. 34 Huggins, *Sport and the upper British classes*, p. 365. 35 David Cannadine, *The decline and fall of the British aristocracy* (New Haven, 1990), p. 385.

12.5 The golden wedding anniversary of George Wyndham's parents, Percival and Madeline, at Clouds, 1910.

the twentieth century, when Wyndham was a regular guest of the Meath and Ward Union hunts:

> So, I was obliged to hunt, however little heart I had for it. Because if you didn't hunt in Meath you might as well be dead. The whole life of the country centred around that occupation. During the hunting season no one talked of anything else.[36]

She emphasized the importance of hunting in developing relationships between men and women:

> You can see out hunting whether a man is selfish or considerate, whether he is a braggart or has courage. And there are many moments when people can be alone together, easily and naturally, with the country about them ... there is – I repeat it, as I have often repeated it – no better test of the man you consider as a husband than to spend a day hunting with him.[37]

Yet hunting remained a largely male preserve and was often characterized by intense rivalries between individuals and groups.[38] Wyndham's letters attest to this, with numerous references to his and his son Percy's prowess at riding (fig. 12.6):

> It is jolly to find that twenty years cannot abate one's huge delight in riding to hounds; and the added joy of seeing Perf [Percy] always in the first flight and often cutting out the work exquisite. If I can keep my place of old days I am pleased – like a boy. If he beats me I am in seventh heaven.[39]

His letters also contain many references to competitions between various hunts and military regiments and convey the impression that sport to Wyndham represented a form of social Darwinism underpinning the values and status quo of an athletic, aristocratic caste. Sport also afforded an opportunity for the social elites to differentiate themselves from their 'social inferiors'. Given the emergence of a powerful *nouveau riche* class, sport became a means of defining class along cultural rather than economic lines. The traditional values that elite sports espoused of simple rural life, patriotism and national strength allowed participants to hark back to a golden age when everyone knew their proper place and the might of the British empire rested on the masculine shoulders of the

36 Pamela Hinkson (ed.), *Seventy years young: memories of Elizabeth, countess of Fingal* (Dublin, 2009), p. 75. 37 Ibid., p. 120. 38 Huggins, *Sport and the upper British classes*, p. 382; J.A. Mangan, *Athleticism in the Victorian and Edwardian public school: the emergence and consolidation of an educational ideology* (Cambridge, 1981), p. 151. For an exception, see the hunting career of Edith Somerville documented by Laura Servilon Browne in this volume. 39 GW to Guy Wyndham, 18 Jan. 1907, *Letters of George Wyndham*, ii, p. 561.

landed classes.[40] In a letter to the poet Hilaire Belloc in 1902, George Wyndham reflected on such a world:

> The coursing of hares … is the oldest sport. And now alas fewer farmers can afford to hunt the fox – it is what they love. They breed the greyhounds and have, as a rule, only two outlets for their skill and keenness. They read the ½d Press about the Waterloo Cup and have one rotten, betting-bedevilled meeting. But when you welcome them all on to the land and have a lunch of sandwiches in a barn and a bottle or so of vintage port, why then you feel that in the South Country we have not been jewed out of the England of Shakespeare and Chaucer.[41]

Buried within his distasteful anti-Semitism was a cultural and political nostalgia. Riding-out remained hugely symbolic to the aristocracy. It conveyed an image of militaristic power, courage and strong leadership. Such a view was in keeping with the fact that cavalry regiments such as the Dragoons, Lancers and the Hussars were the most highly regarded by upper-class families when considering military careers for their sons. Wyndham's letters contain many references to riding-out on military manoeuvres, such as when he 'went to Salisbury Plain and played at soldiers' in October 1908.[42] Riding-out was the physical manifestation of the ideologies of athleticism and manliness inculcated by the public-school system and a Corinthian ideal. At Eton, Harrow, Rugby, Winchester and Westminster young men acquired a spirit of amateurism, athleticism, manliness, patriotism and Britishness. These schools fostered a sense of 'shared educational experiences', and were powerful forces in the process of socialization particularly centred around sporting events.[43] Public schools lay at the very heart of the British imperial mission and provided a strong link with the military tradition and Wyndham's correspondence highlights how military service and sporting prowess were integral aspects of patrician life.

Huggins has argued that the real symbolism of hunting related to the great emphasis that was placed on equestrian bloodlines and breeding, which supported the hereditary principle of wealth and entitlement enjoyed by the landed elites.[44] The best Irish hunts attracted the upper echelons of Irish and, indeed, British society. In January 1905, the *Leinster Leader* reported that 'The duke of Westminster and the marquess of Cholmondeley attended the Meath Hunt on Saturday.'[45] That same month, the attendance at the Kildare Hunt included such notables as the earl of Mayo, Colonel St Ledger Moore of Killashee House, and Percy La Touché of Harristown House.[46] While he was in

**40** Huggins, *Sport and the upper British classes*, p. 367. **41** GW to Hilaire Belloc, 22 Dec. 1911, *Letters of George Wyndham*, ii, pp 713–14. **42** GW to Philip Hanson, 5 Oct. 1908; ibid., p. 617. **43** Mike Huggins, 'Athleticism in the Victorian and Edwardian public school', *International Journal of the History of Sport*, 18:4, p. 149. **44** Huggins, *Sport and the upper British classes*, p. 366. **45** *Leinster Leader*, 27 Jan. 1905. **46** Ibid., 22 Apr. 1905.

**12.6** A young Percy Wyndham on his pony, Heart's Delight, *c.*1897.

Ireland as private secretary to Balfour and later as chief secretary, Wyndham often hunted with both the Meath and the Kildare packs. He also witnessed from the late nineteenth century how fox hunting found itself at the front line of tensions between the landed classes and land agitators, as the rural supremacy of the landed elites was seriously challenged by the newly emerging nationalist Catholic middle classes.[47] At the annual general meeting of the Kildare Hunt in 1901, the chairman, the earl of Mayo (a cousin of George Wyndham), gave profuse thanks to the local farmers for facilitating the hunt on their lands, and it was agreed that they should be encouraged to participate in the forthcoming season's hunts.[48] However, by 1905 it was clear that political muscles were being flexed when the nationalist dominated Naas urban district council rejected for

47 On this aspect of the Land War, see L.P. Curtis Jnr, 'Stopping the hunt, 1881–82' in C.H.E. Philpin, *Nationalism and popular protest in Ireland* (Cambridge, 1987), pp 349–402; and for the revolutionary period, William Murphy, 'Sport in a time of revolution: Sinn Féin and the hunt in Ireland, 1919', *Éire-Ireland*, 48:1–2 (Spring/Summer 2013), pp 112–47.
48 *Nationalist and Leinster Times*, 9 Nov. 1901.

the first time the renewal of the hunt's lease for the use of the town hall for its social and administrative gatherings.[49] This rejection was made after the hunt had offered to pay an increased rent of £25 per annum and a contribution of £140 towards planned renovations.[50] Matters were not much better for the Kildare Hunt's near neighbour, the Ward Union Hunt in County Meath. In March 1901, the Dunshauglin rural district council unanimously passed a resolution stating:

> That we strongly object to the disgraceful practice of riding horses on footpaths, thereby spoiling their appearance and rendering them unfit for use by pedestrians and that a copy of this resolution be sent to the secretary of the Ward Union Committee.[51]

It was not a case of open aggression, but rather a subtle rebuke. George and Guy Wyndham were regular participants with the Ward Union and would, therefore, have been acutely aware of this conflict with the democratically elected and predominantly nationalist district council. In Ireland, social-class issues and local politics had a sectarian dimension. The principal officers of the various hunts were aristocrats and local gentry who were predominantly Protestant, while the increasing numbers of farmers were mainly Catholic. In the long term these tensions also affected hunting in Ireland.[52] The changes in hunting and attitudes towards the sport provoked by the Land War were a case in point, where sport very much reflected the changing social and political dynamic in Ireland and would have sent signals to Wyndham, whose ambition as chief secretary was to settle the Irish question.

## CONCLUSION

Sport and leisure activities in the late nineteenth and early twentieth centuries should be viewed in the context of the profound changes that were enveloping political, social economic and cultural life. The changes brought about by the rapidly industrializing world, increasing urbanization, growing democratization, and the emergence of powerful commercial elites as well as a maturing middle class, would have a deep and lasting effect on society. The once presumptive claims of the aristocracy were being curtailed and the elite to which George Wyndham belonged was experiencing what Ellenberger has described as 'fierce competition in national politics' and indeed in wider spheres of influence.[53]

49 *Leinster Leader*, 28 Jan. 1905. 50 *Leinster Leader*, 11 Feb. 1905. 51 *Meath Chronicle*, 19 Jan. 1901. 52 For sectarian issues relating to the Meath Union, for example, see *Meath Chronicle*, 18 Mar. 1905; *Drogheda Independent*, 1, 8 Apr. 1905. 53 Nancy Ellenberger, 'Constructing George Wyndham: narratives of aristocratic masculinity in *fin-de-siècle* England', *Journal of British Studies*, 39:4 (Oct. 2000), p. 490.

Within these cultural, political and social contexts and shifts what did sport mean to a patrician politician like George Wyndham, and by extension to his peers? In his memoirs, published in 1932, the 9th duke of Devonshire recalled that 'sport has appealed to me more strongly than brain work, which may have been one of the reasons why I have not succeeded in making any money'.[54] Wyndham clearly found fox hunting an exhilarating pursuit that provided the body with great recuperative powers, as he boasted to Hilaire Belloc:

> I have steeped my body and brain in wind and rain. For I have hunted five days last week and four this and always got soaked to the skin. But in the ancient riding coat, leather breeches and boots this does a man good.[55]

He also saw sport, and particularly fox hunting, as a respite from his stressful life in politics. Writing to his sister Mary in 1907, he stated: '[P]ersonally I detest the job [politics], and prefer hunting and the society of the people I am fond of, whether dead and embalmed in books, or alive and pleasant for their beauty and keen wits.'[56] Indeed, Wyndham's frustration and disillusionment with politics, and his need to find comfort in sport and its cleansing qualities, are even more evident in a letter to Belloc in December 1911:

> I escaped from the cut-throat cage of politics, in which slime usurps the place of gore, last Friday. I became once more an animal and a man. I shot rabbits with two neighbours on Saturday. I hunted the fox with neighbours on Monday, Tuesday, Wednesday and today.[57]

To George Wyndham and, indeed, many of his beleaguered class, sport in the closing decades of the nineteenth and early twentieth centuries was one of the few arenas where they could socialize and feel a secure sense of belonging in an ever-changing world. It afforded them an opportunity to hark back to what they might have considered a simpler age, when social order prevailed, and all was well with the world, at least until the invasion of the new wealthy elite.

This essay opened with a quote from the social historian Harold Perkin that 'The history of societies is more widely reflected in the way they spend their leisure time than by their work or politics'. If that be so, then the sport and leisure activities of the landed elites in the decades before and after the turn of the twentieth century reflected entitlement, privilege and the acceptance of a rigid class structure. While possibly true, this was a reflection on a society whose position was rapidly becoming untenable in the face of the great economic, political and social upheavals that were convulsing the new century.

**54** Duke of Devonshire, *My candid recollections* (London, 1932), p. 86. **55** GW to Hilaire Belloc, 29 Dec. 1911, *Letters of George Wyndham*, ii, p. 715. **56** GW to Mary Elcho, 1 Feb. 1907, ibid., pp 566–8. **57** GW to Hilaire Belloc, 22 Dec. 1911, ibid., pp 713–14.

# Lady Castletown's scrapbook: making memories for leisure

MAEVE O'RIORDAN

Lady Clare Castletown (1853–1927) was born Ursula Clare Emily St Leger, the daughter of the 4th viscount Doneraile, Hayes St Leger, and Mary Lenox Cunningham (granddaughter of George Lenox Conyngham of Springhill, County Down). Clare became the sole heiress to the Doneraile estate by virtue of her brother and sister dying in infancy and girlhood. The Doneraile estate were large and profitable, with lands in Cork and Waterford, including the village of Doneraile and the seaside resort of Tramore, as well as a house in fashionable Grosvenor Square in London. The family seat, Doneraile Court, still stands within sight of the village in north Cork. Lady Castletown had a captivating personality (as well as personal wealth) and drew many friends and acquaintances. Her movements, dress, and attendance at events were reported in newspapers and she must have been one of the most desirable matches in Ireland before her marriage in 1874. She married 'Barney', Bernard Edward Fitzpatrick, the future Lord Castletown of Granston Manor, and he appears to have been an equally dynamic and popular person within their world. He was a reasonably outspoken Conservative MP before he inherited the title of Lord Castletown, afterwards continued to have an interest in Irish land reform, and later was one of the leading Irish landlords active in the attempt to find a place for their class in the new Irish state. During their marriage, the Castletowns remained a popular couple and they travelled widely on the American and African continents as well as in Europe, including Scandinavia. In her marriage settlement, Lady Castletown was guaranteed an income of £1,000 per annum during her married life.[1] Their expected children were to inherit both estates.

Marriage was a life-changing step for women of the landed class in Ireland and Britain at this time. When a woman married, she left her parents' home and established herself as the mistress of her own family, gaining greater freedom of movement and independence in the process (provided that she was not married to an abusive or overbearing man). Many women of the landed class would begin a new photograph album or scrapbook that would accompany them on their new life as a married woman. The scrapbook could serve both as a remembrance of those family members that they would no longer see regularly, as well as a means of documenting new friendships (and children) that would arise from married

1 Marriage settlement of Lord and Lady Castletown (NLI, Doneraile papers, MS 34,139/14).

life. Scrapbooks had been popular among the social elite for some time before the 1870s. The hobby demanded a disposable income and disposable time.

'Friendship books' and 'sentiment albums' invited contributions from within the owner's social network. The items in these albums were treasured because of their association with loved or admired people.[2] For example, the Trench family album was created over a thirty-year period from *c.*1845 to 1871 and passed down through the generations. It contained 130 photographs, as well as prints and drawings. In 1948, Leo Coote recorded that 'This book was collected by my Grandmother.'[3] Christine Chichester, who was a member of the wealthy Catholic family from Runnamoate, County Roscommon, kept a scrapbook where she invited family, friends, and acquaintances to sign their names beside their photographs, which she cut out and pasted in various patterns; for example a series of floating heads surrounding a house where they had all stayed.[4] The book also contained sketches and memorabilia from visits and international travel. It also had obvious social importance as it allowed her to display her personal connections.

Scrapbooking was a layered leisure activity. Firstly, the scrapbook might be a means of recording the owner's leisure hours, pastimes or sporting activities. Secondly, the action of physically making the scrapbook – of sourcing, cutting and pasting in pieces – was in itself a leisurely and prolonged activity that could be carried out over days, months or years. Requesting contributions from friends and connections was a means of emphasizing the importance of each personal relationship. Lastly, the act of 'reading' the scrapbook, leafing through the pages and associated memories, became an individual leisure activity, which could evoke for the owner happy memories of an event, or of the activity of scrapbooking. The scrapbook could, in turn, be shared and displayed within the owner's friendship group. Through the creation of a scrapbook, the owner promoted a version of themselves and their activities and relationships that highlighted (for themselves or others) the most desirable aspects of their lives and their memories.

## THE SCRAPBOOK: UNDERSTANDING HERSELF

Lady Castletown started a scrapbook around the time of her 1874 wedding. The red leather-bound scrapbook was a purpose-made, pre-gummed book in the style of Mark Twain's 'pictorial scrap-book', which was patented in 1872. An

2 Katie Day Good, 'From scrapbook to Facebook: a history of personal media assemblage and archives', *New Media and Society*, 15:2 (2013), pp 557–73, 562. 3 Trench Family Album, ALB393, Trench Estate Collection, National University of Ireland, digitized, http://catalogue.nli.ie/Record/vtls000245425#page/1/mode/1up, accessed 21 Dec. 2018. Sincere thanks to Mary Broderick for introducing me to the digitized album collection. 4 Christine Chichester, autograph book (UCC, Grehan Estate Collection, Boole Archives, IE

advert for this type of book claimed that 'the arrangement of pictures in this book is one of the most agreeable and entertaining pastimes'.[5] It was no small feat for Lady Castletown to create this scrapbook; she pasted 325 items into the 110 pages, with a further 18 items loosely inserted. The large number of items pasted into the book is a reflection both of her wide range of interests, and also the time and care she put into creating it; she did not give up after a few months. A scrapbook is more than the contents within it, as each item was chosen above countless other newspaper articles, hand-drawn sketches, mass-produced cartoons and personal letters that the owner would have interacted with. Some emotive response – whether it was irritation, desire, love, lust, nostalgia or self-importance – drove the assembler to select each piece. Each item in turn gained a further layer of meaning in how it was placed in the scrapbook: it might be placed with other items to form a narrative, it could be annotated or defaced in some way or it could be juxtaposed in a seemingly haphazard manner to reveal a wide range of interests. Each item within a scrapbook has greater meaning than if it was preserved in isolation.[6]

Lady Castletown's scrapbooking style could be described as 'entangled', combining 'several layers of text with images of different sizes and shapes on a single page … eschewing any chronological ordering of materials or treating the album page something like a drawer in which to store random objects'.[7] The items pasted into the book are from a wide range of sources and authors. There are 107 newspaper and magazine clippings, 97 handwritten items, 37 drawings or original art works, 85 printed items such as postcards and pamphlets, 8 annotated printed items where Castletown corrected the words in print and just 5 photographs – reflecting a lack of interest in a hobby popular among many of her peers. It is possible that she had another photograph album that has not survived, but the scrapbook offers no evidence of an interest in photography. However, the lack of photographs of herself in this album did not mean a lack of self-reflexive interest. Newspapers reported on her physical appearance and her dress at various society events, and she cut out and preserved these descriptions. In 1881, she wore a white dress with a white parasol flamboyantly decorated with 'an acre and a half of buttercups and daisies' to attend Ascot (the premier horse racing event).[8] She and her fashion choices were discussed in at least three newspapers, while Lord Castletown, or another admirer, wrote a verse about her dress. To be singled out for comment in the society papers suggests that in 1881 Lady Castletown was at the forefront of fashionable society. In the same year, Lady Ardilaun, half of one of the wealthiest couples in Ireland, held a ball in her

BL/EP/G/1506). 5 Advert for Mark Twain's scrapbooks at the end of his *Punch, brothers, Punch! and other sketches* (New York, 1878); British Library, 'Mark Twain's scrapbook and earworm', https://blogs.bl.uk/americas/2015/12/mark-twains-scrapbook-earworm.html, accessed 21 Dec. 2018. 6 Sharon Marcus, 'Sources', *Theatre Survey*, 54:2 (May 2013), pp 283–307 at p. 284. 7 Ibid., p. 293. 8 Untitled newspaper clippings and poem, 1881, Lady Castletown scrapbook, p. 21.

13.1 Illustration of 'Mouscadine', the character of Lady Castletown at Lady Ardilaun's fancy-dress ball, 11 Feb. 1881.

St Stephen's Green house. Lady Castletown attended dressed as 'Mouscadine', wearing a stylized eighteenth-century dress with a bicorn hat, and she included a sketch of her outfit in the scrapbook (fig. 13.1). The event was covered in the press, but not exactly as Lady Castletown would have liked; the newspaper reported that she wore a powdered wig, but she corrected the article writing 'own hair!' in the margin.

Lady Castletown's introspective interest also led her to commission an analysis of her handwriting in order to determine her personality type. An analyst using the nom de plume 'Mirage' deduced that she was

> Most ambitious with an extraordinary strong will & a determination to gain her ends … exceedingly clever, diplomatic … Independent, self-reliant, careless of small matters & having too little respect for public opinion – Possessed of an exceedingly passionate nature …

As with newspaper descriptions of herself, Lady Castletown 'corrected' these descriptions before pasting them into the book. As the owner of the scrapbook she was at pains to ensure that she was presented in a way which she saw as true. Her annotations (in italics) of the analysis of her hand registered her disagreement with some of the observations:

> Yours is Possessing marked independence and fierce with a strong will, and a firm belief in your own powers *(stuck up)* … to gain your ends, or to attract any one whom you consider worth it, you will take a great deal of trouble, & exercise considerable diplomacy & might perhaps to be somewhat unscrupulous as to the means employed *(murder if necessary)* for [you] possess a passionate emotional nature, with great capabilities, … but are equally strong in your dislikes, & somewhat intolerant in your judgements – you are an invaluable ally *(beware!)* & a formidable enemy, very energetic, and extremely quick-witted, with much power to grasp a subject, & a good head for business details *(alas! no!)* … You are somewhat wanting in sympathy, expect people to be interested in your pursuits, rather than being capable of entering into theirs *(brutal)*, and although fond of society, you are perfectly sufficient to yourself and quite happy alone.[9]

The character that emerges from this analysis did not possess the feminine trait of passivity and grace, but was presented as 'a strong character, firm and self reliant'. The anonymous reader offered to predict Lady Castletown's future for the sum of two shillings. The reading was completed in 6 Earlsfort Terrace 'about 1887'. In 1887, Alexandria College, the newly founded progressive higher education school for girls, was housed at this address, but it is unclear why Castletown was at the college, or why anyone there was predicting the future for the price of two shillings.

9 Handwritten text pasted into Lady Castletown scrapbook. Text in italics denotes annotations by Lady Castletown.

RECORDING SOCIAL NETWORKS

Most of the items in the scrapbook are anonymous to the modern reader. Conveniently, Lady Castletown had a distinctive curvy handwriting style that makes identifying any of her unsigned documents possible with a reasonable degree of certainty. It is not so with her artistic style, and it is harder to be certain whether any drawings or sketches are her own creations unless annotated by her in some way. For example, there is one page opening with five examples of 'fold-over butterflies' the type of creations this author made while in school in the early 1990s. These are created by blobbing different coloured paints into the centre of a page, folding over, and pushing the paint outwards. In the corner of one of these fold-over butterfly images the words 'New York' can be faintly seen in pencil. It may be that these were created while she was in New York, or perhaps they were posted to her as a gift; without other evidence it is impossible to determine. However, her decision to paste in all of these simple, repetitive pieces implies that the time spent creating and recording them was of some importance to her (fig. 13.2).

Lady Castletown used the scrapbook to record the admiration she evoked in men. Sixty-two items were dedicated specifically to her. Poetry featured heavily in the volume, with sixty-nine poems and verses, many of them political or

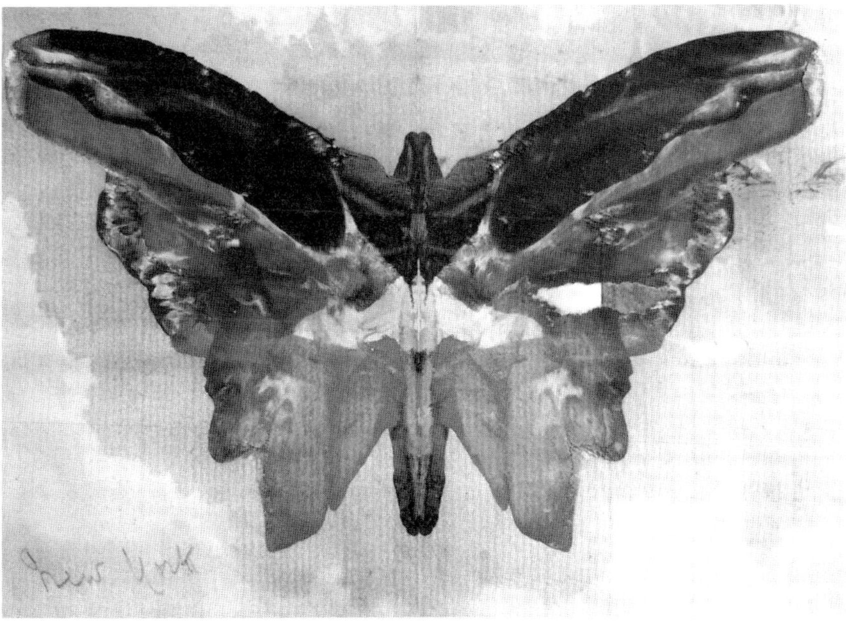

**13.2** One of a series of five 'fold-over butterflies' marked 'New York', attributed to Lady Castletown, n.d.

romantic in nature.[10] The content of several of the poems and letters written for, and preserved by, Lady Castletown was sexual, with different men vying for her attention, sometimes on the same page. She evidently enjoyed the power she felt in her attractiveness, and may have derived pleasure from these poems, long after any of the relationships had ended. An admirer, known only as 'H.', wrote a poem dedicated to her and two other women in February 1881, which conveyed some of the sexual power that she had over men during that Dublin Season:

> When first we got to Dublin
> And inhaled the Liffy Smell/
> we thought we couldn't be worse off/
> Even if we were in H_ll
> And H_ll it was for 6 weeks
> … down from Heaven 3 Angels came
> Whose looks none could surpass
> They called themselves 'the widows'
> They were, but only grass.[11]
> At all the Balls & dinners
> at the Castle & Stephen's Green
> These 3 bewitching creatures were always to be seen
> There was Clare with the lovely figure
> And Amy with the big black eyes
> And little Mae with the merry laugh
> … Ah! could it always be like this
> Dublin would ne'er be slow
> And instead of pining for London
> I should never wish to go
> But now the Trio's broken up
> The Chaperone is gone
> And we unhappy mortals
> Are left forlorn, alone
>
> Dedicated to the three Grass widows (H.)

The author of 'the pathetic ballad of the patent leather boot' went the furthest in expressing his desire for the young Lady Castletown. He yearned after her 'slender figure'. He recalled how the pair had become separated from the others while hunting; they had returned home together on tired horses as the sun was

10 I coded the following themes, allowing items to relate to more than one item where necessary (i.e. a satirical poem would be coded as politics and poetry): politics, class/servants, imperialist/racist, joke/comedy, sport, art, poetry, drama, personal document, fashion, romance, society, history, foreign language, travel, death notice, other. 11 Their husbands were hunting.

setting. Her companion observed: '[W]ith the motion of the saddle, as it rose and as it fell, I see her dainty patent leather boot … I watched her figure gently sway from side to side.' When they finally returned for tea he 'envied both the teacup and the spoon'. The author of this undated poem is unidentified, but as he wondered 'would she ever – in the future be my Bride' it is possible that it was written by her future husband or another suitor. The inclusion of such an erotic poem in her scrapbook, whether it was directed at an unmarried woman, or whether the term 'bride' was a euphemism for a sexual partner who the author was attempting to woo away from her husband, points to Lady Castletown's pride in her ability to evoke sexual desire in men. The author of the poem was left hoping that in his sleep, 'with the agony of parting less acute – I may dream that I am walking back from Kilashee again beside my Angel's patent leather boot'.

Lady Castletown collected a number of clippings from the magazine *Woman*, which was one of several new magazines that were launched towards the end of the century aimed specifically at a female readership. This particular publication ran from 1890 to 1921, and its outlook represented some of the contradictions within Castletown's character. The tagline of the magazine, '*Forward! But not too fast!*', promised to cater to the modern woman, defining its readership as 'intelligent womanly women';[12] yet, it resisted 'appealing to those who are woman in name only'.[13] A weekly publication that cost one penny, *Woman* was within the reach of women of a different social class to Lady Castletown. The editors assumed that the readership was middle class and of the 'English set', able to afford a servant, but nevertheless unaccustomed to the life lived by Lady Castletown. It is unclear then how she came across the winning essay 'Is a husband worth having?' in the competition run by the serial. *Woman* was known for running essay competitions and the winning authors were paid one guinea per 800 words. The prizewinners were invariably members of the middle classes, though obviously the readership, on this occasion, spread outside this class. It may have been that the pithy response to the essay challenge of 'Well that depends on whose husband it is' appealed to Castletown's sense of humour, and indeed her own lifestyle. However her scrapbook also preserves more moralistic and idealistic pieces which argued that

> marriage is the highest state for both man and woman on physiological, social and moral grounds; and the wise woman will consider a husband worth having if she can find one she can truly love, and who will add to her happiness through life.

12 *Woman*, 1 Jan. 1891, quoted in *A magazine of her own*, p. 174. 13 *Woman*, 11 Jan. 1890, quoted in ibid.

DOCUMENTING HER WORLD

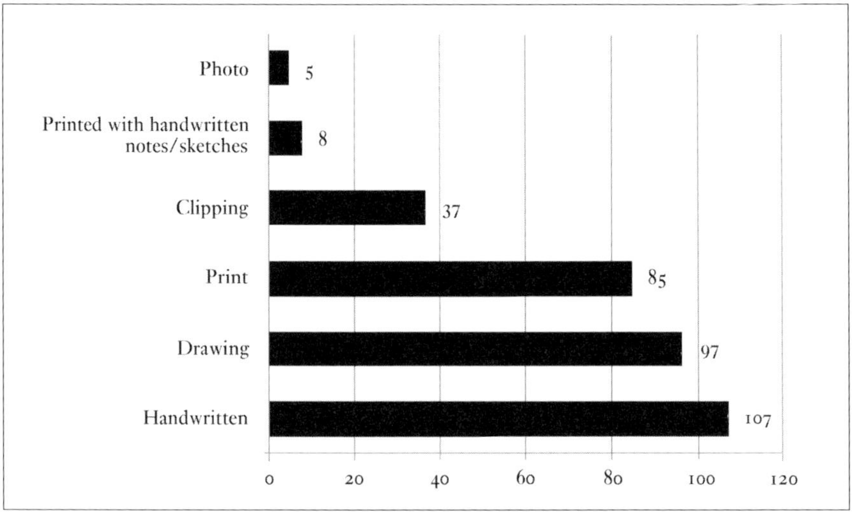


13.3 Breakdown of scrapbook entries by type.

The scrapbook is both a deeply personal document (in that all of the items were either created, collected by or gifted to Lady Castletown), and an outward-looking one with 106 items referring to politics, class relationships or imperialism. Newspaper and magazine clippings were the single biggest source of material for the scrapbook. While the majority of the newspaper clippings cannot be positively identified, those that can come from a range of English and Irish, local, national and special-interest newspapers which reflect her political and social outlook. These were the *Times* and *Irish Times*, the *Pall Mall Gazette*, *Punch*, *Woman*, *St James' Gazette*, *Cork Constitution*, *Cork Examiner*, *Carlow Sentinel*, *Field*, *Vanity Fair*, *Daily Mail*, *Daily Telegraph* and the *World*.

Gladstone was criticized throughout in manuscript verses, cartoons and satires.[14] The scrapbook preserves ephemera from the Land War, including letters from tenants; items of ephemera relating to Lady Castletown's fundraising and organization work on behalf of the Curtin sisters, whose father had been shot at their County Kerry farm; and handbills she found on the street in Dublin (fig. 13.4).[15]

14 For examples, see Lady Castletown scrapbook pp 29, 44, 46, 49, 58, 68, 71, 83, 109.
15 Patrick Emporer, tenant to his landlord Henry H. Barry, 7 July 1887, Lady Castletown scrapbook, p. 88; items relating to Curtin family, ibid., pp 68, 81; 'Notice £10 reward will be given to any person who can give sufficient information of any tenant farmer having paid any rent since the no-rent manifesto was issued by the executive', 'picked up in a street in Dublin', 2 Jan. 1882, Lady Castletown scrapbook, p. 31.

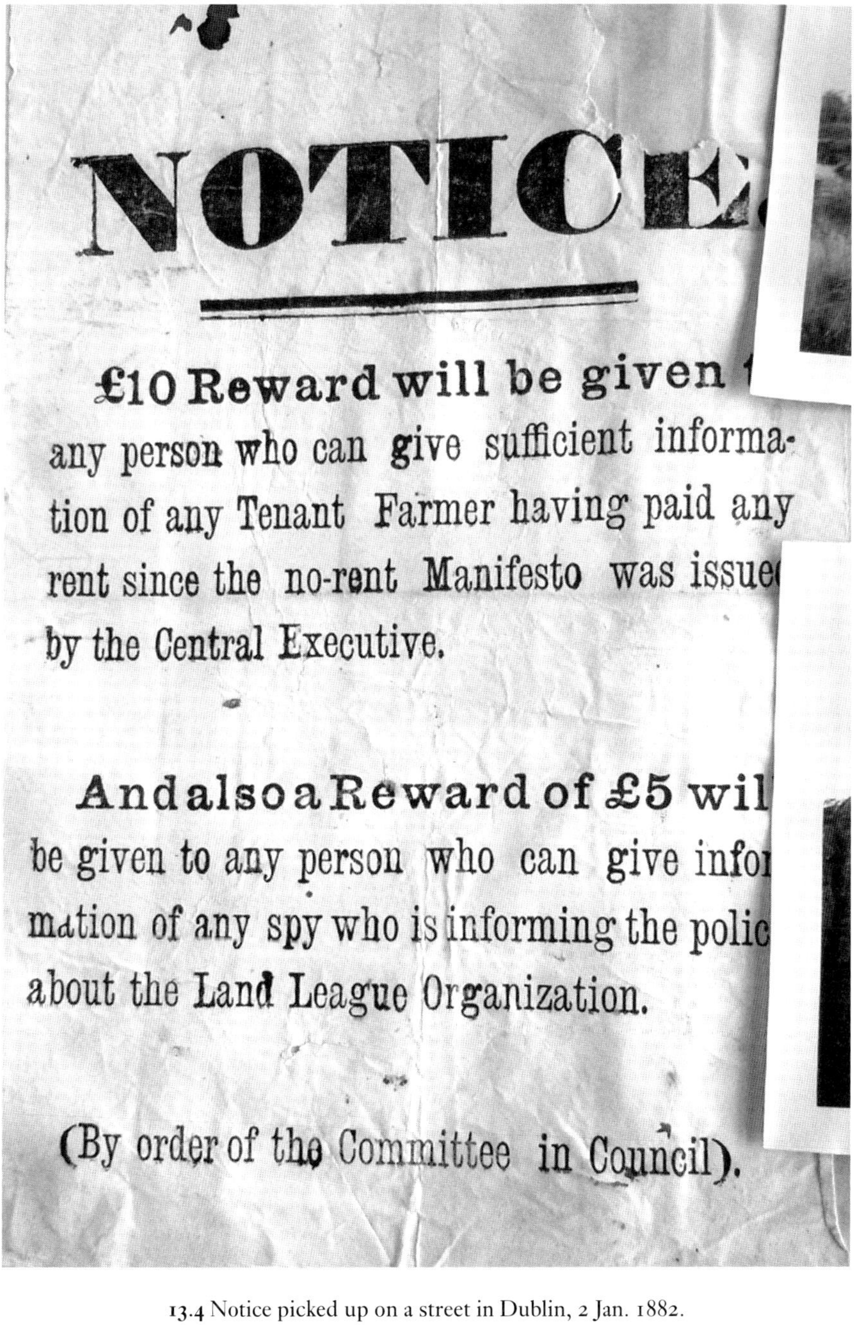


13.4 Notice picked up on a street in Dublin, 2 Jan. 1882.

Many of these items present the plight of the landlord in a satirical way, such as the 'order of sale' for the 'thoroughly broken' Irish landlord 'by order of C.S. Parnell',[16] and the beleaguered status of the landlord class is apparent. The newspaper clipping headlined 'Threatening notices from Doneraile' reproduced a notice aimed at her father that was pinned on the door of the local petty sessions house:

> Doneraile, you Orange dog, beware and take care, for your term in this world is nearer the end. The bullet or dagger you will have before many days that will put an end to Rossmoreism and landlordism in our midst. By order of the secretary I.I.S.

A representation of a coffin and a gun are added and the piece ends with – 'Woe to the man who tears this down. Irish Invinciple [*sic*] Society.' While another read:

> All members of the above society are to assemble at the usual meeting place, under pain of death on Friday at eight o'clock, to consider the necessary steps for the removal of that tyrant, Lord Doneraile. Signed R I B, Secretary.[17]

Lady Castletown's interest in land politics is understandable, as was her antipathy towards Gladstone, and she may have enjoyed sharing satirical postcards and poems with fellow members of her class as one means of dealing with their continued loss of wealth and status.

From the pages of the scrapbook there emerges an image of a confident and elitist woman of the empire who embraced expansionist British aims on the African continent. Some of the content is difficult for a modern readership as it would now be considered racist. However, these examples do provide an insight into attitudes towards imperialism among members of the Irish elite. The British empire was very much their empire, and the battles and wars in India, Afghanistan and Egypt were their own, fought by sons of Irish landed families. Cartoons and drawings depict war as a game for rich white cavalry men to play as they happily hunted down and killed Sudanese foot soldiers and pillaged local monuments. Pictorial representations of these events were sent to Lady Castletown in the form of Christmas cards.

Commercial Christmas cards were first sent in 1843 in England, but the period 1878–88 has been described as a time when 'new efforts were made to raise the art of the card'.[18] Some cards pasted into this scrapbook depict Pre-

16 Undated, Lady Castletown scrapbook, p. 22. 17 News clipping, 29 June 1884, Lady Castletown scrapbook, p. 74. 18 Gleeson White, quoted in Patricia Zakreski, 'The Victorian Christmas card as aesthetic object: "Very interesting ephemeræ of a very interesting period in English art-production"', *Journal of Design History*, 29:2 (1 May 2016), pp 120–36.

13.5 Christmas card, n.d. (*c.*1882).

Raphaelite-style princes and princesses, others are handmade and some are 'humorous', such as the series that depict a hunter with poor eyesight shooting a woman's cat rather than a crow. But there are also several cards that comment directly on the British military campaign in Egypt. A repeated trope was to depict a British soldier sitting on top of a (sometimes destroyed) Egyptian pyramid. One Christmas, Lady Castletown received such a card from her husband, which depicted him dressed in a red military coat smiling and sitting on top of a damaged and partially dismantled pyramid (fig. 13.5). An illustration of a distant city-view of the Cairo skyline was inserted in the corner, and 'Seasons Greetings' is written in a festive font across the card.

That her husband could send her such a card meant that personalized stationary like this was easily obtainable in North Africa for British soldiers. Pages 54–5 of the scrapbook hold seven undated Christmas or New Year's Eve postcards illustrated by Alfred Grey and presumably sold to members of the British Army as jingoistic celebrations of campaigns against African nations. One is entitled 'Lord Charles Beresford's Little Game', and depicted Lord Beresford (1846–1919) firing a cannon at a seaport, happily killing many defending soldiers, who were depicted as minstrels. Lord Beresford was the son of the marquess of Waterford and was certainly known by reputation if not personally to Lady Castletown. He moved in similar circles to her and was born just six years before her. The seaport depicted is Alexandria, where Beresford led a bombardment in 1882.[19] Other postcards depict named battles such as *Kassassin – heroic charge of the guards*, *Tel-el-Kabir – attack on Arabi's entrenchment* and *Tel-el-Kabir – route of the Arabi's army*.

The victory at Tel-el-Kebir on 13 September 1882 was an imperial propagandist's dream. As the town was surrounded by flat desert, the imperial forces marched overnight and attacked before dawn, utterly surprising the defences, who were forced to flee after a short battle. Fleeing soldiers were chased by the cavalry for about twelve miles, who continued to kill all they could.[20] The battle resulted in an estimated 2,000 Egyptian deaths compared to 57 British soldiers, as well as the capture of ammunition, stores, animals and valuables looted from the town.[21] Reports by British soldiers of the battle were steeped in masculine bravado and eerily reflect the representation in Castletown's cartoons. One likened the fleeing soldiers to the fox they hunted at home, while another reported shooting 'a man's head clean off'.[22] Sergeant Healey of the Royal Irish Fusiliers reported how 'we bayoneted all who came in our way … It was something terrible … We followed them for a couple of miles, halting ultimately to let the Artillery and Cavalry perform their part of '"not a bad day's work".'[23]

The event was widely reported in newspapers – not surprisingly, as General Wolseley arranged for news to be telegraphed immediately, ensuring that he was able to shape the communiqué.[24] The battle was the subject of several works of art, including *Tel-el-Kebir* (1883), an epic painting by Alphonse de Neuville, whose depiction of the battle was very different to the cartoons collected by Castletown. Both could be perceived as propaganda, but each worked in a

**19** Richard Hawkins, 'Beresford, Lord Charles William de Poer', *DIB*. **20** Edward Spiers, *The Victorian soldier in Africa* (Manchester, 2004), p. 90. **21** Ibid., pp 90–1. **22** Ibid., p. 90. **23** Ibid., p. 89. **24** Ibid., pp 92–3.

different way. In Neuville's depiction of the Highlanders, he stressed the difficulty of the terrain and the bravery and camaraderie among the soldiers as they helped each other climb through a trench, pulled their wounded comrades to safety or, in the case of the bagpiper, serenely marched through the field of battle while concentrating on his own patriotic task. The enemy forces are barely visible, with two Sudanese and perhaps three Egyptian soldiers observable, all of whom are dead or dying. The danger to the British soldiers was represented by the smoke of gunfire and the enemy soldiers defending a position to the right, out of the picture frame.[25] Lady Castletown's cartoons did not represent any real danger to the British forces. Instead, war was reduced to a game as the assumed mental, physical and tactical superiority of the imperial forces was emphasized. The soldiers did their killing with smiling faces.[26]

Imperial warfare was a serious business, but it was treated with the same levity as fashion choices for a fancy-dress ball in Lady Castletown's scrapbook. This was not a reflection of her misunderstanding of political issues, but rather a reflection of the view taken of the empire by members of the social elite in Britain at the time. She was perfectly capable of presenting content in a serious manner when it related to issues that might affect her personally, such as her husband's political career, his being robbed at gunpoint by the IRA or the threats by the Ancient Order of Hibernians to her social order. For Castletown, despite her husband being in the British Army, and serving, albeit away from the front lines, in North Africa, and later South Africa, these battles were an interest and a form of entertainment, rather than a matter of serious concern for her. Her interest in Africa as an imperial subject led her to travel to South Africa while her husband was assistant adjunct-general in 1900–2.

There is a sense that Castletown was consciously recording history 'as it happened' when it came to the Land War in Ireland and imperial expansion in Africa. However, this was not so in relation to gender politics. Some items can be read as misogynistic, particularly a poem criticizing various women for their use of cosmetics in an attempt to appear youthful.[27] Castletown was interested in female suffrage, and corresponded with the doyenne of Irish suffrage, Anna Haslam, on the subject of running for election.[28] There is no reference to this in the scrapbook. There are no records of women gaining the right to vote in 1918, for example; instead, any feminism that was presented was shown through her active participation in sport. Her obituary in the *Church of Ireland Gazette* stated that Castletown 'was a lady of many parts, a splendid horsewoman, a great traveller, and a big game shot'.[29] Hunting, and particularly shooting, were radical pastimes for a woman. Each demanded physical strength and competiveness, and

**25** Alphonse Marie de Neuville, *The storming of Tel-el-Kebir*, oil on canvas (221cm x 382.5cm), National War Museum, Edinburgh, M.1952.50. **26** Lady Castletown scrapbook, pp 54–6. **27** Anon., 'The Ball', n.d., Lady Castletown scrapbook, p. 48. **28** Anna Haslam to Lady Castletown, 15 June 1896, NLI, Doneraile papers, MS 34,166/7. **29** *Church of Ireland* involved killing creatures for sport. Castletown's horse-riding skills were renowned and she and her husband were intrepid travellers. They went on big-game shooting expeditions around the world and reportedly honeymooned while yachting in the Antarctic.[30] One handwritten poem pasted into the scrapbook alluded to the controversy that surrounded women being accepted as members of the Kildare hunt:

> For what happened was this, on one day in December
> A Lady became, of the Hunt Club a member,
> Now such an affair In the County was rare
> And people said words which sound just like a swear.[31]

Neither did she use the scrapbook as a means of engaging with the First World War in any meaningful way.

## READING THE SCRAPBOOK

Just as most of the items are anonymous, only a third of the 339 items are dated. They cover every decade of her married life, as well as four posthumous items inserted by her husband, and three pieces which are dated from long before she was born. These are a copy of a 1559 inscription on a tombstone of a knight in Kent, a reproduction of a comic 'receipt [recipe] to make a jockey' from 1785, and an original copy of the 'Proclamation by the lord lieutenant disolving the parliament in Dublin [*sic*]' dated 11 July 1797, which even in 1874 must have had some historic significance and was presumably a family heirloom of some sort. This was given pride of place in being pasted inside the front over.

Most of the 114 dated items belong to the 1880s, with 27 items in 1881, 16 dated in 1882 and 10 from 1886. They do not point conclusively to which years or decades she was most active in assembling her scrapbook, although she was certainly busy collecting material during her husband's time in Africa with the British Army during the 1880s. Items are organized neither thematically nor chronologically. The first pages relate directly to her marriage, but after that items appear to have been pasted in almost at random. For example, on page 67,[32] there is a painted sketch, which was possibly a self-portrait, of an unhappy woman dancing with a corpulent man in red coat-tails, dated 16 January 1884 (fig. 13.6), along with a newspaper report on the 'Thirteenth Club' dated 15 January 1894. On page 104 there are four clippings reporting the theft of Lord Castletown's gun in August 1920, a 1919 poem criticizing Lloyd George and

*Gazette*, 8 Apr. 1927. **30** Death notice, *Daily Telegraph*, 12 Mar. 1927. **31** Anon., n.d., Lady Castletown scrapbook, p. 36. **32** Pages are not numbered, but I allocated numbers to pages in conducting this research and can share them upon request.

**13.6** Possible self-portrait depicting dancing couple at Kells, 16 Jan. 1884.

**13.7** (*below*) Page of scrapbook showing clippings relating to robbery of Lord Castletown's gun in August 1920, a 1919 poem criticizing Lloyd George and Bonar Law, an undated sexualized poem fetishizing a woman's riding boot called 'the pathetic ballad of the patent leather boot' and a list of female subscribers to the ILPU.

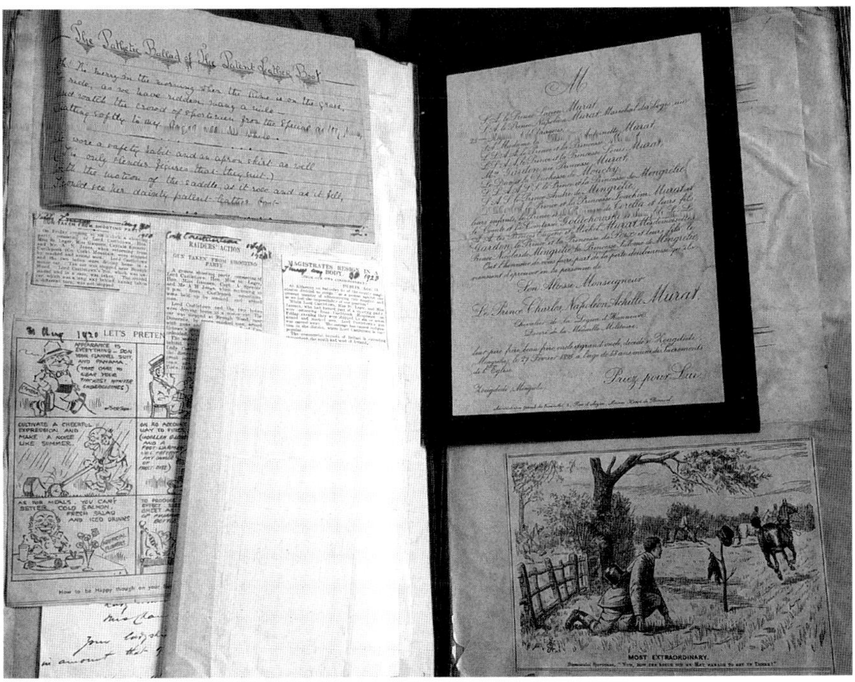

Bonar Law, the undated 'pathetic ballad of the patent leather boot' and a list of female subscribers to the Irish Loyal and Patriotic Union to which Lady Castletown donated £714 19*s*. 6*d*. (fig. 13.7).

Items were only occasionally collated thematically, and it would not be unusual for a serious report on Land League outrages to share a page with a sketch or some society gossip. This was a reflection of her wide and varied interests, and the long time frame over which she created the scrapbook; as it filled up, it was necessary to go back and squeeze items into any available space. Of the eighteen inserts, six relate to Lady Castletown's death, including the order of service at a London memorial service, as well as obituaries and death notices from various newspapers. The scrapbook was therefore in active use at the time of her death, and these inserts imply that it was, to some extent, a shared document with her husband, who chose to add these pieces. He may even have returned to the scrapbook in later life as a means of reminiscing about their time together.

The modern reader was never intended as an audience for this scrapbook, and while we cannot identify the author of each handwritten piece, it is likely that each was instantly recognizable to Lady Castletown by the handwriting or its subject matter. Likewise, while we might be at a loss to understand why certain items were grouped together, we cannot know whether they were truly random additions, or whether there was some meaning in their arrangement that was known only to her. She could 'read' the scrapbook in ways that are no longer possible, and if she decided to show specific items or openings to her circle of friends, they might too have been able to identify handwriting styles or references. If she so chose, Lady Castletown could have revealed the authors to these fellow viewers. The primary readership for this scrapbook, however, was herself. While she did not publish a memoir, this scrapbook can be read as memoir created for herself, as a form of autobiography. It allowed her to construct a version of her life and times preserving selected elements while leaving out many other things. The narrative that was constructed is multifaceted. She shows herself to have been a fashionable and desirable woman with wide-ranging interests, proud of her husband's service in the British Army; at the same time, she was a member (as she saw it) of a persecuted class of Irish landlords under attack from successive Liberal governments, and targeted by a violent and ungrateful Land League, who were destroying previously harmonious class relationships.

Lady Castletown was bedridden in her last years after a serious riding accident and later illnesses took their toll on her health. It was during these years that the scrapbook could take on a second life as a leisure activity. She was no longer gathering large numbers of articles to paste into it but she could look back at her version of her life. In her last bedridden years she associated that time with hardship and isolation; physically debilitated and feeling vulnerable on account of her husband's position in the new Irish state, she may well have derived a nostalgic pleasure from reviewing the contents of the scrapbook, which would have acted as an aide memoire to the 'happier days'. An insight into her thinking at this time can be found in a postcard and letter sent to one of her long-term correspondents, the American judge Oliver Wendell Holmes Jnr, who served on the US supreme court 1902–32:

> [V]ile murders being committed all over this wretched little country with apparent impunity & everybody more or less up in arms about everything –
>
> I rather wish we could go & settle for the rest of our days in California & never set foot in Ireland again – life has become so utterly futile and hopeless & generally disgusting here … Fancy this being Ascot week! & oh the merry days that we used to have there 100 years ago when all the world was young … I think the longer one lives the less one likes living –[33]

## CONCLUSION

The practice of scrapbooking might be dismissed as a feminine craft by some. It cannot quite be classed as art: the sketches within its pages are informal illustrations of romantic poems or rough likenesses of people or circumstances Lady Castletown was familiar with. Its value lies in its credibility as window into the multifaceted interests of its compiler. Lady Castletown cherished her scrapbook to record her personal relationships in a way that could be read by her, but not necessarily by others. She also used it as a means of making sense of her world and the political changes in her lifetime. It demonstrates that, far from being divorced from politics, an elite woman like Lady Castletown could partake in political discourse through her assembly of satirical poems and cartoons. Who exactly saw, read or comprehended the scrapbook is something that will never be known. However, its very existence, not to mention survival, suggests that within the female spaces of the Irish country house there could be discussions that might encompass imperial policies, menus, fashion and conversations of a romantic or sexual kind.

This scrapbook allowed Lady Castletown to express her sense of social, racial and intellectual superiority over the tenant and servant classes, Liberal politicians, Irish nationalists, and most severely, Egyptian and Sudanese soldiers. The majority of the material in the book appears to have been collected within 'her time', when she was described by her handwriting analyst as 'exceedingly quick witted, with a lively imagination, [and] marked capacity to grasp a

33 Lady Castletown to Oliver Wendell Holmes, 14 June [?]; quoted in G.E. White, *Oliver Wendell Holmes Jr* (Oxford, 2006), p. 247.

situation intuitively'. In compiling the scrapbook she was 'careless of small matters', something that is highlighted by her lack of interest in dating or attributing so many items. The absence of any such key hides the personal significance of much of the contents from all but her very closest social circle. Lady Castletown undoubtedly spent many hours compiling the scrapbook, which is a record of her leisure activities, the relationships she valued and the political developments she witnessed. The fact that her husband kept copies of her obituaries in the pages of the scrapbook would suggest that reading and reminiscing through the scrapbook were active leisure activities for Lady Castletown in her last days. It would also suggest that he used this scrapbook as a means of memorializing her and their privileged life together after she, and their best days, were gone.

# 'Ill-gotten acres': the GAA and the Irish country house

CIARÁN REILLY

> I was riding with an Irish Irelander through one of the rare wooded spots in the great ranch district when a few glimpses of the demesne by which we were passing, caught through gaps in the crumbling walls along the wayside, caused me to suggest a halt. On every side were signs of fallen fortunes, of neglect and poverty and ruin. The park was evidently a vast rabbit warren and the sward was overrun by whins. The groves were wide tangles of underbrush. The grand avenue was grass-grown and mossy. The 'big house' itself still made a brave show, but the out offices were woefully dilapidated. Under some of the giant elms and beeches to the rere of the mansion, the bare gables of a ruined kennel showed where the foxhounds had once fed and yelped and slept. The lodge at the grand gate was untenanted and neglected. The gate itself was rickety, and swung half-open on its crazy hinges. 'Who lives here?' I asked, wishing to know the name of the person or persons whose residence had seen better days … 'A member of the Broken Down', replied my comrade, mentioning a name there is no need to repeat. 'They were great people once, but times have changed for them, and, as you see, they are aground on the shoals of adversity'. 'What do they live on?'. 'Rabbits, principally, and three-weeks of old illustrated papers sent to them … They are all hard up. If it were not for their pride and lack of brains, they'd be dead long ago. Their pride keeps the best side out, and their lack of brains prevents them from understanding the emptiness and fatuity of their lives.'[1]

The above conversation, whether real or imagined, recounted in the *Sinn Féin Weekly* newspaper in 1907, was in many ways representative of the wider nationalist attitude towards Irish landlords at the turn of the twentieth century. Such attitudes were particularly manifest during the period of agrarian agitation known as the Ranch War, 1906–9, when the United Irish League (UIL), unhappy with the progress of the 1903 Wyndham Land Act, sought to have untenanted lands and demesnes redistributed or sold. Less than twenty years later, sporting organizations across the country, including the Gaelic Athletic Association (GAA), looked on with interest as the demesnes and lands of the

1 *Sinn Fein Weekly*, 26 Jan. 1907.

14.1 Carlow GAA players Sean Murphy, Sean Gannon, Chris Nolan and Marty Kavanagh, pictured at the ruins of Ducketts Grove, Carlow, January 2018 at the unveiling of the new county jersey and sponsorship by IT Carlow. Courtesy of Pat Moore.

Irish country house were redistributed to uneconomic landholders and others under the terms of the 1923 Irish Land Act. The use of these vast country-house demesnes was particularly apparent to Barney Fay, secretary of the GAA's Ulster Council, who in 1929 made a clarion call to members in which he alluded to the many problems the association faced. Among the challenges which the County Cavan official highlighted was the association's 'inadequate' playing facilities. According to Fay the problem was exacerbated by the fact that

> those who own demesnes have never been too anxious to place their ill-gotten acres at the service of the 'mere Irish'. They never called this a 'ban' only just keeping the natives in their place.

Fay's comments may have encapsulated nationalist attitudes towards Irish country houses that had grown out of the Land War,[2] but did it reflect reality with respect to the use of demesne lands by the GAA? In fact, on the contrary,

2 See for example R.V. Comerford, 'Foreword' in Terence Dooley and Christopher Ridgway (eds), *The Irish country house: its past, present and future* (Dublin, 2011), pp 11–13.

this essay argues that from its formation in 1884 the use of demesne land was often central to the development of the GAA at a local level.[3] From Curraghchase in County Limerick, where the local team were known as the Home Rulers, to Ardfert in County Kerry where the landowner Talbot Crosbie was among the GAA's most prominent supporters, the early development of the GAA depended on the use of demesne land for the hosting of their games and this fostered an unusual alliance between Ireland's largest sporting organization and a number of country-house owners (fig. 14.1).

Historically, the development of demesnes in Ireland occurred much later than in Britain, where it dated from the medieval period.[4] However, by the eighteenth century there was a preference among country-house owners for 'hilly sites, distant vistas and rolling lawns, [and] a view of water was now particularly esteemed'.[5] Over the course of the next hundred years or so demesne land was significantly added to and improved. According to Terence Dooley, by the middle of the nineteenth century about 6 per cent of the country consisted of demesnes, which ranged from 100 to 1,500 acres in size.[6] Many demesnes included a home farm and extensive woodland or plantation within their boundaries but, most importantly, gardens and lawns were laid out for pleasure and sporting purposes. Far removed from the local communities that surrounded them, the demesne was the country-house owner's veritable paradisiacal retreat. Often enclosed by high stone walls, they were regarded as symbols of an alien culture, and by the early twentieth century viewed with antagonism by nationalist writers such as William Bulfin, who concluded in 1907 that they were

> parks and game preserves, remnants of the broad domains [*sic*] that were robbed from the chieftains … and given to the foreigners who fought the Irish for spoil, or the weaklings who sold themselves to the reavers.[7]

But that is not the full story. From the 1830s onwards country-house owners had begun to open their demesnes to local communities, or at least to the more respectable classes, for sporting and recreational pursuits. In many instances, this involved the playing of cricket, such as at Capard in Queen's County (Laois) and Coolattin, in County Wicklow, where pitches were provided for local teams comprised of estate workers and others. Elsewhere, at the beginning of the twentieth century, some landlords opened their demesnes to facilitate the

3 *Fermanagh Herald*, 13 Apr. 1929. 4 For more see Vandra Costello, *Irish demesne landscapes, 1660–1740* (Dublin, 2015); Finola O'Kane, 'Design and rule: women in the Irish countryside, 1715–1831', *Eighteenth-Century Ireland: Iris an Dá Chultúr*, 19 (2004), pp 56–74; Terence Reeves-Smyth, 'Demesnes' in F.H.A. Aalen, Matthew Stout and Kevin Whelan (eds), *Atlas of the Irish rural landscape* (Cork, 2011), pp 278–86. 5 David Dickson, *Old world colony: Cork and south Munster, 1630–1830* (Cork, 2005), p. 197. 6 Terence Dooley, *The Big Houses and landed estates of Ireland* (Dublin, 2001), pp 126–7. 7 William Bulfin, *Rambles in Eirinn* (Dublin, 1908), p. 207.

revolutionary growth in other sports and leisure activities.[8] For example, at Ballyfin in Queen's County, Sir Algernon Coote provided his grounds to the local community for sports including cycling and athletics,[9] as did Patrick Greville-Nugent at Clonyn, near Delvin in County Westmeath.[10] In 1908, in County Kilkenny, E.K.B. Tighe gave his demesne at Woodstock for the 'amusements of the people of the district',[11] while the duke of Leinster had frequently opened the grounds of Carton to excursionists from the late 1880s.[12] Capard, located at the foot of the Slieve Bloom Mountains, provides an example of how local communities frequently used the demesne in the closing decades of the nineteenth century; from the early 1870s, groups including the Tullamore Total Abstinence Society and the Geashill Temperance Society held picnics on the front lawn, taking in the 'beautiful and picturesque scenery'.[13] Other visiting groups reflected the great cultural reawakening that characterized late nineteenth-century Ireland; in 1902, for example, over 130 members of the Tullamore Celtic Literary Society were 'entertained on the lawn to a full luncheon', while other cultural and literary groups from Maryborough (now Portlaoise) regularly visited.[14]

Following its formation in 1884, the GAA, founded in Thurles, County Tipperary, by Michael Cusack and others to cultivate and preserve national games and athletics, quickly emerged as the largest of the cultural nationalist bodies engaged in the Irish revival.[15] The reasons for its initial success were varied but in some cases, and this has not often been acknowledged, it did include support from country-house owners. Indeed, the playing of native Irish sports on demesnes long predated the founding of the GAA. In a number of midland counties, landlords had long been prominent supporters of what was known as 'summer hurling', a game played with a broad camán, or hurley. As early as 1826 Valentine Bennett gave part of his Thomastown demesne in King's County (now Offaly) for the purpose of playing native games. Known as 'the Hurling Park' this pitch was marked on the first Ordnance Survey map in 1838, and today continues to be used by the Drumcullen GAA club. At nearby Kinnitty Castle, the Bernards and their agents, the Manifolds, were also supporters of the native game, as were the Moonys of Doon. As time passed, the GAA could even rely on country-house owners for use of public buildings; at Donard, in County Wicklow, for example, Mrs Goddard gave the use of the town hall for the GAA to hold its annual ball, a fundraiser that was a vital source of income for the local club.[16]

8 For the development of sport in Ireland see Paul Rouse, *Sport and Ireland: a history* (Oxford, 2015); James Kelly, *Sport in Ireland, 1600–1840* (Dublin, 2014). **9** *Leinster Express*, 4 Aug. 1900. **10** *Westmeath Independent*, 2 Apr. 1898. **11** *Kilkenny People*, 5 Sept. 1908. **12** See for example *Freeman's Journal*, 12 May 1887. **13** *King's County Chronicle*, 31 July 1873, 27 Aug. 1891. **14** Ibid., 14 Aug. 1902. **15** See Mike Cronin, William Murphy and Paul Rouse (eds), *The GAA, 1884–2009: a history* (Dublin, 2009); Mike Cronin, Mark Duncan and Paul Rouse, *The GAA: a people's history* (Cork, 2009); *idem, The GAA: county by county* (Cork, 2009). **16** See *Leinster Leader*, 18 Sept. 1915.

Nevertheless, from its inception, the very nationalist ethos of the GAA meant that the organization and landlords were strange bedfellows. From the outset, the GAA was closely aligned with separatism; several of the founding members were Fenians and members of the Irish Republican Brotherhood (IRB).[17] Moreover, within twenty years of its formation the GAA introduced a number of 'bans' which precluded its members from playing or attending 'foreign games'.[18] In addition, GAA pitches were not to be used for these so-called 'foreign games', which included rugby, soccer and cricket, while another rule banned members of the Royal Irish Constabulary and the military from any involvement in the association.[19] By extension, this meant that country-house families, most of whom had connections to the military, the police or British administration in their local communities were precluded from involvement with the GAA. In a sense this created a conundrum. One of the biggest problems that faced the GAA in its early years was the lack of playing pitches. More often than not they depended on the loan of playing fields which were hard to secure; Irish farmers were often reluctant to provide their land, worried about the damage it might suffer, or because a fee for its use could not be agreed upon. Where they did have their own pitches the GAA could adhere to its rules but where they did not they were more than happy to flaunt them and use demesne lands, embracing, sometimes deferentially, the local landlord. By the same measure, landlords were happy to embrace this fledgling organization if it meant communal harmony – only during periods of political animosity was support withdrawn, and then only temporarily.

One of the earliest recorded GAA games played on demesne land occurred in August 1885, less than a year after the GAA's establishment, when over 7,000 people gathered at Hillpark in County Galway to watch a hurling match between the local side and Labane.[20] The following year at Devon Castle in Newcastle West, County Limerick, over 4,000 people attended games on the demesne of the Curling family.[21] These matches suggested to GAA officials that demesne land was highly suitable for hosting games, particularly where the crowd could be controlled and charged an entrance fee through the demesne gates. In 1889, the Queen's County (Laois) championship final was played on Webber's demesne at Kellyville, near Ballylinan, attracting a large crowd and providing a handsome profit for the county board.[22] In 1910 Leigh White of Bantry House, County Cork

17 See Paul Rouse, 'Gunfire in Hayes's Hotel: the IRB and the founding of the GAA' in Fearghal McGarry and James McConnell (eds), *The black hand of republicanism: Fenianism in modern Ireland* (Dublin, 2009), pp 72–85; David Hassan and Andrew McGuire, 'The GAA and revolutionary Irish politics in late nineteenth and early twentieth-century Ireland', *Sport in Society*, 19:1 (2016), pp 51–61. See also Gearóid Ó Tuathaigh (ed.), *The GAA and revolution in Ireland, 1913–1923* (Cork, 2015). 18 See for example *Leinster Leader*, 20 Mar. 1926. 19 For the history of these bans see Paul Rouse, 'The politics of culture and sport in Ireland: a history of the GAA ban on foreign games, 1884–1971', *International Journal of the History of Sport*, 10:3 (1990), pp 333–60. 20 *Connaught Tribune*, 31 July 1909. 21 *Freeman's Journal*, 20 Sept. 1887. 22 *Leinster Express*, 3 Aug. 1889.

was thanked for allowing the GAA the use of his Glengarriff demesne, and for allowing them to make improvements on the playing area – fencing off the pitch – amounting to over £40.[23] Given the entertainment and pageantry that surrounded these games it was hardly surprising then that country-house owners were often present: in 1895 the Adare Desmonds and the Curragh Chase Home Rulers played in front of members of the Limerick gentry including the Monsell and De Vere families.[24] At Kildangan Castle in County Kildare, Dominic More O'Ferrall took great pride in the local GAA club, using his demesne for their games, rejoicing that he was descended from the Gaelic Irish chieftain Rory O'More of Laois.[25] Others such as Lord Cloncurry regularly attended matches played on his demesne at Lyons, near Celbridge in County Kildare. The GAA also promoted athletics and cycling, and these sports too were accommodated on demesne lands, such as Lissanelly in Cappagh, County Tyrone,[26] and at Lissadell in County Sligo thanks to the support of the Gore Booths.[27] At Lissadell in 1905, the organizers of a sports day included Frank Dineen who had served as the fourth president of the GAA (1895–8), and is the man credited with having purchased the site for the association's headquarters at Croke Park.

However, one of the best-known landlord patrons of the GAA in its early years was Charles Stewart Parnell, the leader of the Irish Parliamentary Party.[28] He frequently provided his demesne at Avondale to the local Rathdrum club and others. The earliest games at Avondale were played in 1886 between Rathdrum and Brittas. On this occasion, Brittas adopted what modern commentators would lament as 'a blanket defence', but it was reported that the crowd of several thousand still enjoyed the game.[29] The following year, on returning from Westminster, Parnell rode over the Avondale demesne, where he witnessed the semi-final of the Wicklow Championship, which was played on 'an elevated lawn' in front of the house. According to various newspaper accounts, 'there was a great concourse of people' present and special trains were laid on, with several bands in attendance who played nationalist airs, including one which made reference to the 'Plan of Campaign'. Parnell, it was reported, 'followed the play with great interest'.[30] Over the course of the next decade or so Avondale continued to provide a home for the local GAA club. In 1896, five years after Parnell's death, spectators flocked to Avondale for GAA matches, although it was reported that more were interested in viewing the house than in attending the game. Avondale had become something of a shrine where hundreds of visitors delighted in the chance to go through the house and see the many artefacts associated with the career of the 'Uncrowned King of Ireland. Others picked flowers, acorns, beech nuts, holly, oak and every sort of shrub growing in the demesne'.[31]

**23** *Skibbereen Eagle*, 10 Feb. 1910. **24** *Evening Herald*, 5 Sept. 1895. **25** *Leinster Leader*, 12 May 1934. **26** *Ulster Herald*, 1 July 1905. **27** *Sligo Champion*, 22 July 1905. **28** See Tom Hunt's essay in this volume. **29** *Freeman's Journal*, 18 Oct. 1886. **30** *Belfast News-Letter*, 10 May 1887. **31** *Wicklow People*, 3 Oct. 1896.

Occasionally, the hosting of Gaelic games on demesne land was followed by a public address to the owner. In 1904, Lindsay Talbot Crosbie was thanked for providing his grounds for the 'sport loving people of historic old Ardfert'. The address concluded with the call for:

> Gentlemen of your class to bring themselves more into touch with the people in burying old feuds and helping to contribute to a universal goodwill and fellowship amongst all classes in Ireland.

The address to Talbot Crosbie was replicated elsewhere. In 1909, at Cloyne (later the club of the famed Christy Ring) in County Cork, Colonel Mountifort J.C. Longfield was lauded for his 'kindness and patronage of these genuine Irish pastimes' by allowing the use of his demesne at Castlemary.[32] However, it seems that such kindness was forgotten when in 1920 the IRA burned Castlemary. The same was true of Kinnitty Castle in County Offaly and Devon Castle in Newcastle West, County Limerick, whose owners had been local patrons of the GAA in the past, and both of which were burned during the revolutionary period, 1920–3.

It is important to note that the GAA did not covertly use country-house demesnes. Games were widely advertised in local and national newspapers. Matches held in country-house demesnes were regularly accompanied by entertainments provided by bands of musicians, while excursion trains were organized for the events. In 1901 at Rostellan in County Cork, for example, trains carried passengers towards the home of Mrs Thackwell, while the Cork Workingmen's Band played 'a choice selection of music' in the demesne.[33] In 1913, the Lusk Pipers, then the 'Champions of Ireland', serenaded spectators at GAA matches in Swords demesne.[34] Even the GAA's patron, Thomas Fennelly, the archbishop of Cashel, was present at Lord Kenmare's demesne in 1908 when, amid considerable excitement, the Kilkenny and Cork hurlers played in the 'picturesque grounds of the Earl of Kenmare's demesne, just at the Lake's edge, and commanding a full view of the Earl's beautiful mansion'.[35] In July 1922, when the Ulster Football Championship semi-final between Monaghan and Armagh was played at Ballybay, the spectators were said to have 'found themselves transported into a veritable fairy land in the Leslie demesne amidst scenes of sylvan splendour'.[36] In this instance it is not certain what say the Leslies had in the matter given that the IRA had burned the house thirteen months earlier. However, a few years later, in post-independence Ireland, Ballybay Pearse Brothers' permanent home was created on the Leslie demesne after it was divided by the Irish Land Commission.

32 *Skibbereen Eagle*, 17 Apr. 1909. 33 *Cork Examiner*, 20 July 1901. 34 *Wicklow People*, 30 July 1910. 35 *Kerry People*, 1 Aug. 1908. 36 *Anglo-Celt*, 22 July 1922.

Perhaps the most scenic setting for GAA games was at Glin, County Limerick, the home of the FitzGeralds, knights of Glin. While the demesne was occasionally used by the GAA in its formative years, it was really only during the early 1920s that it became a more permanent venue for local matches. During the truce period in 1921, for example, the knight of Glin allowed the demesne to be used for several matches. These games were played 'within touch of the castle' while the local company of IRA volunteers 'held a gate collection and maintained order'.[37] This was seen as a remarkable turnaround as the previous summer there had been consternation in Glin when a Sinn Féin flag was removed from the old Glin castle.[38] In 1924, at a football match between Glin and Listowel, a Sinn Féin band attended and a 'good sum was realised at the gate'.[39] Such was the setting at Glin that it was regularly favoured by the GAA's Munster Council for fixtures. In April 1930, it played host to Limerick and Waterford in the National Football League, which was attended by over 3,000 people, and in the same year Limerick and Kerry also played in the demesne. The Kerry team on this occasion included legendary footballers Con Brosnan and John Joe Sheehy, members of the Kerry IRA, who had been on opposing sides in the Civil War. The presence of the IRA and the local Sinn Féin branch at these events at Glin, and indeed other venues across the country, suggests a much more complicated relationship between the Big House and local republicanism during the early 1920s. In September 1920, during the War of Independence, the *Sligo Champion* lauded Major R.W. Hillas for allowing GAA games to proceed on his lands and, it was suggested, that 'if other gentlemen ... would follow the good example set by Major Hillas the GAA in the county would be better patronised'.[40]

But, of course, not all country-house owners were as favourably disposed to the GAA. Owing to the GAA's ban on members of the police or military attending or playing Gaelic games, some owners refused to permit matches to take place on their demesnes. In 1905, the marquess of Sligo refused to give the use of Westport demesne to the local GAA club specifically because police and soldiers were not allowed to compete.[41] His decision was quickly backed by the earl of Lucan, who refused to allow games in Castlebar, while the following year there was controversy in Athenry, County Galway, when 'Gaels' policing the playing fields refused to admit members of the military.[42] At the annual Ardfert GAA sports day in July 1904, there was consternation when the Union Jack was flown at the Talbot Crosbie demesne in County Kerry and it appeared as if the event would have to be cancelled. After a long impasse, a deal was reached when it was agreed that the flag at the demesne gate could be left, but the one inside had to be taken down since GAA rules prohibited competing under the Union Jack.[43] A few years before, there had been controversy during the Second

37 *Irish Examiner*, 10 Oct. 1921. 38 *Killarney Echo*, 31 July 1920. 39 *Liberator (Tralee)*, 24 May 1924. 40 *Sligo Champion*, 4 Sept. 1920. 41 *Irish People*, 1 Sept. 1906. 42 *Sinn Fein Weekly*, 15 Sept. 1906. 43 *Kerry Evening Post*, 9 July 1904.

Anglo-Boer War (1899–1902) when a number of GAA clubs were named in honour of Boer generals. These included Athenry de Wets in Galway, Buffers Alley in Wexford, Tuam Krugers in Galway, Lahorna de Wets in Tipperary and the Irish Transvaal Brigade GAA club in Killorglin, County Kerry. In September 1901, the *Irish People* argued it was hardly surprising that many landlords would withdraw the use of land to the GAA given the almost unanimous support of country-house families for the British war effort in South Africa.[44]

In the years following independence many country-house demesnes were taken over by trusts and town councils, which oversaw grazing rights and the use of the land by the local community. Although these were intended as communal spaces, in many cases the GAA ended up exclusively using the land for the playing of their games.[45] In 1925, at Castlerea in County Roscommon, the GAA decided to play the 1925 Connaught Championship game between Galway and Leitrim on the former Sandford demesne, cementing the local club's claim that it was their field.[46] Such action by local GAA clubs often led to acrimonious disputes; one of the best publicized was at Macroom in County Cork.[47] In 1924, Lady Ardilaun had handed over the family demesne to a trust for the people of Macroom and for the local golf club. Very quickly, a group of youths erected goalposts, claiming that the field belonged solely to the GAA.[48] There were many who disagreed. According to the chairman of Macroom Golf Club, R.C. Williams, in 1925:

> We invited the GAA locally to make an offer for the renting of the football pitch annually, throwing out the suggested idea that, in order that turf should be in proper order for important engagements, it should be played upon only on Sundays, and the Town Park used for practices during the week. Our committee realised the advantages to be derived from periodical football and hurling matches from the point of view of business … and we hoped to receive their co-operation in a manner, which would be to our mutual benefit and to the benefit of the town. Unfortunately, their only answer was to enter the castle grounds without authority and play there indiscriminately. Recently they had adopted the practice of arranging and holding matches in the grounds without permission from the committee and charging an entrance fee at the castle gates. In this matter a serious legal responsibility has been incurred by the representatives of the football club and I hope they will realise the position.

The dispute between the clubs continued, and as late as the 1970s it was still unresolved.[49] There was also considerable rancour in Newcastle West in County

44 *Irish People*, 28 Sept. 1901. 45 See for example *Connacht Tribune*, 6 Oct. 1928, 12 Apr. 1930. 46 *Leitrim Observer*, 4 July 1925. 47 *Limerick Leader*, 7 June 1941. 48 Quoted in *Southern Star*, 1 Sept. 1990. 49 See for example *Irish Examiner*, 4 Mar. 1972; *Southern Star*,

Limerick between the local GAA club and the town trust who had been appointed to oversee the former demesne lands.[50] The dispute wrangled on for many years and during one fiery exchange in 1941 it was claimed that it would be better to provide the demesne for 'milch cows' since the GAA could not bring their affairs to order.[51]

In other parts of the country the arrangements between the GAA and country-house owners after independence were more amicable. In 1924, there was great delight in Roscommon when Strokestown GAA, known as Lord Edwards, returned to their 'old battlefield' in Pakenham Mahon's Strokestown demesne. The playing of games here had stretched back to the late 1880s, an era of great contests between local clubs, but these had been halted owing to the presence of the British Army during the War of Independence.[52] The Lord Edwards club was supported by the Pakenham Mahon family, and indeed the family's historical association with the club continues to this day, with the Strokestown jersey sporting on its crest the celebrated Gothic arch that stands at the entrance to Strokestown Park House. As late as 1939 the GAA in Glin were still reliant on the FitzGeralds for the provision of playing pitches. According to club officials: '[M]any Gaels are not so favoured as to be privileged to hold their league football tie in the demesne of a local Knight and within view of his lordly residence.' The *Limerick Leader* agreed that the playing of games in the demesne 'plainly shows the advance of the Gael, and Limerick Gaeldom appreciates highly the Knight of Glin's kindness to the local Gaels.'[53] Old animosities were also cast aside in the pursuit of playing pitches. In 1944, for example, the republican priest Fr Thomas Burbage was more than happy to use the grounds of Capard House in County Laois for the hosting of camogie matches and Gaelic League classes, publicly thanking the owners in the process.[54]

During the 1920s and 1930s, GAA officials across the country waited to see how the conditions set down by the 1923 Land Act, which empowered the Irish Land Commission to compulsorily acquire untenanted estates and demesnes, would be beneficial to their cause. Following on from this, in 1925 the GAA's Central Council initiated proceedings with the Department of Lands and Agriculture 'to procure a share of the ranches which were being divided up', and in its early stages was able to report an 'encouraging and sympathetic hearing'.[55] Among the earliest recipients of demesne land was Rhode GAA in County Offaly, who had started to play football on the former Beaumont Nesbitt demesne at Tubberdaly.[56] The house had been burned in April 1923 during the Irish Civil War amid intense agrarian agitation. The local GAA club also secured the use of the former estate dance hall for fundraising activities.[57] There were

1 Sept. 1990. **50** *Limerick Leader*, 8 Apr. 1940. **51** Ibid., 7 June 1941. **52** See for example *Roscommon Messenger*, 22 Nov. 1924. **53** *Limerick Leader*, 18 Mar. 1938. **54** *Nationalist and Leinster Times*, 11 Aug. 1945. **55** *Irish Independent*, 7 Dec. 1925. **56** *Offaly Independent*, 7 Nov. 1925 and 28 Nov. 1931. **57** Ibid., 4 May 1935.

considerable tensions locally concerning the division of the demesne, and who was to get land, but Rhode GAA, whose secretary was Christopher Jones, the chief protagonist in the burning of Tubberdaly, was given a pitch by the Land Commission.[58] The process in other areas was less problematic. The Ardclough club in County Kildare had Lord Cloncurry to thank for help in their discussions with the Land Commission regarding the allocation of lands, thereby allowing for a seamless transition that avoided local tensions.[59] The exact number of GAA clubs granted playing pitches by the Land Commission has yet to be established. It would make for yet another revealing study if the Land Commission papers were ever to be made publicly accessible. Likewise, it would be valuable to know how many clubs did not bother with democratic methods but instead simply seized untenanted land according to the dictum of Barney Fay that it was morally correct to reclaim 'ill-gotten acres'.

58 Ibid., 15 Jan. 1927 and 28 Oct. 1933. 59 *Nationalist and Leinster Times*, 8 Jan. 1938.

# Keepers, pheasants, poachers, religion and politics: the Rhiwlas estate, Bala, Wales

EINION WYN THOMAS

Friday, 23 September 1892, was not a particularly illustrious day in the scholastic history of Capel Celyn Board School. Returning from his lunch, the headmaster found that all the eldest boys bar one had disappeared. In his log book he noted down the reason for this strange disappearance: 'Mr Price's [Rhiwlas] gamekeepers called at dinner time and induced the bigger boys to go with them to drive the grouse on the mountain.'[1]

Complaint was worthless since Rhiwlas owned nearly all the farms in the valley; the gamekeepers could take children from school secure in the knowledge that nobody would utter a word of dissent. No mention is made in the log book of the boys being punished for this act of truancy. This story illustrates the power that the estate had over people's lives, a power not fully appreciated today, but one that was based on deference and fear.

One of the largest estates in the old county of Merioneth, Rhiwlas, near Bala in north Wales, became an important sporting estate from the mid-1860s onwards. How the tenantry viewed this development was bound up with their fears as to how they would be affected by a change, which they saw as being potentially detrimental to their livelihood. One method of resistance they would use was poaching, not only as a means of attacking the estate in reaction to the introduction of game, but also as a way of warning the landlord against putting political pressure on them during election time. From the opposing perspective there was a landlord with progressive ideas, attempting, in the teeth of strong opposition, to set up a new viable business venture to improve his revenues.

This was a time of great political turmoil in rural Wales, especially in the county of Merioneth, and particularly on the Rhiwlas estate, where a rising Liberal/Nonconformist middle class began seriously to challenge the political power of the Tory/Anglican landlords. The struggle was for the most part peaceful and constitutional, with religious leaders from the Nonconformist denominations leading the attack on the landlords. Allied with this was the growth of a Welsh-language pro-Liberal press, especially Thomas Gee's *Baner ac Amserau Cymru*, which was first published in 1859.[2]

1 Capel Celyn Board School Logbook (Meirionnydd Record Office, Dolgellau, ZA/14/37).
2 The editor, the Revd Thomas Gee, exercised great influence on the political, social and religious life of Wales. He was heavily involved in the anti-tithe movement of the 1880s. In

The town of Bala, on which the estate was centred, was viewed as the intellectual focal point of Dissent in north Wales with two Nonconformist training colleges located there.[3] Students from these colleges would be instrumental in carrying the Liberal message to congregations in rural and remote chapels. For the Anglicans, the town was viewed as being especially hostile to the Church of England. As the editor of *Y Cymro*, an Anglican publication, stated in 1860: '[W]hat Rome is to Italy, Bala is to North Wales. The mother of all evil, "the city of destruction". The place where the poisonous seeds of Nonconformity and Republicanism are sown!'[4]

## THE RHIWLAS ESTATE

The Rhiwlas estate had been established in the second quarter of the sixteenth century when Cadwaladr Prys moved from the family home in Pentrefoelas, Denbighshire, and built a house on the banks of the river Tryweryn opposite the town of Bala.[5] The Prices were a typical Welsh gentry family who took an active and leading role in their community and over the years served as members of parliament, high sheriffs and justices of the peace for the county of Merioneth. They were also known for being patrons of the Welsh bards, and numerous praise poems and elegies composed in their honour showed the esteem in which the family were held.[6] However, by the eighteenth century they had become more anglicized in their outlook, and their knowledge of Welsh culture and of the Welsh language had diminished.

Expansion and growth occurred when Richard Watkin Price inherited the estate in 1794. With prudent financial management, he increased the size of the estate from 9,000 acres to over 15,000 acres. Between 1828 and 1859, he bought fifty-four farms around the Bala area, for which he paid well over £103,000, borrowing most of the money from London bankers and local businessmen.[7] By 1873, following further purchases of land, the estate comprised 17,881 acres, though most of it was moorland with an estimated value of less than 10 shillings

1886 he established the Welsh Land League and through his newspaper he attacked landlordism with vigour. 3 Revd Michael Jones, the principal of the Independent College, was a fiery Welsh nationalist who founded the Welsh colony in Patagonia in 1865. An advocate of land nationalization, he shared a platform with Michael Davitt, the Irish land reformer, when he first visited Wales in 1886. Revd Lewis Edwards, the principal of the Welsh Calvinistic Methodist College, was more measured in his response to events. He was not comfortable in mixing religion with politics, though after the 1859 general election and the political evictions that followed, he fully endorsed the Liberal cause. 4 Quoted by Ieuan Gwynedd Jones, 'Radicaliaeth (Radicalism)' in Geraint Bowen (ed.), *Atlas Meirionnydd* (Bala, 1974), p. 140. 5 John Edward Griffith, *Pedigrees of Anglesey and Carnarvonshire families* (Horncastle, Lincolnshire, 1914), pp 267–8. 6 A. Lloyd Hughes, 'Rhai o Noddwyr y Beirdd yn Sir Feirionnydd', *Llen Cymru* (Caerdydd, 1968–9), x, pp 190–4. 7 Memorandum book of Richard Watkin Price, 1826–59, National Library of Wales (NLW), MS, A40.

an acre.[8] It could be argued that financial considerations, due to the low value of the land, were among the reasons that game rearing was undertaken by the estate, but, above all, it was Price's passion for hunting that was the main impetus.

## GAME AND POLITICS

There is a wealth of evidence documenting the development and impact of game and game preservation on the Rhiwlas estate, in particular the later findings of the royal commission on land in Wales and Monmouthshire, which in September and October of 1893 took evidence at Bala from tenant after tenant who stated how their livelihoods had suffered due to the adverse effect of Price's development of a game estate. John Jones, the tenant of Ty'n Celyn, a farm of forty-two acres, testified that 'a cause of loss to the Rhiwlas tenants is the way pheasants are scattered through the woods on the estate … from there they get over to the cornfields and potato fields and cause great damage'.[9] His predecessor had been ruined by the game and had left the farm owing £80 to the landlord, a debt Jones paid off. He also commented on the arrogance of the gamekeepers towards the tenants, and how he kept losing his cats and dogs to the traps they set. Another tenant, David Roberts, stated:

> In 1866 I took a farm called Llannerch Eryr in the parish of Llandderfel on the Rhiwlas estate … My father-in-law was a previous tenant to me, and he was ruined in consequence of the number of rabbits. It was with great difficulty that I could produce on my farm sufficient to keep four cows, four calves and two horses.[10]

Llannerch Eryr was a farm of 138 acres and regarded as one of the best farms in the district for growing corn. Yet, Dafydd Roberts complained how small the yields were and how once he had lost six acres of corn due to rabbits. For this loss he was given £12 in compensation even though he had made a loss of £200 while a tenant. The farm would ultimately be turned into a rabbit warren.[11] Thomas Davies, the tenant of Fedwlwyd farm, was quite forthright in his answer when asked if there were any complaints about the game on the estate, stating: '[T]here were very great complaints on the Rhiwlas estate, exceptional complaints in fact.'[12] As he left the stand there was loud applause.

When Price was asked by the commission if there had been any tension between himself and his tenants over the issue of game, Price answered in the

8 John Bateman, *The great landowners of Great Britain and Ireland* (London, 1878). 9 John Jones, *Minutes of evidence of the royal commission on land in Wales and Monmouthshire (RCLW)*, 1894, vol. i, 8163, p. 327. 10 Evidence of David Roberts, ibid., 16542A, p. 761. 11 On 11 Oct. 1883, eight guns shot a total of 1,190 rabbits on what was by then called the Llannerch Eryr beat. 12 Thomas Davies, *RCLW*, vol. i, 8141, pp 326–7.

negative. That was not true. But there were also other causes of landlord-tenant tensions. In 1859, relationships had been severely strained when those who had the vote refused to support the Conservative candidate as directed by their landlord in instructions given to them individually in the Bull Hotel in Bala a few days before the election.[13] Despite the threats and intimidation, twenty-one of the Rhiwlas tenants abstained, two voted for David Williams, the Liberal candidate, and eleven voted for William Watkin Edward Wynne, the Conservative candidate.[14] On 12 May, the full county result was declared, with the Liberals polling 351 votes and the Conservatives winning with 389 votes. Price's reaction was immediate and unexpected; five out of the twenty-one tenants who abstained were evicted from their farms.[15] Between the harassment and the evictions, Price and the other landowners browbeat the tenants into submission. This would become apparent in the election of 1865 when there was no revolt. Yet a great deal of ill feeling had been created between tenant and landlord. Over thirty years afterwards, Thomas Ellis Snr recalled that the 'evictions had created a gulf between landlord and tenant. Neither the Ballot Act or time has healed this breach.'[16]

## RICHARD JOHN LLOYD PRICE

It was in this atmosphere of mutual suspicion that R.J. Lloyd Price inherited the estate on the death of his grandfather on 14 June 1860. Aged 17,[17] educated at Eton and later Oxford, he was a young man in a hurry, full of new ideas.[18] Crucially, hunting rather than agriculture was his passion, and during the following years his tenants must have agreed with the editor of *Baner ac Amserau Cymru*, who commented: '[H]ow sad it is to see a young man place so much emphasis on hunting to the detriment of his tenants.'[19]

Price's aim was to turn Rhiwlas into one of the best sporting estates not only in Wales but in Britain. He appealed to the northern English industrialists with time and money to spare, arguing there was no need to go to Scotland when

13 For a detailed study see Ieuan Gwynedd Jones, 'Merioneth politics in mid-nineteenth century: the politics of a rural economy' and D.G. Lloyd Hughes, 'David Williams, Castell Deudraeth and the Merioneth elections of 1859, 1865 and 1868', *Journal of the Merioneth Historical and Record Society (JMHRS)*, 5:4 (1965–8), pp 273–326, 335–51. 14 Wynne was a High Church Puseyite which was another reason why the staunchly Nonconformist tenants found it difficult to vote for him. 15 Evidence of Thomas Edward Ellis, *RCLW*, vol. i, 16910, p. 785. 16 Evidence of Thomas Ellis, *RCLW*, vol. i, 17544, p. 829. 17 He achieved full possession of the estate on his twenty-first birthday, 17 Apr. 1864. 18 J.H. Lloyd, 'The lost industries of the Rhiwlas estate', *JMHRS*, 4 (1961), pp 128–39. One of his most interesting business ventures was the establishment of the short-lived Welsh whisky distillery in the village of Frongoch in 1887. Between June and December 1916, the abandoned distillery was used to intern Irish rebels following the Easter Rebellion. 19 *Baner ac Amserau Cymru (Banner and Times of Wales)*, 29 Jan. 1868.

Wales was within easier travelling distance of the great industrial cities of England.[20] Crucial to the success of this venture was the expansion of the rail network.[21] With the opening of the Corwen to Bala railway in August 1868, there was a direct link between Bala and the north-west of England, and travel time was being reduced from one day to two hours.[22] Development of game estates during this time was not a new phenomenon, but what was remarkable was the enthusiasm and energy with which Price undertook the task. As Tom Ellis would later state:

> [T]he whole paraphernalia of game preserving was set up – a hierarchy of gamekeepers, strict sporting clauses in the agreements, coverts, rabbit warrens, pheasantries, the killing of dogs and cats, the pursuit of poachers, and the confiscation of their guns and nets.[23]

Coverts and woodlands were planted and there would ultimately be fifty-six of them on the estate, covering an area of 612 acres. Three large rabbit warrens were created, the largest being that at Eglwys Ann. This warren measured 350 acres of enclosed rough ground on land formerly belonging to the neighbouring farms; each of the tenants received a reduction of 2*s.* an acre in their rent to compensate for their loss.[24] Price would later argue that poor rushy land was more profitable when given over to rabbits than to sheep, estimating that he could make between 10*s.* and 18*s.* per acre but only 2*s.* 6*d.* when grazed with sheep.

Two major pheasantries were established, where pheasants were reared in pens before being either released onto the estate or sold to other estates. Boxes of rabbits, hares and pheasants were conveyed to Bala railway station and from there to game merchants in England. Pheasants were also reared in hutches and placed in fields on various farms causing considerable annoyance to the farmers and hampering their work, especially during harvest time. Hutches could be easily disturbed by dogs or sometimes farmers' children, who would then incur the anger of the keepers. Pheasant eggs, partridge eggs as well as live rabbits and hares were sold to other estates. To feed the pheasants Rhiwlas Game Meal could be obtained for £1 per hundredweight. Near the head keeper's cottage there was a large storehouse and a cold store built for storing game. To attract potential customers the estate was heavily advertised in the *Field, Sporting Times* and the *Morning Post* and huge hoardings were placed on the side of the railway advertising the Rhiwlas game farm. This was one of the concessions Price

20 R.J. Lloyd Price, *Dogs, ancient and modern and walks in Wales* (London, 1893), pp 37–8. 21 The spread of the railways also aided the poacher with sympathetic railway employees willing to take the game to potential buyers. 22 Such was the importance of the railways that train timetables were printed on the backs of shooting cards. National Library of Wales, Rhiwlas Estate Collection, (Sporting) Battue Cards: 1869–1908. 23 Thomas Edward Ellis, *RCLW*, vol. i, 16911, p. 786. 24 Rhiwlas Estate Collection, Meirionnydd Record Office, MS, Z/DDD/2/155.

extracted from the railway company for giving them the right of way through his lands.

Those who took up the offer to shoot on the estate could expect to pay on average £250 to £300 rent per annum. The Rhiwlas Home Beat, consisting of about 3,000 acres, was let for £300 per annum, with the landlord paying for two keepers and the rates.[25] Five grouse moors were also let, usually on a five-year lease for £250 per annum.[26] There was an important business undertaking here which was vital to the financial well-being of the estate. In 1880, the gross rental of the estate was £13,579, of which £2,782 was derived from the shooting estate.[27]

## GAMEKEEPERS

To look after and protect the game, Price needed gamekeepers. According to the evidence of Tom Ellis to the Land Commission: '[A] crowd of English and Scotch gamekeepers were introduced and dotted all over the estate. I cannot describe the repugnance and loathing caused by the overbearing conduct of these gamekeepers.'[28] All kinds of ills were ascribed to them, especially in the popular press, the most common being that they carried tales to the landlord, a point made by David Roberts in his evidence, when he explained that the reason they were detested was 'because they told lies as between the tenant and the landlord'.[29] In 1868, *Baner ac Amserau Cymru* described the Rhiwlas gamekeepers as being 'men of low character', and said that R.J. Lloyd Price spent his time 'with the lowest order of men while ignoring his responsibilities and duty to the community at large'.[30] Price, according to the popular press, was in danger of alienating himself from his tenants. However, in his evidence to the Land Commission, he rebutted these charges, stating that as a resident landlord he knew all his tenants and their families well and had good relations with them, and to his knowledge game rearing and the employment of gamekeepers had not caused any unpleasantness.[31] Despite Price's assertions, there was universal hatred towards the gamekeepers and it was not uncommon for them to be threatened, attacked, or even shot at. In 1875, Henry Weetman, a keeper employed by Price, described in court what happened when he came across a gang of poachers: 'Two pointed guns at me and said they would fire if I came nearer – a shot was fired and passed very near my right side.'[32] Thomas Storer, another keeper, was left in no doubt what his fate would be when the warning 'Thomas Storer shall be murdered' was painted on a wall in August 1873.[33]

**25** Rhiwlas Estate Collection, Meirionnydd Record Office, MS, Z/DDD/1/196. **26** Ibid., Z/DDD/1/195. **27** Ibid., Z/DDD/4/7 and Z/DDD/4/8. **28** Thomas Edward Ellis, *RCLW*, vol. i, 16911, p. 786. **29** David Roberts, *RCLW*, vol. i, 16584, p. 763. **30** *Baner ac Amserau Cymru*, 29 Jan. 1868. **31** R.J.L. Price, *RCLW*, vol. i, 8165–78, 16261–449, pp 328–30, 744–55. **32** Evidence of Henry Weetman, 14 Dec. 1875, minute book Penllyn court of petty sessions, Merionnydd R.O. ZPS/51/3. **33** Evidence of Thomas Storer, 6 Sept. 1873;

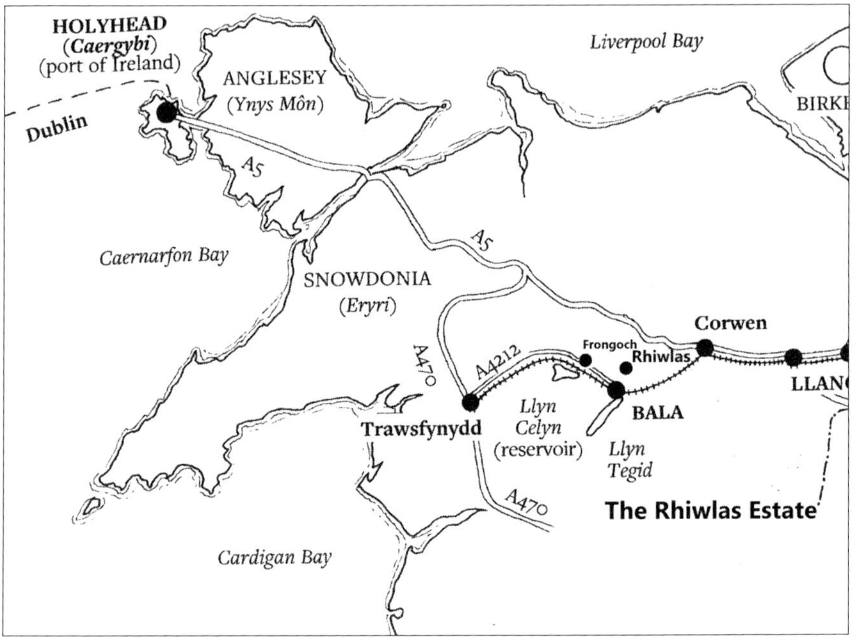


15.1 Map of north Wales showing where the Rhiwlas estate is situated. Courtesy of Gwasg Carreg Gwalch, Llanrwst, Conwy, Wales.

The 1861 census for the parish of Llanfor showed that only one keeper was employed by the estate, John Davies, aged 55, from the neighbouring parish of Llangower. By 1871, things had changed dramatically, with fourteen keepers now listed in the parish. Only two were Welsh; ten came from England and two from Scotland.[34] This would support the accusation that Rhiwlas, like many other estates, had a deliberate policy of not employing Welshmen. Even the Welsh keepers were not local men; the nearest, Evan Jones, came from Glyndyfrdwy, some twenty miles away. Dispersed all over the estate to keep an eye on things, they were largely non-Welsh-speaking churchmen,[35] who did not see the virtues

ibid., ZPS/51/3. 34 Census return for the parish of Llanfor, County Merioneth, 1871.They were Henry Smith, Sutton, Chester; Edward Millichap, Shrewsbury, Shropshire; George Webb, Norfolk; Austin Collins, Blachford, Dorset; James Gregory, Henley in Arden, Warwick; Alfred Storer, Drayton Basset, Stafford; George Bamford, Shrewsbury; Thomas Strangwood, Stourport; James Fowls, Worthingbury; John Lloyd, Oswestry; George Straiton, Scotland; Duncan Mackintosh, Scotland; Evan Jones, Glyndyfrdwy, Merionethshire; Llywelyn Hookes, Ruthin, Denbighshire. 35 Their adherence to the established church tends to be borne out in the surviving church registers for the area. See marriage register, 1837–1952, Llanfor (Merionnydd R.O., ZPE/21/3); baptism register, 1813–1930, Llanfor (ZPE/21/12); baptism register, 1872–1914, Frongoch, Llanfor (ZPE/31/1). The Anglican church held their services in both Welsh and English, therefore it was natural for those gamekeepers who were not Welsh and did not speak the language to follow their employer and attend the Anglican church.

15.2 Richard John Lloyd Price of Rhiwlas (1842–1923).

of temperance; these were the figures that the Welsh speaking, Nonconformist and generally, teetotal tenantry faced.[36]

## POACHERS

On the other side of this divide were the poachers. A romantic and popular perception of poachers saw them as defending the rights of the people to hunt where and when they wanted. Yet they were condemned not only from the bench

36 By 1885, there were a total of twelve Nonconformist chapels located on the estate, all of which held their meetings in Welsh. The religious census of 1851 suggested that in Merioneth, out of a population of 51,307, 93.7% attended a place of worship, the overwhelming number being Nonconformist. See Ieuan Gwynedd Jones and David Williams

15.3 Thomas Edward Ellis (1859–1900), MP for the county of Merioneth, 'the Parnell of Wales'.

but also from the pulpit; many feared that imprisonment, transportation or even the gallows would be their eventual fate.[37] In 1860, when the coroner for Conwy delivered his verdict on the death of a poacher, he described him as a member of 'the most disreputable class on the face of the earth'.[38]

(eds), *The religious census of 1851: a calendar of returns relating to Wales*, ii: *North Wales* (Cardiff, 1976), pp 229–81. On the question of the Welsh language and religion see Ieuan Gwynedd Jones, *Mid-Victorian Wales, the observers and the observed* (Cardiff, 1992), pp 54–79. 37 A good example of this is a short story by the Revd J.R. Roberts, 'Ned y Poacher', which appeared in the first editions of a radical Welsh language weekly newspaper *Y Dydd (The Day)* in June and July 1868. At the end of the story Ned is hanged for killing a gamekeeper, but there is sympathy for his plight. Ned was portrayed as the victim of the stupidity of the landlords in creating game estates and the harshness of the game laws. 38 Quoted in S.C. Ellis, 'Observations of Anglesey life through the quarter sessions rolls, 1860–1869', *Transactions of the Anglesey Antiquarian Society and Field Club*, 75 (1986), p. 132.

15.4 The Rhiwlas gamekeepers. Courtesy of Archifdy Meirionnydd, Dolgellau, Gwynedd, Wales.

Instances of poaching in Wales were at their highest in the period 1865–80 and the evidence suggests this was certainly the case on the Rhiwlas estate. Shortly after the death of R.J.L. Price in 1923 an article written by 'Gohebydd Achlysurol' ('Occasional Reporter') appeared in *Y Seren*, a local weekly newspaper in the Bala area, in which the author remembered poaching being rampant on the estate from the mid-1860s onwards. This is substantiated by the number of poaching cases that came before the Penllyn court of petty sessions.[39] Between 1867 and 1878, 70 cases were heard by the Bala bench alone. Of these, 10 were to do with illegal fishing, 11 with poaching on other estates in the area and the remaining were all cases related to the Rhiwlas estate.[40] By contrast between 1860 and 1865, only 16 cases of poaching had been dealt with for the whole of the county of Merioneth.[41] The press blamed Price and his obsession with hunting and game preserving for this rise in poaching cases arguing that without game there would no poachers and by definition no breaking of the law. It was a simplistic argument but carried much weight and reflected the popular

39 This article appeared in *Y Seren* on 27 Jan. 1923 and was critical of R.J.L. Price and his passion for hunting. Price had died a few weeks earlier on 9 Jan. 1923, aged 81. The identity of the writer was never revealed. The Penllyn court of petty sessions covered the parishes of Llanuwchllyn, Llangywer, Llanycil, Llanfor and Llandderfel. 40 Minute books, Penllyn court of petty sessions, 2 vols, 1867–78 (Meirionnydd R.O., ZPS/51/2; ZPS/51/3). 41 R. Gwynedd Parry, 'Trosedd a chosb ym Meirionnydd yn Chwedegau Cynnar y Bedwaredd Ganrif ar Bymtheg: Tystiolaeth Cofnodion y Llys Chwarter' ('Crime and punishment in Merioneth in the early 1860s: evidence of the court of quarter sessions'), *Cymdeithas Hanes*

attitude towards the game laws, for as the *Caernarvon and Denbigh Herald* stated: '[L]aws that make private property out of public vermin tend to break down the respect that should be felt for all laws.'[42]

'Gohebydd Achlysurol' provided an insight into why people poached and who they were:

> [P]oaching during this period was different – it was not the poacher catching a rabbit for food but rather it was poaching by a gang of young men, the sons of responsible and respectable farmers. Poaching was a means of protest against the unprincipled English gamekeepers sent to the country to terrorise the people.[43]

Tom Ellis made the same point in his evidence to the Land Commission, describing 'how bands of young farmers used to go about the fields at night, maintaining terrible fights with keepers, not for the mere purpose of poaching, but as a protest against the system which had grown up'.[44] Poaching was for neither food nor financial gain but was motivated out of revenge especially against the English gamekeepers. There was a common belief that poaching was not the same as stealing, and that poaching as a crime had been created by the law, and that the law was in the hands of the landowners.[45] As one Welsh poacher stated: 'I am a poacher … [but] I never stole anything in my life. I am a gentleman, the son of a gentleman, but still I am a poacher.'[46] It could be said that these men viewed poaching as a sport and that it was carried out not only by those living on the margins of society but also by the middle classes, especially the sons of tenant farmers.

Those accused of poaching could depend on alibis being given by friends and

*Cyfraith Cymru*, 2 (2002), p. 109. **42** Quoted in S.C. Ellis, 'Observations of Anglesey life through the quarter sessions rolls, 1860–1869', *Transactions of the Anglesey Antiquarian Society and Field Club*, 75 (1986), p. 132. **43** *Y Seren*, 27 Jan. 1923. **44** Thomas Edward Ellis, *RCLW*, vol. i, 16958, p. 793. **45** See, for example, P.B. Munsche, *Gentlemen and poachers: the English game laws, 1671–1831* (Cambridge, 1961); Harry Hopkins, *The long affray: the poaching wars in Britain* (London, 2008). For contemporary discussions on the game laws see, William Cobbett, *Rural rides* (London, 1830; [2001]), pp 394–402; Anon., *A letter on the game laws by a country gentleman* (London, 1815); Richard Griffiths Welford, *The influence of the game laws, being classified extracts from evidence taken before a select committee of the House of Commons on the game laws, and some introductory remarks: with an appendix and an address to the tenant farmers of Great Britain* (London, 1846). See also Mary Augusta Ward, *Marcella* (1894; repr. Peterborough, Ontario, 2002). This novel, where the ethics of game preserving are discussed at length, is based on the true story of the killing of two gamekeepers by three poachers, two of whom were later executed, near the village of Aldbury, Hertfordshire in December 1891. Also in Daniel Owen, *Gwen Tomos, Merch y Wernddu* (*Gwen Tomos, the daughter of Wernddu farm*) (Mold, 1894; repr. Wrexham, 1948); set in north-east Wales, there is hatred of the game laws and sympathy for the poachers even though a gamekeeper is killed by one them. **46** Griffith Evan Jones, *Confessions of a Welsh salmon poacher* (London, 1877), p. 7. Based in the upper reaches of the rivers Severn and the Wye in mid-Wales, Evans stated that he only became a poacher due to the passing of the Salmon Fisheries Act, 1861 (24 & 25 neighbours, even though some of these did stretch credulity. In November 1867, Thomas Hughes, accused with others of poaching salmon in the river Tryweryn near Capel Celyn, was provided with an alibi by his neighbour, John Roberts. In his statement, Roberts claimed that he was with Hughes in his home on the night in question. Asked what he was doing there, Roberts replied: 'I was reading my Bible!'[47] It is questionable whether Roberts would have provided an alibi if his neighbour had been accused of stealing. There was passive support for poaching from the chapels, with ministers less vocal in their condemnation of poaching than they would have been of other transgressions committed by their congregations.[48] There was even support for poachers who had committed murder. In November 1868, the earl of Lisburn's head keeper on the Trawscoed estate in Cardiganshire was killed by a poacher. Despite a reward of £100 for his capture, William Richards, who had allegedly shot the keeper, managed, with the aid of friends and family, to escape to the United States.[49]

## THE TYNFFRIDD POACHING CASE

Hatred of the keepers and the game laws, coupled with political activity, produced an inflammatory situation on the Rhiwlas estate. One case clearly illustrates the point. In the early hours of 19 November 1867, at a farm called Tynffridd just outside Bala, a gang of twelve poachers came face to face with six keepers. No attempt was made by the poachers to escape and they held their ground. A graphic description was given in the testimony of one of the keepers as to what happened next:

> As we neared them, they called out, 'stand back' (they spoke in English) … Edward Owen held up a gun and the others shouting 'shoot, shoot'. Edward Owen did fire a shot. The shot passed me. I took hold of the gun immediately it was fired. Edward Owen and I had a struggle during which we both fell. I received a blow to the head as we fell. Edward Owen and I struggled on the ground for some time. He would not give up the gun. George Straiton came to my assistance and we got possession of the gun.[50]

Vict. c. 109), which he regarded as an infringement on the custom and practice of the people to catch salmon when and where they wanted. See also David Jones, 'The second Rebecca riots: a study of poaching on the Upper Wye', *Llafur: Journal of Welsh People's History*, 2 (1976), pp 32–56. **47** Minute book, Penllyn court of petty sessions (Meirionnydd R.O. ZPS/51/2). According to the keepers, there were fourteen poaching on the river that night but only five came before the court: Thomas Hughes, tenant farmer; Morris Jones, tenant farmer; Richard Jones, son of a tenant farmer; Rowland Jones, farm servant; and Edward Roberts, labourer. The case against the five was dismissed. **48** D.J.V. Jones, 'The poacher: a study in Victorian crime and protest', *Historical Journal*, 22:4 (1979), p. 859. **49** Bethan Phillips, *Dihirod Dyfed* (*The scoundrels of Dyfed*) (Cardiff, 1991), pp 1–16. According to tradition, William Richards hid in the local Nonconformist chapels. **50** Statement of Evan Jones; minute book, Penllyn court of

A running battle then ensued, shots were fired by both sides and of the twelve poachers, three were caught and taken to the lock-up at Bala – Edward Owen (21 years old), the son of a tenant farmer; Evan Jones (16) another son of a tenant farmer; and John Roberts (25), weaver – while the rest of the gang managed to escape.

On 23 November, committal proceedings were held at Bala, where the three were charged with 'poaching at night being armed'. Feelings were running high against the keepers, and the courtroom was full of those supporting the defendants; more than once the magistrates had to threaten to clear the chamber. Since this offence carried a prison sentence of up to three years the justices bound over the defendants for a £50 surety each until the next assize court to be held in March 1868.[51]

Before then, on 6 January 1868, one of the defendants, John Roberts, took an action against eight of the Rhiwlas keepers for 'assault and highway robbery', alleging that while walking home on the night of 4 January at around 11pm, he was attacked and a gun he was carrying stolen.[52] On the day of the trial, there was great excitement in the town with the police out in force. Things were made worse by the fact that the public was barred from the hearing. As an eyewitness would later write: '[D]id the Justices fear that the people would show their feelings as they did before?'[53]

The keepers were found not guilty and immediately the verdict became known there was widespread belief that the justices were colluding with the landlords, and that justice had been denied. The fact that Price was one of the justices was ample confirmation for many.[54] Letters appeared in the press condemning the justices: one argued that in the light of this miscarriage of justice a stipendiary magistrate should be appointed for Merioneth, while another wrote: '[B]efore the people will respect the law, they have to be convinced that the landlords are playing fair.'[55]

With ill feeling and suspicion running high, the case against the three poachers was heard at the assizes on 12 March 1868. They pleaded guilty and were discharged on bail for good behaviour. A deal had been struck and, significantly, Price was one of those who had argued that mercy should be shown to the defendants. In a statement read out in court, he admitted that there was ill feeling in the area due to his game operations and he recognized that the poaching that had taken place was not for financial gain but rather an attack upon himself. He hoped that things would settle down and that he could become a

petty session (Meirionnydd R.O., ZPS/31/2). 51 *Baner ac Amserau Cymru*, 4 Dec. 1867. 52 Minute book, Penllyn court of petty sessions (Meirionnydd R.O., ZPS/SI/2). Since John Roberts was one of the three defendants in the Tynffridd case, there could have been an element of harassment in the actions of the keepers. It was commonly believed that Rhiwlas gamekeepers would seek revenge against anyone who dared to cross them. 53 *Baner ac Amserau Cymru*, 8 Jan. 1868. 54 Ibid., 22 Jan. 1868. 55 Ibid.

popular landlord like his grandfather.[56] *Baner ac Amserau Cymru* welcomed his statement and expressed the hope that Price would now work with his tenants and would be more willing to listen to their complaints, especially as regards game. Interestingly, at the end of the article there was a veiled threat that he and the other landlords should refrain from putting political pressure on their tenants in the forthcoming election, 'lest something worse happens to them'.[57]

## THE GENERAL ELECTION OF 1868

A general election was called for 17 November 1868. Rumours began to circulate towards the middle of October that once more pressure was being exerted on the Rhiwlas tenants to vote for the Conservative candidate. On Bala fair day, 24 October, the agent was caught pressurising some tenants to vote with their landlord. That night a band of armed men went to a covert near Rhiwlas and killed as many pheasants as they could find. The local press reported that 'it was such a powerful and determined body of men that no keeper dared to try and stop them'.[58] Nobody was taken to court for this attack.

For the tenants this election was not going to be a re-run of 1859 or of 1865. Reports started circulating that the sons of tenants were travelling around the farms warning those who were undecided in their support for the Liberal party that 'matches were cheap'. The editor of *Y Dydd* did not condone the attacks but stated that the landlords would do well to remember 'that if they carried on with intimidation of the voters then this could lead to imprisonment, transportation or even the gallows'.[59] The message was clear: if landords were going to regain the trust of their tenants they would have to refrain from forcing them to vote contrary to their conscience, or they would have to face the consequences.

On Saturday 7 November, several Rhiwlas tenants met at Bala to discuss 'this dangerous situation', as they called it. They drafted a letter to Price, which they later published in *Baner ac Amserau Cymru*, condemning the poachers who had attacked the coverts, noting that 'Mr Price had behaved in a gentlemanly manner towards the three respectable young men last March, and his promise to lessen the game on the estate.' They concluded with the hope that poaching might now cease. The editor of *Baner ac Amserau Cymru*, Thomas Gee added a footnote: 'It is good to see that Mr Price draws closer to his tenants and is ready to listen to their complaints.'[60] Not a word was said about the election but the insinuation was that if intimidation of the tenants continued there would be further attacks on the estate.

**56** Ibid., 18 Mar. 1868. **57** Ibid., 21 Mar. 1868. **58** *Y Dydd*, 13 Nov. 1868. 'Herwhela, Y Sgriw a Beca yn y Bala' ('Poaching, the screw and Rebecca in Bala'), an interesting title that harked back to the Rebecca riots in west Wales in the mid 1840s when toll gates and some game preserves were attacked. **59** Ibid., 13 Nov. 1868. **60** *Baner ac Amserau Cymru*, 14 Nov. 1868.

Yet the writing was on the wall for the Conservatives in Merioneth. As a consequence of the Second Reform Act of 1867, and the hard work of the Liberals in ensuring that those eligible to vote were registered, the number of voters in the county of Merioneth had risen to over 3,000. Faced with defeat, on 14 November, three days before the poll, the Conservatives withdrew their candidate, leaving the seat open for the Liberals. As one disgruntled Conservative supporter wrote in his diary: 'Dissenting preachers and that class of men have replaced the old county magnates.'[61]

## CONCLUSION

For R.J.L. Price, the development of a game estate was financially advantageous, especially to an estate that was heavily encumbered with debt.[62] However, the tenants viewed this development with trepidation. They felt alienated and betrayed by their landlord, and harassed by gamekeepers, who they regarded as their social inferiors. Edward Owen, one of the three defendants in the 1868 case, left Wales in 1874 for the Welsh colony in Patagonia, citing harassment by the keepers of himself and his family as the primary motivation for their emigrating. The tenants felt that the landlord put sport before their interests, and regarded poaching as a way of attacking a system they regarded as oppressive. Game was in a real sense threatening their livelihoods, even though Price and other landlords claimed that any tenant who had a just grievance would be compensated. The reality, according to the Land Commission report, was that many were nervous of complaining for fear of incurring the wrath of the estate. As one witness stated: '[I]t is understood that some landlords are ready to give compensation for the loss caused by game, but it is equally understood by farmers that it is an offence to claim compensation.'[63] The Ground Game Act of 1880, which had been strongly resisted by the landowners, curtailed the power of the landlords to reserve the killing of ground game for themselves and gave the 'occupier an inalienable and concurrent' right to shoot hares and rabbits, but not winged game, on his own land. This did alleviate some problems, but tenants were still afraid to enforce their legal right under the act for fear of antagonizing

61 Diary of Hugh Revely of Bryn Gwin Dolgellau, 17 Nov. 1859 (microfilm copy, Meirionnydd R.O.). The power and authority that the Nonconformist ministers had over their congregations is explored in Mathew Cragoe, 'The problem of preacher influence: chapel politics' in Mathew Cragoe, *Culture, politics and national identity in Wales, 1832–1886* (Oxford, 2004). 62 Financial problems blighted the estate over the years and many attempts were made to remedy the situation. The most remarkable was in 1887 when Price placed a huge bet on a horse called Bendigo running in the Kempton Jubilee stakes that year. The horse won and with part of the winnings Price built a mausoleum for himself and his family in Llanfor churchyard. Above the door he had the following carved: 'As to my latter end I go/ To seek my Jubilee/ I bless the good horse Bendigo/ Who built this tomb for me.' 63 *Report of the royal commission on land in Wales and Monmouthshire* (1896), pp 515–17.

their landlord.[64] On the Rhiwlas estate the tenants were permitted to use only ferrets and nets to catch rabbits; no guns were allowed.[65] Replying to the accusation that he was acting against the spirit of the act, Price replied that this was the proper way to kill rabbits and that he did not think that his tenants 'cared to use firearms, they are very much afraid of them as a rule'.[66]

Yet a shift was beginning to appear in the balance of power. This was a tenantry growing in self-confidence, and poaching, or the threat of poaching, was used against the estate to stop it putting political pressure on its tenants. This growth in self-confidence had its roots in the Nonconformist chapels that dotted the area. These chapels and chapel organizations played a major part in their lives, and the leaders of this society were the chapel elders. Democratically elected by their respective congregations, they were seen as being the natural leaders of their community. Here a literate, knowledgeable and politicized tenantry found its voice. Of the five tenants evicted following the 1859 election, four of them were elders in the local chapels.[67]

For contemporary commentators on both sides of the divide, game and game preservation was viewed as part of the Welsh land question. It was a visible issue: the game and the damage that it did could be seen and measured, the gamekeepers were a constant threat and the sporting tenants could behave in a high-handed and arrogant manner.[68] For the tenants, these were all very real grievances. Above all, game preserving – as has been noted before – was viewed as being alien to the country, not least of all because its language and terminology was English. It was a pastime that a strongly Nonconformist society saw as wasteful and childish, diametrically opposed to their work ethic. The landlords, on the other hand, viewed the topic as an excuse by the Welsh-language press to attack them. According to J.E. Vincent, a strong supporter of the landlords: 'The "great game question" is one of those subjects … upon which Radical newspapers … can easily incite furious articles.'[69] Vincent had a point. The Welsh press saw game as an easy target. They attacked what they saw as the undue harshness of the game laws, and supported poachers who were prosecuted, and, in some cases, they even issued veiled threats to landlords. In 1885, the editor of *Y Celt*, commenting on the fact that Lord Penrhyn had sacked two quarrymen for poaching, reminded him how lucky he was that he did not live in Ireland, where agrarian agitation and violence was widespread during the era of the Plan of Campaign.[70]

**64** Ibid., pp 510–13. **65** Rhiwlas Estate Collection (Meirionydd R.O., Z/DDD/7/8). **66** R.J.L. Price, *RCLW*, vol. i, 16378–82, pp 751–2. **67** Ieuan Gwynedd Jones, 'Merioneth politics in mid nineteenth century: the politics of a rural economy', *JMHRS*, 5:4 (1965–8), pp 287–92. **68** *RCLW*, 1896, pp 499–520. **69** James Edmund Vincent, *The land question in north Wales* (London, 1897), pp 192–8. Vincent was secretary of the Landlords Association of South Wales and Monmouthshire and counsel for the North Wales Property Defence Association. He claimed to have been present at all the public meetings of the Land Commission. **70** *Y Celt*, 27 Feb. 1885.

In 1883, the appointment of Edward Watkin, a Welsh speaker and a Nonconformist, as agent on the Rhiwlas estate, helped ease tensions. The concerns of tenants regarding damage done by game began to be addressed sympathetically, or so Watkins claimed, with compensation given if complaints were proved. Those who suffered sustained losses saw reductions in their rents. For example, the tenant of Ty'n Celyn farm had his rent reduced from £56 p.a. to £36 p.a. due to the proximity of the farm to coverts.[71] Yet, Tom Ellis asked: '[W]hat compensation can there be for the agony and irritation of a tenant at seeing his crops eaten and destroyed by game?'[72]

Nonetheless, the estate was becoming popular and recognized as one of the premier game estates in Wales. Its heyday was between 1880 and 1914.[73] This was the era of the huge hunting parties with correspondingly huge bags.[74] Poaching continued and tensions sometimes flared up into violence. In April 1910, five young farmers were jailed for three months for attacking and wounding three of the Rhiwlas gamekeepers.[75] There was strong local support for the five and after the guilty verdicts were given there was uproar in court and a determined but unsuccessful attempt by the crowd to rescue the prisoners.[76] Yet, in the main, hatred towards the keepers was less virulent than before as they and their families became more assimilated into Welsh society. The Guests, a gamekeeping family originally from Kent, and the Tees, originally from Pontefract, would in time become as Welsh as the Welsh themselves, and would play their part in the social, political and cultural lives of their respective areas.

71 Edward Watkins, *RCLW*, vol. i, 16832, pp 779–80. 72 Thomas Edward Ellis, *RCLW*, vol. i, 16911, pp 785–6. 73 Lord Walsingham and Sir Ralph Payne-Gallway, *Shooting, field and covert* (1900; repr. Southampton, 1987), pp 27, 213. 74 On 7 Oct. 1885, ten guns shot a total of 5,046 rabbits on the Eglwys Ann warren. One of the guns was Earl de Grey, regarded at the time as being the finest shot in Britain. This mass slaughter did attract criticism, see *Vanity Fair*, 17 Oct. 1885. 75 Merioneth court of quarter sessions, Easter sessions, Bala, 5 Apr. 1910 (depositions, uncatalogued, Meirionnydd R.O.). 76 *Yr Wythnos a'r Eryr*, 6 Apr. 1910.

# Sport on the wall: the nineteenth-century boom in sporting taxidermy

ANNIE TINDLEY

In his 1952 novel *Men at arms*, Evelyn Waugh captured an experience that will be familiar to many country-house visitors and owners: coming face to face with a large, and sometimes somewhat shabby, taxidermy display. The hero, Guy Crouchback, is on training exercises in the remote Scottish islands when he encounters the castle of Colonel Hector Campbell of Mugg:

> The Campbells of Mugg had never been rich but at some moment in the middle of the nineteenth century a marriage, or a sale of property on the mainland which was being transformed from moorland to town, or a legacy from emigrant kinsmen in Canada or Australia – by an accession of fortune of some kind common amongst lairds, the Mugg of the time got money in his hands and proceeded to build. The fortune melted but the new castle stood. The exterior was German in character, Bismarckian rather than Wagnerian, of moderate size but designed to withstand assault from all but the most modern weapons. The interior was pitch pine throughout and owed its decoration more to the taxidermist than to sculptor or painter.[1]

The setting for Waugh's wry if not wholly unaffectionate portrayal of the house of Colonel Campbell was likely to have been in part inspired by Kinloch Castle on the Isle of Rum. Like many such properties, a new house was built on the site of a much older edifice in 1897, with a heavy emphasis on Romantic architecture, featuring battlements and interior taxidermy settings emphasizing native British birds and animals, principally what was being shot or caught locally.[2]

For families with deeper pockets or imperial connections, their taxidermy displays could be much more exotic. It is the case that taxidermy of all types – and it is a hugely various art form – became extremely popular as an interior design trope in the Victorian and Edwardian country house. Taxidermy was just one of the many expressions or trappings of the cult of field and commercial sport, and the architecture of the houses and lodges as well as the taxidermy collections proudly displayed in them were offerings made on the altar of that cult.

1 Evelyn Waugh, *Men at arms* (London, 1965 ed.), p. 361. 2 Robin Noble, *Castles in the mist: the Victorian transformation of the Highlands* (Glasgow, 2016), pp 55, 58, 60, 62.

16.1 Interior of Kinloch Castle, *Scottish Field*, 2014.

This essay takes a somewhat tangential approach to the theme of sport and leisure in the country house, by examining one of the most ubiquitous after-effects of field sports: displays of taxidermy that continue to dominate country-house interiors to the present day. Field sports including trout and salmon fishing, deer stalking, grouse and pheasant shooting, fox hunting and big-game hunting were among the most dominant leisure activities of the landed and aristocratic classes, and this is recorded not just in the archives of game books or paintings and photographs, but in the creation of tableaux of preserved animals that adorned most country houses at some time (fig. 16.1). The popularity of taxidermy knew no national bounds, and a visitor is as likely to find it in Derbyshire as in Connemara or Sutherland. That said, it is particularly dominant as an interior feature in Scotland, Yorkshire and the west of Ireland: the meccas of hunting, shooting and fishing in elite culture.

Much of this type of sporting taxidermy display was developed in the mid- to late nineteenth century as techniques and materials improved, although it drew on deeper roots, as this chapter will outline. Taxidermy's origins lie in the development of natural history and zoological collections put together by the landed elites and their wider scientific and cultural networks, well before it ballooned into a key element of nineteenth-century interior design in country houses.[3] From relatively scholarly beginnings it evolved into the height of

3 Alexis Turner, *Taxidermy* (London, 2013), pp 70–1.

fashion for all social classes, but the charge was led by the landed and aristocratic, who spent the most time and resources on field sports and had large houses to fill. Field sports of all kinds were a global activity by the nineteenth century. Easier access via speedy transport to the empire, plus trend-setting by figures such as the prince of Wales, meant that big-game hunting and the resulting conversion of the dead animals into tableaux and even more exotic features for the drawing rooms, billiards rooms, hallways and other areas of country houses became relatively commonplace. However, it is important to ask what it was for, and what it said about the class who commissioned and displayed it in their houses. As stalking, shooting and fishing became dominant leisure pursuits of the elite and landed classes, taxidermy provides a fascinating insight into elite class formation, identity and purpose. One could push the argument a little further and note the declining fashion and appeal of taxidermy from the 1920s to the 1990s, mirroring in part the relative decline of the landed classes and their country houses. Taxidermy came to be seen as old-fashioned and, by the 1940s and 1950s, even symbolic of the regressive nature of the landed classes – no longer truly leisured in those difficult decades but still surrounded by the spoils of their preferred leisure activity. However, taxidermy has seen a major cultural and interiors revival in the twenty-first century, again perhaps symbolic of the resilient nature of the country house and those who own, live and visit it. This essay will unpack this trajectory, examining the origins of taxidermy practice and display, then discussing its rise alongside that of field sports, its use, marketing, creation and what it can tell the historian about the history of sport and leisure as well as the landed and aristocratic classes that led the way in its creation.

## ORIGINS AND DEVELOPMENT

The origins of taxidermy in country houses lie in the late seventeenth and early eighteenth century, when small displays of rare specimens were carefully collected and displayed in cabinets and rooms of curiosity, often consisting of ensembles of insects, birds, horns and eggs. These were rare and often exotic items, often sourced from overseas, increasingly reflecting the commodities of the imperial territories. Sometimes they were fashioned to be legendary items – narwhal tusks as unicorn horns, phoenix eggs or philosopher's stones.[4] These displays were carefully curated to demonstrate the learnedness and scientific-collecting credentials of the owner, rather than being presented as fashionable items of interior decoration. In order to build these collections, their owners needed the right contacts and had to be part of small but highly influential networks of natural historians, geologists, botanists and explorers.[5] Thus, the

4 J.M. MacKenzie, *The empire of nature: hunting, conservation and British imperialism* (Manchester, 1988), p. 35. 5 P.A. Morris, *A history of taxidermy: art, science and bad taste*

landed classes were leaders in the developing discipline of natural history, devoting their resources to furthering scientific endeavour. In Scotland in particular, this was part of a mania for improvement and the spread of Enlightenment thought to which the landed and aristocratic classes contributed significantly.[6] These collections were symbolic of a fundamental shift in the nature of the political, economic and cultural character of the landed and aristocratic classes, away from their traditional military roles and into the leadership of civil society. They had the resources to pay for the collection and presentation of these early taxidermy specimens and enough room in their houses to display them. Their collecting mania was underpinned in this period by their educational and intellectual ambition.[7]

To take one famous example: John Stuart, the 1st marquess of Bute (1744–1814), alongside a notable political career, counted Joseph Banks as a friend and colleague, and with Banks was one of the founding personnel of the botanic gardens at Kew. Bute was at the heart of worldwide scientific networks established by the end of the eighteenth century, networks which were as symbolic of British imperial power as they were the pursuit of knowledge.[8] Taxidermy specimens sourced via these networks were about the dominance of culture over nature, and the powerful over the powerless, whether in the imperial colonial context or the class-defined context of Britain and Ireland.[9] By the later nineteenth century, this trend had extended exponentially, and hunting expeditions set up for the explicit purpose of establishing natural history collections across the world were common. Most of these would have included trained taxidermists who preserved the specimens in the field.[10]

From these private-museum-like origins, specialized skills and craftsmanship in taxidermy began to develop across Britain and Ireland, for instance, in the pioneering work of John Hancock of Newcastle-upon-Tyne. He took advantage of new materials and techniques that ensured a longer shelf life for taxidermy, but he also developed a number of artistic and aesthetic modes that would become commonplace, such as setting specimens into naturalistic, often exciting, tableaux with painted scenery and plants. As well as being visually engaging, contemporaries regarded these tableaux as assisting public education and understanding of the animal world, whether indigenous and familiar or the exotic and little understood habitats, animals, reptiles, birds and insects of the growing imperial territories.[11] Aristocratic and landed patrons who took an interest in natural history were important clients for the main taxidermy firms,

(London, 2010), pp 257–9. 6 Ibid., pp 252–3. 7 MacKenzie, *Empire of nature*, p. 36. 8 Joseph Sramek, '"Face him like a Briton": tiger hunting, imperialism and British masculinity in colonial India, 1800–1875', *Victorian Studies*, 48:4 (2006), pp 661–2. 9 Ibid., p. 662. 10 Ashley N. Cotu, 'The elephant in the room: mapping the footsteps of historic elephants with big game hunting collections', *World Archaeology*, 47:3 (2015), p. 490. 11 John Wilson Foster, 'The culture of nature' in J.W. Foster (ed.), *Nature in Ireland: a scientific and cultural* which were established by the 1830s on the back of this patronage.[12] A firm's commercial success could be made by securing a customer like Edward Thomas Booth (1840–90), a man of independent means who bought a house and land near Brighton in order to set up a specially built museum for a major taxidermy collection of British birds. In doing so he gave regular and valuable employment to four Brighton-based taxidermy firms: Saville, Pratt, Swaysland and Braznor.[13] This type of taxidermy for collectors dominated the early decades of the art, but the rise of field sports as the dominant pursuit of both old and new landed wealth from the 1840s fundamentally changed the nature and scale of its use and display in country houses.

## TAXIDERMY, LANDED IDENTITY AND COUNTRY-HOUSE INTERIORS

From around the 1840s to the 1920s, taxidermy became one of the defining features of the interior design and decoration of country houses and lodges, particularly in important sporting regions, such as western Ireland, Yorkshire and rural Scotland. It emerged out of dedicated cabinets and small, specially designed rooms, moving into the rest of the house – hallways, dining rooms, drawing rooms, billiard rooms and libraries. Few public spaces escaped this rash of stuffed creatures. Taxidermy became part of the fabric, the wallpaper of houses, rather than something rare and specifically intended for the display of taste, power and wealth. This steep and comprehensive rise was of course linked to the massive increase of field sports from the 1830s. Deer stalking, grouse and pheasant shooting and fishing for salmon and trout became among the most popular of aristocratic and plutocratic leisure activities, and entire estates were economically, architecturally and culturally reconfigured to meet the appetite for hunting, shooting and fishing, and then decorated with the spoils.[14]

The trend required a few champions for it really to take hold: the west Highlands landowning family of Ellice of Invergarry, friends with the up-and-coming animal painter Sir Edwin Landseer, as well as Albert, the prince consort, who developed new techniques in deer stalking once Balmoral had been purchased in 1852.[15] The prince of Wales was a later champion, although he preferred the less energetic activity of grouse shooting, particularly in his later years.[16] Leisurely activities including all types of sport were seen as a veritable duty of the British and Irish upper classes, as well as an important outlet for emotion and aggression in an elite culture that was expected to demonstrate little

*history* (Dublin, 1997), pp 619–20. 12 Morris, *History of taxidermy*, p. 258. 13 This later became a public collection when Booth donated it to Brighton corporation in his will: Morris, *History of taxidermy*, pp 264–5. 14 Foster, 'Culture of nature', pp 600–1, 616. 15 MacKenzie, *Empire of nature*, pp 32–4. 16 Alastair Drurie, '"Unconscious benefactors": grouse-shooting in Scotland, 1780–1914', *International Journal of the History of Sport*, 15:3

of either.[17] Leisure was seen as being an attitude more than an activity: training for social and political leadership.[18] The importance of sport can be demonstrated in the significant proportion of time it absorbed: for many country gentlemen and landed aristocrats, half or more of their time would be taken up with the seasonal field sports, with the rest left to public and political life.[19] Sport was also constructed as being beneficial for the wider social and common good, whether through eradicating 'vermin' species, or by extending hospitality and displaying landed power, leadership, skill and wealth, at home and overseas.[20] In 'controlling' nature – first by breeding it, then by killing it and lastly by displaying it – the landed were making a clear statement of intent about how they perceived their role in society.[21] Through field sports, they were able to physically display their landed estates in a controlled and constructed way: a display of property, the foundation stone of their position and British and Irish society.[22] Sport, of course, also supported the vital social networking and mixing required to maintain the culture, marriage alliances and identity formation which had always been important, but was especially so by the mid to late nineteenth century, when growing challenges were darkening landed horizons.[23]

It was not just old money that became enamoured of field sports; new money did too, and old money was happy to make hay while this particular sun shone. The 3rd and 4th dukes of Sutherland reconfigured most of their vast northern estates to attract and accommodate high demand from sporting tenants, a trend that endures into the present. Sheep farms were turned over to shooting lets; new lodges were built, complete with kennels, ice houses and fleets of both indoor servants and the gamekeepers, river bailiffs and pony and dog men required to generate the right experience outdoors, all for fat annual rents.[24] Land and river management was revolutionized to support the appetite for salmon, trout, deer and game birds of all kinds.[25] The sheer popularity of the Scottish Highlands as a sporting destination was expressed by the *Field* in an editorial of 1872: 'If you could throw a net over the Highlands in August, you

(2007), pp 59–60. **17** Thomas Cox, 'Diplomacy on dangerous ground: aristocratic hunts in nineteenth- and twentieth-century Nepal', *Journal of South Asian Studies*, 33:2 (2010), p. 264. **18** Nicola Drucker, 'Hunting and shooting: leisure, social networking and social complications' in Terence McDonough (ed.), *Was Ireland a colony? Economics, politics and culture in nineteenth-century Ireland* (Dublin, 2005), pp 125–6. **19** See Richard Hoyle, 'Introduction: field sports as history' in Richard Hoyle (ed.), *Our hunting fathers: field sports in England after 1850* (London, 2007), p. 2. Note too Anthony Trollope's leading man in the Palliser series of novels, Plantagenet Palliser, who abhors field sports, much to the distress of the rest of his landed, wealthy family. But even Plantagenet sees the value in maintaining sporting facilities on his estates. **20** Cox, 'Diplomacy', pp 265–6. **21** Ibid., p. 270; Hayden Lorimer, 'Guns, game and the grandee: the cultural politics of deerstalking in the Scottish Highlands', *Ecumene*, 7:4 (2000), p. 405; Sramek, 'Face him like a Briton', p. 665. **22** Hoyle, 'Introduction', p. 12; Drucker, 'Hunting and shooting', p. 130. **23** Ibid., pp 118, 131–3; Hoyle, 'Introduction', pp 24–31. **24** Drurie, 'Unconscious benefactors', p. 58. **25** Specialist property letting agencies were also set up to manage the annual influx of wealthy sportsmen seeking lodges to lease: Grant Jarvie and Lorna Jackson, 'Deer forests, estates and would catch nine-tenths of the genius and glory of Britain.'[26] The development of associated technologies – not just taxidermy – was also critical to supporting the spectacular rise in popularity of commercial sport.[27] Gunsmiths, telescope manufacturers, specialist clothing providers, fishing rod and bait specialists – all were constantly expanding and innovating to keep up with sporting demand.[28] Taxidermy was just one of a range of technologies and crafts that underpinned sport and those who devoted their lives to its pursuit.

One of these was the duke of Westminster, described as one of 'the greatest of Victorian sportsmen'.[29] He had a passion for horse racing and fox hunting but was also a superb shot and maintained no fewer than four shooting lodges in Scotland, with some of the best deer stalking and salmon and trout fishing in the world. His 'bags' were prodigious: by the 1890s, between 5,000 and 6,000 pheasants per season were shot at his Cheshire seat, Eaton Hall, alone.[30] Sport was an elite activity, and the spaces and environments it was carried out in exclusive spaces.[31] Sport was also an activity that new money could partake in and excel in, with the hope of social acceptance. Certainly, the famous hunters of the day, such as Captain Frederick Courteney Selous and Chauncey Hugh Stigand, gained an entrée into aristocratic society via their sporting exploits, recorded in wildly successful publications and, of course, taxidermy collections.[32] The Industrial Revolution saw an explosion of new wealthy families seeking social acceptance in landed and aristocratic society, and they leveraged participation in sporting activities to do so.[33] For those old landed families clever or fortunate enough to take advantage of industrial and imperial wealth, their means of pursuing sport also increased.[34] The passion for sport would be instilled in the great English public schools and ancient universities, where it was seen as a useful route to the promotion of manliness and muscular Christianity.[35] Selous gave a lecture at Rugby School in 1879 on travel and adventure in South Africa, illustrating his talk with his hunting rifle and the heads and skins of six lions.[36] The impact is easy to imagine.[37] Taxidermy became a defining expression of landed, elite culture, highlighting their residual military and leadership roles after they had been effectively replaced in that milieu by the professional military classes. Instead, they exercised their military prowess in sport, and displayed the trophies of this new 'war' on their walls. As such, taxidermy in country houses

the aristocracy', *Sports Historian*, 18:1 (1998), pp 32–3. **26** Cited in Drurie, 'Unconscious benefactors', p. 57. **27** Hoyle, 'Introduction', pp 31–8. **28** Drurie, 'Unconscious benefactors', pp 60, 68. **29** Mark Girouard, *The Victorian country house* (London, 1979 ed.), p. 3. **30** Ibid. **31** Lorimer, 'Guns, game and the grandee', pp 406–7. **32** MacKenzie, *Empire of nature*, p. 38. **33** J.A. Mangan and Callum McKenzie, 'Privileged education, hunting and the making of martial masculinity', *International Journal of the History of Sport*, 25:9 (2008), pp 1112, 1120. **34** Girouard, *Victorian country house*, p. 5. **35** Mangan and McKenzie, 'Privileged education', p. 1106. **36** J.A. Mangan and Callum McKenzie, 'Martial conditioning, military exemplars and moral certainties: imperial hunting as preparation for war', *International Journal of the History of Sport*, 25:9 (2008), p. 1154. **37** The same enthusiasm was seen across public schools at this time: MacKenzie, *Empire of nature*, pp 45–6.

provides vital pieces of material and cultural history, as do the game books that keep the same record in an archival format.[38] For many of the landed elite, hunting was a still-respected function of chivalric integrity, and the taxidermy that resulted from it was an interior reminder of their history and identity.[39] It also served a practical purpose: country houses, particularly new Victorian and Edwardian houses, could be colossal and, frankly, needed to be filled and decorated. Taxidermy was one form of interior furnishing that reflected landed roots and respectability – for new or old money – as evidenced by the careful design and positioning of displays for maximum aesthetic appeal and evidence of tasteful discernment.[40]

Stags heads (trophy heads) were most common: either stuffed or boiled. The search was always on for the great 'royals' – those with fourteen points on their antlers.[41] These displays could appear in almost any room or space in the country house by the Edwardian period, such was the cult-like status of sport. However, they were most likely to be found in the great hallways and staircases, as at Balmoral, Royal Deeside or Mar Lodge, Aberdeenshire.[42] Mar Lodge in fact still houses no less than 2,435 skulls and antlers of deer.[43] The dominance of sport soon changed country-house organization and layout in more fundamental ways, however, with gun rooms and gentlemen's sitting rooms displaying cases of stuffed game and fish caught on the estate.[44] This chimed with the late Victorian trend for muscular and masculine architecture in country houses, particularly in the Gothic style.[45] This material culture of sport was fuelled by the notions of a chivalric aristocratic class found in the novels of Sir Walter Scott (set in Scotland but wildly popular across Europe), but heightened and mythologized, with 'mighty Nimrods' to the fore.[46] Cultural constructions of their hunting prey also highlighted this. As well as having pleasingly medieval and royal origins, the hunting or stalking of stags was seen as a worthy activity because the stags themselves were regarded as aristocratic beasts.[47] It also took stamina and skill to stalk, making the 'trophy head' an object in the country house that served as a memory and marker of the prowess of the stalker.[48]

The most important taxidermy firms operating in the nineteenth century were well aware of these cultural trends and exploited them cannily to secure high-paying and returning custom among the landed classes. One of the most

38 Drucker, 'Hunting and shooting', p. 127; Mackenzie, *Empire of nature*, p. 35. 39 Mangan and McKenzie, 'Privileged education', p. 1110. 40 Olive Cook, *The English country house: an art and a way of life* (London, 1974), p. 212. 41 Michael Forsyth-Grant, *Deer stalking in the Scottish Highlands, 1940–1990* (Edinburgh, 1999); MacKenzie, *Empire of nature*, p. 35. 42 Girouard, *Victorian country house*, p. 43. 43 Noble, *Castles in the mist*, p. 63. 44 Girouard, *Victorian country house*, p. 37; Lorimer, 'Guns, game and the grandee', p. 410. 45 Girouard, *Victorian country house*, p. 56. 46 Mangan and McKenzie, 'Privileged education', p. 1110; Lorimer, 'Guns, game and the grandee', p. 406; Stephen Taylor, *The mighty Nimrod: a life of Frederick Courteney Selous, African hunter and explorer* (London, 1989). 47 Lorimer, 'Guns, game and the grandee', pp 408–9. 48 Mangan and McKenzie, 'Privileged education', pp 1108–9; Lorimer, 'Guns, game and the grandee', pp 412–13, 418–19.

famous taxidermists of the day, Rowland Ward, set up a showroom in London called 'The Jungle' to showcase his best work, with a heavy emphasis on the exotic and 'trophy' trades.[49] Ward Ltd also produced handsome catalogues and lists of services, beautifully illustrated, with marketing specifically aimed at country houses in magazines and publications for the country set.[50] They provided a total wraparound service, calling themselves 'Practical and artistic taxidermists, designers of trophies of natural history, preservers and adapters of all specimens of animal life'.[51] Taxidermists such as Ward, Gerrard and Peter Spicer regarded themselves as artists, turning wildlife into an aesthetic of slaughter, and Ward deliberately associated himself with figures such as Millais and Landseer.[52] Ward, for example, created miniature sculptures of his most famous taxidermy works, had them cast as bronzes and sold them as a lucrative sideline.[53] Ward's 1917 catalogue contained a section titled: 'Decoration of special rooms in country houses,' promising that

> trophies of the hunting field, of favourite horses, of the gun, of the fishing rod etc. can be characteristically grouped and arranged to decorate smoking rooms and libraries or special rooms devoted to trophies of sport.[54]

Taxidermy firms were also aware of the increase in dedicated masculine spaces and rooms in country-house interiors, where their specimens were most likely to be displayed.[55] One of Ward Ltd's main competitors, Edward Gerrard & Sons, knew the value of networks when dealing with landed and aristocratic clients, and made sure to advertise the fact they prepared specimens for luminaries such as Lords Curzon, Cromer, Kitchener and Captain Selous to generate business.[56] By 1891, there were no fewer than 369 taxidermists employed in London alone, and, interestingly, the occupation was listed under 'house decorations'.[57]

Revealingly, taxidermy was an expression of a global elite culture of big-game hunting, where the landed and wealthy British and Irish made long trips to hunt wild animals and then display them at home. Big-game hunting and the resulting taxidermy were essential parts of comprehending the reach of global empire in

49 P.A. Morris, *Edward Gerrard & Sons: a taxidermy memoir* (London, 2004), p. 34. 50 P.A. Morris, *Rowland Ward: taxidermist to the world* (London, 2003), pp 21, 30. 51 Catalogue of Rowland Ward Ltd, 1917, cover page (Castle Howard archive). The author would like to thank Christopher Ridgway for drawing her attention to this source. 52 The painter Millias' son, J.G. Millias, became a renowned bird collector and travelled the world collecting specimens and publishing books about it: Hoyle, 'Introduction', p. 23; Morris, *Rowland Ward*, p. 16. 53 Morris, *Rowland Ward*, p. 19. 54 Catalogue of Rowland Ward Ltd, p. 7. 55 Cook, *English country house*, pp 214, 218; Girouard, *Victorian country house*, pp 37, 43; Turner, *Taxidermy*, p. 71. 56 Morris, *Gerrard & Sons*, p. 36. The firm created a rug for Lord Kitchener made from forty bears. The marketing techniques must have worked, because when Ward died in 1912 he left an estate of £150,000; Morris, *Rowland Ward*, p. 18. 57 MacKenzie, *Empire of nature*, p. 41.

**16.2** Elephant's foot fashioned into a drinks cabinet by Rowland Ward Ltd. Castle Howard Archives, Rowland Ward Ltd catalogue.

the metropolis.[58] Those landed families with direct imperial connections as administrators, governors or members of the armed forces began this trend, classically seen in rugs (usually tiger or lion) in country houses. More unusual items were also highly popular, as Ward Ltd's elephant's foot crafted into a drinks cabinet demonstrates (fig. 16.2).[59]

**58** William Beinart, 'Review article: empire, hunting and ecological change in southern and central Africa', *Past and Present*, 128 (1990), pp, 162–86; Lorimer, 'Guns, game and the grandee', pp 414–46. **59** For other examples of more unusual taxidermy, see Turner,

16.3 Interior of the museum at Dunrobin Castle, Sutherland. Author's image.

The 5th duke of Sutherland (1888–1963) was an avid big-game hunter, and he set up his trophies with great care in a special museum in the grounds of Dunrobin Castle, Sutherland, mixing native British mammals with exotics from the African savannahs and the plains of India (fig. 16.3).[60]

Getting the animal specimens from the imperial hunting grounds to remote country houses was a significant feat in itself.[61] The effort was reflected in the final cost of mounting exotic animals. In 1905, Ward Ltd charged £300 for a fully mounted hippopotamus and £235 for a giraffe.[62]

In some of the imperial territories, British and Irish landed sportsmen found indigenous sporting and hunting traditions already in place, and utilized these specific cultural and practical circumstances. Tiger hunting in India, Nepal and Burma, for example, had a long aristocratic tradition that predated the arrival of the British.[63] For many younger sons of the landed classes, a career in the empire

*Taxidermy*, pp 73–4. **60** Lorimer, 'Guns, game and the grandee', p. 414. **61** Cotu, 'The elephant in the room', pp 487–8. **62** Morris, *Rowland Ward*, p. 32. These prices in 2018 values are roughly equivalent to £23,500 for the hippo, and £18,400 for the giraffe. **63** Cox, beckoned, to remove pressure from the estate rental rolls and family resources. A common consolation for them was hunting and sport; from pig-sticking in India to tiger hunting in the Terai, the spoils came back and peppered country-house interiors in the same way Chinese plate and Japanese lacquer work had in the eighteenth century.[64] The conquest and display of imperial nature was symbolic of British imperial identities and their fitness to rule over colonized peoples and helped to consolidate and keep in place elite social cohesion in new contexts.[65] The trend for photographs of British aristocrats, dignitaries and royals standing over piles of dead tigers and elephants exemplifies this cultural construction.[66] Some, however, were motivated by Victorian notions of conservation and scientific understanding, taking more from their eighteenth-century forbears than a desire to express individual qualities of martial manliness. Lastly, the cultural construction of distance was critical: as in remote areas of the Scottish Highlands or western Ireland, the sheer distances involved in getting to lodges for sport kept the riff-raff at bay, and this was a trend only intensified in the imperial context, where the best big-game sport might involve weeks of expensive travel to reach hunting grounds.[67]

Arguably, the imperial taxidermy trend denotes another shift in the role and culture of the landed classes, away from the actual levers of power to a more ornamental role, as David Cannadine has pointed out.[68] Hunting is nothing if not time-consuming and could be argued to be an indicator of the decline of the hard power of the aristocratic classes, and its slow replacement with soft or symbolic power, that of culture, heritage, symbolism – an echo or shadow of their former dominion. Other scholars have argued the opposite case: that sport, particularly in Scotland, became and remains the necessary precondition for a dutiful and worthwhile public life, and is evidence of the successful adaptation of the landed and aristocratic classes, cushioning their transition into the twentieth and even the twenty-first centuries.[69]

## CONCLUSION

Taxidermy collections have left sometimes uncomfortable legacies for property owners in the twenty-first century. They became passé and seemed in almost comically bad taste. By as early as the 1920s collections often lay neglected with sometimes catastrophic results. Taxidermy was beginning to be seen – and still often is seen – as an appalling legacy of an age and class that did much to endanger

'Diplomacy', p. 262; Sramek, 'Face him like a Briton', pp 668, 675. **64** MacKenzie, *Empire of nature*, pp 186–9; Drucker, 'Hunting and shooting', pp 135–6. **65** Mangan and McKenzie, 'Martial conditioning', p. 1137; Drucker, 'Hunting and shooting', p. 138. **66** Sramek, 'Face him like a Briton', p. 659. **67** Drurie, 'Unconscious benefactors', p. 63; Mangan and McKenzie, 'Martial conditioning', p. 1144. **68** David Cannadine, *Ornamentalism: how the British saw their empire* (London, 1997), pp 1–17. **69** Jarvie and Jackson, 'Deer forests, estates and the aristocracy', pp 24–5.

many species and habitats. There are practical considerations too: taxidermy needs to be carefully maintained and requires a good deal of space to display to full effect. As country houses came under existential threat in Ireland and Britain, with many being abandoned, attacked, demolished or turned to institutional use, the natural habitat of taxidermy collections came under threat.[70]

Take the Cotton-Powell Museum at Quex Park in Kent, for example. It was the brainchild of Percy Horace Gordon Powell-Cotton, who spent twenty-six years in Africa to build up one of the most important private taxidermy collections in Britain.[71] He opened the museum to the public in 1896, and visitors could gaze at 6,000 mammal specimens, including eight dioramas of 500 game animals set in their natural habitats, some over 20 metres long.[72] Although a significant feat, the collection constitutes something of a challenge to the Quex Park curators today, in part due to its size, but mainly due to ambiguous public attitudes to taxidermy. The collection does offer an opportunity for visitors to reflect on the culture that underpinned its creation, however. The same experience can be had at Calke Abbey in Derbyshire. When the National Trust took over the ownership and management of the property in 1985, they were faced with the important taxidermy collection of Sir Vauncey Harpur-Crewe, including racks of roughly skinned birds and 400 cases of completed specimens.[73] Perhaps happily for contemporary property managers, the largest zoological collection ever assembled by one man – the 2nd baron Rothschild – in Hertfordshire, was sold in the early 1930s to the American Museum of Natural History. It took 185 crates to ship the collection, which had been created by a dedicated on-site taxidermist, with some special pieces by Rowland Ward, including Britain's first full-mount white rhinoceros.[74] However, after a spell of deep unfashionability, taxidermy has become à la mode again, and now among different social groups.[75] This fashion is less about aspiring to be like the landed classes, and more about the twenty-first century pursuit of authenticity and irony. But perhaps it offers an opportunity. A critical re-examination of this common yet almost invisible material culture is long overdue and would be valuable in developing an understanding of the self-expression and self-understanding of the landed classes, through the sport on the walls of their houses. In an age where species and habitats are in many cases under critical pressure, it seems an opportune time to develop a better understanding of the origins and intellectual framework of country-house taxidermy collections, as well as what they might contribute to future conservation efforts and public education.

70 Reflecting the changing context, the once-dominant firm of Rowland Ward Ltd closed in the 1960s, due to a combination of changing attitudes to wildlife, particularly now endangered species, as well as the end of empire. Morris, *History of taxidermy*, p. 269; Peter Mandler, *The fall and rise of the stately home* (London, 1997), pp 1–6. 71 Morris, *History of taxidermy*, p. 254. 72 Coutu, 'Elephant in the room', pp 491–2; Morris, *History of taxidermy*, p. 282. 73 Morris, *History of taxidermy*, pp 253, 270. 74 Ibid., p. 271. 75 Kirk Wallace Johnston, *The feather thief: beauty, obsession and the natural history heist of the century* (London, 2018).

# Open spaces, the landed classes and the Boy Scouts, 1908–39[1]

ALLEN WARREN

Founded in 1908, the Boy Scouts were a social phenomenon in the years before 1914 and have remained a prominent civic presence ever since throughout many parts of the British Isles and around the world. In rural areas, they were widely supported by the aristocratic and landed classes. The suggestion is that this endorsement by rural counties is part of a wider redefinition of public service among the landed classes, which to some extent mimics parallel developments through which the royal family have gradually developed into what might be called a 'public-service monarchy' in the twentieth century. Just as the political, governmental and imperial power of the aristocracy declined, those among the landed, aristocratic and gentry families inclined to social and political engagement locally found new ways of contributing in an increasingly democratic society. The St John's Ambulance, the military service charities, the Anglican church, the prisons and justice service, the fields of conservation and preservation, along with the Boy Scouts and Girl Guides, were all in a way an answer to the question: what was the point of the upper classes in Britain and Ireland between 1880 and 1945, and beyond?[2]

1 The author would like to thank the Archives Department of the Scout Association, Gilwell Park, Chingford, London E4 7QW for their help in researching this essay. I have also been assisted by 1st Keynsham Scout Group making their archive readily accessible to me and to the Group Scout Leader, Ian Carter, in particular. Most of the local material consulted was through the British Newspaper Archive (BNA), and, particularly in the Somerset section, from the *Western Daily Press* (*WDP*), the *Taunton Courier and Western Advertiser* (*TCWA*), the *Wells Journal* (*WJ*) and the *Bath Chronicle and Weekly Gazette* (*BCWG*). The BNA search engine enables fragments of evidence to be recovered easily and from these shards a broader narrative can be created. Only the more significant items have been referenced. **2** The records of the Scout Association have been quarried more for illustrative material, supporting a broader social or cultural argument, than in an attempt to explain the continued existence of such bodies for over a century. The only history of the Boy Scouts, as distinct from biographical studies of its founder Robert Baden-Powell, is Henry Collis, Fred Hurll and Rex Hazlewood, *B-P's Scouts* (London, 1961). See also: John Springhall, *Youth empire and society: British youth movements, 1883 to 1940* (London, 1977); Allen Warren, 'Sir Robert Baden-Powell, the Scout movement and citizen training in Great Britain, 1900–1920', *English Historical Review*, 101:399 (1986), pp 376–96; *idem*, 'Citizens for the empire: Scouts, Guides and an imperial ideal, 1900–1940' in John M. Mackenzie (ed.), *Propaganda and empire: the manipulation of British public opinion, 1880–1960* (Manchester, 1986), pp 232–56; *idem*, 'Popular manliness, Baden-Powell, Scouting and the development of manly character' in J.A. Mangan and James Walvin (eds), *Manliness and morality: middle class masculinity in Britain and America, 1880–1940* (Manchester, 1989), pp 191–219; *idem*, 'Baden-Powell: two lives of a hero,

17.1 Boy Scouts storm Windsor Castle, *Punch Magazine*, 5 June 1911. Scout Association Archives.

To help answer that question this essay looks through the prism of the growth of the Boy Scout movement across the British Isles, and the role of the upper classes in that growth. It has two specific areas of focus.

The first looks at some of the wider developments in national life as they affected the landed classes and how they became associated with the unconventional training scheme for boys and later girls, launched in early 1908 through the publication of the handbook *Scouting for boys*. Written by a career soldier, Robert Baden-Powell, who had accidentally acquired a popularly heroic status during the siege of Mafeking early in the Boer War, the book was

or two heroic lives?' in Geoffrey Cubitt and Allen Warren (eds), *Heroic reputations and exemplary lives* (Manchester, 2000), pp 123–41.

supported by the publisher and philanthropist Arthur Pearson, and was a runaway success. Within two years, the Boy Scouts had some 100,000 members across the UK. As a result of the enormous public interest, the figure of the Boy Scout became a sort of icon for society and its potential (fig. 17.1).[3]

The second focus looks at a single rural county, Somerset, so as to illustrate the earlier national themes by way of a number of individual narratives.

With regard to the wider national developments, at the top of society there is the royal family in relation to its public-service identity. What is important is the immediate endorsement given to the Boy Scout scheme by Edward VII. As he moved around the country after 1908, groups of Boy Scouts in their distinctive uniforms would form up at railway stations in unplanned guards of honour, which the king acknowledged. He sent an official message of support to the first ad hoc gathering of Scout supporters at the Crystal Palace in September 1909, and authorized the use of the term 'King's Scout' for those boys who had won a particular combination of public-service badges in the training scheme, for example: first-aider, life-saver or messenger. Baden-Powell was himself knighted in 1909. There were cartoons of the king in a Scout uniform conferring the honour, and he was scheduled to review a rally of Scouts in the week he died in 1910 (fig. 17.2).[4]

Edward VII's brother, the duke of Connaught (1850–1942), was also a supporter. He had come to know Baden-Powell quite well earlier in their army careers in India in the 1880s. He actively supported the Scouts as governor general of Canada (1911–16), and became the first president of the Boy Scouts, following the grant of a royal charter in 1912. Under that charter, the king was *ex officio* patron, and a leading member of the royal family would be president; a pattern that continues up to the present in both the Scouts and Guides.[5]

George V honoured his father's personal commitment. All of his children took on public roles in the Boy Scouts or the Girl Guides. The prince of Wales became chief Scout of Wales in 1911, later appearing in a Scout uniform at significant national Scouting occasions, most notably at the World Boy Scout Jamboree at Arrowe Park, Birkenhead in 1929, at which he camped overnight.

3 For the *Punch* cartoons on the Boy Scouts, see the Bernard Partridge cartoon image of the capture of Windsor Castle, Scout Association Archives (hereafter SAA), the *Headquarters Gazette* (hereafter *HQG*), July 1911. 4 Edward VII, for king's message to the Scouts and their leaders, attending the Crystal Palace Rally, Scout Association Archives, *Headquarters Gazette*, Sept. 1909 (hereafter SAA, *HQG*). For requirements for king's Scout badge, SAA, *HQG*, Nov. 1909. On Baden-Powell's knighthood, see G.Whitelaw cartoon, SAA, *HQG*, Dec. 1909 (originally published in the *Glasgow Evening News*). 5 For the duke of Connaught's earlier friendship with Baden-Powell, see Tim Jeal, *Baden-Powell* (London, 1989), pp 111–12. For Connaught becoming the first president of the Boy Scouts Association, see SAA, *HQG*, June 1913 and his address, as governor general of Canada, in support of the Boy Scouts as a non-militaristic movement. Connaught is reputed to have claimed that his influence deterred the Canadian government from introducing compulsory cadet training, which had been introduced into Australia in 1911.

17.2 Cartoon of Edward VII knighting Robert Baden-Powell, *Headquarters Gazette*, Scout Association Archives.

His sister, the princess royal, countess of Harewood, was an active president of the Girl Guides, as was the present queen's late sister, Princess Margaret, both of whom were members of the Buckingham Palace Guide Company during the Second World War. The duke of York, later George VI, himself an enthusiast for camps for boys of different backgrounds during the 1920s, was also honorary commissioner for Scouts in London. The royal family could not have made a stronger signal of how the upper classes might like to emulate their sovereign. They took the hint and rapidly became commissioners in their own counties. To give just three examples among many: Lord Glanusk (Brecknockshire), Earl Fortescue (Devon), the earl of Albermarle (Norfolk).[6]

George V also kept his father's promise to review the Boy Scouts in July 1911, at a camp of over 30,000 Scouts in Windsor Great Park. Once again, the message was clear: Windsor Great Park was a royal park, others lucky to own parkland should take note and offer their land for camping by Boy Scouts. Large gatherings of Boy Scouts were good publicity for both parties, as parkland could be used easily and at little or no cost to the owner. These local occasions took various forms. In Somerset, the county-wide structure renewed in 1919 decided to hold a county camp, or jamboree, each Whitsun holiday weekend in the districts by rotation, building upon earlier camps in 1911, 1912 and 1917. This pattern continues to the present, with local landowners in the particular district hosting the event.[7] The same convergence is seen in the giving or leasing of land to the Scouts for camping. Marginal land in particular had little financial value during the interwar years and the Boy Scouts wanted such 'rough' sites for their camping and backwoods activities. Again, to take the example of Somerset, the Dyke Acland family, keen supporters, had allowed Scouts to camp on their land at Horner Water on Exmoor. This has continued ever since, consistent with the family's decision to give the whole of their Exmoor estate to the National Trust in 1944.[8] Similarly, the Taunton Scouts acquired a district camping ground locally at Huish Woods in the Blackdown Hills from the Gore-Langton family, one of whose members was the county commissioner from 1936.[9]

The second national feature is the significance of outdoor recreation and fresh air after 1900. The impact of dense urban living on the health and welfare of children and young people became matters of considerable social and political concern, leading some commentators later to broaden the analysis and to attribute the break down in international relations in 1914 to over-civilization and urbanization.[10] After 1918, hiking, rambling, cycling, camping and caravanning all grew in popularity.

A radical version of this is represented by John Hargrave (1894–1982) in his book, *The Great War brings it home* (1919). A charismatic volunteer in the Boy

6 The king's rally on 4 July 1911 was well orchestrated, coming shortly after the coronation in May. For account, pictures and cartoon of the event, see SAA, *HQG*, July 1911. For the Prince of Wales' public identification with the Boy Scouts, see his welcome home after his imperial tour during 1922 (SAA, *HQG*, Oct. 1922), and his overnighting at the world jamboree at Arrowe Park in Birkenhead, August 1929 (SAA, *HQG*, Aug. 1929), along with the extensive national press coverage. 7 For instance, Lord Hylton (1896–1967), lord lieutenant of Somerset (1949–64) and president of the Somerset Boy Scouts, hosted three such county jamborees at Ammerdown Park, in 1942, 1953 and 1964. 8 The Acland family, based at Killerton, Devon were also active supporters of the Boy Scouts in that county, and Colonel Alfred Dyke Acland, distinguished soldier and director of W.H Smith, became national treasurer of the association in 1922. 9 Gore Langton of Hatch Park, near Taunton, county commissioner for Somerset 1936–52, facilitated the acquisition of Huish Woods as the local Scouts' district camp site. 10 Early pre-1914 examples would include the Fresh Air Fund,

Scouts and a woodcraft enthusiast, he was appointed as the headquarters commissioner for camping and woodcraft by Baden-Powell in 1918. At first, it worked well as the two men had much in common and were of a similar character. But Hargrave was too unorthodox and came into conflict with Baden-Powell. He was sidelined, moving on to found the woodcraft organization Kibbo Kift Kindred, which after many transformations became the present-day Woodcraft Folk. But the woodcraft enthusiasm was a significant element in the Boy Scouts in the 1920s.[11]

More practically, under the 1918 Education Act, local authorities were able to make provision for camping grounds and sports fields; this was colloquially known as 'the Boy Scout clause'. Baden-Powell himself became president of the Camping and Caravanning Club in 1919, succeeding belatedly Scott of the Antarctic.[12] After 1918 camping generally came to acquire an almost quasi-religious status, whether in small gatherings of adults or children in brotherly commune with nature, or in huge international camps, or Scout jamborees as symbols of international harmony – a realization of a League of Nations of the world's youth.[13]

The third national theme relates to family. Among the upper classes, the word can be misleading to modern ears. Often it is used by them as a related network or even dynasty – a group of interconnected, interrelated families, which could at times be colloquially expressed as 'he or she is a sort of cousin of mine'. Similarly, families defined in this way had a whole stock of houses and estates, grand and less grand, in which the extended family lived. The involvement of families with the Boy Scout movement could come about in a variety of ways.

To take some northern examples. The Orde-Poulett family home was at Bolton Hall in Wensleydale. The Hon. Percy Orde-Poulett (1894–1915), the heir presumptive and grandson of the 4th baron Bolton (1845–1922), was an undergraduate at Trinity College, Cambridge in August 1914. Enthused by the Boy Scout movement in London through the Trinity College mission, and in his native county where he ran the village troop, he enlisted in August 1914 and was killed in France the following May.

In 1922, when Percy Orde-Poulett's father succeeded as the 5th Lord Bolton, later becoming lord lieutenant (1935–44), he assumed the presidency of the North Riding Boy Scouts. At the same time, Lady Bolton became president of

Clarion Cycling Clubs, the Camping Club, the YMCA and the Boys Brigade. 11 See Springhall, *Youth*, pp 110–20. Two survivals of that enthusiasm are the naming of the adult training scheme, still called the Wood Badge, and the role of the campfire in the camping programme – a mixture of songs and sketches outdoors in which some participants use highly decorated blankets to keep warm. 12 Education Act 1918, c. 39, s. 17, 'to provide social and physical training'. 13 For education and the open air after 1918, see Robert Skidelsky, *English progressive schools* (London, 1969). See also the websites of the Ramblers Association, the Cyclist Touring Club, the Youth Hostels Association, and the Camping Club of Great Britain and Ireland, of which Baden-Powell became president in 1919.

the Girl Guides. The Girl Guides still have a camping ground on Bolton estate land.[14]

In the case of Christopher Vane, 10th Lord Barnard (1888–1964), of Raby Castle in County Durham and possessed of over 71,000 acres in the county, the Scouting connection proved life-long. The Vane family had provided the Scouts in the nearby village of Staindrop with a site on which to build a headquarters in 1914, on which the present headquarters still stands. On succeeding, Lord Barnard became county commissioner for Scouts in 1929, with Raby Park becoming almost an unofficial county camping ground during his tenure as county commissioner, which lasted for the next twenty-nine years until 1958, when he became lord lieutenant.

In the case of the Catholic Fitzalan-Howard family, dukes of Norfolk, forty years later, it came from experience in the school troop at Ampleforth, north Yorkshire. In the case of Martin and Mark Fitzalan-Howard in the 1970s and 1980s, they became deputy county commissioner in north Yorkshire and national treasurer of the Scout Association, respectively.

With the family of the earls of Clarendon in Hertfordshire, courtiers and ministers since the seventeenth century, the connection may be directly attributable to Edward VII's private visit to the Clarendon home, The Grove, in Hertfordshire in the company of Mrs Keppel in 1909, when he was greeted by a Boy Scout guard of honour at the railway station. We do not know any more about the visit, except that when a local troop was formed it was called 'Lady Hyde's Own'. But on the death of Lord Clarendon's grandson and presumptive heir, Lord Hyde, as a result of a shooting accident on 27 April 1935, we learn from the obituarist that while at Eton, the young Lord Hyde had had a transforming effect on the Eton College Scout troop, before becoming probably the only heir to an earldom who was also a member of the Oxford University Rover crew. On graduation, he continued that Scouting involvement in Hertfordshire until going to South Africa in 1931 as an ADC to his father as governor general and *ex-officio* chief Scout of the dominion.[15]

A similar case is the Philipps family, long established among the Pembrokeshire gentry, and raised to the peerage in 1908 and subsequently to a viscountcy in 1918. The second son of the first baron, the Hon. Roland Philipps, was educated at Winchester and New College, Oxford, before deciding to have some time in London settlement work, initially as a resident in Oxford House. One of the many settlement social programmes was running boys' camps.

14 For Percy Orde-Poulett, see Keith Taylor, *Wensleydale remembered: the sacrifice made by the families of a northern dale, 1914–1918 and 1939–1945* (Bakewell, 2004), pp 68–70. For the Trinity College, Cambridge Mission, see Lawrence Goldman, *Trinity in Camberwell: Trinity College mission, 1885–1985* (Cambridge, 1985). 15 For Edward VII visit to Watford and The Grove, home of Lord Clarendon, and his acknowledgement of the 1st Watford Scouts ('Lady Hyde's Own'), see BNA, *Watford Observer*, 24 July 1909. For Lord Hyde's membership of the Oxford University Rover crew, see Bodl. Libr. MSS Top Oxon d328/1–3.

Roland Philipps quickly became a passionate enthusiast for the ideas and methods of the Boy Scouts, in effect, becoming the full-time volunteer commissioner for east and north-east London, his family purchasing a house from where he could base his operations on Stepney Green. He enlisted in August 1914 and was killed on the Somme on 7 July 1916.[16] The house in Stepney was left to the Boy Scouts, becoming their own East End settlement, and only closing in 1982.

Finally, to conclude with a Somerset example. Lieutenant John Wethered Power of Thurloxton Manor, near Taunton, had been educated at Eton and Trinity College, Cambridge and was also later killed on the Somme. His obituarist commented that he had been a familiar figure at the University Settlement and the Trinity College Mission in the East End and a keen supporter of the Waifs and Strays Society and the Boy Scouts.[17]

The fourth national theme is that of the retired military man on half-pay in rural England. It is well known that younger sons of the landed classes, especially the gentry, followed military careers, which in the late nineteenth century were almost exclusively within the British empire. Later, they were joined by a more extensive network of colonial officials, lawyers, engineers and businessmen overwhelmingly educated within the public school system. Unless they were going to the top, they retired between the age of 45 and 55 on half-pay. Returning home, they were well suited to supervising the dispersed operations of the various county or regional bodies that interested them. In this context, it is not surprising that they frequently became commissioners within the Boy Scouts, either at district or county level. The emerging Boy Scout structure had many similarities to that of the modern St John's Ambulance, founded in 1876, with its county-based structures of uniformed commissioners, officers and cadets, linked to a public service function and a youth and adult training scheme.[18]

The fifth theme is the education of the upper classes after 1880. Paradoxically, just as the traditional classes were losing political authority and economic confidence, the education of their sons and those of the successful professions and business classes was being forged into an extended, integrated and reformed system of public schools. Among the many achievements of the Victorians, for good or ill, was the fashioning of an elite education system linked to the reformed ancient universities, traditional professions and the Anglican church, which remained very little challenged until the 1960s. Its significance has been

16 Hon. Roland Philipps MC (1890–1916), second son of Lord St Davids, lord lieutenant of Pembrokeshire, was killed on 7 July 1916. In addition to his Scout work, he was also Welsh secretary for the Boys Country Work Society and the prospective Liberal candidate for South Glamorgan. There are many references to Philipps' work in the SSA, *HQG*, 1910–16. 17 John Wethered Power (1895–1916), see BNA, *BCWG*, 23 Sept. 1916. 18 The monthly lists of Boy Scout commissioners in SAA, *HQG*, 1909–14 and in the local press make this point very clearly. See also, Edward Spiers, *The army and society, 1815–1914* (London, 1980).

underestimated. If only one example was allowed, it might be the fact that between 1940 and 1955 the leaders of the two main political parties were: first, Winston Churchill, grandson of a duke, an old Harrovian and colonial journalist before his election to Westminster; second, Clement Attlee, son of a middle-class solicitor, educated at Haileybury and University College, Oxford, later secretary for Toynbee Hall, the pioneering East End Settlement, and mayor of Stepney, before becoming a Labour MP for Limehouse in 1922.[19]

For our purposes, the most significant aspect of this before 1914 lies in the emergence of the settlement movement in London and major cities. These voluntary associations brought young men and women from privileged backgrounds together in a mixture of social action on broadly Christian foundations, political and moral idealism and a developing practical awareness of poverty and deprivation. For many, not having or wanting to make definitive career choices, working for a period in a settlement mission was today's equivalent of a 'gap year', giving a preparation for ordination, bar exams, the military or going into the family's business or managing the estate. It is not surprising that it is during this period that the Anglican diocese of Southwark acquired its reputation for social radicalism, which has lasted into the twenty-first century. The history of the settlement movement deserves to be more studied and understood.[20]

Boys' work, as it was called, was a prominent part of the settlement ethos, and *Scouting for boys* was written very much with that constituency in mind. The settlement experience had influenced the likes of Percy Orde-Powlett, Roland Philipps and John Wethered Power to engage in Scout work before 1914.

The last national theme is the idea of public service itself. Here, the experience of the Great War at home is crucial. Before 1914, the historian can catalogue a whole range of voluntary and social actions taken up by the upper classes, men and women, growing out of Victorian views on philanthropy – religious, educational, welfare, rescue, and animals. What we would now call the voluntary sector had much energy, but few unifying assumptions or shared experiences. The First World War changed that dramatically, engaging the whole civilian population for the first time, and in unanticipated ways. Coincidentally, the same was true for the Boy Scouts with their ethos of citizens' service, popularly represented as the daily 'Good Turn' for each young member. Even before 1914, the provincial press featured incidents in which Boy Scouts had lent

**19** J. de S. Honey, *Tom Brown's universe: the development of the public school in the nineteenth century* (London, 1980). Only a small number of secondary schools before 1914, day or boarding, had Scout troops, although some preparatory schools did. After 1918 a much larger number adopted Scouting, usually independent boarding schools or maintained grammar schools, thereby continuing the exposure of the established classes to Scout programmes and activity. **20** Tower Hamlets Record Centre, Oxford House Collection, *Oxford House Magazine*, July 1910–12, I/OXF/A/4/3/1–3. For Toynbee Hall, see J.A.R. Pimlott, *Toynbee Hall: fifty years of social progress, 1884–1934* (London, 1935).

17.3 Ernest Stopford Carlos, *Coast watching*, Scout Association Archives.

a hand, putting out fires, providing messenger services, distributing leaflets and so on. A compelling example relates to rescues from drowning, which was very common at a time when popular swimming away from the coasts was in rivers, often near weirs. One of the key Scout tests for boys wishing to gain the first-class badge was to be able to swim fifty yards clothed, not only for self-preservation but to save others. On a short stretch of the river Avon in north Somerset, there were about five or six swimming incidents yearly, some involving drownings or rescues by Scouts or their leaders.[21]

The public was already conscious of this element of public service in the Boy Scouts, and it was a new development in work with boys. The other agencies – the Brigades, the Sunday schools and the Girls Friendly Society – were, in the main, denominational organizations aimed at extending individual religious or moral understanding, or were clubs providing recreational or trade training for working-class lads or young women. The citizen-training element in the Boy Scouts enabled it to recruit adult leaders more widely, and broadened the social appeal to boys with the distinctiveness and variety of its programmes.

The outbreak of war in August 1914 fully confirmed this. Coming upon the civil authorities unexpectedly, the first two months were confused. Widespread fears of spies and saboteurs led to Boy Scouts guarding bridges, signal boxes and

21 For example, BNA, *WDP*, 31 Apr. 1911, 4 Dec. 1912.

telephone lines. In Bristol, all Scoutmasters were immediately summoned to their city headquarters to co-ordinate how they might assist the civil authorities, and over the next few months Scouts and their leaders performed a range of functions.[22]

The first direct impact on towns and cities of hostilities was the arrival of thousands of Belgian refugees for whom there was no ready infrastructure of support. In the case of Taunton in Somerset, the whole of the Belgian refugee reception was organized by the town's Boy Scouts, including housing and recreation, something that, perhaps uniquely, continued throughout the war in association with the civic authorities. Nationally, the Boy Scouts manned the coast-watching service, sending older boys for periods of six weeks to work with the coastguard, a practice that also continued throughout the war. These contributions were widely recognized, leading the *Times* to devote a whole chapter in its history of the war to the civilian service of the Boy Scouts (fig. 17.3).[23]

By 1920 the Boy Scouts had become a distinctive part of the social landscape in both towns and the countryside across Britain and they have remained so. The relationship with the royal family has continued, with Scouts taking a recognized part in public ceremonies such as royal jubilees and coronations, distributing programmes and acting as uniformed stewards – and on Remembrance Sunday at the Cenotaph providing the guard of honour outside the Foreign Office as the royal party appears, and also taking part in the British Legion's march past. In return, the monarch or royal representative since 1935 has reviewed King's/Queen's Scouts in the quadrangle at Windsor Castle, prior to the national Scouts St George's Day service of rededication in St George's chapel, a pattern replicated across the country.[24]

Many of the themes outlined above might be found in small and medium-sized towns across the country. The town of Keynsham, between Bristol and Bath, serves as a good example. The Scouts had played a modest civilian role during the war years, collecting salvage for recycling, distributing pamphlets and fliers, and raising funds for charities. In appreciation, the town presented the troop (about twenty boys aged between 11 and 18) with a trek cart. Scouts paraded with the British Legion on 11 November every year, as they still do, as part of the public tribute but also in remembrance of the many former Scouts

**22** BNA, *WDP*, 23 Dec. 1914 contained a feature on the Boy Scouts' efforts in the city of Bristol. In addition to some 58 leaders and 200 Scouts recorded as enlisting, Scouts had had signalling duties on the Bristol Channel, relief duties at depots, were cycle messengers for the Red Cross, acted as orderlies in local hospitals, collected salvage and some thirty had spent time guarding tunnels and bridges. Fifty had volunteered as collectors for Chocolate Day, with Bristol gathering more chocolate for the troops than any other city. **23** For a synoptic view of the Boy Scouts' contribution to the civilian war effort, see *The Times history of the war* (London, 1918), xviii, ch. ccliii, pp 145–80. **24** For the first King's Scouts St George's Day Parade at Windsor in 1935, reviewed by George V and Queen Mary, see *Pathé News* coverage.

who had lost their lives. Public service of a 'civic' kind continued. The Scouts built the jubilee beacon on the top of Lansdown, near the town in 1935, they delivered logs to the elderly, sang carols to the residents of the former workhouse at Christmas, and during the 1930s regularly put on a pantomime in the town. They were not unique.[25]

But what of Somerset's landed classes and those individuals who were actively supporting now both the Boy Scouts and Girl Guides? Six examples will have to suffice. First is Colonel William Leir (1840–1916), the founding county commissioner from 1910 until his death in 1916. From a long-standing gentry family, based at Ditcheat Priory, near Shepton Mallet, Leir was an active man and a keen sportsman with interests also in amateur dramatics. In retirement he particularly supported tennis and hockey in Somerset and the west of England, most notably establishing the regional framework for women's competitive hockey, a model subsequently developed nationally. He was immediately enthused by the Boy Scout scheme, and took a personal initiative in helping to co-ordinate the local associations around the county, which in towns were largely promoted by the YMCA, before he was confirmed as county commissioner by the national headquarters in early 1910. He began organizing county-wide camps of Boy Scouts, two of which were held in 1911 and 1912 at Freshford, south of Bath. Later, Leir, writing about the camps, made it clear that they were organized on strictly non-militaristic Baden-Powell lines, with troops camping in a dispersed pattern, rather than the more orderly pattern used in Territorial or Boys' Brigade camps.[26]

The second example is Lady Constance Ryder (1871–1950), younger sister of John, 5th earl of Harrowby, of Sandon Hall in Staffordshire. Lady Constance moved to west Somerset with her sisters in the early 1920s to The Knowle in the village of Timberscombe, near Minehead. She became a Scouting enthusiast, founding a Boy Scout troop and a Rover crew in the village, and later became the district commissioner for west Somerset as well as acting county secretary. She was also a benefactress to the parish church's fabric, where she played the organ and ran the choir, and to the Boy Scouts, donating a small woodland camping site that is still used to this day. A magistrate, she bred prize-winning cattle, was an active unionist and was an enthusiast for folk dancing (a major activity in her Rover crew), appearing in an elaborate Elizabethan tableau at nearby Dunster Castle in 1931. For many years one of the trophies competed for annually at the Somerset Boy Scout county jamboree was the Lady Constance Ryder Trophy for camping standards (fig. 17.4).[27]

**25** 1st Keynsham Scout Group archives. **26** For Leir, see BNA, *WG*, 14 Jan. 1910, *BCWG*, 13 July 1912, 22 May 1916; SAA, *HQG*, May 1910, Jan. 1913. **27** See Lady Ryder's comments on the positive elements of being a female Scoutmaster, BNA, *WDP*, 7 May 1927; for Somerset Scout activities 1924–39 as Scoutmaster for Timberscombe and district commissioner; for west Somerset see BNA, *TCWA*, 4 Feb. 1939, 4 Mar. 1950. See also memorials in St Padroc's Church, Timberscombe. Photographs and memorabilia in the West

The third example is by way of contrast, but is introduced to make the point that public service and the voluntary work were sectors of rural life that had the potential to be a meeting ground between the traditional landed classes and rural businessmen. Herbert H. Shepherd (1869–1938) was the owner of a successful hemp-spinning business near Ilminster in south Somerset, founded by his father. They were among the largest employers in this highly rural area, and their hemp was integral to carpet manufacturing in neighbouring Axminster. Educated at Harrow and Magdalen College, Oxford, Herbert Shepherd trained as lawyer before joining the family business. The family did not obviously join local county society by acquiring an estate, but lived in a large 'gentry-style' house in Ilminster, The Shrubbery. But both father and son became magistrates and acted as the local representative on the newly established county council, usually running unopposed. Herbert was a magistrate for over thirty years, a county councillor from 1907 until 1936 and chairman of the county education committee from 1924 to 1936, while simultaneously serving as county commissioner for Scouts from 1919 to 1935 and chairman of the county Nursing Association and many other local charities. In a curious way, his public persona had parallels with those of the 5th marquess of Bath (1862–1946), lord lieutenant of Somerset (1904–46), president of the Somerset Boy Scouts (1919–46) and chairman of Wiltshire county council (1906–46). Their paths would have crossed frequently in Somerset affairs.[28]

The fourth example is very different: Sir Richard Paget (1869–1955) of Cranmore Hall, near Shepton Mallet. In many ways a traditional member of the long-established Somerset gentry, he was also a barrister and scientist, whose most significant work was in phonetics and the technique of vocalization. This research inspired a commitment to deaf and mute people, which led him to pioneer modern sign language. Prior to 1914 he was supporter of the Boy Scouts and he was also for a time the local district commissioner for Mid-Somerset in the 1920s, taking a particular interest in the rapid growth of the Wolf Cub section for 8- to 10-year-olds.[29]

Two final examples are from the north of the county: the Strachey and Wills families. The Stracheys had lived at Sutton Court, near the village of Stowey, since the Middle Ages. They were Liberal in politics, with Sir Edward Strachey, 4th Baronet, being MP for South Somerset from 1892 to 1911, when he was ennobled. His second son was St Loe Strachey, well-known editor of the *Spectator* from 1887 until 1925, and elder brother to Henry Strachey, 'artist, musician and Scouter', as his memorial in Stowey Church puts it. Henry had been art critic of the *Spectator* from 1896–1922 and all were kinsman of Lytton Strachey.

Somerset Folk Museum, Allerford. **28** Herbert H. Shepherd (1869–1938); see BNA, *WJ*, 11 Mar. 1938. **29** Sir Richard Paget (1869–1955); see *ODNB*, 42, pp 368–9, BNA, *BCWG*, 12 June 1920.

17.4 Lady Constance Ryder and her Scouts, West Somerset Rural Life Museum, Allerford, Somerset, Scout Association Archives.

Henry Strachey, after a period as a working artist in London, settled in Somerset and became enthused with Scouting, founding and running a village troop in nearby Bishop Sutton before 1914. More importantly, he was one of the first adults to undertake the adult training scheme, the Wood Badge, with a curriculum devised by Baden-Powell personally, in which the adults were trained in a typical camp setting and followed a programme of activities as though they were a youthful Boy Scout patrol. Strachey became the adult directing the Wood Badge courses in Somerset under canvas at a site in the Mendip hills in Ebbor Gorge. He also continued painting until his death, and a number of his murals were a commission for the White House at Gilwell Park, the camping headquarters of the Scout Association. He also painted a number of rather idealized pictures of Boy Scouts in camp. His nephew, Edward, 2nd baron Strachey, followed a more conventional path as a soldier, seeing service in the Somerset Light Infantry from 1911 until 1920. On retiring, he also became supportive of the Boy Scouts, and one of the field organizers for the international Scout jamboree at Arrowe Park in 1929.[30] He and his uncle, Henry,

30 See *BCWG*, 2 Nov. 1940; *Shepton Mallet Journal*, 8 Nov. 1940.

were the district commissioners for north-east Somerset from 1923 – with a brief intermission in 1930 – until Henry's death in 1940.

The Wills family were heirs to the Bristol tobacco barons W.D. Wills and H.O. Wills. Enormously wealthy, the Wills family were now an extended dynasty with houses, farms and estates in north Somerset, Gloucestershire and the Highlands. Here the example is Captain Ronald Dewhurst Wills (1891–1937) of Hill House, Corston, just outside Bath, who had been educated at Marlborough and Trinity College, Cambridge before serving in the Somerset Light Infantry throughout the First World War. Having no need to earn a living, he took an active interest in the Bath Young Men's Christian Association and in Bath Orthopaedic Hospital. It was probably through the 1st Bath (YMCA) troop that Wills became acquainted with the Boy Scouts, becoming an assistant district commissioner in Bath and, briefly, in 1930, district commissioner for north-east Somerset. He was a significant local benefactor, hosting the Baden-Powells at the south-west of England Boy Scout jamboree at Corston in 1932, paying for the firework display and for the aerial photographs of the camp, which was on his land. He also paid for the purchase of a small piece of land in the centre of nearby Keynsham, on which the first Scout hut was built in 1928, and which, with later land acquisitions, is still the site of the group today. This original headquarters was opened by the district commissioner in 1928, his Somerset neighbour the honourable Edward Strachey of Sutton Court (fig. 17.5).[31]

Unsurprisingly, the Boy Scout movement fared variously across the British Isles as a whole, as it did within Europe before 1914. This was not because the landed classes thought differently in Scotland, Wales and Ireland; it was more that the nations' historic cultures and physical geographies were less receptive.[32]

Scotland provides the closest parallel. Perhaps unexpectedly, the Boy Scouts were popular, despite the vigour and strength of the Boys' Brigade in Glasgow and the west of Scotland more generally. Both were positively supported by the civic authorities across Scotland and by the landed elites in the rural areas. It is an intriguing question as to how both could co-exist and Scotland's youth history deserves more research.[33] The Boys' Brigade was both explicitly Christian and quasi-military; the Boy Scouts, by contrast, were non-denominational and patriotic in a distinctive Scottish way. The Boy Scouts in Scotland also had what might be called the 'Balmoral' factor, with prominent Scottish families following the example of those south of the border. For example, four of the five chief Scouts of the United Kingdom after 1945 were Scottish. Until 1974 the chief Scout was also chief Scout of the commonwealth, with its imperial headquarters in London. Three of those four ultimately were made Knights of the Thistle,

31 Ronald Dewhurst Wills (1891–1937). See *BCWG*, 25 Sept. 1937. 32 SAA, *HQG* Feb. 1911 gave national statistics for boy members as of 30 Sept. 2010: England, 81,267; Scotland, 14,815; Wales, 3,614; Ireland, 1,651. 33 John Springhall, Brian Fraser and Michael Hoare, *Sure and steadfast: a history of the Boys' Brigade, 1883–1983* (London, 1983).

17.5 Colonel Hon. Edward Strachey, district commissioner, opening the Keynsham Scout Headquarters, 1928, 1st Keynsham Scout Group, Scout Association Archives.

and the fourth a Knight of the Garter, with Lord Rowallan also becoming governor of Tasmania and Sir Charles Maclean lord chamberlain. The present Lord Airlie, Scottish neighbour, friend and relation of the royal family, declined to be considered as a potential Chief Scout, but as a leading banker in London, was the treasurer of the Scout Association for many years, and also a later lord chamberlain.

In Scotland, the Boy Scouts were able to give their own distinctive gloss to the style of the movement – national, civic and imperial. Not that this was without tensions, including, significantly, over the uniform. The increasingly non-militaristic uniform of the leadership, with adults adopting shorts, was generally not a problem in Scotland, with its tradition of the kilt. But headgear was a different matter, with young leaders and Rover Scouts in the west of Scotland, in particular, being determined to wear the bonnet in the early 1930s.

Baden-Powell was not impressed, wanting the Scout hat to be a unifying element in the UK Scout movement. The Scottish Rovers threatened to break away, but Baden-Powell gave way.[34]

The experiences in Wales and Ireland were very different, with the Boy Scouts making little impact before 1914. In Wales, the closeness of Nonconformity and nationality meant that the Boy Scouts were seen as marginal, and especially so in the Welsh-speaking parts of north Wales.[35] These factors should not imply that the landed classes did not make the attempt. Once again, the royal family led the way, with the prince of Wales becoming chief Scout of Wales, following the Windsor Rally in 1911. While Wales did not have a Balmoral, the family home of the lords Glanusk near Crickhowell, acquired some of the same qualities, with the 2nd Lord Glanusk, an early supporter of the Scouts, becoming chief commissioner. His son, the 3rd baron, and in turn, his son-in-law, Bill Legge-Bourke, also supported the movement in London and Wales. Bill was chairman of the finance sub-committee of the national association. His widow is presently lady-in-waiting to the princess royal and lord lieutenant of Powys, while their daughter, Tiggy, was nanny to Princes William and Harry. But Scouting had little wider national impact, especially after the emergence of a distinctive cultural movement for young people in Wales, the URDD, in 1922.[36]

If the cultural landscape in Wales was difficult, in Ireland it was virtually impossible outside the Protestant north-east. There, the association took root quite quickly, rather as it had in the west of Scotland. Beyond Ulster, Dublin and Cork, where there were significant small Protestant communities, the Boy Scouts made little impression. The success of the Gaelic Athletic Association, with its close association with the Roman Catholic church through the parish and educational systems, meant that the Boy Scouts stood little chance before 1922 (fig. 17.6).[37]

The UK Scout Association found it very difficult to establish any national, provincial or county structure. Initially, the earl of Shaftesbury became the chief commissioner, building on the fact that as an Ulster as well as a Dorset landowner, he had Irish connections, and had been the first lord mayor of Belfast – but nothing much happened following the announcement. Eventually,

34 SAA, minutes of the committee of the council, 14 Oct. 1932 (private minute book), say that Lord Hampton should suggest to Baden-Powell that he had to give way. 35 In the first national survey in 1910, Wales recorded 3,898 members. 36 On Lord Glanusk, see feature in SAA, *HQG*, Nov. 1912, in which he enthuses about adult leaders wearing shorts and how in Wales, the Boy Scouts have to overcome Nonconformist fears about militarism. This source records that he had founded the troop in Crickhowell, with pictures of Lord Glanusk and the troop in camp in Glanusk Park. The Glamorgan Scouts held a camp in Glanusk Park in the summer of 1910, SAA, *HQG*, Sept. 1910. For URDD see organization's website. 37 Baden-Powell commenting on Scouting in Ireland after a visit; see SAA, *HQG*, June and Aug. 1911, in which he initially endorsed what were called Nationalist Scouts, who did not take the oath to the king. Among many things, it shows how naïvely optimistic he could be.

17.6 Scouts on duty at the Eucharistic Congress in Dublin, 1932, National Library of Ireland.

the veteran earl of Meath took on the role, but as the founder of the Empire Day movement and a man of many opinions, it was unlikely that he would have much impact.[38] Of the Irish aristocracy, only the earl and countess of Powerscourt gave significant public support, with Lady Powerscourt becoming chief commissioner of the Girl Guides. The Powerscourt grounds were made available for camps and field days; it is no coincidence that Powerscourt is not far from Dublin.

There was a paradox here in relation to the Irish Roman Catholic church's reaction to Scouts across Europe generally. In the rest of the United Kingdom,

38 Meath was still attending the committee of the council in London in June 1922 (aged 81) when he suggested that, given the fluid political situation, no Scout promotional material should presently be used and that the Scout uniform should not be worn close to the border with the newly established state of Northern Ireland. The committee decided that local commissioners should be able to suspend Scout activity until the situation became clear and further instructions could be given. SAA, minutes of the committee of the council, 8 June 1922. See also Marnie Hay, 'The foundation and development of Na Fianna Éireann, 1909–16', *Irish Historical Studies*, 36:141 (May 2008), pp 53–71; and J.A. Gaughan, *Scouting in Ireland* (Dublin, 2008).

the Roman Catholic hierarchy quickly identified with the Scouting approach, most notably Cardinal Bourne of Westminster and his adjutant, Bishop Butt. As the English public-education system fully accepted denominational elementary education, there was no difficulty over 'closed' Roman Catholic Scout troops. On continental Europe, the Catholic churches endorsed Scout training in various ways, so much so that at the end of the First World War, in a spirit of collaboration, an international conference of Catholic Scouts was set up. Ireland was not a member.[39]

This situation could not alter until the twenty-six counties formally became the Irish Free State, and after the conclusion of the Irish Civil War. Then it changed quite rapidly as a new, distinctively independent Irish religious, political and governmental identity was fashioned. Probably the initiative came more generally from the Catholic teaching orders like the Christian Brothers. Certainly, Fathers Tom and Ernest Farrell were important in this process. By the time of the Eucharistic Congress in 1932, the Catholic Boy Scouts of Ireland was firmly established. If there could be any doubt, the photographic record of that extraordinary demonstration of public religiosity shows Boy Scouts lining the processional streets and serving refreshments to the young first communicants.[40] But it was a very different world from that of the elderly Henry Strachey running his village troop in north Somerset and his Wood Badge courses in Ebbor Gorge.

**39** For the Roman Catholic hierarchy's support in the UK of Catholic troops, see SAA, *HQG*, June 1912. For the opening of the first Catholic troop in Bristol, 24th Bristol, see *WDP*, 25 Sept. 1912. **40** The Catholic Boy Scouts of Ireland was founded in 1927 as a separate Catholic Scout movement in the Free State as a result of experimental programmes and campaigning by Fathers Ernest and Tom Farrell. Endorsed by the hierarchy, Catholic Scouts featured in the centenary celebrations of Catholic emancipation in 1929, and most publicly during the Eucharistic Congress in 1932. The International Catholic Conference of Scouting was set up as an umbrella organization at the time of the first world Scout jamboree in London in 1920 and endorsed by Pope Benedict XV in 1922.

# Amateur astronomy in the nineteenth-century Irish country house: the observatory at Monksgrange, Co. Wexford

LESLEY WHITESIDE

In 1876, Edward Richards of Monksgrange, Co. Wexford, bought a small second-hand telescope for his 21-year-old daughter Adela. Within weeks of its delivery, father and daughter found it inadequate for what they called 'studying the moon' and 'stargazing' and they began a lengthy search for a superior instrument. It was not until November 1878 that a better telescope was installed in the observatory which Edward built in front of the house at Monksgrange (fig. 18.1).

Edward had been born at Monksgrange in 1826, the second son of Goddard and Dorothea Richards. As a second son, not expecting to inherit the estate, he trained as an engineer and worked on the construction of the Waterford-Limerick railway line before emigrating to America in 1848. Edward married there and had three children but by 1860, his son, infant daughter and wife had died and Edward was left to bring up Adela, who was 5 years old. Father and daughter developed a particularly close relationship, which can be seen in the large volume of correspondence between them, starting in her childhood and continuing until his death in 1911.

In America, Edward worked for ten years as a railway engineer before becoming a pioneer farmer in Kansas. In 1860, his older brother, John Richards, died and Edward inherited Monksgrange but it was not until 1866 that he returned to Wexford and took over the management of the estate. Having spent her childhood in the wilds of Kansas, it was difficult for Adela to adjust to life in Ireland but she was greatly helped by her paternal grandmother, Dorothea, who moved back to Monksgrange after the death of her second husband, Richard Sargent of Waterford. Dorothea soon persuaded Edward to send Adela to school in Paris, where she could receive an excellent education. At home and abroad, Dorothea introduced Adela to European *mores*, and encouraged her to draw and paint, to play the piano and to sing. Dorothea's determination to give her granddaughter every advantage was expressed in the purchase of a new piano for her in 1870 and in travelling with her on the Continent at an age when most grandmothers would have stayed at home.

Accompanied either by Dorothea or an American artist companion,[1] Adela learned French, German and Italian, attended concerts, lectures and the theatre,

1 Adelia Gates was a decorative water colourist, who later became a scientific botanical illustrator. Some of her work is in the collections of the Smithsonian Institution, Washington.

18.1 Monksgrange, showing the observatory. Courtesy of Monksgrange Trust.

and visited museums, galleries, archaeological sites, notable buildings and gardens. She subsequently spent long periods in France, Germany and in sophisticated Italian cities such as Siena and Florence. This experience of European culture broadened her mind and stimulated an interest in science and the arts. Adela later became a prolific writer. In addition to numerous articles and short stories, she published three novels, two of which were based in Kansas, the third being set at the time of the 1798 rebellion in Ireland.[2]

The rich archives at Monksgrange give an interesting insight into the leisure pursuits of the family. It is important to examine the choice of astronomy in the context of other pastimes, the distinctive way in which a growing interest was put into practice and the involvement of Adela, considering how typical she and her father were of gentry families in Ireland. Leisure pursuits required free time and many inhabitants of the Irish country house enjoyed this in abundance. The Richards family did not share the passion for hunting, which could take up four days a week in season, leaving little time for more cerebral leisure pursuits, such as music, art and science. The huntsman was in many ways a different type of person from the musician, artist or scientist. The hunt was a very sociable activity, for which it was important for both rider and horse to be immaculately presented. In contrast, the typical scientist or naturalist, often dressed in old clothes, spent long hours alone, the one in a laboratory or workshop, the other

2 She is included in Rolf Loeber and Magda Loeber with Anne Mullin, *A guide to Irish fiction, 1650–1900* (Dublin, 2006).

18.2 Adela as a young girl. Courtesy of Monksgrange Trust.

outdoors. The astronomer was likewise dressed in old clothes and was primarily concerned with keeping warm. Art was also largely a solitary occupation, as was music, unless playing in an ensemble.

It seems that people engaged in the more robust sports primarily for fun, while others played music, drew and painted as an expression of a creative urge, and another cohort became amateur scientists. These pursuits were not, of course, mutually exclusive and it was, for instance, a great advantage for a botanist, entomologist or astronomer to be able to draw. Edward Richards drew with the precise skill of the engineer, while Adela was a keen art student, who exhibited and sold some of her works. As early as 1872, Adela spent considerable sums of money on photographs and while there was a family interest in photography, it is possible that these early purchases were photographs of paintings for the purposes of study. Music also played a large part in life at

Monksgrange, with the family frequently gathering round the piano to sing, or combining their talents in ensemble playing.

A young woman like Adela might enjoy solitary pastimes, such as astronomy and art, *and* sociable activities, including hunting or, in her case, tennis. While Adela was sociable, Edward was too much of an individualist to enjoy hunting or team sports, both of which he considered to be a waste of time. He did, however, enjoy long solitary walks, believing that they provided the best form of exercise, and using them to think through personal problems. As might be expected in such an active family, there was no shortage of other pursuits, including archery and ice skating on the pond at Monksgrange. The enthusiasm for skating emanated from the experience of winters in America; it was typical of Edward that he sometimes made the skates himself. Cycling was quite a passion and there is in the archives a photograph of Edward's second wife, Ellen, with a new bicycle, wearing a dress designed for her by him.

Although Adela became a keen gardener at an early age and professed a taste for natural sciences, there is no evidence that she was interested in the 'soft' sciences, such as botany, entomology and ornithology. It was easy for a young woman to pursue such interests, for one had only to step outdoors onto the family estate to find specimens all around. Furthermore, a joy of these sciences was that one needed very little equipment or formal teaching. Armed with a pencil and notebook, a ruler, specimen jars and a hand lens, one could discover and record the richness of wild flowers, butterflies and other insects. Children of gentry were often taught to draw and paint in watercolours, so identification of an unrecognized specimen could be resolved later in the comfort of the house. Identification sometimes required the use of a microscope but many amateurs pursued their interest without one. For most people, it remained a leisure pursuit rather than a serious science; they looked for flowers, insects and birds for the sheer pleasure of doing so. Their chief requisite was not a microscope or telescope but patience in observing.

The low-tech nature of botany and entomology made it easy for women to be involved but some women pioneered the use of specialist equipment. Mary Ward took her childhood interest in butterflies and other insects to another level through the use of a good microscope given to her by her parents when she was 18. Combining microscopy with her skill as an artist, she produced several books, including *A world of wonders revealed by the microscope – a book for young students, with coloured illustrations*, published in 1858. Mary, countess of Rosse, through her pioneering photography in the 1850s, opened new possibilities for women and men alike. While photography was regarded as an art form, it also involved delicate chemical processes in the darkroom.

The participation of women in science often stemmed from a father's encouragement. Richard Lovell Edgeworth of Edgeworthstown in Co. Longford encouraged all his children to perform simple chemical experiments from an early age, and his daughter Maria had a life-long passion for the subject.

Likewise, Dr Robert Ball, a well-known amateur naturalist, fostered an interest in science in his children. While his three sons had distinguished professional careers, his daughters Mary and Anne made important contributions in botany and zoology, although their findings were usually published under the name of their brother, Robert, or were passed to other distinguished men, who incorporated them in their own publications.

What these amateur scientists had in common was curiosity about the natural world. Many, however, saw more than the beauty and diversity of nature: they saw it as a wondrous part of God's creation and their pursuit of their discipline was in search of a deeper understanding. This was particularly true of astronomers, of whom a remarkable number were clergy or sons of clergy. The close link between the church and astronomy had been demonstrated in 1790, when Richard Robinson, archbishop of Armagh, established an observatory there. It would be difficult to better the explanation for his enthusiasm which William Parsons, 3rd earl of Rosse, gave to a scientific gathering in 1843:

> The love of truth; the pleasure which the mind feels in overcoming difficulties; the satisfaction in contributing to the general store of knowledge; the engrossing nature of a pursuit so exalted as that of diving into the wonders of creation …[3]

By the 1870s, however, when Edward and Adela Richards became interested in astronomy, religious motivation was not universal; for freethinkers, such as Edward and Adela, it was impossible to ignore the debate around Charles Darwin's writings. Whatever the motivation, the pursuit of deeper understanding through astronomy was in some cases channelled into an obsessive counting of stars, mapping of moon craters and modifying equipment. Astronomy's appeal to the obsessive nature was elegantly expressed by John Joly, professor of geology and mineralogy in Trinity College, Dublin, when he wrote of 'the spell which the greatest and most imaginative of the sciences casts upon every thoughtful mind'.[4] Many leading Irish astronomers of the nineteenth century fell under this spell and Edward Richards was not immune.

A significant point arises in the context of astronomers: this essay excludes those whose interest was professional rather than amateur, the term 'amateur' being used in the original sense to denote one who pursues an activity for the love of it. There was, of course, a thin line between a leisure pursuit and a profession. For the 3rd earl of Rosse, whose Leviathan telescope at Birr depended on his exceptional engineering skills, it would have been inappropriate

3 Rosse's address, as president, to the British Association in 1843 was printed in the *Report of the thirteenth meeting of the British Association for the Advancement of Science held at Cork in August 1843* (London, 1844), pp xxix–xxxiii. 4 John Joly, 'William Edward Wilson, 1851–1908', *Philosophical Proceedings of the Royal Society*, 83A (1909–10), p. iii.

to become a professional engineer but several young men of gentry birth whom he employed as recorders subsequently became professional astronomers or engineers. Given Edward Richards' engineering skills, it might have been expected that he would be interested in astronomy but it seems that it was Adela who first evinced an interest. She was by no means the first young woman of the Irish country house to be interested in astronomy. Maria Edgeworth knew the leading astronomers of the time, notably the famous John Herschel. The highlight of her visit to him in England in 1822 was the time they spent looking through his telescope. After four days at the observatory in Armagh in 1831 with its director, the Revd Thomas Romney Robinson, she wrote excitedly: 'He showed me all the experiments in the polarisation of light which Herschel showed us with an excellently contrived apparatus of his own …'[5] Mary, countess of Rosse, and her husband's cousin, Mary Ward (née King), were also interested in astronomy and the former's earliest photography was related to her husband's telescope at Birr Castle.

Although she did not come from the Irish country house, Agnes Clerke occupied a prominent position in nineteenth-century astronomy. She and her sister Ellen inherited this interest from their father, a Cork bank manager, and they both wrote books on the subject. Like Adela, Agnes Clerke spent a lot of time in Italy in the 1870s and attained a fluency in European languages, which enabled her to read astronomical writings in the original. Clerke's *Popular history of astronomy during the nineteenth century* was reprinted as recently as 2003, when it was described in the foreword as 'an unrivalled source of readable, accurate information on a great age of revolution in astronomy'.[6] As Allan Chapman has pointed out, one should not underestimate the merits of this publication on the grounds that it was a 'popular' history, for at the time 'the word meant "no equations or higher mathematics" rather than "dumbed down"'. He adds:

> her *History* is a formidable piece of scientific scholarship … displaying a minutely detailed knowledge of astronomy, spectroscopy, stellar and solar physics, optics and gravitational mechanics as they were understood in the 1880s.[7]

5 Valerie Pakenham, *Maria Edgeworth's letters from Ireland* (Dublin, 2018), pp 279, 317. Robinson married Maria's youngest half-sister, Lucy, in 1842 and Maria used every opportunity to question him about his work. 6 Mary T. Brück's foreword to a facsimile edition of Agnes Clerke, *A popular history of astronomy during the nineteenth century* (Decorah, IA, 2003). 7 Allan Chapman, 'William Parsons and the Irish nineteenth-century tradition of independent astronomical research' in Charles Mollan (ed.), *William Parsons, 3rd earl of Rosse: astronomy and the castle in nineteenth-century Ireland* (Manchester, 2014), pp 285–6.

Clerke's accomplishments show what could be achieved by a woman who had an education similar to Adela's. It is possible but unlikely that Adela had the ability to master the same range of disciplines as Clerke did; Adela's focus was more on the arts than on science.

Clerke, whose most ambitious book was *Problems in astrophysics* (1903), was elected an honorary fellow of the Royal Astronomical Society in 1903 at the same time as that other outstanding woman astronomer, Margaret Huggins. Born Margaret Murray, the daughter of a Dublin solicitor, she derived her interest in astronomy from her Scottish grandfather. Like Adela, she was a good artist and musician but it was her marriage to the famous English astronomer William Huggins that enabled her to develop her skills. It was she who conducted the experiments with photographic plates that allowed husband and wife to become pioneers of spectroscopic astrophotography. They are regarded as founders of the science of astrophysics and it remains striking that, as a woman, Margaret achieved such recognition in the late nineteenth century.

While many of the prominent nineteenth-century astronomers were friendly with one another, Agnes Clerke and Margaret Huggins were close friends. They were, however, unusually placed, for there were major barriers to women who were interested in astronomy. The first was the need to have honed their mathematical and engineering skills. Even if one purchased one's equipment, one had to make constant adjustments and complicated calculations. The second barrier was cost: the price of a high-grade telescope was very high. A first-rate telescope that was 13.3 inches in diameter, bought in Paris in 1831, cost Edward Cooper of Markree Castle, Co. Sligo, the enormous sum of £1,200. Cooper bought it from Robert Aglaé Cauchoix and then gave Thomas Grubb of Dublin one of his first astronomical commissions in providing an equatorial mount for it. Cooper made a notable contribution to astronomy by his stellar mapping of the zodiac region of the sky. His four-volume *Catalogue of stars near the ecliptic* was a major undertaking, the fruit of more than 72,790 observations in seven years and eight months. His catalogue gave the locations of 60,066 stars, of which 51,101 were previously unknown.

William Wilson of Streete, Co. Westmeath also devoted money and time to astronomy. His contribution in astronomical photography and photometry was achieved firstly with a fine 9-inch refractor telescope and later with a 24-inch reflector, both from Grubb of Dublin.[8] Thomas Grubb had established a foundry at Charlemont Bridge in which he made cast-iron billiard tables and some specialized machinery. He was interested in both optics and astronomy and had his own private observatory with a 9-inch telescope. It was, therefore, not surprising that in 1833 he eagerly accepted a commission from Thomas Romney

8 A recently published book on Wilson recognizes the significance of this little-remembered astronomer. Ian Elliott and Charles Mollan, *William E. Wilson (1851–1908): the work and family of a Westmeath astronomer* (Dublin, 2018).

Robinson to build a 15-inch reflector telescope for Armagh Observatory. With the completion of this and Edward Cooper's equatorial mount, Grubb was launched on a career that made him and his son Howard the most important instrument makers in Ireland. The firm received commissions from Ireland's leading astronomers and its telescopes also went to observatories worldwide, including in Greenwich, Vienna and Melbourne.

A brief explanation of the difference between a nineteenth-century refractor and reflector is necessary: because the refractor used glass lenses to bend light into focus it was limited in size and had problems with various aberrations. (It was impossible to make a glass lens bigger than 20 inches because it would distort at the edges.) Being smaller, more portable and easier to maintain, it was the more common type of telescope and was good for studying the moon and planets but was inadequate for seeing deeper into space or examining faint objects, such as galaxies and nebulae. The reflector, in which a silvered metal speculum (mirror) reflected light into focus, could be made larger and more powerful. In telescopes, size is everything, and the bigger the diameter, the more light is collected, enabling better resolution and permitting fainter and more distant objects to be seen.

It was to see such objects that William Parsons, 3rd earl of Rosse, built the massive reflector known as 'the Leviathan' at Birr in 1845. The pre-eminent example of astronomic instruments in Ireland, with a diameter of 72 inches, it was the largest in the world and was not exceeded in size for seventy-five years. Rosse could not have built it without the considerable fortune of his wife Mary, who, as we have seen, shared his interest in astronomy.

Its construction was a major feat of creative engineering, particularly as he even cast the speculum himself. Most amateur astronomers commissioned their telescope from a maker such as Grubb but Rosse made his own. Being 'a skilful engineer, an experienced founder and an ingenious optician', he trained all his workmen himself.[9] For the construction, he utilized a laboratory, extensive workshops and a foundry and even had to build a small railway line to transport the huge speculum to and from the workshops. His great reward was that the telescope was the first to reveal the spiral nature of the galaxies and hundreds of enthusiasts visited from far and wide to see for themselves. The telescope is still a notable feature in the park at Birr Castle and the estate is at the centre of new developments with the I-LOFAR (Irish Low Frequency Array) project, a new radio-telescope connected to the international LOFAR telescope network. Unlike the Leviathan, which towers above the ground, this is a flat installation in a large circle on the ground.

9 Robert S. Ball, *Great astronomers* (London, 1895), p. 273. Ball was the scientific assistant at Birr in his youth and later became director of Dunsink Observatory.

18.3 The Leviathan. Postcard from the collection of Charles Mollan.

There were far more private observatories in England than in Ireland. In 1861, George Frederick Chambers' *Handbook of descriptive and practical astronomy* listed observatories in the United Kingdom and recorded only three in Ireland: at Birr, at Markree and at Ravensdale Park, near Dundalk, the estate of Lord Clermont. By the 1870s, there were more observatories but few owners are known to have made a significant contribution to astronomy. Although Edward and Adela were not among Ireland's leading astronomers, the story of the Monksgrange observatory is significant nonetheless. The telescope which Edward bought for his daughter in November 1876 from London opticians Horne and Thornthwaite, at a cost of £10, was a 3-inch refractor. He had seen it advertised in the *English Mechanic and World of Science* in an issue of 3 November 1876. This publication, which appeared weekly from 1865, was a prolific source of information for people who were interested in the various branches of science and technology. Not only did it print illustrated articles on everything from electricity to photography, from plumbing to astronomy, but it published advertisements for pieces of equipment and included a queries and answers column, used by amateur astronomers to source everything from telescopes to eye pieces and to exchange information and observations. Edward Richards used it not only in his pursuit of astronomy but also in connection with his various engineering projects at Monksgrange. The magazine also carried reports of such scientific bodies as the British Association for the Advancement of Science, the most important organization for scientific enthusiasts in Britain and Ireland.

It may have been their common membership of the British Association or the fact that they both read the *English Mechanic* which made Edward, an Irish country gentleman, feel that he could write that same month to the illustrious amateur English astronomer, William Birt, seeking advice on how to proceed. Edward wrote: 'Touching your advt in the *English Mechanic*, my daughter is about studying the moon with a three-inch [telescope] … She wants a good map. I am quite ignorant on the subject.'[10] Birt, whose major work was in upgrading the lunar map, clearly posted a helpful reply and the two corresponded for some years. It is frustrating that Edward destroyed almost all incoming letters and consequently one sees only one side of the correspondence. Over a decade, Edward wrote hundreds of letters about astronomy at Monksgrange but they were only a fraction of the letters, business and social, which he wrote every week. This is a significant point when one is considering the use of time in the country house, for he was typical of country gentlemen in writing copious letters to suppliers in Wexford, Dublin and England, in relation to the estate, and to family members and friends in Ireland and abroad. Letter writing consumed a lot of Edward's time, especially during Adela's absences, when he wrote to her very frequently.

Edward and Adela approached astronomy with characteristic thoroughness. They read journals such as the *Astronomical Register* and bought some of the most important books for amateurs. Among them was Thomas Webb's *Celestial objects for common telescopes* (1859), the standard guide on using a telescope and on what could be observed with a small refractor. Another purchase was *The moon* (1874), by Nasmyth and Carpenter. A recent publication, it was one of the earliest collections of moon imagery and had a major impact on lunar study.

By January 1877, Edward and Adela were exasperated with the telescope. Edward wrote again to Birt, saying:

> My daughter is absent or she would write … I know enough to see that the [telescope] I got for her will not be satisfactory if one goes on with the stargazing. Besides, I have got interested in the matter myself and should like to join her in observing.[11]

Edward also asked if Birt could give him the address of some amateur observers who had good instruments near Dublin or London and who would allow him to visit and decide on what would be suitable for Monksgrange. Adela's absence was not unconnected with their search for a better telescope. While staying with her Orpens cousins in Dublin, she obtained an invitation from Robert Stawell Ball, professor of astronomy, to visit Trinity College's observatory at Dunsink but recognizing the need to see a good *amateur* astronomer's equipment, Edward

10 Edward Richards to William Birt, 27 Nov. 1876, letter book, Aug. 1876–Sept. 1880, p. 80, Monksgrange Archives (hereafter MGA), I/BB/2b. 11 Edward Richards to William Birt, 25 Jan. 1877, MGA, I/BB/2b, p. 109. Birt was secretary to the lunar committee of the British Association for the Advancement of Science.

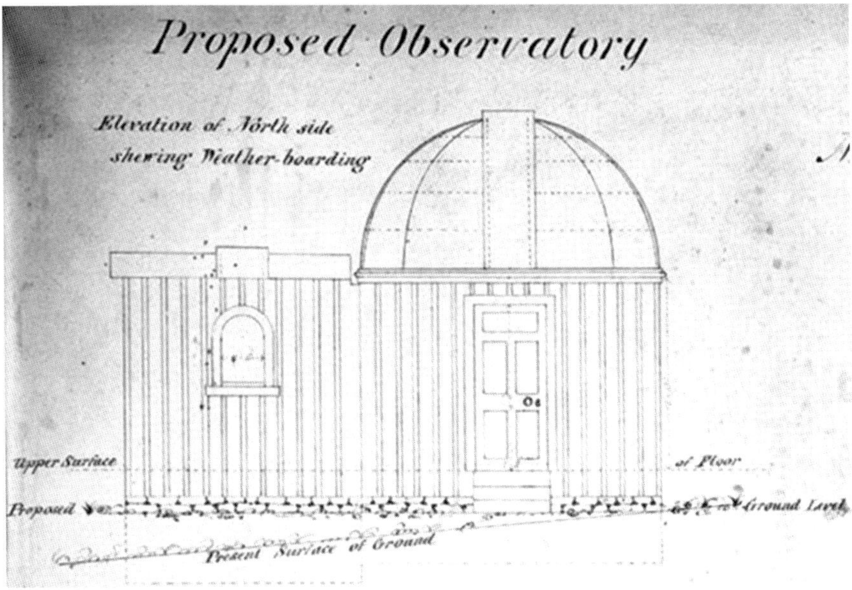


18.4 Design for an observatory by T. Cooke of York. Courtesy of Monksgrange Trust.

told her to discover the name and address of one 'S.T.', who was known to have had a telescope some years earlier. He advised her: 'get an introduction, see the instrument and find out all you can … the Orpens must know some amateur astronomers, see their instruments if possible & learn what you can … Lose no time about it.'[12] The first line of inquiry proved a vital connection for them, as the Revd Sterling Tomlinson welcomed visits and provided detailed advice on the choice of telescope, as well as the mount and the construction of the observatory.

While amateur astronomers were generous in offering guidance, Edward suffered from a lack of contact with Ireland's leading astronomers. A self-reliant man of independent disposition, he had not been interested in establishing a wide social circle upon his return to Ireland and did not partake in the endless round of hospitality which prevailed in many Irish country houses. Had he been a graduate of Trinity College he would have known many of the Irish astronomers, the more illustrious of whom were linked through their membership of the Royal Irish Academy or one of the English-based learned societies. He became, however, a member of the Selenographical Society, founded early in 1878 by fellows of the Royal Astronomical Society with a particular interest in lunar work.

Edward relied on his own engineering skills to put into practice the advice he gleaned. He was a skilled carpenter, was proficient with his lathe and already had

12 Edward Richards to Adela Richards, 15 Jan. 1877, in correspondence between Edward Moore Richards and Adela Richards, *c.*1860–1880, MGA, I/J/7.

a well-equipped workshop in which to make items for his observatory. Over the next year, Edward corresponded with a number of instrument makers and amateur astronomers, both in England and Ireland. Early in 1878, he was on the point of buying a 4.5-inch telescope from instrument makers T. Cooke of York but opted instead for a 5-inch refractor from Howard Grubb. In the archives at Monksgrange, there are drawings for the design of an observatory which were sent to Edward by Cooke (fig. 18.4).[13]

Having ordered his telescope in March 1878, Edward waited impatiently. Although he had paid a deposit of £44 3*s*. 4*d*., 'a third of the price of the telescope',[14] he later asked several times for modifications and was fortunate that the final price was not higher. In preparation for the new telescope, Edward and Adela avidly read up on the subject and, one imagines, made the most of opportunities to talk to astronomers of the British Association at its annual meeting, held in Dublin in August 1878. Edward also joined the association's visit to Birr on 22 August to see the Leviathan.

The observatory he built was closely modelled on Cooke's designs but he sought advice from Tomlinson and others on specific details. Adela would not have had the skills to carry out this work and there is no evidence that she helped her father. His correspondence shows him in his element, more than happy to work on his own. His mother's journal records that 'During the past summer and autumn Eddy has been busily engaged putting up an observatory in the lawn – he has worked at it … with the greatest energy.'[15] The 5-inch telescope, which Edward described as 'Class C, modified for the better',[16] was finally ready in November 1878 and was installed in the observatory. It was a considerable improvement, which enabled Edward and Adela to make better observations.

While Adela enjoyed observing, astronomy was already an obsession for Edward. An engineer at heart, both the planning of his observatory and the process of observing gave scope to his sharp mind and his drawing skills. Ultimately, as he once wrote to Adela, 'science workers must labour for the love of it'.[17]

At Monksgrange, there is a painting in oil on board depicting the interior of the observatory, completed in 1879 by Adela for an amateur art exhibition in Dublin. In it, one can see the telescope, a finder and mount in the foreground and, at the work station, a recording notebook and candle. On the wall is a view of Saturn as seen through a telescope. When it was exhibited in Dublin the following winter, the painting was praised for its skilful representation of conflicting moonlight and candlelight. In the success of this picture lies a key to

13 One of the designs for an observatory sent to Edward by T. Cooke, MGA, uncatalogued. 14 Edward Richards to Howard Grubb, 28 Mar. 1878, MGA, 1/BB/2b, p. 292. 15 Journal of Dorothea Sargent, 21 Nov. 1878, MGA 1/BB/1c. 16 Edward Richards to the Revd R.S. Hutchings, 7 Aug. 1886, letter book, May 1883–Sept. 1886, p. 471, MGA, 1/BB/2d. 17 Edward Richards to Adela Richards, 6 Sept. 1877, in correspondence between Edward Moore Richards and Adela Richards, *c.*1860–1880, MGA, I/J/7.

18.5 The interior of the observatory. Courtesy of Monksgrange Trust.

Adela's diminishing interest in astronomy. By the 1880s, she was spending more and more time painting and writing and there is little evidence of her active stargazing after her marriage to Goddard Orpen in 1880 and their subsequent move to London. She still considered herself an astronomer, however, writing that the transit of Venus on 6 December 1882 'was to have been a great day for all astronomers, ourselves included' but the skies in London had been clouded.[18]

Edward, however, worked assiduously and grew in confidence. During 1880, his letters to Birt show that he was following the latest developments in astronomy while recording his own observations and adding to his equipment.[19] He was even bold enough to contest the observations on moon craters by a well-known astronomer, Frank Dennett, submitting drawings of his own.[20] In February 1880, Edward wrote to the treasurer of the Selenographical Society: 'If you think my assistance would be of any help (as I am only a new hand at observing) I should be willing to cooperate in mapping any part of the moon you wish.'[21]

18 Journal of Adela Orpen, 7 Dec. 1882, MGA 1/BB/5d. 19 Edward Richards to William Birt, 28 Jan. 1880, 23 Mar. 1880, 29 May 1880, MGA, I/BB/2b, pp 617, 651, 684. 20 Edward Richards to William Birt, 28 Jan. 1880, MGA, I/BB/2b, p. 617. 21 Edward Richards to the Revd W.J.B. Richards, 11 Feb. 1880, MGA, I/BB/2b, p. 631.

**18.6** Adela, hoeing a garden bed, and Eddie, in front of observatory. Courtesy of Monksgrange Trust.

While Edward was enthusiastically making observations with his telescope, during that year, Land League agitation had led his tenants to stop paying rent. Edward's vociferous opposition to the Land League made him a potential target for discontents and by late December, he was preparing to install a defensive steel turret over the front door, was reviewing his stock of guns and had taken the precaution of dismantling the telescope. That month he wrote to Howard Grubb: 'We are on a loaded mine that may explode at any moment.'[22] After a while, he used his telescope again but the political situation did not improve in the 1880s and the loss of rents left him short of money. In January 1886, he advertised his telescope in the *English Mechanic* in words that must have puzzled some of the English readers. It ran: 'Believing … prominent loyalists will be little likely to get compensation for malicious injury to their property, I am anxious to sell my astronomical instruments at once.'[23]

Having found a buyer for the telescope, he sent it to Howard Grubb for cleaning and wrote several letters urging him to do the necessary work as soon as possible, as 'I much need the money.'[24] Adela's explanation of the sale of the telescope appeared in the *St James's Gazette* (London) in December 1888. She adopted the voice of the Monksgrange silver urn facing imminent sale:

22 Edward Richards to Howard Grubb, 21 Dec. 1880, letter book, Sept. 1880–May 1883, MGA, I/BB/2c, p. 57. 23 Edward Richards to *English Mechanic*, 7 Jan. 1886, MGA, I/BB/2d, p. 386. 24 Edward Richards to Howard Grubb, 11 Oct. 1886, letter book, Sept. 1886–July 1892, MGA, I/BB/2e, p. 9.

> During the Land League years we gradually fell away from our former estate. Rents which had cheerfully been paid for sixty and eighty years were suddenly declared 'impossible' and were not paid at all. My master never had been extravagant; he did not keep racers; he never even hunted; but as he got hardly any rents he was soon as much hampered for money as if he had previously wasted his substance. First it was the telescope that was sold … because he did not dare to use it at night for fear of being shot at through the windows of the observatory when star gazing … After the telescope went the lathe; then in quick succession the servants, the horse and the jaunting car. And now the worst must be told. I, the chief of the family plate – I, the Silver Urn of 150 years – must go too to meet necessary expenses.

Edward handed over the estate to Adela in 1900 and she and her husband, Goddard Orpen, moved there permanently. Goddard spent much time researching and writing his history of Ireland under the Normans (published 1911–20) but the management of the estate left Adela little time for many of her pursuits. With their children, Iris and Eddie, they maintained a strong interest in gardening and music. Goddard was an extremely good photographer, whose large collection remains in the archives. It has provided the Monksgrange illustrations for this essay. While astronomy proved only a passing phase, the large volume of extant papers gives great insight into the way in which a leisure pursuit was conducted. The observatory stood for many years, a sad reminder of more carefree days.

# Contributors

**Kerry Bristol** is a senior lecturer in the School of Fine Art, History of Art and Cultural Studies, University of Leeds. She is currently researching and writing a book on everyday life in the eighteenth century at Nostell Priory, West Yorkshire.

**Laura Servilan Brown** is a PhD candidate and Hume Scholar in the Department of History at Maynooth University and has just completed her thesis on the social context of the Anglo-Egyptian Sudan, 1899–1956.

**Fergal Browne** is an accountant by profession but has published extensively on the great houses of County Cork. He has recently published a history of Belgooly Mills and Distillery in the *Journal of the Cork Historical and Archaeological Society*.

**Philip Bull** is adjunct professor, La Trobe University, Melbourne, and visiting professor, Centre for the Study of Historic Irish Houses and Estates, Maynooth University. He recently published *Monksgrange: portrait of an Irish house and family, 1769–1969* (Dublin, 2019).

**Oliver Cox** is Heritage Engagement Fellow at the University of Oxford, where he is a member of the Faculty of History. He is the founder and director of the Thames Valley Country House Partnership.

**Ian d'Alton** was a visiting fellow at Sidney Sussex College, and a senior research associate, Peterhouse, Cambridge and is currently a visiting research fellow at the Centre for Contemporary Irish History, Trinity College Dublin. He has recently co-edited (with Ida Milne) *Protestant and Irish: the minority's search for a place in independent Ireland* (Cork, 2019).

**Terence Dooley** lectures in the Department of History at Maynooth University, where he is also founder and director of the Centre for the Study of Historic Irish Houses and Estates. His most recent book is *Monaghan: the Irish revolution, 1912–23* (Dublin, 2017).

**Eugene Dunne** is a retired member of An Garda Siochána and a PhD graduate of the Department of History, Maynooth University.

**Brian Griffin** is senior lecturer in history at Bath Spa University. His main research interest is the social history of nineteenth- and early twentieth-century Ireland, with a particular focus on policing, sport and crime. He is the author of *Cycling in Victorian Ireland* (Dublin, 2006).

**Tom Hunt** holds a PhD degree in history from De Montfort University, Leicester. He specializes in the history of Irish sport and is the author of *Sport and society in Victorian Ireland: the case of Westmeath* (Cork, 2007).

**Antonia Laurence-Allen** has worked in museums and galleries in Scotland, the USA and Canada. Her areas of interest include visual art collections and society in the nineteenth and twentieth centuries. Since 2014 she has been employed with the National Trust, Scotland.

**Tony McCarthy** is a PhD graduate of the Department of History, Maynooth University. He is also a qualified accountant with an MBA from University College Dublin. He is the author of *The Shaws of Terenure, a nineteenth-century Dublin merchant family* (Dublin, 2010) and is currently working on a book on George Wyndham in Ireland.

**Maeve O'Riordan** is lecturer in women's and cultural history at University College Cork. She is the author of *Women of the country house in Ireland, 1860–1914* (Liverpool, 2018).

**Ciarán Reilly** is a historian of nineteenth- and twentieth-century Ireland based at Maynooth University. He is author of the best-selling *Strokestown and the Great Irish Famine* (Dublin, 2014) and *The Irish land agent, 1830–60: the case of King's County* (Dublin, 2014). His book on Capard House in County Laois will be published in 2019.

**Christopher Ridgway** is curator at Castle Howard, Yorkshire, co-founder of the Yorkshire Country House Partnership and adjunct professor in the Centre for the Study of Historic Irish Houses and Estates, Maynooth University. His books include *Castle Howard and Brideshead: fact, fiction and in-between* (2011); *The Morpeth Roll, Ireland identified in 1841* (Dublin, 2013); and *Duty calls, Castle Howard and the Great War* (2014).

**Einion Wyn Thomas** is a native of Bala in north Wales. He was university archivist at Bangor University, 2002–15, where he was also co-founder of the Institute for the Study of Welsh Estates.

**Annie Tindley** is senior lecturer in history at Newcastle University, where her research focuses on modern rural British history, with particular expertise on landed estates and aristocratic families. She is the founder and associate director of the Centre for Scotland's Land Futures.

**Allen Warren** is co-founder (with Christopher Ridgway) of the Yorkshire Country House Partnership and former head of the History Department at the University of York (1996–2003). He has published on late nineteenth-century government and politics in Britain and Ireland, the history of youth movements, as well as country houses in Britain and Ireland.

**Lesley Whiteside** has written on a wide range of historical subjects, including the histories of two of Ireland's oldest secondary schools. Her biography of George Otto Simms is a key resource for the history of the Church of Ireland.

# Index